THE CHURCH HISTORICAL SOCIETY

New Series, Sources: Number Two

———

AN ANGLICAN TURNING POINT

Documents and Interpretations

AN ANGLICAN
TURNING POINT

Documents and Interpretations

BY

STEPHEN FIELDING BAYNE, JR.

Executive Officer
of the Anglican Communion,
1960-1964

THE CHURCH HISTORICAL SOCIETY

Austin, Texas

1964

Printed in the United States of America
by Gillick Printing, Inc., Berkeley, Calif.

102434

Acknowledgments

The Officers and Executive Board of The Church Historical Society are profoundly grateful to Bishop Bayne for this collection of his papers that record so significant a half-decade in the history of the Anglican Communion, to which he has contributed such outstanding leadership in his position as first Executive Officer. We are also in debt to Archbishop Lord Fisher of Lambeth for his contribution to the volume, prepared in the midst of a busy itinerary in the South Pacific area.

Generous and ready permission to reprint a number of Bishop Bayne's published addresses and articles during these recent years has been given us by the following publishers and editors—to whom we extend our most sincere thanks:

The Seabury Press, New York City, for No. 2—the address given by Bishop Bayne at the Anglican Congress in Toronto, and published in *Anglican Congress 1963, Report of Proceedings.*

The Bishop of Connecticut, as Editor of *Pan-Anglican,* for No. 19.

The Editor of *Anglican World,* for Nos. 3, 6, 7, 14, 25, 28.

The Editor of the *Canadian Churchman,* for No. 23.

The Editor of *The Living Church,* for Nos. 8, 9, 10, 13, 15, 16, 17, 18, 20, 21, 22, 26, 29, and 31.

The Editors of *Lutheran World,* and its corresponding German edition, *Lutherische Rundschau,* for No. 30.

MASSEY H. SHEPHERD, JR.
President

Abbreviations

ACMS	The Advisory Council on Missionary Strategy
CACTM	Central Advisory Council of Training for the Ministry (Church of England)
CCSEA	Regional Council of the Church of South East Asia
CIPBC	The Church of India, Pakistan, Burma, and Ceylon
CMS	The Church Missionary Society
DWME	Division of World Mission and Evangelism, World Council of Churches
PECUSA	The Protestant Episcopal Church in the United States of America
SPCK	The Society for Promoting Christian Knowledge
SPG	The Society for the Propagation of the Gospel in Foreign Parts
UMCA	Universities' Mission to Central Africa
WCC	World Council of Churches

Contents

Part One: Documents

I.

Historical Note

IT IS DOUBTLESS PREMATURE to think of either a personal memoir or the publication of confidential correspondence relating to the appointment of the first Anglican Executive Officer. It seems appropriate, however, to prepare a brief sketch of the appointment and its background, including some relevant excerpts from correspondence.

The Anglican Executive Officer is responsible to the two principal inter-Anglican bodies, the "Consultative Body" of the Lambeth Conference and the "Advisory Council on Missionary Strategy." The composition of these two groups is presently governed by Resolutions 60 and 61 of the 1958 Lambeth Conference. In broad terms, the Consultative Body is composed of the Primates or Presiding Bishops of the Anglican churches and provinces, or their episcopal alternatives; the Advisory Council includes those and also the other metropolitans, and allows for lay or clerical alternates. In April, 1964, a "meeting of metropolitans" was held which included the membership of the Consultative Body and three additional metropolitans, from Australia, Canada and the United States, as well. This group—perhaps best viewed as an enlarged meeting of the Consultative Body—is intermediate in size between the Consultative Body (22) and the Advisory Council (36). Whether this meeting established a pattern for the future is not yet known.

In any case, the constitution of both groups is necessarily informal. The authority for their existence and their terms of reference is that of the Lambeth Conference alone; and it is well understood that the Conference has no legislative or constitutional power. *De facto* recognition is no doubt given them by the agreement of the churches and provinces to provide financial support for the Executive Officer, and to receive and consider their recommendations; but neither has coercive or constitutional authority over any church or province. But this

is unimportant. Each group is, essentially, a meeting of the churches
and provinces, in the persons of responsible leaders, for consultation
and planning. Each church or province must take appropriate action,
in its own way, before any recommendation can come into effect (as
far as that jurisdiction is concerned). Thus the dynamics of the
Anglican Communion remain clearly rooted in the authorities of the
constituent churches and provinces. This is in accord with the description of the Anglican Communion adopted by the 1930 Lambeth
Conference, that it "is a fellowship, within the One Holy Catholic
and Apostolic Church, of those duly constituted Dioceses, Provinces
or Regional Churches in communion with the See of Canterbury,
which . . . are bound together not by a central legislative and executive
authority, but by mutual loyalty sustained through the common
counsel of the Bishops in conference" (Res. 49).

The Lambeth Conference is the supreme expression of the
"common counsel" referred to. Both the Consultative Body and the
Advisory Council are of the nature of continuation committees of
the Conference. Indeed this is explicitly stated in the first case (Res.
61; 1958 Lambeth). The Advisory Council, considerably broader in
membership (even to the deliberate inclusion of the laity as possible
alternate members), is not so directly related to Lambeth; it represents
rather a continuing, consultative relationship among the churches of
the Anglican Communion; as such, nevertheless, it is an extension,
in a special area, of the same "common counsel."

The origins of both these bodies lie in the second Lambeth
Conference, in 1878. In the case of the Consultative Body, the Encyclical Letter of that Conference suggested that a "Committee might
be constituted, such as should represent, more or less completely, the
several Churches of the Anglican Communion; and to this Committee
it might be entrusted to draw up, after receiving communications
from the Bishops, a scheme of subjects to be discussed" (by the
Lambeth Conference). This suggestion was followed, in 1897 (Res. 5),
by a firm recommendation that such a "consultative body" be constituted. In 1908, "the existing Central Consultative Body" was reconstituted, on much the present pattern (Ress. 54, 55 and 56). In 1920,
further clarification of membership and responsibility was given (Ress.
44 and 45), and the committee concerned was "of opinion that the
position of the Consultative Body of the Lambeth Conference should
be strengthened . . . that (it) may be increasingly regarded as a real
living Body, to which any question of Faith and Order may be
referred, as an authority of great moral weight, providing a voluntary

nexus for the whole of the Anglican Communion though possessing no power to enforce its decisions." In 1930 (Res. 50) the Conference again revised and broadened the statement of the "usual duties" of the Consultative Body. This sufficed, apparently, until 1958, when the Conference once more gave considerable attention to the Consultative Body, and adopted the following resolution (61) which presently governs its activity:

> The Conference, while reaffirming the opinion expressed in Resolution 44 of the Lambeth Conference of 1920 that the Consultative Body is of the nature of a Continuation Committee of the Lambeth Conference, recommends that its duties and composition should be redefined as follows:
>
> (a) The duties of the Consultative Body shall be:
>> (i) to carry on work left to it by the preceding Conference;
>> (ii) to assist the Archbishop of Canterbury in the preparation of business of the ensuing Conference;
>> (iii) to consider matters referred to the Archbishop of Canterbury on which he requests its aid and to advise him;
>> (iv) to advise on questions of faith, order, policy, or administration referred to it by any Bishop or group of Bishops, calling in expert advisers at its discretion, and reserving the right to decline to entertain any particular question;
>> (v) to deal with matters referred to it by the Archbishop of Canterbury or by any Bishop or group of Bishops, subject to any limitations upon such references which may be imposed by the regulations of local and regional Churches;
>> (vi) to take such action in the discharge of the above duties as may be appropriate, subject to the condition that with regard to churches, provinces, and dioceses of the Anglican Communion its functions are advisory only and without executive or administrative power.
>
> (b) The Consultative Body shall consist of:
>> (i) The Archbishop of Canterbury as ex officio Chairman and the Archbishop of York;
>> (ii) The Primates or Presiding Bishops of National or Provincial Churches in the following countries or areas:
>> Wales; Ireland; Scotland; U.S.A.; Canada; India, Pakistan, Burma, and Ceylon; Australia; New Zealand; South Africa; West Indies; Japan; China; West Africa; Central Africa; Middle East.
>> (iii) Such Members to represent other dioceses under the jurisdiction of the Archbishop of Canterbury as he may appoint.
>
> Each member shall have the right to nominate a bishop to take his place at any meeting which he is unable to attend.

(c) The Archbishop of Canterbury with the approval of the Consultative Body shall appoint a secretary to serve under the directions of the Archbishop, who may, if the Advisory Council so agrees, be also the Secretary of that Council.

(d) The Consultative Body shall meet when summoned by the Archbishop of Canterbury or on his behalf; and in between meetings may conduct business by correspondence. All minutes and papers shall be sent to every member and if so desired to alternates also.

(e) Expenses incurred on behalf of the Consultative Body shall be borne by the fund provided for the Advisory Council on Missionary Strategy, if that Council so agrees.

The Advisory Council on Missionary Strategy equally was foreshadowed in the Encyclical Letter of the 1878 Lambeth Conference. The Committee was "of opinion that it is desirable to appoint a Board of Reference, to advise upon questions brought before it either by Diocesan or Missionary Bishops or by Missionary Societies." They suggested that the details of the establishment of such a Board be referred "to the Archbishops of England and Ireland, the Bishop of London, the Primus of the Scottish Episcopal Church, the Presiding Bishop of the Protestant Episcopal Church in the United States of America, with the Bishop superintending the congregations of the same on the Continent of Europe, and such other Bishops as they may associate with themselves."

Very likely the suggestion was premature. At any rate, no such Board was formed, and sixty years and two world wars passed before the establishment of the Advisory Council on Missionary Strategy. The intervening years were by no means barren in this respect. The immense dislocation of both wars called for unusual co-operative arrangements—particularly between Britain and North America—which gave confidence to those who were in due course to press for the Advisory Council. The realignment of political and economic structures consequent on the wars, and the parallel, vigorous self-consciousness of the "Younger Churches," added force to the impulse. The Lambeth Conference in 1948, meeting after eighteen years of isolation, brought together an unprecedented number of bishops, most of them unfamiliar with older patterns of overseas relationship and eager to move toward a fuller and more vigorous expression of Anglican interdependence. The Committee on the Anglican Communion proposed an "Advisory Council on Missionary Strategy"—a proposal adopted in Resolution 80. Additionally, in Resolution 81, the appointment of liaison and communication officers by each national or regional church was urged, "to promote closer co-operation and a clearer understanding between the different parts of the Anglican Communion."

This latter recommendation was not implemented. But the Advisory Council was established, and in fact functioned during the following decade, meeting as occasion offered—notably at the Anglican Congress at Minneapolis in 1954. By 1958, when the Lambeth Conference again met, it had become clear to many that the existence of the Council alone could not guarantee the fulfillment of the hopes which had given it birth. The Committee on Progress in the Anglican Communion accordingly recommended that a full-time officer be appointed and that the membership of the Council be revised. New procedures and terms of reference were suggested. Most significantly, it was recommended that the cost of carrying out these plans be "borne by the whole Anglican Communion in such proportion among its parts as the Advisory Council shall decide."

These recommendations were accepted by the Conference (Res. 60), which also, in the following Resolution, after reconstituting the Consultative Body, agreed that, if desired, the same officer might serve both the Consultative Body and the Advisory Council, support for the combined operation being supplied by the budget of the Advisory Council. These two resolutions were implemented at once. At a meeting during the Conference itself, agreement was reached by the metropolitans on a just proportion of costs, a tentative budget was established; it was decided that the same officer should serve both bodies, and a short list was prepared of names to be considered for the new office. A note of urgency had been expressed in Resolution 60, requesting action "by His Grace the President as soon as possible." On the basis of the agreements mentioned above, the Archbishop then pursued the matter; and in due course wrote to me, October 17, 1958, broaching the possibility of my considering such an appointment.

Not having served on the Committee in question nor, of course, shared the subsequent exploration, the invitation was both startling and unsettling. Besides, I had a candidate of my own. But I wrote to the Presiding Bishop that I felt the proposed office was "potentially at least one of the greatest usefulness in the deepening and development of our Communion and our common life ... perhaps its greatest usefulness lies in the fact that it is not an administrative job, really, and has no 'authority.' Its immense possibilities lie in the chance to imagine and win support for a great degree of common strategy and planning and study and life, which I think all of our Anglican people are hungry for . . ." (October 26th) .

There were difficulties—financial, personal, and constitutional—to be met. Not until February 24, 1959, was the way clear for the Archbishop to write more specifically about the office and its responsibilities. With his permission, I quote some paragraphs from that letter. Apropos of a recent conversation with another metropolitan, he wrote:

> There is a sense in which it is true to say that the preparations of the Agenda for the 1968 Lambeth Conference began the moment the 1958 Conference ended. I said . . . that I thought that an immense amount of the value of the 1968 Conference would rest upon the work done from now onwards by the holders of this office, and I believe that is true. Already since the Lambeth Conference (two Metropolitans) have gone; there are other Metropolitans who before too long will go, and certainly before 1968 I shall have gone: and yet an enormous amount of an indefinable kind has rested and does rest upon the personal links between the existing Metropolitans all looking to Lambeth. In any case I have long been aware of the fact that the Archbishop of Canterbury cannot himself as Chairman of the Conference do the kind of necessary donkey work or organize the necessary liaison which holds the Anglican Communion together. The Executive Officer I regard as the immediate personal assistant to the Archbishop of Canterbury for all this work. In a sense he will make his own job: it certainly will not mean just sitting in an office in London. It will often mean sharing personally in the outlook and interests of all the Provinces of the Anglican Communion.
>
> Let me specify two examples:
>
> (a) The North India Plan: a lot has happened since the Conference ended. The C.I.P.B.C. is putting the Lambeth proposals to the North India Negotiating Committee, and doing it very clearly . . . now there ought to be somebody with me who knows all about this battle here; who can keep in touch with our people in India, and who knows also what some people in the United States are thinking, and whether there ought to be some active consideration of these problems done on behalf of the Episcopal Church. You see what I mean? We have got a very good set up in the Church of England now to deal with Inter-Church questions. There is, however, a hostile element: it exists here: it has links with the United States and with many other parts of the Anglican Communion: somebody ought to help me to see that other Provinces are aware of what we are trying to do, and able to see whether it ought to be done in other Provinces. Otherwise we wait until North India goes through, and then half of us back it and the other half condemn it. I am putting all this tersely, but you can see what I mean.
>
> (b) Then there is another thing to be watched: Resolution 76 of the Lambeth Conference told me to set up an Advisory Committee to prepare recommendations for the structure of the Holy Communion service. I can easily set up a committee here: in fact we have got one called the Liturgical Commission, but somebody must work out some kind of liaison system between people here and people in

the other Provinces who are interested in this particular problem, and again I think it is for the Executive Officer to keep an eye on that: get the right system working and see that it goes on working.

I have not even mentioned the concerns which fall to the Executive Officer in connection with the Anglican Advisory Council on Missionary Strategy, but certainly things arise there, and I think the Executive Officer will also have to know something about what part all the various Provinces are taking in ecumenical discussions on the World Council of Churches. In fact his experience would become as wide as that of the Anglican Communion itself, and it would be for him to pick out at any given moment the problem, great or small, which wants some pulling together. I am perfectly sure that this would mean visiting from time to time Anglican Provinces overseas, not merely to impart some information but to find out what is biting them.

This letter was followed, March 2nd, by a final invitation "to accept the post of Executive Officer." The Archbishop added "The Lambeth Conference Report indicates that your duties are partly to the Anglican Advisory Council on Missionary Strategy and partly to the Consultative Body of the Lambeth Conference. In both capacities and particularly in the last it means, in fact, that you are directly Assistant to the Archbishop of Canterbury in his responsibilities towards the Anglican Communion and the Lambeth Conference in particular."

On March 5th I responded, saying that I did not see how I could decline, but outlining the steps I had still to take, and suggesting the coming Easter as a target date for a final answer. It may be of interest to quote some paragraphs from my letter, which responded to the two previous ones from the Archbishop:

Let me say that I appreciated most deeply your thoughts in your long letter, and that the examples you cited were exactly the sort of thing in my own mind. Another such area would be that of preparation for the next Anglican Congress—quite rightly, the initiative in that ought to be taken by the Canadians; but the needful and anticipatory study could be helped a good deal by the Executive Officer. Indeed my own committee at Lambeth felt very strongly that both in preparation for the Congress and the next Lambeth and also in following up what we did last summer, the need for concerted inter-Provincial study was clear and sharp; and we rejoiced at the Conference resolutions which seemed to implement this.

Much of the new officer's work, I think, would be in the realm of communication—weaving a new intensity of unity among the bishops and the churches. You have done an enormous service in your personal relationships; and what is needed is some way to reap the fruits of that on a permanent basis.

Much more of his work, I'm sure, must lie in helping to develop concerted missionary plans and perhaps specific inter-Anglican proj-

ects for new areas. Here I imagine there can't help but be some
tricky corners, and much need for patient and imaginative pioneer
work with our various church groups and missionary societies. Yet
I find, among our American clergy at least, the greatest enthusiasm
imaginable for the possibility of new and fully-inter-Anglican missionary work; and in our church, at least, we need badly to have a fresh
missionary enthusiasm.

Most of all, I think the new officer must be one who will believe
without weariness and without doubt in the vocation of our Communion and in the dream all of us share in some degree of what our
common life and witness can be, under God . . . believe in it and
keep putting words to it everywhere he can. The trouble with us is
that we have our high points, as at Minneapolis and at Lambeth,
when those of us who are together see a dim vision of what could be
and ought to be and must be; but we have lacked any way to hold
on to that in the years in between and to clothe it with some kind
of reality. I should imagine that the new officer's chief task would
be here—*how* to do it I do not know, but I would have perfect confidence that we can find the ways, if the substance of the dream is
true. . . .

Of course I understand that I am directly assistant to you. You
know what I can and cannot do, and you know the needs of our
Communion far better than anyone else; and I am content to look
forward to whatever degree of responsibility and autonomy you see
fit. My only strong feeling would be that there ought to be a certain
degree of looseness, enough to make it clear that this new post is not
an *English* invention, nor merely an extension of your own office—
I say this knowing that you share it and understand the issues
involved. Indeed the whole point of the office, as I see it, is to give
articulation and expression to the corporate life of our whole Communion, and to give it at a new and deeper level than our present
patterns afford. Do you agree?

I know also that there will be inescapably a degree of experimentation in fitting in the various facets of this post—the missionary job,
the Lambeth job, and the European churches. The post confers three
hats, and this is not the easiest thing in the world. But I have enough
confidence in the whole plan to feel that the details of it will be
worked out in due course; you have administrative skills and experience second to none, and I'm sure will see the ways to fit this puzzle
together. . . .

His gracious and patient response of March 13th was characteristic.
I quote two paragraphs from it which carried a bit further the clarify-
ing dialogue about the rather puzzling relationships of the new office:

> I must not now go again into the possibilities of the office which are
> as vast as they can be, and I am thankful that you see the vision
> of them. When I last wrote I really forgot to say that the Anglican

Advisory Council on Missionary Strategy will keep you supplied with important work, and I have already got one topic ready waiting for you which . . . I promised to put to the Executive Officer concerning the proper Anglican provision for the whole South American Continent and the Caribbean: there is a task!

Only one other word: you mention your own strong feeling that there ought to be a certain degree of looseness in the new post making it clear that this is not an English invention, nor merely an extension of my office. With that I wholly agree. I might have been guilty of describing it as a kind of auxiliary office to me: I really never meant that, but I did realize that I should be unloading many things on to you to my own great relief which at present I carry almost entirely on my own shoulders. But, of course, in this office you are entirely your own master, responsible to the Anglican Advisory Council on Missionary Strategy for any tasks that you take on at their request, and responsible to the Consultative Body of the Lambeth Conference for any assignments you take on at their request (which means in effect at my request): so there we are.

Finally, April 3rd, it was possible for me to write him and the Presiding Bishop that I could accept the invitation with a full and free heart. During the next fortnight, there were many practical steps to take. I had earlier (in March) opened the whole matter to my Standing Committee, who with startling unanimity felt I must accept. On April 16th I told my clergy. On April 19th, as I was beginning a preaching mission in a New England parish for one of my former priests, public announcement was made.

The bones of the announcement, as made by the Archbishop, were in the following terms:

ANGLICAN EXECUTIVE OFFICER

At the request of the Lambeth Conference, 1958, the Metropolitans of the Anglican Communion have appointed a new officer with the title of Anglican Executive Officer.

The chief duties are on the one hand to act as controller of the Anglican Advisory Council on Missionary Strategy, and on the other hand to exercise a general supervision on behalf of the Consultative Body of the Lambeth Conference on all matters affecting the Anglican Communion which call for attention between the decennial Conferences.

As the office is a new one it will be for the first holder of it to discover how best to fulfill these duties and to render his best service to the various Provinces of the Anglican Communion in their joint concerns.

My own announcement to my flock was in the form of a letter read in each congregation on that Sunday morning. It may be worth noting, parenthetically, that the bond between a bishop and his diocese in the American Church is probably more personal and intimate than anywhere else in the Church. It is traditional to say that we "marry" our dioceses. We are elected by the mutual choice of the clergy and laity. In most cases, I should imagine, we are largely supported from the annual budget of the diocese. The tradition against the translation of diocesan bishops is profoundly deep. Thus a tie is established, for better or worse, which is almost never broken except by retirement or death. This is not the place to debate this matter. I only state the fact, which of course colored my feelings intensely—I remember vividly coming home from the gathering of the clergy, feeling as if I had just divorced a dearly-loved wife! But I quote part of the letter which was read in the congregations for whatever value it may have as expressing my view of the task I was to undertake:

> You will ask what this new ministry is. I cannot answer easily, for it has never existed; and what it is to be must depend very greatly on what those who launch it make of it. But I think I can say quite clearly what is needed.
>
> Last summer, at Lambeth, the bishops came to a united mind that unless our Anglican Communion learned how to work together far more closely than we now do—work together, think together, plan together—we must increasingly fall short of the vocation with which we are called. Our world with its harsh problems and divisions, is far too complex and changes far too fast and is far too closely woven together, for us Anglicans to continue in our present isolation from one another. Here we are, forty million Christians gathered in three hundred and thirty-one dioceses, in fifteen self-governing Churches the world around—if we are to bring to our world the witness to Christ and His truth with which we are entrusted, we need far more than a meeting every ten years or so. We need to plan a common missionary strategy; we need to keep thinking together (as we do now only at Lambeth and the Anglican Congress); we need to learn to act together more and more as a world Church rather than merely as a group of national Churches of the same tradition.
>
> As the report of Bishop Gray's Committee said, "It has become evident that this Communion . . . is destined for greater and perhaps more dangerous responsibility . . . It can bring to the modern world conflict a tempered wisdom and a spiritual stability which can re-inforce the hopes and aspirations of the human race in its pilgrimage. It is obvious, however, that it will not fulfill this task unless it takes cognizance of some of its weaknesses . . . It needs to be reminded in all its parts that no one lives to himself, and that as a body with a common life, the whole is always something greater than the sum of those parts . . . If the responsibilities of a world-wide Communion are to be grasped and its resources mobilized, fuller expression must

be given to four vital principles of corporate life—co-ordination, co-operation, consolidation, cohesion."

Sharing this conviction, the bishops established a new office to begin this task of learning to think and plan and act together. The new Executive Officer will have two central responsibilities. One will be to the Advisory Council of Missionary Strategy, the central planning group for our missionary work, which we established in 1948 and then greatly enlarged last summer. The second responsibility will be to the Consultative Body of the Lambeth Conference, the continuing committee whose job it is to function during the intervals between Lambeth Conferences, to carry out what is decided, and to plan for coming Conferences.

Thus at the very outset the new officer must be concerned with a bewildering variety of different matters—with such widely varying concerns as new missions in New Guinea or South America or the industrial areas of Africa with the fulfillment of plans for the new United Church in North India, with the draft of a new model liturgy of the Holy Eucharist to guide future Prayer Book revision, with joint international study of population problems, with the establishment of new seminaries in the "younger churches" of our Communion, with the new Regional Council of our dioceses in the western Pacific . . . you see how wide our concerns are, and how greatly the bishops hoped that this new office would be a help in our common task.

If it were to be an administrative office or establish a new bureaucracy, it would fail utterly of its purpose. We do not need new machinery, nor could our Anglican witness be given simply by multiplying secretaries and committees. What is needed is some superman who can hold all these diverse interests together, in his mind and heart, who could help each part of the whole Church to be mindful of the whole, who could excite and interest our clergy and people to see and do the common work of our household together, who would be able to dream and imagine and speak for possibilities which have never yet existed, who would have the patience and persistence to bring together the needs and hopes and insights of all our scattered brotherhood, who would be set free to think of nothing save our family as a whole, and the work our Lord has given us all to do, in this dark world.

I am trying to put into words the great hope we all shared last summer when we established this ministry. Long before we had any thoughts about who could do all this, if anyone could, we saw what needed to be done. How this is to be fulfilled, what the unimaginable pattern of this work is to be, is a question to which we could bring no settled answer at all. Nor can we now; if you were to ask me today where I shall start, I could not answer you. Yet the needs and the hopes will speak for themselves, God willing, and the ways will be found, if there is flexible imagination enough in me, and if there is a united will among ourselves in our Communion to support this new work and co-operate with it.

In due course the diocese chose the Rt. Rev. William Fisher Lewis (then missionary Bishop of Nevada) as Bishop-coadjutor; the months slipped away with Bishop Lewis increasingly carrying the responsibilities of the diocese; and on New Year's Eve, Mrs. Bayne and our two youngest children and I set out for London. We left an hour before my resignation became effective, but the diocese was content and did not cut my pay.

I include also an *aide-memoire* summarizing a long conference with Archbishop Fisher at Lambeth, in September, 1959, which gave me my first procedural guides. Much has changed in the organization of the Church of England (and in the frontier of Anglican life as well) since then, but the outline of duties and relationships is not without interest:

ANGLICAN EXECUTIVE OFFICER

Aide Memoire given to Bishop Bayne, 18th September, 1959

Bishop Bayne has a double duty, first to the Consultative Body of the Lambeth Conference, and secondly to the Anglican Advisory Council on Missionary Strategy.

On matters concerning the Lambeth Conference it will be the Bishop's duty to keep in touch with the various Provinces of the Anglican Communion, acting therein on behalf of the Archbishop of Canterbury as Chairman of the Lambeth Conference and responsible to me.

So far as keeping in touch with the Church of England is concerned he will have many sources of information, but his official sources will be the Archbishop of Canterbury and the Archbishop of York.

Taking up from the Lambeth Conference 1958, the Bishop should have in mind the following things:

I. GENERAL

(a) The follow-up of matters arising out of the 1958 Conference.

(b) Preparations for the Anglican Congress in Toronto in 1963.

(c) Arrangements for a meeting of the Consultative Body two years before the next Lambeth Conference for discussion of the agenda. (For urgent reason other meetings of the Consultative Body could be called).

(d) Co-operation with the Archbishop of Canterbury in making arrangements for the next Lambeth Conference, presumably in 1968.

(e) Questions arising under Resolutions 16 and 17 of Lambeth 1958.

(f) Occasional Papers: after the 1948 Conference I issued from time to time what were called Occasional Papers to all overseas bishops, making reports chiefly of a factual kind on progress in the various matters arising out of the preceding Conference. There were three such Occasional Papers (q.v.). It is for the Bishop to consider whether, when and how Occasional Papers should be produced in the future. Lambeth will be ready to do anything required to help, including the expense of distribution.

II. PARTICULAR

Taking the Five Committees of the 1958 Lambeth Conference in order, the following things may be noted:

Committee I.   The Bible

No particular question arises.

Committee II.   Church Unity

In England the Bishop's chief contact should be with the Bishop of Chelmsford as representing the Church of England in general. He was Chairman of Committee II. He is my chief confidant on Church Unity matters; he is Chairman of the Church of England Council on Inter-Church Relations; he is also Chairman of a group consisting of the Chairmen and Secretaries of the last named Council plus the Overseas Council of the Church Assembly, and the Council for Ecumenical Co-operation. This group is designed to keep these three Councils in touch with matters concerning Church Unity inside or outside the Anglican Communion.

(The officers of these three Councils are as follows:

Church of England Council on Inter-Church Relations:
  Chairman: The Bishop of Chelmsford.
  Secretary: The Reverend J. R. Satterthwaite.
Church Assembly: Overseas Council:
  Chairman: The Bishop of Liverpool.
  Secretary: The Reverend J. G. H. Baker.
Council for Ecumenical Co-operation:
  Chairman: The Bishop of Guildford.
  Secretary: The Reverend David Paton.)

Particular questions to be watched, arising out of Committee II from a Lambeth Conference point of view:

(a) Ceylon Scheme and North India and Pakistan Plan.

(b) The Spanish and Lusitanian Churches.

(c) Anglican policy towards the Roman Catholic Church: (i) on the Continent, and (ii) in other parts of the world.

(d) Questions arising in the World Council of Churches.

(e) Church of Sweden resolution on Women priests.

Committee III.   Progress in the Anglican Communion

(a) Resolutions 58–72 concerning the Advisory Council on Missionary Strategy and the Consultative Body, see above. The Advisory Council on Missionary Strategy has no form and no existence, and for practical purposes cannot meet except at the time of an Anglican Congress or a Lambeth Conference. Its practical existence is in the Bishop as Anglican Executive Officer, and in his contacts with the missionary work of the Anglican Communion in various parts of the world. There has already been discussion between us about what are the chief problems arising at the moment in this field. So far as the Bishop's contacts with the Church of England in this field are concerned, his chief reference will be to the Overseas Council of the Church Assembly: but it is not to be forgotten that the Overseas Council is linked with the Church of England Council on Inter-Church Relations and the Council for Ecumenical Co-operation through the group referred to above.

(b) For questions concerning ministries and manpower in the Church of England, consultation will be with the Bishop of Bath and Wells as Chairman of C.A.C.T.M. (Central Advisory Council of Training for the Ministry).

(c) Prayer Book: I suppose the first task here is to keep in touch with the various Provinces and see what they are doing about Prayer Book Revision. Here in England the Bishop's main contact must be with me. There is a Liturgical Commission of the Church of England dealing with Prayer Book Revision under the Chairmanship of the Dean of Lincoln. Secondly, under this heading, reference must be made to Resolution 76. I have not discussed this Resolution with anybody, and I am not at all sure what should be done about it.

Committee IV. Reconciling of Conflicts

Nothing is needed here except to note whether at any time some joint discussion between one or more Provinces of the Anglican Communion is needed on some current international issue. The Church of England's chief touch with such matters is through the British Council of Churches.

Committee V. The Family

So far as I know no action is needed here.

G. C.

18th September, 1959

Finally, an indication of the scope of the new officer's work, as seen at the outset, may be gained from a memorandum prepared for the ACMS in 1963. The Lambeth Conference in 1958 had bequeathed a number of concerns to the ACMS and the Consultative Body, in various reports and resolutions, and these properly provided an initial agenda for me. In preparation for the ACMS meeting at Huron College, Canada, in 1963, I drew up a paper commenting on the status of the main tasks with which I had begun work. (The references to things identified as "ACMS 63/something" are to reports and working papers on specific matters—some thirteen in all—provided for the meetings of the ACMS and the Consultative Body):

CHECK-LIST OF PRIORITIES

Introduction

This is a summary of the situation, in mid-1963, of the various tasks and concerns specifically identified by the 1958 Lambeth Conference as priorities for the ACMS and the Lambeth Consultative Body, and the responsible officer of those two groups. This summary does not take account of developments since 1958; it is a report on what Lambeth itself suggested for the attention of its two continuing bodies. I have been principally guided by these recommendations in organizing my work. After three and a half years, it may be useful to look at them, to see what progress has been made in each particular and perhaps chiefly, to evaluate priorities for the future.

I. ACMS

A. Organization:

The Conference (Res. 60) accepted "the recommendations of the Committee on Progress in the Anglican Communion concerning the ACMS, and respectfully requested that action be taken by His Grace the President as soon as possible." Action was taken accordingly; the desired officer was chosen; the ACMS was reconstituted on the suggested basis; and a plenary meeting of the Council is being held in connection with the Anglican Congress.

B. Areas of Special Urgency:

The Committee identified nine areas of "special urgency" for the careful consideration of the ACMS. They, and an indication of the action so far taken, follow:

1. *African Townships.* No specific program has been developed in this respect. Africa and our strategic necessities there, however, have been the subject of a special study by the Overseas Council of the Church of England, and specific programs may be expected to arise out of that. (ACMS 63/2.)

2. *South America.* A full study of South America, from the point of view of the Anglican Communion, has been carried out by PECUSA, and a report and recommendations are submitted from a four-church consultation in Mexico in 1963. Some action has already been taken to implement these recommendations. (ACMS 63/1.)

3. *Chinese Dispersion.* No intensive study of this area has been felt necessary. The largest concentration of Chinese people outside of continental China is in South East Asia; and the CCSEA has taken an increasing initiative in this respect. A brief survey was made by CCSEA in 1961; PECUSA has released a third of its reserve China Funds for work at the discretion of CCSEA; a publications committee has begun work; a bishop has been assigned to Taiwan; and in other ways, significant beginnings have been made on various sectors. The CCSEA seems the appropriate jurisdiction to take primary responsibility for this work. (ACMS 63/11.)

4. *New Guinea.* Primary responsibility for this area rests with the Church in Australia, and with the South Pacific Regional Council. Recommendations are currently being made with respect to New Guinea and the whole South Pacific island area, to strengthen our relationships and common planning. (ACMS 63/3.)

5. *Middle East.* A report is being made on the Archbishopric in Jerusalem, drafted by the Archbishop. Progress has been made in planning and priorities in the area. (ACMS 63/7.)

6. *New Provinces and Councils.* (See also Res. 66.) Two provinces —East Africa and Uganda—have come into existence since 1958, and the necessary preliminary studies are going forward with respect to two more—Brazil and South East Asia (the dioceses of Jesselton, Kuching, Rangoon, and Singapore and Malaya). The Council of the Church of South East Asia has been greatly developed and reconstituted. The South Pacific Anglican Council is presently being carefully studied, in relation to the problems of our mission in the South Pacific area. (ACMS 63/3 and ACMS 63/11.)

7. *Missionary Dioceses.* Where problems in this connection have been referred to the ACMS, appropriate action has been taken by myself. No general consultation on this subject has been held.

8. *Restrictions on Religious Freedom.* (See also Res. 67.) No action has been taken by ACMS in this matter, and little of any consequence by myself.

9. *Possible conflicts with governments.* Little action has been taken in this respect beyond the confidential circulation of background material as appropriate.

C. Resolutions of direct reference:

1. *Channels of communication (Res. 62).* Attempts have been made to deal with this in four principal ways. First, through my own direct efforts in writing and speaking. Second, through the development of additional channels of communication, as *Anglican World, Compasrose, Exchange* and the like. Third, by the stimulation of inter-Anglican working groups of various kinds, notably liaison among public relations and information officers, etc. Fourth, by the general circulation of news and papers of interest to particular groups, to "Consultants," etc.

2. *Exchange of materials, skills, etc. (Res. 63).* Development in this area, so far, has been almost entirely through correspondence or personal visits. No specific program or channel, with the exception of *Exchange,* has so far been developed.

3. *Polygamy (Res. 120).* No action has yet been taken in this respect.

D. Resolutions of indirect reference:

1. *Bible study (Res. 12).* Some churches have developed programs for this; my own activity has been limited to (a) general cognizance, (b) putting people into touch with one another, where indicated.

2. *Stewardship (Res. 64).* Again, any activity on my part has been limited to general cognizance and communication. A consultation on the laity, including this theme, has been planned for the post-Congress weekend in Toronto.

3. *Movement of peoples (Res. 65).* No action has been taken by myself or the ACMS in this respect beyond participation in conferences and the like dealing with the problem.

4. *Anglican Congress (Res. 68).* I have tried to give all possible assistance to the Canadian Church in planning the 1963 Congress.

5. *Cycle of Prayer (Res. 69).* Publication of this Cycle has been continued by the Overseas Council of the Church of England, and commended by myself for widest possible use. Studies have been made of the eventual re-design of the Cycle, and a paper prepared on this subject for discussion by the ACMS. (ACMS 63/10.)

6. *Pan-Anglican (Res. 70).* This valuable periodical has been carefully studied by its father and sponsor, the Bishop of Connecticut, and is presently being published on a new basis, designed to fill a vacant area in our communications.

II. Lambeth Consultative Body

A. Organization:

Resolution 61 of the 1958 Lambeth Conference suggested a reconstitution of this body; and the Archbishop of Canterbury took action accordingly, including the appointment of myself as the responsible Executive Officer.

B. Areas of Direct Responsibility:

1. *Wider Episcopal Fellowship (Res. 16).* A preliminary meeting of Anglican and non-Anglican representatives was held during the WCC Assembly in New Delhi, in 1961, and it was then agreed to plan the Conference sought by Lambeth. Since then, plans have been completed for such a conference to be held in April, 1964.

2. *Lambeth Conference (Res. 17).* No action has yet been required on this subject.

3. *Ceylon/North India/Pakistan (Ress. 20–24).* Full attention has been given this matter, beginning with the publication of a volume containing the relevant documents and material, and continuing with the periodic circulation of additional material—all designed to further the recommendations of these resolutions.

4. *West Africa (Ress. 31–34).* A plan for a united church in West Africa has been developed and is now ready for consideration by the churches concerned. Copies of the current edition of the plan are being circulated, for the purposes contemplated by the resolutions.

5. *Jerusalem Archbishopric (Ress. 35–37).* No official action has been required under these resolutions.

6. *The Holy Communion Service (Res. 76).* No action has yet been taken to form the Advisory Committee proposed in this resolution. A beginning of common study has been made through the circulation of a draft African liturgy which has been studied by most of the churches separately, and on a joint regional basis by PECUSA and the Canadian Church. The results have been communicated to the author of the liturgy, the Archbishop of Uganda. A list of "Liturgical Consultants" has been developed, and correspondence opened between churches on liturgical matters. A Consultation on

Liturgical Affairs is planned for the post-Congress weekend in Toronto. It is hoped that, helped by all these activities, it may be possible to move toward the fulfillment of Resolution 76.

7. *Mutual Exchange of Information (Res. 131)*. No action has yet been taken to implement this resolution, except for the development of a proposed study program on the family, by the appropriate agencies of three churches—Canada, England, and the USA. This proposed program has not yet been set in motion, pending further consideration of the whole field of inter-Anglican study.

C. Areas of Indirect Responsibility:

1. *Unity negotiations (Ress. 44 et al.)*. All that has been done so far, in these matters generally, has been to develop a list of "Consultants" in ecumenical affairs, and to circulate relevant information to them and the authorities of the respective churches. A Consultation on Ecumenical Affairs is planned for the post-Congress weekend in Toronto.

2. *St. Augustine's College (Ress. 95–99)*. The College Consultative Council has continued to function, although its communication with the Anglican Communion as a whole is tenuous. The budget agreed to by the Lambeth Conference of 1958, calling for grants totalling £14,000 from the provinces of the Anglican Communion, has been met in full, beginning with 1961. This budget covered the minimum operating costs as estimated in 1958. A paper on St. Augustine's will be circulated (ACMS 63/13).

3. *Industrial Society (Res. 111)*. No action has been taken, or apparently needed in this respect.

4. *Divorce Legislation (Res. 118)* and

5. *Marriage Discipline (Res. 119)*. No action has been needed or taken so far, on these allied resolutions.

STEPHEN F. BAYNE, JR.

ACMS 63/9
June, 1963

A POSTSCRIPT

By ARCHBISHOP LORD FISHER OF LAMBETH

THE HISTORICAL NOTE written by Bishop Bayne admirably sets out how the office of Anglican Executive Officer came into existence and how it came about that he should be offered and should accept the invitation to be first holder of this office. The following brief notes are perhaps needed in order to complete Bishop Bayne's picture, with the general outlines of which I wholly concur.

It is true that origins of both bodies, the Consultative Body and the Advisory Council, can be found in the second Lambeth Conference in 1878. But in 1948 the former entered into a new kind of existence and

the latter was created *de novo* to meet new circumstances. My first
contact with the Consultative Body was in 1946 or thereabouts when I
summoned it, according to precedent, to consider the Agenda for the
1948 Lambeth Conference. All there was to work on was the draft
agenda prepared by Archbishop Lang with a view to the Conference
due in 1940 but prevented by the outbreak of war in 1939. There were
at Lambeth few supporting papers of any substance, and no chaplain
who had had any touch with previous conferences or any knowledge of
their working. Bishop Bell, Bishop Haigh and others gave me of their
great knowledge and experience with utmost generosity. But Lambeth
had to work it all out afresh before the Consultative Body met. And
the Body was a cumbrous thing. It was meant to be composed chiefly
of Primates and Presiding Bishops. Because of the difficulty and cost
of travel at that time, it consisted in fact chiefly of Bishops resident
in England—some as diocesans, some representing overseas Primates
and Presiding Bishops. An agenda was prepared, submitted to all overseas diocesan bishops, revised at Lambeth and promulgated. Meanwhile
Bishop Haigh and I had to consider what preliminary documents ought
to be prepared and circulated before the Conference met; and the translation of all this into actual documents, and the circulation of them
in time was the work (part of the work) of my staff at Lambeth. The
same procedure was in general followed before the 1958 Conference;
but by then I had had larger experience of my office; and I was able
with my advisers to see quickly what topics (great or small) were of
pressing importance and what documents setting them out would be
needed. Even so the pressure upon Lambeth alone was intense. All
that, and the growing importance of the matters needing to be kept
in view with mutual understanding and consultation by Primates and
Presiding Bishops *between* the ten yearly conferences, lay behind the
Resolution 61 adopted by the 1958 Conference and quoted by Bishop
Bayne.

Then there is the development of the Advisory Council on Missionary Strategy. Bishop Bayne finds a foreshadowing of it in the Encyclical
Letter of the 1878 Conference; but I doubt whether any of us concerned with the establishment of the Advisory Council were aware of
this foreshadowing. Resolutions 80 and 81 of the 1948 Conference arose
straight out of an immediate situation. The idea of an advisory council
grew, I suppose, from many contributory sources, but not least from
the two following:

Missionary work in England had always been done by independent
societies within the church and not as a direct activity of the Church

of England as such; and splendid work they had done. But such people
as the late John McLeod Campbell, secretary of the Church Assembly
Missionary Council, who had a grand strategic vision, were convinced
that these Societies, all represented on the Missionary Council, must
be brought to work together, sacrificing some degree of their separate
independence, working under the Missionary Council, to a unified
strategic plan. Canon McLeod Campbell did splendid work; but he
was always conscious of a feeling of frustration because the Missionary
Societies were so loath to reveal, let alone to co-ordinate, their plans or
even to act overseas under the controlling authority of the dioceses
overseas which they served. There was a growing need for strategic
vision in this field at home.

At the same time, in the Anglican Communion great regional
churches were often entirely ignorant of what other churches were
doing in establishing infant regional churches or indeed of what areas
they were working in. And misunderstandings were arising. Some
bishops of missionary dioceses in Africa or elsewhere would go on
expeditions to the United States or Canada to plead the cause of their
own diocese on compassionate grounds of urgent local need. They did
it with great effect, and won large sums from the generous-hearted
Anglicans to whom they went. But they did nothing to reveal to them
the general field of Anglican missionary endeavor or to educate them
in the principles of missionary strategy or in the most pressing general
needs of the moment. It was not surprising that there was some resentment in the United States at this itinerant begging for particular
dioceses, cashing in as it seemed on American wealth and American
generosity; and embarrassment was often caused to us at home when
without the consent, often without the knowledge, of authority at home
(except perhaps for the authorities of a particular missionary society)
bishops of missionary dioceses, most of whom were in fact English and
supported entirely by the Church of England, went on these money-
raising expeditions.

It was out of such a situation that the need for an Anglican Advisory
Council came to be realized. And of course, as soon as such a possibility
was seen, there came into view all the positive and constructive possibilities which it has been the particular task and privilege of Bishop
Bayne to work out and translate into the realities of inspiration and
application.

One further historical note may be added. The proposal for an
Advisory Council on Missionary Strategy was put to the appropriate
committee of the 1948 Conference and recommended by it to the whole

Conference, which approved of it in Resolution 80. Resolution 81 recommended the appointment of liaison and communication officers by each national or regional church. Bishop Bayne says that this latter recommendation was not implemented. That is not quite true. Canon McLeod Campbell was appointed secretary of the Advisory Council, and all the regional churches appointed their representatives to the Council. The machinery was there. But Canon Campbell was also full-time secretary of the Church Assembly Missionary Council (as it was then called). The Lambeth Conference gave him no money and no extra staff with which to fulfill his duties to the Advisory Council, and the members of it were scattered all over the world. So it inevitably led a very desultory existence. When the Anglican Congress at Minneapolis in 1954 was approaching, Canon Campbell and I decided that there must be a meeting of the Advisory Council (one to be attended by the Primates and Presiding Bishops in person)—its first meeting—and we prepared an Agenda. The time had not come when such an idea as a budget for the Council and contributions on an agreed scale from all the regional Anglican churches to support it could be suggested. We were still well content with "here a little, there a little" by way of money and organization.

But at Minneapolis the Advisory Council did two things, both pregnant with purpose and hope. It invited all the regional churches to contribute their due (and allocated) share to two Anglican projects, significant for the whole Communion. One was to sustain and improve the stipend of the Bishop in Jerusalem, soon to be made Archbishop in Jerusalem, where he represented in the Holy City the whole Anglican Communion. (The Archbishop is appointed still by the Archbishop of Canterbury, but only in his capacity as Chairman of the Lambeth Conference and after consultation with and gaining the approval of his fellow Primates and Presiding Bishops for the appointment.) The other project was to sustain and improve the income of St. Augustine's College, Canterbury, which had already begun its beneficent life as a central college of study for clergy from all parts of the Anglican Communion. In due course every regional church without demur, and indeed with generous appreciation, accepted its assigned obligation for these two primary examples of organized Anglican co-operation. The Conference of 1958 gave the Council for the first time a Chief Officer and a staff.

February 1964

II.

Reports of the Executive Officer

1960

February 6, 1961

My Lord Archbishop,

It is a very pleasant, if somewhat perplexing task, to report to your Grace, and through you to the churches of our Anglican household, at the end of the first year of my duty as Anglican Executive Officer. It is pleasant because it does not often happen that a man in middle life is privileged to break entirely new ground in such a pioneering ministry as this. But it is equally perplexing to explore an uncharted country of inter-church relationships and to venture into untried experiments in our common life. I resolved, a year ago, to move very slowly in attempting to define duties or describe functions too closely, and I am still of the same mind. Nevertheless, the year has brought some unavoidable and irresistible clarification, which has been welcome, and which is reflected, to some degree, in this report. But the major point, I think, is not that time itself has done this but that the needs of our common life have made themselves felt—if at the cost of more perplexities, still with the added assurance of a job infinitely worth doing.

Housekeeping

In assigning degrees of importance to tasks undertaken in 1960, I must assign first place to the very unromantic details of simply opening a new office. The elemental necessities of assembling a staff, finding house and office space, purchasing equipment, establishing an identity, working out the essential routines of correspondence, and generally opening for business, occupied a heavy proportion of time and energy.

25

Thanks to your Grace, it was possible to take our first steps at Lambeth. With the summer came the decision to center both our home and office at 21 Chester Street, where the Leasehold was purchased by the Central Board of Finance, who are reimbursed from the annual budget of the Executive Officer. I am most grateful to many, notably to Captain Doig, Secretary of the Central Board of Finance, for immense help given in this matter.

The costs of modifying and adapting the house for dual use amounted, in 1960 to some £800, of which approximately £200 was paid from my Executive Officer budget, £325 by the Protestant Episcopal Church appropriation for my work as Bishop in charge of the American Churches in Europe, and £275 from gifts made to me by friends in America. The expense of furnishing the offices, in the same period, totalled £1,125, of which £1,030 came from gifts from friends in America. Office machinery purchased in 1960 cost about £1,600. Once again, I was glad to have had a gift fund from which to make these necessary purchases; £1,250 came from this source, £270 from my own budget and £75 from the funds of the American Churches in Europe. In summary, it required about £3,570 ($10,000) to launch the new office and supply the basic tools with which it must work. I feel I must express particular thanks to my own countrymen and Church in this, for so imaginatively foreseeing such needs and helping to meet them.

In closing the accounts for 1960, I add heartfelt appreciation for the warm and brotherly way in which each of our churches has met its share of the budget. 1960 was the first year of such a voluntary and highly experimental matter, and it is gratifying to know that with only tiny and accidental exceptions, every expectation was met in full. By good fortune, the Episcopal Church in the United States had made provision for its share of the budget in 1959 as well as 1960, which thus made it possible for our moving expenses from Seattle to London to be met without having to tax the 1960 budget. Thus the full amount given in 1960, £11,000 in round numbers, could be devoted to 1960 operation, and we were able to end the year with all bills paid. Estimates for 1961 and succeeding years are already in your Grace's hands and will, I understand, be circulated to the churches in due course. It is my earnest hope that the small increase requested may be met, for, after one year's experience, it is clear that some readjustment of our 1958 estimates is essential.

I add a comment about staff, which is pertinent at this point. Almost from our arrival February 15th, it became clear that we would need at least one more office secretary than we had guessed, simply on account of the enormous correspondence which flows steadily in and out of the office. I do not regret this in the slightest, for such mail is in large measure the blood-stream of our church's life. But it does lay an unremitting burden on my office staff, particularly in a year in which everything was new and everything had to be solved for the first time; and I cannot possibly express my deep gratitude to Mrs. Irvine and our secretaries for all they have so loyally and selflessly done.

Future staff requirements must wait until priorities are clearer than they are now. In general, I have tried to avoid assuming responsibility for anything which could possibly be done by somebody else—and this policy will continue. I am aware of the steady danger of "bigness," of over-centralization, and I mean to resist in every possible way. Yet it is clear that some inter-Anglican tasks can be done by one agency so much more effectively and wisely than by many, that it will be foolish not to accept the necessity for some central staff. Certain levels of research, for example, or the establishment and maintenance of common study programs are the sort of activities which, in time, may rightly claim provision on my staff. But I am not yet prepared to make specific recommendations in this area.

Specific Tasks

The Lambeth Conference in 1958 assigned responsibilities to the Consultative Body or to the Advisory Council on Missionary Strategy, in 31 different areas. Of these areas of responsibility, 19 are of direct and immediate concern to myself, as Executive Officer of these two bodies. These areas in turn have defined most of my work in this first year. I cannot say that all of them have had equal—or even nominal—treatment; but we have tried at least to explore each area, and to do a little tentative fishing; and in 15 instances, at least some progress has been made.

In terms of time, first priority has rightly gone to areas of special concern in missionary strategy. Here I conceive my basic task to be that of preparing the studies and material needed by the Advisory Council on Missionary Strategy, if it is to function in depth and with an adequate horizon. I have taken it for granted that the first opportunity for a full-dress meeting of the Advisory Council would be in 1963, at the time of the Anglican Congress in Toronto. Thus I have planned this part of my work on a three-year basis, with the hope of having adequate material ready by 1963, on which the Advisory Council can base the kind of broad, long-range, corporate decisions for which all our churches pray. The areas in which these decisions must be made are necessarily largely those established in the report of Committee II of the 1958 Lambeth Conference. Five geographical areas were selected for special emphasis—the African industrial townships, South America, the Chinese of the Dispersion, New Guinea, and the Middle East. Studies are already underway in three of the five areas, and I hope that by the end of 1961 the other two areas will also be under study. Two other matters—those concerning the establishment of new provinces and of new missionary dioceses—are clearly interwoven with the area studies themselves. Both South America and Africa are continents calling for the most careful thought, looking toward a redistribution of our missionary work and for new organization to help us meet unprecedented needs.

The three studies already underway, to some degree, are those in South America, South East Asia, and in Africa. In South America, the American Church has already made a preliminary survey, at my request, and now has undertaken responsibility for major area studies. In South East Asia, the South East Asia Council itself has undertaken responsibility for this work, with financial help from both the American Church and the Church of England. Africa, with its soon-to-be five provinces, and with the interplay of separate missionary societies, is a more complex area of study. However I am proposing to the Overseas Council of the Church Assembly of the Church of England that they undertake this study, with a view to assembling and interpreting the vast accumulation of data already in the possession of our churches and missionary societies, to prepare suitable proposals for the future.

All of these missionary studies, of course, are really, and increasingly, matters which might better be described as "inter-church relationships." Our Anglican policy has always been that of the establishment, as soon as possible, of fully indigenous, national or regional churches. Thus we pray to see established precisely such a family of churches as that in which we now have the privilege of ministering. This does not ease the problems of concerted missionary strategy. To arrive at such strategy requires the most responsible planning and partnership on the part of the churches concerned. And while each of our constituent churches is moving toward such responsible planning, we are still in a transition phase in which dependence on older missionary alignments—both those of societies and of national churches—sometimes hampers responsible self-study and decision. I need hardly say that this is not by design— it is simply an inescapable cost of strong support and nurture—but it does not make it any easier to move from this inherited pattern into the loftier and more mature level of responsible relationship, church to church. Yet this is precisely our Anglican direction and destiny.

Such responsible partnership implies and requires, in each constituent church, a degree of local and provincial responsibility which we do not always have. Thus our task of co-ordinating missionary strategy for our world-wide communion is far more than merely a matter of assembling demographic and social data. There are concurrent tasks— those of awakening responsible self-reliance and developing the necessary organs of common life—which are of equal and urgent importance. It is all very well to talk about the provincial system, and the desirability of establishing autonomous provinces as soon as possible. But provincial status, by itself, can be almost meaningless, unless the province is willing to accept, and is equipped to accept, the full obligations of a constitutionally independent church.

I have dwelt on the areas of missionary responsibility, because they are the most urgent, in terms of time. Many of the recommendations of the 1958 Lambeth Conference, however, had no direct reference to missionary affairs at all. Of these I may instance such matters as (a) "the wider episcopal fellowship," (b) the establishment of a central liturgical committee or (c) our various unity negotiations—notably those in India, Pakistan and Ceylon. While trying to maintain an intelligent relationship with all of our various unity conversations, the North India-Pakistan-Ceylon proposals have claimed rightful priority on my time in 1960. Almost immediately after assuming this new office, the Metropolitan of Calcutta sent to each of our churches a question as to their relationship with the proposed united churches of North India, Pakistan, and Ceylon, should those unions be effected. It seemed clear to your Grace, as it did to me, that my essential part in this was to make available to all the churches concerned, all the basic documents which must guide their answers. Thanks to the imaginative generosity of SPCK, it was possible, during the spring and summer of 1960, to assemble this material and publish it in a form readily available to all concerned. The booklet as published does not pretend to answer the question involved; it is intended simply as what I called an "exercise in brotherhood"—a way of fulfilling some of Lambeth's hopes for deeper and better communication within our household.

To a lesser degree I have tried to follow up Lambeth's recommendations with respect to the "wider episcopal fellowship," to a common study of liturgical and other matters, to the important matter of the exchange of material, skills, personnels, etc., and to the development of such interesting and useful improvisations as the regional councils. The

South East Asia Council is perhaps the most vivid example of this—a council which brings together the dioceses of four separate provinces, all sharing one common life and a common geography. The vitality and co-ordination of this regional association prompts me to believe that some such informal, conciliar pattern may be a most promising solution in other parts of the world, where again we have provincial interests somewhat oblique to one another, or even overlapping.

Finally, Lambeth also bequeathed certain specific obligations, such as those involved in the Anglican Congress, St. Augustine's College, and the pioneer journal of our affairs, *Pan-Anglican*. I have tried to meet the immediate necessities of each of those situations as they arose. The Anglican Congress plans are well in hand, thanks to the initiative of the Canadian Church. I have been fortunate in being able to meet with their Committee twice in 1960, and give such counsel as I could to assist in their planning. I need not speak of the importance of this capital appointment for 1963, in Toronto. St. Augustine's College, one of our three major inter-Anglican concerns, has had serious financial problems to face which will, I believe, be happily met in the event that the proposed new apportionments for our inter-Anglican financial commitments are acceptable. The loss of Canon Sansbury to the Diocese of Singapore and Malaya has caused all friends of St. Augustine's great concern; his leadership—almost from the inception of St. Augustine's College—has been unique in our Anglican history. Of *Pan-Anglican* I would only express what I know is the universal feeling of all of us, a sense of immense indebtedness to Bishop Gray for the extraordinary and vivid leadership he has given through that periodical. With the establishment of *Anglican World* it has been felt wise to discontinue *Pan-Anglican* as a regular periodical, and to rethink its place in our Anglican life. But our indebtedness to it remains very great indeed.

Since the 1958 Lambeth Conference, the Archbishop in Jerusalem has announced the establishment of a second inter-Anglican center of studies—that of St. George's College in Jerusalem. The new center is in a highly experimental phase at the moment, and the clarification of its vocation will be one of the first tasks of its new staff. But I do not doubt that it will meet the same warm welcome that St. Augustine's College did, and will fill an equal place. It illustrates the moving and significant way in which inter-Anglican projects are born. We do not establish them because we think such projects would be desirable. They are born in the initiative of this or that individual or church, and they commend themselves to our corporate thought and conscience because they serve deep purposes. Such, I pray, is also the nature of my own office and appointment.

Communication

During 1960, since we left Seattle on New Year's Eve, 1959, I have travelled just under 130,000 miles. The first six weeks of the year, Mrs. Bayne and I and two of our children were en route from Seattle to London, coming by way of Honolulu, Japan, South East Asia, India, Jerusalem and Rome. This long trip seemed helpfully to mark a clear break with our American diocesan life, and to plunge me at once into the wide world of our Anglican household. During those six weeks, it was possible for me to learn something of our churches in Japan, the Philippines and Borneo, and make briefer calls in Hong Kong, Djakarta, Singapore, Calcutta and Jerusalem. Since our arrival in London, February 15th, I have made four trips to North America and two to South Africa, as well as a dozen briefer ones to the continent of Europe and elsewhere. A fair proportion of this travel was in connection with my collateral duties as Bishop in charge of the seven American (Episcopal) congregations in Europe, and of the Episcopalian personnel in the United States Armed Forces in Europe. In the course of all this journeying, I have been able to make official visits to our churches in Scotland, the United States, Canada, South Africa and Japan, and to the Philippine Independent Church. I do not anticipate any less travel than this in 1961. It is quite clear that personal knowledge and communication at first hand is an indispensable ingredient in this ministry; and while I regret the fact that I can be in London less than half the time, there is no alternative, at least for the present.

Parenthetically, I note my gratitude for the above-mentioned collateral appointment as Bishop in charge. Even in the busiest times, it is a great refreshment of the spirit to be able to visit congregations and military bases, and to live again, however briefly, the life of a diocesan bishop. Whether it would be wise or fair to this sizeable American flock to continue a part-time episcopate indefinitely is an open and troubling question. But for the moment, it is a matter of warm thanksgiving to me that I have this privilege, all the more because, in my dual role, I may be able to help toward breaking down the quite absurd nationalistic wall of partition between the American and British congregations in Europe. As long as these congregations (both British and American) are considered merely as chaplaincies and not as authentic, full, Christian congregations, no question of "jurisdiction" arises. What causes such division (where it exists) is not jurisdiction but homesick national tradition, for the most part, and only the discovery in depth of the essential unity of the Church in Christ is needed to heal such separation. As we grow in depth, and in a common understanding of our vocation as Christian congregations, questions of jurisdiction will be easily solved, as will the sometimes-encountered suspicious peering at one another across national walls. This discovery in depth goes on apace, in every part of the world, I rejoice to learn; and true international or supra-national Anglican unity becomes daily more of a fact.

I speak of "personal knowledge and communication" as the essential elements in my travels, and this is so. The occasion may be a meeting or conference or lecture or whatever, but what happens is orientation and the interpretation of one part of our companionship to another. This is indeed the heart of the Executive Officer's work. Important as the missionary studies are and the chance to deal with the myriad inter-Anglican affairs, the one imperative function of this ministry is what could be broadly called "communication."

This may take the form of exciting and sponsoring the valiant new periodical *Anglican World*, or of setting up trans-Atlantic conferences on public relations, or of writing a monthly article for the church press, or of private letters to fellow bishops, or of an address in England or South Africa or Manila, or of the book on Ceylon, North India and Pakistan, or of any other of the multitude of projects which have engaged our thoughts in this first year. In every case, the thing itself, whatever it was, was simply an opportunity for a deeper awareness of our common Anglican life—its needs, its strength, its hopes—all the things which in the deepest sense are to be communicated.

Doubtless there are many instrumentalities yet unexplored, such as radio and television, moving pictures, common study programs, a better use of our magazines and periodicals, and the like. I am myself convinced that the first new step must be in the establishment of regular, monthly newsletters, to all my brother bishops, and this I hope to begin in the near future. Then, beyond that, lies the open and inviting field of a steady increase in planned visiting and exchange, of clergy, laity, students, businessmen—so that there will be many doing what I do, in helping to establish by personal knowledge, a new and deeper sense of the Anglican family.

For the great treasure our household holds in trust, to give, God willing, into the wider unity of the Church and the world, is a certain secret of unity. I need not dwell on it for it has often been described— a unity born not out of people thinking alike as much as people acting together. It is a unity nourished by acts rather than by opinions, by sacraments far more than catechisms. It is a unity which permits, indeed welcomes, a wide diversity in cultural and liturgical matters because the poised and balanced and responsible freedom at the heart of it needs few outward props of dress or custom. I know, for I was one of the bishops who voted for the establishment of this office and longed for what it might do and mean, how deep the hope is, in every part of our Anglican Communion, for precisely this new, deep sense of what has been given us. My task is to find every possible way in which this healthy and wholesome Anglican self-consciousness can be deepened, and to speak for it, and do what I can to represent it as strongly as I can.

And in all this, I must remember that we and our Communion are not an end in ourselves, but only a passing, historical configuration. The time must come when we will be able to pour all our gifts into a greater treasury, with the gifts of all others, that God may be glorified in a united Body. Thus we are never to be satisfied with what we now have or are; our destiny and our duty is eventually to disappear, as a separate company of Christian people, in the only real unity there is, that of the Holy Catholic Church. Thus every Anglican must learn to walk delicately, aware of the glorious heritage which is his (not by his own deserving)—yet equally aware that it is a talent entrusted to him, and not to be buried.

Here that bit of jargon, "confessionalism," needs mentioning. I am quite prepared to find myself useful, now and then, in being able to represent our wide household in this or that inter-church matter. But I resist being identified in any sense as a "confessional" officer—indeed, I resist any tendency to think of the Anglican Communion as a "confession." It would be good for us Anglicans if we had more of the courageous and uncompromising witness of the "confessional" churches of the world, as they grow in self-conscious loyalty in the face of persecution. But it would not be good for us or for any Christians to become a unitary sect of people who sought above all for clear, denominational, doctrinal tests or thought overmuch about our imperial, institutional possessions at home or overseas. The only Church we Anglicans believe in is the one described in the Creeds; into that we are baptised; that Church ordains us and feeds us sacramentally; that is the only Church which has the right to command our entire obedience. Thus we are uneasy at "confessionalism," at least as far as that word connotes an eternity of conflicting denominational families, each with "its own" world-wide power structures. It is impossible, I think, to be a good Anglican without at the same time being most deeply concerned about ecumenical life and problems. It is only those who do not take the Creeds seriously who are able to speak easily about "churches." To the great, historic brotherhoods of Christians, such as our own, the Church cannot be many, but only one. And the ecclesiological significance of my office must be found against that background.

I close this section with the hope that, as the months go on, I can find ever-increasing ways to make the reality and the nature of our Anglican household clearer to ourselves as well as others. Curiously, it often seems that the Mother Church of England knows the least about our Communion of all our Anglican fellowship. Here especially I mourn the necessity for so much absence from England, for I long for the chance to stir and awaken the mind of the Church of England to know what its leadership and devotion have given to the world, in the 350 years since the first overseas Anglican Church was established, in Jamestown. We who come from the younger churches know very well what has been given us, and give thanks for it, and for the growing partnership which gleams and brightens ahead of us. How I wish that something of this same sense might be equally shared by the oldest partner. It is disconcerting to feel that of all our churches I am the least at home in England (in the sense of meeting any broad understanding of my job, and the inter-Anglican character of my ministry and of our churches' life). This is all the more curious because, of all nations, the British people and the Commonwealth have pioneered in precisely the deep, liberal association of free people which is such an apt political parable of the even-deeper association of Christians in Christ. But we all need to know ourselves and identify our hopes and needs, and my task is to do whatever is possible to do, that the unity of mankind may be somehow strengthened and purified by the life and example of the Church, and of our own Communion within it.

Next Steps

It is still premature, I think, to project any radical new directions. After barely a year of learning, I am not yet ready to trust my judgment about specifics, save as they are forced on me by the course of events.

Certain needs have become clear however, in the course of these early months, and I may mention five of them, because they can be easily met if understood. The first is the unremitting need, on all sides, to recognise the purpose and nature of my office, and to see to it that I am supplied with the information I need to do my work fully and faithfully. There is no blame attaching to any church or person in this; it is simply a matter of becoming accustomed to having a central officer in our Communion. But if that officer is to be what he should be, he must be on the "information" list of every relevant working group—missionary societies, unity negotiating committees, publication boards, or whatever. Sometimes it is kindness which moves people to spare me burdensome mail. Sometimes it is forgetfulness, or lack of awareness that I am interested. But I would be glad to be spared both the kindness and the forgetfulness, for it is most important that I know what is going on, in order to head off duplication, or to suggest or improvise relationships of which we are not easily aware.

Second, this consideration has a particular bearing on inter-church relationships within our communion. Because I am an American, it is natural for those concerned with appeals to the American Church to direct them through me or include me in their proposals. In any case, appeals made to the American Church are, as a matter of routine, referred to me for evaluation before they are dealt with. All this is enormously helpful. But I need hardly point out that the American Church is only one of the soon-to-be-eighteen churches for whom I work, and that the same factors operate in all these cases. If it is important that the American Church take no action in inter-church matters without reference to our central office, then it is equally so with respect to all the other churches. For what we desperately need, as Committee II said at Lambeth in 1958 is "co-ordination, co-operation, consolidation, cohesion"; and the only way to get these things is to build them into our way of living and doing business from the beginning. It is most disconcerting, for instance, to work for hours to excite a bit of study here or a conference there, only to discover—often too late—that this study or whatever it is has already been planned. It is correspondingly heartwarming to have missionary executives, for example, take pains to keep me in touch with what they are doing and thinking, so that my own advice, such as it is, can proceed at least from a general knowledge of the situation.

Third, it is painfully clear that we need vastly more corporate consultation than we now have. It is all very flattering for me to be treated as a lonely oracle, and there are manifest advantages to working for two bodies which rarely meet. Nevertheless, I am only too conscious of my own ignorances and foolishness to wish to see over-much dependence placed on my individual judgment in important matters. It would not be right to delay the necessary decisions on this ground—we must keep going, even if only on an imperfect basis, and I will not hold up a useful and good missionary project, for instance, simply because I cannot fully document my judgment about it. But we must push ahead as swiftly as we can to the time when there is steady and ample consultation among us. The Anglican Communion now suggests what the United Nations would be if it met only once in ten years. What our patterns of consultation are to be is not yet clear, but the need for steady, mutual dialogue grows more clear every day.

Fourth, we have very urgent need to develop planning facilities and organs, even in our smallest churches. Hardly any of our family has made more than a start in this direction, or has begun to think in long-range terms about its vocation, and the program and plan which is needed to fulfill that vocation. All too often in our Anglican history, we have followed a "bird-shot" theory of missionary expansion—firing a number of scattered, small, evangelical pellets so as to sprinkle a society with ecclesiastical operations of little power, often no more than one lonely man far separated from his brothers. This has bred a succession of devoted missionary heroes and of moving stories of persistent bravery. But it has not distinguished us for our foresight and our wise obedience. Many people dislike the word "strategy," as being a sub-Christian word. I do not necessarily quarrel with this; I only say that if we are not prepared to be as prudent as the general making war or the man building a tower, of whom our Lord told us, then we are not very good stewards; and this prudent obedience is precisely what "strategy" signifies. To achieve this means for all of us far more attention to planning—to measuring our objectives and the societies within which we propose to minister, and thoughtfully to organize our task forces to do that job. No central office can do this; a central office can co-ordinate such studies; but until there is in each province, responsible and thoughtful planning and a willingness to accept corporate, provincial responsibility for these matters, our co-ordination will be a feeble thing.

Finally, there is a clear need for all of us to make a frontal attack on provincial and national narrowness. It would be foolish to quarrel with Anglicanism's ancient rooting in national soil. I do not question for a moment the great gains that have come to us precisely because of our local and regional identities. But in a headlong rush our whole world, and we with it, are being tumbled out of the comfortable provincialisms which were tolerable a century ago, into one world where our very life depends on person-to-person knowledge and dialogue. To our shame, the Church often has cherished such narrowness rather than taking the lead in destroying them. At its best, there is rightly a gigantic subversiveness about the Body of Christ in this world, which stirs restlessly under every separation between men; and this we Anglicans must respond to in brotherly obedience. I do not now speak of obliterating national or provincial differences. These are the very subject matter of our dialogue. But I speak of the ignorance, the pride and prejudice, which so often prevents the dialogue from taking place. One church uses the laity more fully than another, for example, and this can become a nourishing point for exchange; it can also become the occasion for silly accusations of "clericalism" on one side, or "protestantism" on another. Again there are healthy differences of liturgical practice, which can become the life-giving substance of mutual strengthening, but often degenerate into mere suspicions of whatever kind of churchmanship we do not like. I do not plead for the millenium; I plead only for a sensitive comradeship which will teach us all, and move us, to learn how to learn from each other, and help us all to know one another better.

For what is at stake, in this whole prodigious Anglican dream, is not that we shall somehow win more people to join our Anglican club, or build a more efficient denominational power structure, or make a bigger splash in the world. The point is unity; the point is that the Church is the one body in the world which is bigger than any human differences; the point is that we have a duty to placard before the world the reconciliation God has worked in us through Christ Jesus. If that reconciliation cannot bridge the superficial differences between Australia and Africa, or Canada and the United States, then the Church is an illusion and the whole Christian enterprise has been a ridiculous dream. What matters is that we shall realize what God has done in making us one in Christ. The Anglican Communion is not the whole Church, nor more than one of the scattered brotherhood within the Church. But it is all we have—all I have at any rate—to begin with. It is my only way of joining redeemed humanity. It has given me all I am and all I have; and through it there has opened a way through which I can somehow learn to surmount the tensions and divisions which break humanity.

But when I think of the nervous suspicion that divides my own country from Canada, for example, or reflect on the tensions which separate the Christian on Taiwan from his cousin in Hong Kong, or read of the heartbreak in Africa, and remember that, despite all this and through it all, God has been giving us the means to find our true brotherhood in the Church, I grow impatient with our pettiness and the failure of our church to remember what it is, or to fulfill what God has begun in us. This is the meaning of my office as I understand it, to be a constant witness and guardian of unity, not for the sake of power or prestige but for the sake of the brotherhood God has already given us. If it is the unity within our Anglican family alone, at the start, which is given to us, at least it is a start, and the best we have. Such has been my guiding principle, in this first year; and I pray it will be so in whatever years may lie ahead.

Respectfully submitted,

STEPHEN F. BAYNE, JR.
Executive Officer

1961

February 14, 1962

MY LORD ARCHBISHOP,

For the second time it is my privilege to report on my year's work as Anglican Executive Officer. 1961 was, like 1960, largely a year of new and uncharted responsibilities, relationships, duties, opportunities, and therefore of steady improvisation. Some progress was made in the direction of "job-description" although I am yet unwilling to attempt any general crystallizing of details in this respect, preferring to reserve any thorough proposals in this area until the Advisory Council and the Consultative Body meet in August, 1963. For the most part, the year was a case of meeting each thing as it came and trying to see how it should be handled. Roughly a third of my time seems to go to matters which could be called "missionary strategy" and another third to those which fall in the general area of the Lambeth Consultative Body. The final third comprises affairs which do not fall into any of our existing channels or patterns and here it is a case of discovering what church or agency should be responsible, or could be, and then exciting the appropriate action.

Personally the most notable event in our corporate life, in 1961, was the retirement of Your Grace's predecessor and your succession to the Archbishopric. Lord Fisher gave a powerful impetus and direction to our Communion for more than fifteen years. He presided over the two Lambeth Conferences, and the Anglican Congress, which were most aware of and deeply involved in inter-Anglican relationships, which produced the Advisory Council on Missionary Strategy and later reconstituted both that body and the Lambeth Consultative Body, and which made specific provision for my office. It was he who called me to this office and established my first guidelines. To have his counsel, almost day-by-day, in the beginning months of my work was a privilege for which I shall never cease to give thanks. We did not always agree; when we disagreed I was often in the wrong, as it proved; but more often the disagreements simply represented the tensions within our Communion itself, between newer and older churches, between churches of varying national and ecclesiastical traditions. Such tensions are not only inescapable, they are a mark of the health of a vigorous community of churches. This Lord Fisher fully understood and welcomed, and his unmistakable and confident leadership, informed by his immense knowledge of the life of our Communion, was a gift beyond price to us all and not least to me.

Corporately, the happiest and most notable event of the year was the launching of our newest province, the Church of the Province of Uganda and Rwanda-Urundi, in April. In a most moving ceremony in the Cathedral in Kampala, the responsible care of the life of its nearly two-million members was entrusted to the new church, until then a congeries of missionary dioceses. It need never be misunderstood that the churches of the Anglican Communion take indigenous leadership and responsibility seriously. From the very outset of our overseas expansion, 350 years ago, it has been our plan and purpose to develop self-confident and buoyant leadership in the newer churches in order that they might the more swiftly take form as self-governing, independent, regional and national churches on their own. To my knowledge, no other Christian bodies have advanced as rapidly as the churches of our Communion in the development of indigenous leadership, and in the achievement of freedom from ecclesiastical "colonialism."

Of all this, the establishment of the new province of Uganda was an important mark. The process is not without its problems. While the Anglican Communion is a pioneer in the establishment of autocephalous, indigenous churches, we have very much still to learn about the relationships of responsible partnership which must then take the place of the missionary relationship with which it all begins. There are troubling questions in this area with which we must wrestle far more radically than we presently do. An autocephalous province is a fine thing in theory. But it may remain only theoretically fine—indeed it may actually weaken our witness and mission—unless it is taken seriously with full understanding and adequate provision for what it must have if it is to be able to assume the responsibilities of independent life. To shift from a diocesan missionary relationship to the far more responsible church-to-church relationship is in itself a transition of very great complexity. To go beyond that, in the establishment of new provinces, and foresee the exacting capital and other needs which the new church must then assume, requires more imagination than has yet been given to it. The next province likely to come into independent existence is that of the Brazilian dioceses, and I have urged the committee of the American Church concerned with this to make a careful study of the new needs and new relationships required, if "provincial autonomy" is to be more than merely a somewhat picturesque phrase. Such a study would be of interest and value to all of us, and would aim directly at what is presently our weakest link.

Travel and Personal

As in 1960, about two-thirds of my time was spent away from England, in various churches of our Communion, or in other duties. My travel totalled about 122,000 miles and included official visits to our churches in Japan, India, South East Asia, Taiwan, Uganda and the United States. In addition, official visits were made to the Ecumenical Patriarch, and to three churches in the "Wider Episcopal Fellowship"—the Lusitanian Church, the Old Catholic Church of Germany and the Spanish Reformed Episcopal Church. Seven journeys included the United States, either for the quarterly meetings of the National Council (the central executive body of the Episcopal Church of which I have the privilege of membership), or for the triennial meeting of the General Convention, of which I am a member of the House of Bishops. As Executive Officer, I am also, *ex officio*, a member of the Strategic Advisory Committee, the American Church's central planning body, which meets three or four times a year, as well.

This extensive travel, conducive enough to reflection and writing, is doubtless an essential ingredient in the Executive Officer's task. It may be that as time goes on, that task will necessarily become more and more of an administrative one, to be performed from a central headquarters. Such a time has not yet come; the work of the Executive Officer now is mainly one of communication and interpretation; and the weaving of this web is done in the field. Yet I must say that I regret the long absences from London, not only for what they cost in family relationships and in the added burden on my office staff, but also because of the curious rootlessness of our life, in consequence. Over the year I am in England about one week out of every three. This means, inescapably, that my relationship with the Church of England and the life of this island is thin indeed, and I long for the time to come when I can feel as identified with the Church of England as I do with Japan, say, or Canada or South East Asia.

All the more welcome then are the opportunities which occasionally come to take part in the life of England and its Church. It was a joy to be able to address diocesan conferences last year in Birmingham, Canterbury, Hereford, Manchester, Sheffield, Worcester and York, as well as to preach or speak to special gatherings in Chelmsford, Exeter, Guildford, Liverpool and London. Two American clergy conferences— for the Bishops of Delaware and Virginia—also came my way; I was honored to give the St. John the Divine Lectures in Houston, Texas, and the McMath Lectures in Detroit, Michigan; and finally to preach at special missionary services in Boston, in Detroit at the General Convention, and in Philadelphia at the annual meeting of the Overseas Mission Society. I should also want to mention with appreciation the occasional opportunities to take part in radio and television programs of various kinds, both in Britain and elsewhere. British broadcasting, both of radio and television, unquestionably sets the standard of excellence for the world; it also provides uniquely generous opportunities for Christian witness and the communication of ideas, which I feel lay claim on the Church's best response; and I rejoice whenever opportunity comes to have part in a "Meeting Point" or "Brains Trust" or to take a turn at "Lift up Your Hearts."

A fair share of travel on the European continent, as in 1960, was in connection with my collateral responsibility as Bishop in charge of the American churches in Europe. Although there are only seven civilian congregations in my care, the large and growing number of American military personnel for which I am the ordinary, means for me, in effect, the care of a very considerable missionary diocese in itself. I welcomed this appointment and I still do, for purely selfish reasons— mainly that it gives me a chance, from time to time, to fulfill a bishop's normal ministry. Yet I know that the time must come when, in justice to the care of the nearly two-score priests involved and the thousands of church people, so many of them young men, this work must be better done than on a hurried, part-time basis.

I hope that none of what I write will seem to Your Grace to be grumbling. Despite its rootlessness and its wearying perplexities, I am more convinced than ever of the necessity for such an exploratory ministry as this, in contemporary Anglican life. What it will lead to, in the way of additional inter-Anglican administrative structure, I do not clearly see. But there is every evidence, every day, of the need and place for this work of understanding and the exchange of ideas and resources. And personally I count it a privilege to have had these two years, and the wide and warmly-intimate knowledge of all our Anglican churches which has come to me.

Yet this ministry is perplexing, for it is not one which can be fulfilled or even understood in terms of administrative structure. Before us all, in the Anglican Communion, there rises a dream of a brotherhood of Christians more durable and more sensitive and intimate than any other association this world knows. Yet this brotherhood would be impossible on any basis simply of administrative or executive authority or power. Indeed it exists precisely because it is not based on a "confessional" power structure at all.

Whatever is done through my time and efforts, for example, must be done because the churches of the Anglican Communion freely agree to do it, accepting whatever it is on its own merits, and giving to it the obedience and the support it deserves. This is our way, for better or worse. We are not a unitary world-Church with a "confessional" hierarchy.

Neither are we a shambles of conflicting, national religious clubs. We are a family, called by His name and about His business; and this is of the greatest seriousness and depth; and therefore there is and ought to be the greatest dignity and weight attached to whatever we so freely agree to do, not because there is coercive power to reinforce our decisions, but because we are not children playing at church, but grown people trying to be obedient to our calling.

Finance

There are three family concerns which have been generally accepted as fully inter-Anglican responsibilities. The oldest is our joint responsibility for the operating budget of St. Augustine's College, Canterbury. The second is the share of each church in the budget and the expenses of the Archbishop in Jerusalem. The third is the cost of my own office and work. In 1961, at Archbishop Fisher's request, these three inter-Anglican budgets were brought together, and one figure, representing each church's share of the combined total, was sent to the primates and metropolitans concerned. In most cases the figure given was somewhat larger than the total contributed in previous years. This was partly due to increases in the three separate budgets, partly to recalculation of fair shares (based on the formula agreed on in 1958, with respect to the Executive Officer's budget), partly to the fact that not all churches had previously contributed to all three purposes.

The total thus apportioned, early in 1961, was £28,400 of which £12,050 was for St. Augustine's College operating budget, £2,740 was for the expenses of the Archbishop in Jerusalem, and £13,610 was for my own office budget. A detailed report on these matters will be circulated in due course, when final figures are available. In the meantime, it may be of interest to note that ten of the eighteen jurisdictions were able to meet the new apportionment in full or better, and an eleventh plans to do so in 1962. This very helpful response is all the more appreciated when it is remembered how sharp an increase the new apportionments represented in some cases. While the amounts are not intrinsically large, they do present problems especially to dioceses and provinces which have scanty resources of their own and urgent needs to meet; and my appreciation is very great indeed to all concerned, especially to those churches which successively faced goals in some cases twice or more than had been asked of them in previous years.

The total given by us all (against the apportionment of £28,400) came to something over £26,000. From this the full operating budget of St. Augustine's College was met, also the hoped-for share in the ministry of the Archbishop of Jerusalem. My own expenses in 1961 totalled about £11,700, a saving achieved, quite frankly, by withholding salary increases for my staff, long-merited, by deferring maintenance of the premises at 21 Chester Street, and by restricting other expenses, especially travel. Thus we ended 1961 able to meet the minimum needs for our three family concerns, and hopeful that in 1962 we will be able to reach our full objectives.

I must express the appreciation which I am sure all of us feel for the assistance given by the Central Board of Finance of the Church of England, by Captain Doig and his colleagues, in administering these three budgets. It is a labor of love on a new and untested frontier, and I am all the more grateful for the very great help which has been given in bringing our resources together for our common tasks, and in administering those resources so faithfully and wisely.

Missionary Planning

I would like to turn now from more general thoughts to brief reports on specific areas of the year's work. The first is that of "missionary planning," in the broadest sense. Although there is little yet to show for it, much has happened or begun to happen which promises to bear richly in years to come.

The root need in inter-Anglican missionary life is for responsible, collective church-to-church relationships. During the "missionary" phase (in the technical sense) of the Church's life, much of the planning and deployment of resources necessarily lies with the older church or society. But at a point in the development of the newer churches, as I suggested above in reporting on Uganda, this missionary relationship must give place to another, more mature, more responsible, and requiring a far higher degree of corporate action on the part both of the newer church itself and the sponsoring and helping bodies. There is not much sense in establishing new provinces if they do not have both the will and the means to assume responsibility for their own life and growth. To assume this responsibility—certainly to take the initiative in it—requires certain elements in a province's life which are often not present nor even needed during the first phase of missionary relationship.

Paramount among these needs is that of the will of the new church to take corporate responsibility for its own members. The older missionary relationship may be that of church to diocese, or society to diocese—it may even be a relationship between smaller units. But this fragmentary relationship must end when a province comes into existence. For by definition, a province is a unit of the Church, a microcosm of the whole body; and thus its own first responsibility must be a corporate one, to the members of the body, first of all to its own common life and mission. And this is tested, I believe, by a corresponding willingness of each member of the body to consider its own priorities in relation to those of its companion dioceses. If this will to achieve a common life is not present, there can be little progress in "planning."

The second necessity is that the new province has the means by which to do thoughtful planning. These "means" include both personnel and other resources, chiefly the modest financial provisions required to make meetings possible and to give some measure of facility to central provincial life and administration.

The third need is for the older churches and societies to be willing to take the responsibility of the new province seriously. It is quite impossible for any sponsoring church or society to make a wise judgment about priorities in the life of a new province—our information is too partial and our judgment too limited to let us have the deciding vote in these things. It must be the new church's responsibility to set its own priorities, and ours to meet those as best we can in brotherly support.

Thus the development of responsible missionary planning in our time is largely the problem of building responsible church-to-church relationships. Much progress has been made in this direction during the past year. Perhaps the most notable example was in the Church of the Province of East Africa, one of the newer provinces and also one in which the tradition of corporate responsibility was initially at its weakest. Despite these difficulties, and because of the imaginative and statesmanlike leadership of the archbishop and bishops of the Province, a first beginning on true provincial planning was made, and already the results of this more radical attack are evident. Similar development is going on in other provinces as well, notably in Uganda and in CIPBC.

The mere establishment of a deeper and more responsible relationship between churches does not in itself meet all our problems. It simply makes it possible to meet them; such relationships require as much from the older churches as they do from the newer. This is notably true in the recruitment of men and resources for brotherly inter-church aid. At this stage, it may be that "missionary planning" is as much and as grave a problem for the older churches as it is for the new, in the re-examination of our whole structure of missionary support, of the recruiting and training of missionary personnel, and perhaps most notably, in the provision of massive and adequate capital partnership with the new churches.

The need for manpower, with the best of training and the utmost of devotion, remains. The day of the missionary is by no means past; indeed there may be a greater need now than ever before in our history. Even though the form of the missionary changes and has changed, there seems to be no end to the need for men and women, able and willing to take their place alongside the clergy and laity of the newer provinces. But we must think as deeply and sympathetically about the capital needs of the newer provinces. To set a new provincial church off on its independent life without giving it at least the minimum equipment it needs to meet its own emergencies and provide some power and dignity for its own decisions is a failure in responsible comradeship. Given the best will in the world, in the older churches, to give emergency help or to undertake specific projects, true maturity still would require that we provide the newer churches with at least the essentials with which to administer their own affairs and to implement and fulfill their own basic decisions.

Thus the task of missionary planning is not by any means a task for the newer provinces alone. It is a family responsibility in which every Anglican church has its full part. But I am satisfied that there was measurable progress in both sides of this relationship during 1961, and perhaps the most progress in the most important area, that of seeing the problem itself.

The Advisory Council

Our supreme inter-Anglican planning body is the Advisory Council on Missionary Strategy, established first by the Lambeth Conference of 1948, and then strengthened and re-established in succeeding years. The constitution of this body is still extremely flexible. It may consist of the primates and metropolitans of our churches and provinces, or they may appoint clerical or lay deputies at will. Doubtless experience will teach us whether this flexibility should give way to a more fixed structure. In the meantime, it has been my thought, in which Archbishop Fisher concurred, that the next meeting of the Advisory Council should consist of the primates and metropolitans themselves, just before the meeting of the Anglican Congress in Toronto in 1963. Such a meeting would have the added advantage that it could also make easily possible a parallel meeting of the Lambeth Consultative Body.

The agenda for the 1963 meeting of the Council has not yet been established, but it will inescapably be mainly that of taking the appropriate decisions about missionary planning—particularly in those areas underlined by the 1958 Lambeth Conference as most critical. Most of the studies and planning now going on look toward the 1963 meeting of the Advisory Council, of course. The Council itself, since it is purely advisory, can take no final decisions. What should rather be hoped for, I believe, are broad strategic decisions taken by the primates of our churches in consultation with one another, which can then be relayed to the churches themselves for action. A parallel meeting of the missionary executives of all our churches is also planned for 1963, which will bring to the Advisory Council the added benefit of expert and experienced advisers.

In preparation for this meeting, as I reported last year, extensive studies are being made in particular areas. The Overseas Council of the Church of England has kindly undertaken a general survey of African needs. The American Church has sponsored a study now going on, conducted by the Bureau of Applied Social Research of Columbia University, of the South American frontier. Less elaborate studies are also underway in South East Asia and other parts of the Anglican Communion. The result of these studies will be enormously helpful to the Advisory Council at its meeting, even though no study by itself can answer the problems it uncovers and analyzes.

Inter-Anglican Study

This phrase includes a variety of projects. The Lambeth Conference in 1958, in three separate resolutions (especially 76 and 131) asked for the development of a fully inter-Anglican program of study. Such a program, if it is to be of any importance and depth, is a major project, with fairly drastic requirements in organization and manpower. While it may not be necessary that there be many inter-regional, inter-church meetings, there must be some; travel expense in this case is a fairly drastic matter. Equally complicated is the problem of the planning of study in such terms as are relevant to the different societies in which our churches live.

Nevertheless tiny beginnings have been made in three directions. One was represented by "Ceylon, North India, Pakistan," a collection of the relevant documents bearing on the two church union proposals currently being considered in India and by our Anglican churches. With the generous help of SPCK, this book was published and circulated in 1960, among all our churches, and has greatly aided in providing the background for concurrent study by our whole household of a common problem.

A second instance is that of the liturgical study, which has just been launched, in selected areas of our Communion, based on a proposed African liturgy prepared by the Archbishop of Uganda, after consultation among the five African churches. This proposed liturgy for Africa, in a preliminary draft, has been circulated to all primates and metropolitans with the suggestion that appropriate study groups, especially of a regional and inter-church nature might be asked to examine it and respond to the wish of the Archbishop of Uganda for counsel about it. In addition, a specific program of inter-church study has been planned for North America, where such regional study seems immediately easy to launch.

A third type is still in the planning stages—that is a study of family life in various societies. Consultation among competent authorities in Canada, England and the United States has produced some preliminary sketches, which in due course may well yield a program of most helpful corporate work, perhaps in anticipation of the needs of another Lambeth Conference.

None of these three which I mention begin to satisfy the needs felt by the 1958 Lambeth Conference. They are no more than the barest beginnings. Some of the specific areas instanced by Lambeth, such as divorce legislation, polygamy, the needs of an industrial society, etc., have not yet even been touched. It is my hope that in 1962 and succeeding years, these lacks can be remedied.

Channels of Communication

I cannot pretend, Your Grace, to have made more than a start in this area; it remains sadly true that our communications are not good, by and large, and often limited to questions and answers in personal letters that cross my own desk. This is not satisfactory, nor is the personal contact made possible by the steadily-increasing travel characteristic of our times, however extensive that may be.

We have some good servants of communication. The periodicals in various churches have shown wonderful generosity in publishing news and views about our corporate Anglican life. My own monthly column, feeble though it is, is not without value in this; but far more important, I believe, has been the growing amount of information about other churches which our principal periodicals have steadily published.

Anglican World is doubtless the most notable venture in communication—a private venture, financed and made possible by *Church Illustrated*. An invitation is currently being issued to the dioceses of the Anglican Communion to give it the financial backing it needs, and I pray for the success of that venture. In the meantime, *Anglican World* reaches every part of the Anglican Communion six times a year, with information about our life in our various provinces and with often important ideas for corporate consideration. Its circulation, although small, has steadily increased since it was launched. It is to be hoped that determined and enthusiastic support may be given it in the months to come.

Pan-Anglican, our veteran leader in this field, has decided to abandon regular publication and substitute for it a program of occasional studies of various natures. No Anglican can be slow to acknowledge gratitude to Bishop Gray of Connecticut for his leadership in *Pan-Anglican*, and it may well be that this new chapter of its career again will pioneer an important new development in our life. Also to be anticipated is the publication of Canon Howard Johnson's reflections on his astonishing two-year pilgrimage to every part of our Communion. This book, I understand, is to be available by the end of 1962, in good time to help us prepare for the Anglican Congress of 1963.

It still remains an unfulfilled duty on my part, to provide the missing links in the chain of communication. A beginning has been made in the launching of *Exchange,* a periodical bulletin on missionary affairs, the first issue of which has only lately been sent to those concerned. I plan to continue to trespass on the kindness of our church periodicals monthly, also on that of *Anglican World*. It is also my plan, this year, to begin a regular series of newsletters to my fellow bishops; I have been reluctant to inflict more reading matter on them, since my own inundation when I was a diocesan bishop is still fresh in my mind! But on balance, I am persuaded that the advantage of a newsletter every two or three months probably outweighs the nuisance. I hope so.

Exchange

Exchange, in the language of the 1958 Lambeth Conference, implies much more than a tit-for-tat relationship between churches. It really signifies the deployment of all our resources, wherever they may be within our Communion, to meet our tasks most effectively. It means finding the resources of men and ideas and skills and money, where they are, and then finding the ways to bring them to where they are needed.

Exchange is thus doubtless the heart of my task. It is also the most complex part of my task. For it requires not only a profound knowledge of our needs, and of our resources; it requires also a judgment about priorities, and channels of communication—all of which are by no means easily to be had. Indeed, I should say we have hardly begun an approach to this task.

Yet there are most encouraging stirrings everywhere in our Communion—chiefly in the form of volunteers and suggestions, often coupled with an increasing knowledge of corresponding needs. I speak of this not to call attention to any particular project of exchange, but to underline what I regard as a fundamental truth about our Communion. The truth is, that there is no church which has not something to give and something to receive, that there is no church which has not something to say to the others, and something to hear and learn from them. Another way of saying this, rather more blunt, is that no Anglican church is "right," in the self-righteous sense of that word. I put it that way not to be rude to anybody who thinks otherwise, but only again to emphasize the modesty and eagerness which must be the prime characteristic of our common life, and therefore, par excellence of my own approach to our life and its problems.

Anglo-Americana

The fact that I am an American resident in England, as well as the fact of my collateral assignment as bishop in charge of the American churches and the American Episcopalian military personnel in Europe, makes it both pleasant and inescapable that I should often be involved in specifically Anglo-American matters, notably between the two churches involved. There has been, and there still remains a persistent problem of communication and interpretation between the two nations and the two churches. I need not dilate on the reasons for this, nor on the absolute necessity for knowledge in depth and patient understanding, the indispensable preliminaries to tough and enduring brotherhood.

Within the Church, certainly the best ways to nourish that understanding are personal ways, notably in the exchange visits we make across the Atlantic. For several years now, the "Wates-Seabury Scheme" has meant that, each year, two priests of the Church of England exchange with two Americans, each man undertaking the care of his opposite number's parish for a year and living as closely as possible as his opposite number lives. Thanks to the most imaginative generosity of Mr. Wates the proposer of the scheme, both churches, and indeed both nations, have been enriched by the affectionate comradeship and interpretation given them by these visitors. Of course this is just a beginning, and I pray that the time may speedily come when we will have more qualified applicants than we can possibly handle, instead of the very limited numbers now—in a word, I hope for the same excited eagerness in the hearts of many as there now is among a few of us.

These are not the only exchanges. There are many of briefer duration, privately and informally arranged; and while the effect of these is a good deal less profound than the "Wates-Seabury" partnerships, nevertheless they add measurably to the pool of understanding.

So too do other kinds of visits and exchanges. Notable during the last year was the occasion when the bishop and most of the clergy of the diocese of West Virginia came to England for a month, and found their way into many churches and homes, both in the diocese of Chichester and elsewhere. Similar plans are underway for 1962, in other cases. Another type of visit is that proposed by the young people of Alabama, who plan to come to Coventry during the coming summer. And still other plans, involving even the exchange of visits between the members of parishes across the Atlantic, are in prospect.

Another type of interchange between the two churches is instanced by the proposal now being explored by CACTM and two American theological seminaries, looking toward the formal appointment of ordinands from the Church of England to take two years of their theological training in the United States. It is my hope that this will become an exchange program, and not merely a one-way street. But again, it is an experiment in understanding, in depth; and is to be welcomed and valued accordingly.

I need say nothing of the hundreds of less formal contacts which happen in the course of a year. Nor do I need say, I am sure, that what I write about the United States and England is almost equally true about the relationships between other nations and England, and their churches. The fact is that the Church, and our Communion as a major segment of the Church, is the deepest and surest common life given to mankind, in a world often more and more sharply divided. If we do not express and fulfill that given unity, then we are neither understanding nor thankfully receiving the gift God gives us in His Body. Even so small a thing as the exchanged visits of two families thus gains an immense dignity and meaning, not because of its intrinsic significance, but because of God's Will and His Love.

Regional Councils

Three of these may be mentioned, each at a different stage in its development. Doubtless the most mature is the South East Asia Council, in which dioceses of four different provinces are linked together in warm brotherhood. Rangoon, a member of CIPBC, and Hong Kong, a constituent diocese of the Church in China, join three of Your Grace's overseas dioceses—Borneo, Korea, and Singapore and Malaya—and two American jurisdictions—the Philippines and Taiwan—to compose this regional Council. An annual meeting, either of the bishops alone, or of the bishops together with a clerical and a lay representative from each diocese, is the principal instrument of the Council. However, a liaison and field officer, Canon Lee of Singapore, travels widely through the Council area to implement and fulfill its needs and plans. The Council decides annually on the expenditure of those funds which the American Church puts at its disposal for work among the overseas Chinese, at present $50,000 each year. An executive committee functions during the interim between council meetings, and there is also a special committee particularly responsible for our work among the Chinese outside of continental China.

One of the central problems and opportunities of this Council arises in connection with the question of provincial status for the dioceses which compose it. Geographically the area involved is probably too wide for a single province effectively to function. In addition, Hong Kong already belongs to the Chinese province as may Taiwan, God willing, in due course; the Philippines seem destined in time to become a separate province of their own; and thus there are real difficulties in the way of any simple plan for a united province of South East Asia. In consequence, there has been a special awareness and scrutiny of the nature of the council itself, especially with a view to exploring the possibilities of a simple, synodical organization which might function as a para-Province, until more elaborate organization is possible. Your Grace is already familiar with this matter and has given measured encouragement to this exploration. The question involved is a complex one indeed. It is not simply a matter of sensible obedience to precedent with respect to provincial organization and power. It is also a matter of the way in which, in a highly self-conscious emerging society, due weight can be given to local responsibility and autonomy, even though ecclesiastical jurisdiction rests in several different authorities, and thus involves complicated questions of inter-relationships.

Much has happened in the past few years in South East Asia, chiefly in the steady deepening of affectionate and brotherly comradeship. This comradeship has in turn nourished the conciliar structure, itself a new thing in Anglicanism, and one leading into hitherto unexplored relationships. Certainly the Church cannot contemplate stopping short of the ultimate unity of the national or regional province. But the Council, more and more, seems to be an intermediate association of very great usefulness, and a seed-bed of provincial life of incalculable richness.

A second council is that of the South Pacific area, including the four dioceses of Polynesia, Melanesia, New Guinea and Carpentaria, as well as the small American jurisdiction in American Samoa. Thus three provinces are involved—Australia, New Zealand and the United States —in a very loose association. But here again, the current seems to set toward a steadily-strengthening comradeship, accented in the South Pacific area particularly by the ecumenical activity in the region, and specifically by the proposal to establish a central federal theological seminary in Suva.

Still a third area of council development is the Caribbean, where the bishops of the American missionary dioceses have launched a regional council of their own. For the moment, this council will include only the American jurisdictions, and will provide an intermediate meeting place short of the American General Convention for these dioceses sharing a common region. But it is hoped that this council will ultimately widen to include as well the dioceses of the Church of the Province of the West Indies.

The appraisal of these councils, of course, is still highly tentative and exploratory. I think that all we know is a need for a closer association than we now have, where different Anglican provinces are in close proximity to one another; yet in most instances it must be an association short of full provincial unity. No one can claim that any final answers are yet in sight to the manifold questions which conciliar organization raises. Nevertheless, each succeeding year finds more experience at our command, and more informed and confident expectations.

Other Inter-Anglican Matters

I should like to mention briefly several other concerns for which I have some measure of responsibility. The first is the Anglican Congress, to be held in Toronto in August 1963. The Canadian committee has been assiduous in its thought of every detail, and all plans, both for program and hospitality are well in hand, and full information about them has been sent to all the bishops and churches. What remains is now a matter of preparation on the part of all the rest of us. A useful series of studies, for parochial use, has been prepared by the Canadian committee and is available to all dioceses. But perhaps of far greater significance is the personal and spiritual preparation of all of us, in our separate provinces, for this cardinal event. The choice of delegates, the heightening anticipation of the Congress itself, the expectancy of what will result from this unique gathering—all these things remain yet largely in the future. My own feeling, Your Grace, is that 1962 ought to be an even more critical "Congress Year" than the actual year of 1963 itself. For we shall only gain from the Congress what we have prepared ourselves to gain, and expect to gain.

"The Anglican Cycle of Prayer" continues to be used, and even moderately pressed, in many parts of our Communion. It is disappointing that not all our church periodicals find it possible to include the Cycle in their publications, for it would mean much if every reader of national and provincial and diocesan papers might be confronted, issue by issue, with this reminder of brotherly responsibility and prayer. But an increasing number do; and I rejoice to find cathedrals and parish churches everywhere in the world using the Cycle of Prayer

with increasing regularity. Our appreciation here is to the Overseas
Council of the Church of England who assemble and publish the Cycle;
and that appreciation on my part is very warm and sincere indeed.

St. Augustine's College, Canterbury, remains a matter of central
and thoughtful concern. It is still seriously under-financed. In 1958,
at the Lambeth Conference, it was agreed that St. Augustine's needed
an annual increase of £3,000 in order to balance its minimum budget.
Despite this agreement, little or any of the increase was given until
1961 when, in the revised financial arrangements, the increase was
allocated and paid. In the meantime, with increasing costs and the
accumulation of a deficit, it remains still true that St. Augustine's is
operating at the barest minimum. Its service to our whole Communion
is profound—there is not a corner of the Anglican world which has not
been lighted by its warmth and leadership. But St. Augustine's is in
danger of becoming still one more illustration of an unhappy Anglican
habit, that of sending a boy to do a man's work. Its budget is not
sufficient to permit us to bring enough of our best leadership to join
with the resident staff. Its salary levels are inexcusably low; its household budget is barely sufficient to maintain the existing plant; it is
simply impossible for St. Augustine's to be the central staff college of
the Anglican Communion, which was the dream which gave it birth,
nearly fifteen years ago.

It would be easy to say that this is only a matter of money. But
money follows interest and concern; the churches of the Anglican
Communion are not yet involved in the management and care of St.
Augustine's to that degree which would press the College as an immediate and personal problem to them; and until the full responsibility
for its affairs is lodged effectively in our several churches, Canon Cragg
and his colleagues seem bound to continue laboring against almost
insuperable odds. Despite these stubborn difficulties, the College continues to minister in its extraordinary way to our Communion. The
Church of England is perhaps less excited about it than others, which
is probably not unnatural in view of geography. But I find almost no
province of our Communion in which there is not eager and thankful
awareness of St. Augustine's and what it has meant in the lives of
many of our clergy; and for this we owe immense gratitude to Bishop
Sansbury and Canon Cragg, and to many others who have shared the
leadership of the College.

St. George's College, in Jerusalem, now begins to take form as
perhaps a second major inter-Anglican theological center. At present, it
is simply a concern of the Archbishopric itself, and any decision about

its future status within our Communion must rest with the Advisory Council, no doubt, and the subsequent action of the several churches. In the meantime Archbishop MacInnes has gone ahead to explore the development and vocation of this College, in many ways so uniquely situated with respect to the possibilities of archaeological, biblical and ecumenical study. I am to have the privilege of laying the corner-stone of the building for the College during Holy Week, 1962; and already a modest roster of courses is being offered, both for students from the Archbishopric itself and from overseas.

Wider Episcopal Fellowship

This fellowship, which was the subject of much thought by the bishops at the 1958 Lambeth Conference, and indeed was the subject of a specific resolution, is a way of describing that group of churches with which churches or provinces of the Anglican Communion are in "full communion," or a relation of "inter-communion." Some are national churches, such as those of Sweden or Finland. The Old Catholic Churches are included, both on the Continent of Europe and in the United States. The Church of South India represents a new configuration, the result of a reunion plan involving several traditions. Two of the churches are very small, the Lusitanian and the Spanish Reformed Episcopal Church. The Philippine Independent Church is perhaps one of the largest and, at the same time, one of the least-known in this fellowship.

This informal group has no precise outlines, nor any constitutional structure. It is nothing more than its name indicates—a fellowship within the whole Body of Christ, which holds certain fundamental things in common, such as the historic episcopate. In this they represent a partial fulfillment of what was sketched in the Lambeth Quadrilateral. But the fellowship is not a bloc, or alliance, or union of churches—it is a group of friends who hold certain great things in common. During the year, three events of measurable importance took place within the fellowship, in the completion of concordats between the Protestant Episcopal Church in the United States and the Lusitanian and Spanish Reformed Episcopal Churches and with the Philippine Independent Church. In all three cases, close association and warm friendship had paved the way for the formal agreements now concluded. Indeed the historic friendship of the Church of Ireland with the two churches in Spain and Portugal goes back nearly a century, and made it possible for full communion with them to be a fact long before a formal concordat was thought of.

Another significant event during the year was the preliminary consultation, under Your Grace's chairmanship, of representatives of these churches, at New Delhi. A luncheon meeting provided opportunity for discussion among a score of representatives of Anglican churches and of the churches of the wider fellowship. It has been left that a larger and more formal conference is to be planned for Jerusalem, early in 1964. For myself, I venture to express the hope that this companionship will be thought of in the most wide and generous terms, not in merely legalistic ones, for to me it represents a major stage in the fulfillment of the dream of a fully united body for which we pray and toward which we slowly move. The wider episcopal fellowship itself is not the form of that great Church; it simply provides a common ground and a working association which, under God, may facilitate the more fundamental steps which need to be taken. But it is a fact. Relationships of full communion or inter-communion exist. Anglican churches more and more find themselves involved in the full sacramental blood-steam of other bodies. Our lives increasingly lie side-by-side—even presenting the anomaly, as in the Philippines or the United States, of parallel episcopates. Such an anomaly is clearly one not to be welcomed or perpetuated; and yet the fact that it exists is, at least for the moment, a witness to the way in which Christian unity can outrun our human institutions and limitations. Therefore this fellowship, far from being some interesting, theoretical structure of inter-church relationships or an exclusive society of old friends, is to be taken, I believe, as a present, disturbing, exhilarating vocation of Christ, and so to be received and fulfilled, obediently and thankfully.

Ecumenical Reflections

During the year all our churches and provinces maintained ecumenical activities of some significance. In many of them, specific negotiations and conversations are going on, looking toward church unity. In every case, the ecumenical encounter proceeds at appreciable depth.

The most notable occasion, during the year, of course, was the Third Assembly of the World Council of Churches at New Delhi. There were eighty delegates from Anglican Churches representing all our separate jurisdictions. I may write here with particular appreciation of the generosity of the church people of England, through the Council for Ecumenical Co-operation, who put into my hands a fund with which to subsidize the travel of delegates from our newer provinces, particularly in Africa. Full reports have been made of the Assembly at New Delhi, and no comment is needed from me, save to record the full and wholehearted participation by all our Churches.

One of my own duties during the year was to preside at a consultation on Inter-Communion, called by the World Council of Churches, at Bossey. This is a theme looming steadily larger on the ecumenical horizon; and while the consultation itself was quite inconclusive, it did serve a useful purpose in underlining some of the issues involved, and proposing ways in which the churches might well approach the problem.

In this as in other, more important, matters, Anglicans may well be grateful for the opportunities which come to us for participation in ecumenical dialogue, and for responsibility within the ecumenical movement.

We need not feel, nor do we, that we have a uniquely valuable contribution to make to the dialogue. But we have a unique contribution to make, as do other companies of Christian people in like measure. And it is essential that we take our full part accordingly.

It is of the greatest importance, I believe, that our participation in ecumenical affairs be understood within its proper context. Much is being thought and said these days about "confessionalism," a word which has come into widespread use lately to describe not only churches of a common doctrinal allegiance, but also international structures of church federation, and the like, which are often structures of considerable collective power and durability.

I must confess that the words "confession" and "confessionalism" are somewhat opaque to me. Where Christian people are drawn together in moments of crisis, around a faith which they confess together (as in Germany in the 1930's), then the use of the word is clear enough. But this sense of militant and united witness does not always apply in the contemporary use of the word. It is more likely nowadays to become simply a catch-word, to describe inter-regional and international ecclesiastical organization, based on some common statement of doctrine or of faith which differentiates the group in question from other Christian people.

Used in this sense, I must confess that it is difficult for me to accept it or apply it to my own ministry or to our common Anglican life. The sting of "confessionalism" is a double one—it is the sting of a particular statement of the Christian faith which separates and divides one group of Christians from another—it is also the sting of an international power structure which may cut across ecumenical life, and divide and subvert the deeper current of unity. And neither of these characteristics is true of Anglicanism as I know it. We are a fellowship of regional and national churches, which hold no particular, private doctrinal statement of our own, which look back to no founder save Our Lord, which have no particular theological school or bias of our own, which define as little as possible (within the universal historic definitions of the Catholic Church), in order to be free to offer to our societies the full and unchained faith of the universal Church in its most liberal and inclusive form. I do not say that we always succeed in this. I am simply trying to describe the nature of our Anglican mission and vocation as we understand it.

In order that this mission may be the better obeyed, we believe deeply in the greatest degree of autonomy within each separate church, while at the same time welcoming with all our hearts the comradeship of free churches which our Communion exemplifies. Earlier in this report I had occasion to speak of my own ministry and the fact that it is not an administrative one, dealing with coercive authority, but rather one of interpretation, leading toward the free choice of common action. Insofar as this central ministry is of help in the ecumenical task, I welcome every opportunity to give that help. But it must be given on our terms. We are not a "confession"; I am not a "confessional executive"; and such common action as we are able to offer in the ecumenical task is one which must be fully and freely understood and undertaken by our separate churches, not simply within their own societies, but also in appropriate measure through our corporate action as a world-wide Communion.

All this means simply that I seem obliged to spend a fair amount of time and energy in fending off an easy but inaccurate label, and in trying to make understood the true nature of our Anglican unity. Misunderstanding is not only confusing, it is also painful at times; and there have been moments when precisely this point of misunderstanding has brought pain both to others and myself. I am sorry that that is so, all the more when such misunderstanding has got in the way of the share of ecumenical life which we as Anglicans long to take. This is perhaps more for me to worry about than Your Grace, or Your Grace's colleagues; but I report it, for it weighs heavily on my conscience and heart.

I close this report only too conscious of the immense variety of matters which have gone unreported, and the even greater variety of duties and opportunities which I have not yet even begun to explore. I have had a long and fairly full ministry since my ordination nearly

30 years ago. Never can I remember having had to carry so many things in my head and my prayers, nor to have been so conscious of my own limitations. Perhaps hardest to remember, at times, is the way this immense horizon of duty and opportunity shrinks, in the end, to the measure of one family somewhere—perhaps even one individual. Yet this intensely personal dimension is the true size of all our common effort, I am sure. The point of my job is not that the reputation or power of the Anglican Communion shall be enhanced or glorified, but that one more person, somewhere in the world, may be thereby brought to know Our Lord and so be saved. Such, at any rate, is the size of what I try to do, in my own eyes.

Respectfully submitted,
STEPHEN F. BAYNE, JR.
Executive Officer

1962

January 21, 1963

MY LORD ARCHBISHOP:

Once again I have the honor to report on a year's work as Anglican Executive Officer. 1962 was, like it predecessors, necessarily a year still largely of exploration and improvisation. I had assumed when I undertook this ministry that it would take at least three years to learn enough to prepare a competent job description, and to measure at all adequately the needs and the appropriate expression of our Anglican unity, and this has turned out to be the case. Nevertheless the experience the three years has brought now gives me confidence in the prospect of the planning which will be made possible in 1963 at the meetings of the Lambeth Consultative Body and the Advisory Council on Missionary Strategy.

Itinerary

In the course of the year, travel totalling 147,000 miles included official visits to six of our Anglican family of churches, Australia, Canada, Central Africa, Ireland, the Jerusalem Archbishopric and the Nippon Seikokai. In the first four instances, the visit included a part in the General Synods of the churches. Most memorable in this respect was the synod of the Church of England in Australia, the first of that now-united church under its new constitution. In addition I was privileged to attend meetings of two of our regional councils, those of South East Asia and the South Pacific. In Jerusalem it was a grateful duty to lay the cornerstone of the new building for St. George's College, and in Japan, through the kindness of the Presiding Bishop, it was possible for me to have a most helpful meeting with the bishops of that church.

Two official visits were made to churches with which we are in full communion. In February I was happy to attend, in the Philippines, the formal celebration of the concordat of full communion between the American Church and the Philippine Independent Church. This relationship, which brought together in fullest sacramental brotherhood some six million Christians, has since that time been widened to include nearly a dozen or more Anglican churches where similar concordats are either already concluded or in the final stages of negotiation. In June, in Lisbon, I was privileged to join in the consecration of the Right Reverend Luis Pereira as the second bishop of the Lusitanian Church. His consecration at the hands of the Bishop of Southern Brazil, Bishop Molina of the Spanish Reformed Episcopal Church and Bishop Fiandor, the now-retired first bishop of the Lusitanian Church, was also shared by the Archbishop of Utrecht and the Bishop of Deventer as well as myself, thus uniting episcopal order from both Anglican and Old Catholic traditions. Both the Lusitanian and Spanish Churches, for so long the peculiar care of the Church of Ireland, now have concordats of full communion with the American Church; their Council of Bishops includes Anglican, Old Catholic and Philippine Independent bishops; and they are thus uniquely illustrative of that node of unity called by the Lambeth Conference "The Wider Episcopal Fellowship."

It was also my privilege to visit the Ecumenical Patriarch again, not only renewing a valued personal friendship but also, I pray, thus helping to strengthen the bond of unity between our Anglican household and the great family of the Orthodox Churches. Unlike though we may be in the superficial accidents of culture and history, there is between the Anglican and Orthodox churches a profound unity already evident and a clear vocation to such common life and study as was so movingly described by Your Grace in Athens. Both in Europe and in North America, important conversations between Anglican and Orthodox theologians now are going forward. In the words of our

American bishops, "Our prayer here must be for nothing less than the fulfillment of (our) mutual confidence, in full communion with one another . . . In prayer and in boldness may we swiftly press forward until we break the Bread of Life together in one thankful obedience to the Saviour."

My collateral responsibility as bishop in charge of the American churches in Europe took me to the continent a number of times for visitations to our civilian congregations and the very much larger American military household. It was a particular pleasure to be able to invite the clergy and lay readers from all our Anglican civil and military jurisdictions in Europe, and the Old Catholic, Lusitanian and Spanish Reformed Episcopal Churches as well, for a four-day conference at Berchtesgaden led by the Bishop of Michigan. It is my hope that such a conference may again be possible in 1963, when the distinguished American theologian, A. T. Mollegen, will be our leader.

All the more welcome because of the long periods spent abroad were the days when I could be at home in the United Kingdom. Most of this necessarily was devoted to the business of my office. But it has been a great joy this past year to have been able to preach at the universities of Birmingham, Cambridge, Oxford and St. Andrew's; to lead a clergy conference for the Diocese of St. David's; to lecture at the St. Andrew's Summer School for Clergy; to address diocesan groups in Llandaff, Norwich, Salisbury, and Southwark; and otherwise to take such part in the life of the Church in these islands as is possible for me. Preaching in England, as many Americans before me have discovered, is a most happy experience. One may miss the characteristically boisterous appreciation of an American congregation, where it is a social convention to speak of any sermon that parses as if the author were Chrysostom. But such exuberance is small loss in contrast with England's noble remnants of biblical literacy, and the characteristic thoughtful listening and prayerful companionship in a common task which gladdens a preacher's heart. This year brought opportunities as various as a missionary sermon in Coventry Cathedral, the dedication of a new tower in the Washington family's ancestral church, the ordination of an American priest in Plymouth, and the very great honor of a Sunday in Sandringham Church. All these added immensely to the joy of a busy year.

Finally I must briefly record the fact that I continue as a member of the American Church and its House of Bishops. In our Communion we know of no generalized "Anglican"; as individuals we are each rooted in our separate churches; and in my case this means continuing at least a skeletal participation in the life of the American Church. Of particular relevance to my major responsibilities are membership in the National Council and the Strategic Advisory Committee, two central bodies in the American Church's life, appointment as a delegate to the forthcoming Faith and Order Conference in Montreal, and as a member of the Consultation on Church Union. It was a particular pleasure also in 1962 to be asked to give the Bohlen Lectures in Philadelphia and the Pitt Lecture at the Berkeley Divinity School, and to be the concluding visitor to the Diocese of Honolulu on the occasion of the centennial celebration of their unique Anglo-American history. And I was personally most gratified to return to my sometime diocese last summer, to moderate the interesting gathering of theologians and scientists at the Seattle World Fair.

Financial

I should like to express my warm appreciation again to the Central Board of Finance of the Church of England for their kindness in managing the three inter-Anglican budgets of which I am a somewhat remote watch-dog. As in 1961, the operating budget of St. Augustine's College and of my office, together with the salary and allowances of the Archbishop in Jerusalem, were dealt with as a common Anglican responsibility, and the costs were divided proportionately among the eighteen Anglican jurisdictions. Final figures are not yet available, but it seems clear that the response from the churches will exceed that of 1961. While every Anglican jurisdiction has a fair share in the total combined budget of £28,400, the *amounts* each can give, measured in financial terms, vary greatly. Approximately 80% of any such fairly-divided budget must necessarily be carried by four churches, and less than full response from any of these is bound to be a crippling blow. But three of those four (and ten churches altogether) had met their quotas in full before the end of the year; and it is likely that the final report will bring us a good deal closer still to our goal.

I am concerned in these matters on two scores. One is purely practical. The three budgets included are all at an absolute minimum, and any deficit in support means the loss of an essential service. In 1961, we finally met the minimum needs of St. Augustine's College in full, three years after the bishops at Lambeth had agreed on what that minimum need was. And this was accomplished only by cutting back on my own budget by deferring maintenance and other costs, and by special contributions outside the budget. 1962 presented an even sharper problem with less margin to play with.

More important is the bearing of all this on the future. One result of these first exploratory years has been the unfolding of many possibilities and needs for inter-Anglican action. Many of these are of immediate significance and clearly commend themselves. But the test of any such project in the end must be whether the churches will give it their wholehearted support. Thus I am concerned to try to read our common will as measured in our support of the few things we do together now. One perplexed treasurer wrote me early last year asking if I could tell him exactly what this inter-Anglican budget was worth to his diocese. I could only answer him stumblingly by saying that I guessed it was worth whatever the Anglican Communion was worth. So I must think of these mundane little affairs, I am afraid.

An Ecumenical Year

To many Christians, the Second Vatican Council was no doubt the uniquely-vivid reminder of ecumenical realities and problems in 1962. Not unexpectedly, the first session of the Council was not concerned with ecumenical problems in the stricter sense, but rather with problems of the internal discipline and life of the Roman Catholic Church. Nevertheless so extensive a meeting of the largest body of the world's Christians attracted immense attention, gave substance to the Pope's imaginative leadership, provided a theater for the free play of long-restrained energies and inquiries within the Roman Church and, perhaps most of all, confronted non-Roman Christianity with unfamiliar challenges and new ecumenical frontiers.

Certainly one consequence of all this was a heightening of ecumenical sensitivity on every side. Within our own Communion, the year was marked by both the continuance and development of old relationships and the launching of new ones. Perhaps more significant than these was an evident heightening of concern for the fulfillment of the already-given unity of Christians in Christ. I do not know of any one of our churches, for example, which has not discovered a welcome increase in warm and friendly relationships with Christians of the Roman Catholic obedience. In some instances, surprisingly enough in North America where tensions between Roman Catholics and other Christians have been strongest, the new climate of friendship expressed itself in unprecedented ways—in participation in common study and prayer, in a novel and welcome willingness to join in one another's occasions of public celebration, and the like. It is understood that friendship alone will not solve basic ecumenical problems. But without it there would be no solution; and as far as it goes, it is a true and good expression of the unity of all Christians in Holy Baptism—a basic unity fundamental to all others, I should suppose.

Of far more immediate promise and concern has been the stirring new depth in Anglican-Orthodox relationships, illuminated by Your Grace's visits to the Ecumenical Patriarch, to Athens and to Moscow. Theological dialogue of very great potential significance has begun again between Anglican and Orthodox leaders both in England and in North America. It may be to the point to comment that such parallel dialogue has a particular usefulness because of the differing ecclesiastical structures of the two societies. In North America, Orthodox and non-Orthodox churches live side by side, sharing one common society. Inevitably, the dynamics of dialogue in such circumstances are quite different from those characteristic of a situation where the national churches of different nations converse with one another. It may be hoped that such parallel conversations, each informed by the other, may yield a greater and swifter harvest of obedience to our Lord's will for unity.

Within our own Communion greatest attention, no doubt, is still focused on the choices confronting the Church of India, Pakistan, Burma and Ceylon in Ceylon, North India and Pakistan. 1961 and early 1962 brought a response from other Anglican churches to the Metropolitan's questions which was both confusing and largely negative. The confusion was further compounded by a prevailingly negative decision on the part of the Indian dioceses themselves. In recent months, however, it has seemed to become clear that neither Plan nor Scheme has entirely lost usefulness. While final decisions remain to be made, it appears likely that further negotiation, aided by consultation with theologians from other churches, may permit a fresh attack on what have seemed most stubborn problems. All that can truly be said at this juncture is that our most devoted prayers should be offered for patient and persistent effort on the part of the churches concerned in India.

Significant negotiations are also underway in other parts of the Anglican Communion. In Nigeria, negotiations involving the Presbyterian and Methodist Churches as well as our own dioceses have progressed with warmth and promptness. A notable and most courageous action of the Church of the Province of West Africa highlights this development. The Synod of that Province, meeting last summer, adopted a resolution authorizing the Nigerian dioceses to enter at once into the proposed United Church, should negotiations make the union possible before the next meeting of the Synod. Since the Nigerian dioceses constitute by far the greater part of the strength of the Province, this action seemed to many of us one both of courage and confidence in the Nigerian plans.

Your Grace will know far better than I the situation in England. But I may mention the encouragement that has come to many of us in the Anglican household both at the re-opening of an horizon of Anglican-Presbyterian conversations and also at the evidently buoyant and hopeful dialogue between Anglicans and Methodists in England.

Probably the most elaborate and inclusive conversations are those in the United States, launched in 1962, which include six (and hopefully eight) churches, representative of more than 20,000,000 Christians. The outcome of an initial suggestion from the United Presbyterian Church to the Protestant Episcopal Church, the "Consultation on Church Union," as it is called, now represents almost every tradition in American life from the congregational to the Old Catholic.

But there is hardly an Anglican province which has not evidenced a new stirring of concern for Church unity. In Australia, now that the long process of internal unification has been accomplished, our church is readying itself for participation in conversation looking toward unity. In East Africa, similar conversations including the Moravians, Methodists, and Presbyterians as well as the East African province are underway; and less developed but significant conversations have begun in still other areas, all arising out of the intent ecumenical mood of our times.

Finally, I should refer to one unique ecumenical relationship— that involving the Episcopalian diocese of the Philippines and the Philippine Independent Church. Here are two churches sharing the life of one nation, churches now in full communion with one another and increasingly involved with one another. Full communion could represent a dangerous turn of affairs, for it could mean a paralysis of further effort toward real and costly and Catholic unity. The will of both these churches has been to pass that danger point, and to engage in a thoughtful and determined program of growing-together. It may well take a generation or more before old ignorances and divisions disappear. But the leadership of both churches is determined that nothing shall hinder the full ripening of unity.

The training in common of the ordinands and clergy of both churches is doubtless a cardinal first step, and this has now been the case for a number of years. Approximately equal numbers of ordinands from each church share the life of St. Andrew's Seminary in Quezon

City. Regional councils, representative of both churches, with staff and funds at their disposal, are now being established. Joint programs in special areas are being established, especially for training. The strategic needs of both churches, largely centered as they are in different areas of the nation, are increasingly determinative in planning. Such are some of the practical steps now being taken, under the all-important guidance of the Joint Council of both churches which is the principal planning body.

In some ways the situation in the Philippines is unique, involving as it does parallel episcopates as well as a host of lesser anomalies in church life. But full communion between episcopal churches anywhere is likely to involve precisely these anomalies. And while I am sure that all of us have welcomed the growing partnership in full communion which the bishops at Lambeth called "The Wider Episcopal Fellowship," some at least have been concerned, as I must confess I have, at precisely the danger which confronted us in the Philippines, namely that of accepting full communion as the end of the ecumenical road. For one church to be in full communion with another is an immense step forward in the path of unity. It may be an indispensable stage. But full sacramental communion alone is not unity, where it does not mean the self-denying sharing of one another's life and witness, with all its cost as well as all its strength. If we are not fully responsible for one another—prepared fully to bear one another's burdens and share one another's tasks—then full sacramental communion may mean nothing more than a mere ceremonial courtesy. This is the danger; and the experiment in the Philippines deserves the most careful thought and study by all our Anglican family.

Anglican Congress

A good deal of my work in 1962 has been preparatory to the gathering of our household in Canada next summer. I have indeed no direct responsibility for the Anglican Congress itself, which is being planned for us by the Church of Canada. But it is a grateful privilege to note and express appreciation for all that church is doing as host to the Anglican Communion at this gathering. Close to a thousand bishops, priests and lay people will attend, representing our nearly 350 dioceses; leaders from virtually every Anglican church will take part in the program; the Canadian Church has given $150,000 to assist sister churches in the travelling expenses of delegates; elaborate preparatory studies have been published for use in our parishes. It is a notable and energetic effort on behalf of us all.

It is no secret that the Congress has been viewed with mixed feelings by some Anglicans as well as others, mainly on the ground that it appears to be a "confessional" gathering rather than an "ecumenical" one, and in consequence will be a step backward or to one side along the ecumenical path. This hesitation seems to me, for at least two principal reasons, to be unjustified. First, there is no necessary contradiction between an ecumenical gathering and what is currently labelled a "confessional" one. The Anglican Communion is an expression of Christian unity, a particular historical fulfillment of unity, within the wider if less-intense fellowship of the ecumenical movement as a whole. It is an ecumenical fact of astonishing depth and durability, bringing together Christians of widely-different cultures and traditions, covering nearly the whole spectrum of theological insights. Any meeting of the Anglican Communion is an ecumenical gathering, of very great significance, as will be—to take another instance —the world gathering of the Lutherans in Helsinki. The only possibility of contradiction would lie in some inconceivable decision on our part to withdraw ourselves from the WCC and from ecumenical life generally, in favor of going it alone. And the record of ecumenical participation and activity on the part of all our Anglican churches is far too plain to permit any such possibility.

The second factor is that of the Congress leadership and membership itself. The test of the ecumenical bearing of any gathering of Christians is surely what they talk and think about and what comes out of their discourse. And to prejudge what will be said to us next August and what we shall think about it, seems to me quite irresponsible. I have no doubt myself that the Congress will be a positive ecumenical event of very considerable magnitude.

I have had occasion before this to comment on "confessionalism" and the Anglican Communion, and I need add little to that now. The word itself is part of the problem, I believe, for it is not a useful nor helpful word to describe the whole complex of inter-church problems, to which it is often applied. The different companies of Christian people in this world have different levels and organs of their unity. The depth of their unity varies; the means and expressions of it vary; the degree of conformity to a central pattern or authority varies. Therefore it darkens counsel to seek to identify all these factors with one word.

All the undeniable ache and resentment which flares out against "confessionalism" is grievous enough, and I do not doubt but that there are Anglican aches and resentments just as there are in other

Christian communions. But it is surely less than helpful to try to meet all our different sorts of problems with one word or one fixed idea. What is needed is far more careful and humble study of the problems themselves, such as has now begun in the area conferences sponsored by the WCC, and will doubtless be continued in 1963. And in such study, meetings such as the Anglican Congress play their proper, indeed indispensable, part. For the tensions which are so often lumped as "confessionalism"—tensions between older and newer churches and cultures, tensions arising out of differing patterns of education, tensions inherited from older historical or social situations, tensions born in problems of money or property—all such things are precisely what will be in the background of at least the latter half of the Anglican Congress program.

My direct responsibilities have to do with a series of meetings collateral to the Congress itself. Two important educational consultations will precede the Congress—one concerned with theological education, the other with general education. Two briefer consultations are now planned to follow the Congress—one on Church unity negotiations and a second on liturgical revision. Then a very broad conference of missionary executives is planned in advance of the meeting of the Advisory Council on Missionary Strategy and the Lambeth Consultative Body. The preparatory work for these meetings is going forward on time.

The dual meeting of the Advisory Council and the Consultative Body will, of course, offer me a rare and welcome opportunity to meet my numerous employers collectively. More significantly, it will give the churches of our Communion the first opportunity since 1958 to take counsel together about many things. The agenda for both these meetings, as Your Grace knows, will be crowded; and much of my work this year has been in preparation for this. Not only will there be decisions to be taken about specific areas and problems, such as Africa or South America, or exchange programs or means of communication. There must also be long-range decisions about the future form of my own office and work, and the right development and implementation of that mode of unity which is appropriate for the Anglican Communion. All these matters have furnished opportunity for much thought in the past year.

Regional Councils

1962 saw the adoption of a Constitution defining the Council of the Church of South East Asia—adopted by the eight constituent dioceses

of the Council with the general approval of the metropolitical authorities involved. This action marked another step forward in the
exploration of what is for our Communion a new form of regional,
inter-provincial association. The search for such association grows out
of three principal needs, I believe. One is that for the highest degree of
local initiative and responsibility consistent with the wider unity of the
Church. A second need is that for a deeper level of common life among
Anglican churches of different backgrounds, sharing a given area of
the world. The third is that for every positive step we can take toward
a fully-united Christian body in that region.

Unity is indivisible. The local unity of the Church in any place
cannot be considered separately from its unity across the whole world,
and across the centuries too. The practical problems of Church unity
indeed largely center here, in finding appropriate ways in which this
indivisible unity can be strengthened and more greatly fulfilled in
all its manifestations, without imperilling or impoverishing any of
them. Within our Anglican family, those problems take certain characteristic forms. For example, our normal progression is from the
"missionary" phase of church life, where the initiative is largely in
the hands of the originating church or society, directly to the stage of
the establishment of an autocephalous ecclesiastical province. Generally
speaking, we have had no intermediate pattern, although the dual
allegiance of certain bishops in Japan and China, during the formative
years of those two churches, represented an experiment in that direction. Thus we have often been forced into either a persistent paternalism (or infantilism) on one hand, or into an abrupt and somewhat convulsive autonomy on the other, with consequent cost, either way, to the
full idea of unity.

Again, because of our strongly-national character, our wider unity
has often been established along national lines—"American" Missionary
districts, "British" dioceses, etc.—to the point of the ridiculous, in some
cases, where different Anglican jurisdictions lie in close proximity to
one another. Yet again, perhaps because of our profound sense of full
communion, we have not been as aggressive in seeking the local unity
of Christians as the Church's doctrine rightly should have driven us
to be, with the result that we have sometimes given an impression of
"foreignness" long after any actual control from outside had virtually
ceased to exist.

These are some of our key Anglican problems, whether shared by
other Christians I cannot say. The development of regional councils
has been a response to those problems and an attempt to meet them.

In the case of South East Asia, this development has gone further than elsewhere, probably largely because of regional cultural and historical factors. But what has been demonstrated there has considerable relevance to other parts of the world.

In effect, the Council—consisting of the bishops and at least one clerical and one lay representative of each constituent diocese—is competent to exercise such authority as is given to it, perhaps varying in the case of each diocese and each of the parent metropolitan churches. It is not a substitute for a provincial church. It is both an intermediate step on the way toward provincial status, and also a means whereby two or more provinces may establish an appropriate degree of common, interdependent life in a single region (and "regions" grow larger and larger as the world itself shrinks).

The Council is both an outgrowth of a stronger sense of the local unity of the Church and also a way to nourish that sense and articulate it. It reflects the profound ties of the local church with its parent bodies, yet provides a theater for responsible local leadership, in such a way that the parent bodies are themselves brought together in their children, so to speak. It encourages ecumenical responsibility locally without seeming to violate other existing unities. It provides a most significant stage of corporate church life preparatory to provincial status, a stage wherein it may prove possible better to prepare our churches for autocephalous responsibility than we have done in the past. It makes possible an escape from the limitations of our national tradition without losing the great gifts that tradition has provided.

These are some of the gains I see from this significant and continuing development. It is important, I feel, that the parent churches shall do more than give token recognition to such councils. Financial responsibility and responsibility in self-government should go hand in hand with constitutional recognition, if growth toward a truly virile, indigenous church is to come. I had occasion, in September, to spell out to my American colleagues some of the consequences of the two preceding sentences, in a memorandum which was circulated to all bishops. Doubtless the American Church, with its unique structure of provincial responsibility, has unique problems accordingly in accommodating itself to conciliar structure. But equally I must acknowledge the financial support they have given to the South East Asia Council, and urge parallel confidence on the part of all others concerned.

You are, Your Grace, fully familiar with all this, and it would be superfluous for me to do more than suggest other areas where conciliar development either is progressing or which may offer an invitation to such development. The Caribbean, West Africa and South America have all suggested themselves as regions where similar exploration might well be helpful. In the South Pacific area, a regional council is already operative, providing a similarly flexible framework for the concerns of three churches, those of Australia, New Zealand and the United States.

Communication

The only additional instrument of communication developed in 1962 was the periodical newsletter to bishops, *Compasrose*. This has seemed to find a useful place in our corporate life, as has *Exchange*, an earlier experiment in communication. *Anglican World* has weathered another year, however without the gain in circulation hoped for. Being a private venture, its continuance must depend on the support it gains from subscribers and advertisers, and there is cause for real concern on this score. The reappearance of *Pan-Anglican*, on a new basis, is presently being considered by the Bishop of Connecticut and his advisers, with the hope of perhaps supplying yet another missing level of communication, not as an alternative to any of our existing periodicals but rather at a new level altogether.

The various provincial and national periodicals within our Communion continue to afford great help in this area. 1962 was encouraging, I felt, in the steady increase of information about both Anglican and ecumenical affairs appearing in the different national papers. In this respect, I think I must single out the *Canadian Churchman* which reaches, each month, every Anglican family in Canada with a generous measure of news about the whole Christian world. But it is unjust to single out any one, I am sure. And I owe a particular debt of gratitude to *The Living Church*, which sponsors my monthly opinions.

All this is "communication," in the common sense of that word. I am impressed with our gains in the circulation of information, for such information is an essential ingredient in unity, and unity is the heart of the Anglican Communion. I do not scorn what we have if I say that we need immensely more of it, and in greater depth. It is a good thing to have facts and figures about one another, to know what we are doing and what we hope to do, and we are not yet even at the point of ordinary literacy in this respect. Whenever I feel complacent about us, I remember that the very existence of the Anglican Communion itself is unsuspected by probably the majority of Anglicans, and my complacency disappears.

But what is of far greater importance, I am sure, is the *depth* of our knowledge of each other. We are not communicating at the most important levels, most of the time. If there is unity in the Body of Christ, then it will be true of us who share that unity that we share one another's life, its hopes and pain and needs and strengths, behind or underneath the "images" of one another which we project and receive. This requires, I should imagine, the most personal of relationships—communication in prayer, in individual acquaintance and friendship, in the exploration of one another's ideas, in common enterprises shared, in common judgment accepted.

There are enormous barriers in the way of this deeper communication. The dynamics of history, the intricate pattern of national and cultural rivalry, the relative freedom of the Church from its country and culture—these are conditions within which the unity of the Church must be fulfilled, and there is little we can do to change them. But despite those difficulties, there is much we can do. Personal knowledge of one another—such as is gained by the exchanged visits of the clergy and laity—is no doubt the swiftest instrument of unity. And here we have already seen immense possibilities, in the Wates-Seabury scheme for example. Exchange is not always possible. In such case, we must then work all the harder to prepare our clergy and lay people, when they move from one church and one culture to another, for the embassy of unity which is part of their Christian vocation.

The written word is another pathway to unity, where it is possible for us to penetrate one another's lives and cultures through our books. Here again there are great difficulties, of cost and distribution. But I am satisfied that none of them is insoluble, given the will to share our thoughts. The present modest and tentative "treaty" between the Seabury Press and SPCK is a stimulating first experiment along this line. It is my hope that what has thus begun may continue, until there is—at least within the Anglican Communion—that free market in ideas on which our unity depends.

At another level, CACTM's adventurous proposal to send selected ordinands to the United States for two years of theological training opens new vistas of communication. I pray that this may quickly become an exchange program, not on the casual basis presently obtaining but definitely planned, in order to establish a clear line of communication.

So one could continue, for the avenues of communication in depth are many. This is indeed a field deserving of the full time and energy of some imaginative person, who can bring to it the attention and wisdom it deserves. For I repeat, what is at stake is not simply "better-informed churchmen." What is at stake is the unity of the Body of Christ, of which our Anglican unity is a precious and vivid expression.

Missionary Planning and Co-ordination

It is impossible to report in any detail on this urgent phase of the work of my office in 1962. But I may briefly comment on certain lines of development, and on what they seem to suggest.

In broadest terms, the co-ordination and expansion of Anglican missionary work, desired and sought in the establishment of the Advisory Council on Missionary Strategy and of my office, requires at least these four elements:

1. The development of local or regional planning, by the regional churches themselves, on a corporate basis which would keep in view the common interests and needs and witness of the province or church as a whole.

2. Steady consultation and shared planning by all our churches, "sending" and "receiving" alike, "new" and "old" alike.

3. The exploration and exploitation of new resources, of money and manpower, wherever they may be found, and of ways to use these resources wherever they are needed, anywhere in our Anglican household.

4. Decision in consultation about priorities, so that our obedience to mission represents the best offering we can make, in terms of our own strength, our ecumenical responsibilities, and the needs of the world.

We have made some progress in the development of all four of these elements. The most encouraging developments, I think, have been in the area of the corporate planning of the churches themselves, particularly the "newer" churches. A year ago I had occasion to comment on this aspect of the life of the newer provinces. I said then that paramount among the needs of new provinces "is that of the will of the new church to take corporate responsibility for its own members. The older missionary relationship may be that of church to diocese, or society to diocese . . . but this fragmentary relationship must end when a province comes into existence. For by definition, a province is a unit of the church . . . and thus its own first responsibility must be a corporate one, to the members of the body, first of all to its own common life and mission. And this is tested . . . by a corresponding willingness of each member of the body to consider its own priorities in relation to those of its companion dioceses."

This responsible, corporate planning—often sacrificial in individual cases—has strengthened markedly as the months have gone on. More and more it has been possible to put before all our churches a larger and clearer view of what each church plans and hopes to do, and what the corresponding needs are. Often this planning must be done with only the most rudimentary tools. Often it involves the deliberate postponement or even the scrapping of certain projects for the sake of others which seem more important to a church as a whole. But increasingly there has been an understanding throughout our Communion of our need to rethink both the dimensions and the nature of our interchurch relationships. Along with most other Christians, we are learning how better to express the responsible partnership which must be the pattern of relationship between younger and older churches. And local, corporate planning is the first element in this—planning which is then taken seriously by the rest of the family, and which furnishes the basis for a trusting and responsive dialogue.

I quote some cogent words from Bishop Newbigin. He asks the question "Have we taken seriously enough the clear teaching of the New Testament that witness is an activity of the Holy Spirit and only secondarily and derivatively our action? . . . Or have we been so conformed to this world that we have . . . allowed the work of missions to become assimilated to the processes of western cultural invasion, so that we have made of it an affair in which we were responsible for directing a process of teaching and training for the so-called younger churches until in our judgment they were ready for responsibility?"

Bishop Newbigin goes on to comment "what does not seem to have been noticed is that the question does not seem to arise at all in the biblical situation. There is no period in which the church is independent. From the very beginning every one of these young churches, with all its manifold weaknesses and even scandalous sins, is treated as simply the body of Christ in that place, the dwelling place of the Holy Spirit, and therefore as being not independent and not dependent but always and from the very beginning in a position of reciprocal inter-dependence with the other members in the body of Christ." In those sentences, Bishop Newbigin states in a provocative way a fundamental principle which increasingly has found its expression in our Anglican life.

And we are beginning to respond to such broader and more responsible planning, in broader and more responsible ways. Perhaps the most notable instance of this during the past year was the very large gift of £230,000 to the Church of the Province of South Africa, from SPG, to help meet the enormous cost of new church construction required both by the new frontiers of that province's life as well as the bitter and divisive cost of apartheid. This was, in essence, a church-to-church gift, to put into the hands of the South African province the means to attack an acute and urgent problem. It was a sacrificial gift, and the result of responsible and brotherly planning. If I mention that one gift, it is not to make any invidious comparison. There is hardly any Anglican church or society which has not known a ferment of discontent with the present depth and dimensions of our response to the needs of our fellow Christians. How we shall, corporately or individually, meet these elementary needs of the younger provinces is doubtless something to be discussed and decided when the churches meet in 1963.

The second element I mentioned is that of steady consultation and shared planning. At the moment, our record here is far from satisfactory, although here too there has been growth in 1962. I am myself the chief bottleneck, at this point, for until we can devise some better pattern of consultation, the bulk of it must be channelled through my office. And with the inescapable limitations of my own time and ability, together with the unexpected breadth of inter-Anglican interests in which I have been involved, I am only too clearly aware of the present limitations of our consultative process. I say this not to seek comfort, but to indicate the point we have now reached, which is that of a need for a sufficient enlargement or rearrangement of staff to permit the continuous examination, evaluation and consultation which a central office requires.

I do not suppose that this consultation can ever be done by a central office alone. The point of the central office is to bring the churches themselves into closer and more continuous confrontation and consultation. The Advisory Council, and my office with it, represent not so much an executive or administrative agency as they do a new phase —a process—of constant consultation. This again will be a matter for consideration and decision this coming summer, and I do not doubt but that we shall find the appropriate arrangements needed to make this process possible. In the meantime, I am acutely aware of my own limitations in this respect.

The third of the fundamental elements in inter-Anglican missionary co-ordination is that of the unused or unawakened resources, and the deployment of them where they are needed. Again it would be possible to report some progress in this area. But it is pitifully small, in comparison with the needs.

I have no doubt that there are many reasons for this, perhaps different in the case of every Anglican church. But I think there are certain common problems which are faced by all our Anglican churches. For one thing, we need to re-study our whole decision-making procedure, in all our churches. How are the bonds of brotherhood between churches to be established? How are the channels of common life to be built? How must we order our internal affairs so that the common life of our separate churches can be more fully mingled—so that what each church has and needs can be effectively married to the needs and strengths of another church? With our characteristic Anglican permissiveness in these matters, and our dislike for concerted strategy—both of these excellent qualities in their own way—we have reached the point, in our swiftly-changing world, where we are substantially unable to move as swiftly and decisively as the needs of our churches require. And to the degree that that paralysis is due to our own structure, we all have an obligation to re-examine and redesign our procedures.

More importantly, I have the increasing feeling that we cannot sustain the needs of a world-wide Communion in the 20th century on the basis of an antique caricature of the missionary. I do not speak, of course, of those at the heart of the Church's missionary work, but rather of our failure, throughout the Anglican Communion, to pay enough attention to the education of the clergy and the laity alike in the changing form of mission. Nor have we paid enough attention to the basic theology of mission, which we have all too often thought of as church-extension, as the enlargement of the Anglican Communion, as a process that starts with ourselves, rather than as obedience to Him with Whom all mission begins.

We have now reached the point, in all our churches, where the great majority of our people can make no effective connection between the convulsive world history in which they live and the mission of Christ by Whom all things are made and saved. Mission and missionary affairs seem to most of our people completely unrelated and irrelevant to the world in which they live and the choices they must make in it. Therefore our response to missionary needs tends to be inadequate, childish, unimaginative, and inappropriate. And while I have no doubt that we can greatly improve both our procedures and our response, I am sure that these alone will not begin to solve our major problems of missionary obedience. It is not too much to say that the Anglican churches of the world need to be born again in a profound rediscovery of mission and its meaning and its cost.

Finally, what about priorities? The Advisory Council will meet this coming summer, for the first time in five years. There will doubtless be more than enough on the agenda, and if I have done my job at all adequately, there will be manageable decisions to be taken. Despite the unmet needs of our younger provinces especially—and no one knows these needs any better than I—we have not reached the point of needing to cut back on anything that we presently do. None of our missionary work anywhere does more than scratch the surface of the potential resources we have.

But there are still the greater questions of new missionary frontiers, both at home and abroad. And here questions of priority will inescapably arise. In the Pacific, in South America, in Africa . . . there is no area of the world where we can say that we have done all that is required of us. And the question where our highest responsibilities lie and how we can best corporately meet those responsibilities is the central question of priority before us.

As I close this report, and read again what I have written, it is clear that a central concern of all Anglican life is unity. The Anglican Communion itself is an episode in Christian unity. Mission is only the other face of unity. All that we are and do in our separate national churches is to try to serve unity, both at home and abroad.

Yet we need to be reminded, as Your Grace has more than once reminded us, that unity is not the only note of the Church. And perhaps nowhere do we need this reminder more than in the small and dangerously cosy circle of our own Anglican household. If I am, as I believe, a chief minister of Anglican unity, I perhaps need to be mindful first of all of the vertical dimension in the Church's life. Unity alone, much less Anglican unity, may mean nothing by itself except the huddling together of like-minded people in a hostile world. Obedience, judgment, witness . . . these are the signposts to our salvation, in all the perplexities and busyness of our life.

Respectfully submitted,
STEPHEN F. BAYNE, JR.
Executive Officer

1963

January 31, 1964

MY LORD ARCHBISHOP:

For the fourth time I have the privilege of reporting on a year of duty as Anglican Executive Officer. The central cluster of events in our Anglican year were, of course, the Anglican Congress and the related meetings in Canada, on which I report more fully in a later section. But of great significance also were the Latin American Consultation in Mexico, last January, and some ecumenical events and gatherings of interest. In October announcement was made of my anticipated return to the United States, officially in November, 1964, to succeed the Rt. Rev. John B. Bentley as Director of the Overseas Department of PECUSA. Finally, the closing months of 1963 saw the first steps being taken in "Mutual Responsibility and Interdependence in the Body of Christ."

Itinerary

My travel was somewhat restricted in 1963, mainly because of the intense season in Canada and the long weeks of preparation for those meetings. Some 113,000 miles were covered in trips to various parts of the world including the pleasant novelty of two trans-Atlantic passages by sea. Official visits were made to the Church of Ireland, on the occasion of the Columban Celebration in June, and to the Church in Wales, at the meeting of their Governing Body in September. Several visits were made to the Anglican Church of Canada during the year, apart from the Congress, including a special planning session with the executive group of the Department of Missions of that Church, in connection with their participation in "Mutual Responsibility" proposals. In February I attended an important meeting of the Joint Council of the Philippine Independent-Philippine Episcopal Church, and in May I had the honor of a visit to His All-Holiness, the Ecumenical Patriarch.

Twelve trips were made to the continent of Europe during the year, principally to fulfill my collateral responsibilities as bishop in charge of the American churches and ordinary of the Episcopalian military personnel in Europe. These visits included confirmations in some twenty-five centers, the annual meeting of the Convocation in

Paris, the ordination of a deacon in Frankfurt, and the pleasure of giving hospitality at Berchtesgaden to a conference of clergy and lay readers from Anglican jurisdictions on the Continent and from the churches of the Wider Episcopal Fellowship as well. As a bishop of the American Church, I had also the privilege of an ordination to the priesthood in Oxford, of visits to three of the Wates-Seabury Exchange clergy, and of the dedication of a memorial window in Tollesbury—a unique center of Anglo-American history because of its long association with the series of challenges for the America's Cup. In addition, my membership of the American House of Bishops and the National Council of that Church involved me in six trans-Atlantic journeys in the course of the year.

As in previous years, there were many happy opportunities to share the life of the Church and people of Britain. Two visits to St. Augustine's College gave me some touch with the life of that remarkable institution. I was privileged to preach at diocesan missionary festivals in Leicester and St. Alban's, and to address the Ely diocesan conference. The Clergy School of the diocese of Blackburn also introduced me pleasantly to Mr. Butlin's notable ministry. King's College, London, and Christ Church, Oxford, afforded me welcome hospitality of ideas, and I was glad also to preach at St. Paul's and Southwark Cathedrals, Gray's Inn, Sandhurst, and in some parish churches as well. Once again, St. Nicholas Cole Abbey generously opened its doors to me and an American congregation for the appropriate celebration of Thanksgiving Day.

One is particularly aware, in the intimacy of these islands, of the way in which radio and television, as well as the written word, permit a generous warmth of personal relationship. This was supremely welcome at the time of President Kennedy's assassination; both BBC and ITV, as well as the press, offered to me, as to all Americans in Britain, both heart-warming reassurance and also the chance to share with our hosts the burden we had first thought we were carrying alone. Then (as indeed on other occasions) I cherished the privilege of speaking or writing to many unknown friends. And I must not fail to express to *The Church Times* and other periodicals particular appreciation of their generosity in opening their columns to my occasional rumination. While it seems right to begin now to limit the amount of writing I have attempted to do, it would be ungracious not to record my gratitude for unfailing readiness to make public both thoughts and news. The lack of official channels for such purposes has been more than made up by this thoughtfulness.

The Canadian Summer

July and August saw great numbers of Anglicans in North America, principally in Canada. The fourth World Conference on Faith and Order at Montreal, in July, included an almost-full quota of Anglicans both in its membership and leadership. This was less unprecedented than the warmth of interest shown by the Roman Catholic Church and the positive participation of the representatives of the Orthodox Churches in the conference. Disappointment has been expressed by some at what was felt to be a meager accomplishment by so portentous a group. Yet, as so often in such cases, the fact that these people met and talked may have been more than adequate justification for the Conference, notably so because of the two new strains in the ecumenical dialogue noted above. I regretted very much that at the last minute illness prevented my own participation as one of the four delegates of the American Church.

An impressive series of meetings in the United States as well as Canada were arranged for various groups of Anglicans attending the Congress in Toronto. A "group life laboratory" was held for bishops in July, jointly arranged by the Canadian and American Churches in Cambridge, Massachusetts. This permitted some thirty or more bishops from around the world to explore the techniques of "group dynamics." Again, two concentric consultations on the Church and Education were arranged by the Churches of Canada, England and the United States in Cranbrook, Michigan. These made possible significant policy discussions having to do with both the institutional frontiers of the Church, especially in the new nations, and also the witness of the Church within universities and schools. The reports of these consultations were subsequently adopted and circulated by the Advisory Council on Missionary Strategy.

Another type of meeting was exemplified by the three consultations held in Toronto the weekend following the Congress. Two included the "consultants" in ecumenical and liturgical affairs, nominated by their respective Metropolitans. The third was a gathering of representatives of the laity and of those especially concerned with the laity. In each case, the principal aims were the exchange of information and the discussion of needed new channels and vehicles of communication within the fields concerned. It was felt that these were successful innovations.

At Huron College, London, Ontario, five gatherings were held of supreme importance in our common life. Two were the official meetings of the ACMS and the Lambeth Consultative Body. In addition, the five Archbishops of Africa met in very productive sessions; and the conference of heads of Anglican Theological Colleges met concurrently with the ACMS for helpful discussions. Perhaps the most radical consultation was that of the "Missionary Executives Conference," a week-long gathering of fifty or so representatives of missionary societies and boards, and churches, who spent long hours in surprisingly swiftly-moving discussion of the mission of the Church in all its aspects. From this group came the germ of the proposal, later adopted by the Lambeth Consultative Body, for "Mutual Responsibility and Interdependence in the Body of Christ."

The meetings of the two supreme bodies, ACMS and Lambeth Consultative Body, have been fully reported in the Minutes of the respective groups, and the decisions need not be repeated in detail. Doubtless the most significant action taken was the adoption of the "Mutual Responsibility" document. But other reports and recommendations of significance were also adopted, most of which have since been published together with the main document itself.

All these gatherings, large and small, were made possible mainly because of the Congress itself—the ten days of worship, fellowship and study given our Communion by the immense generosity and imagination of the Canadian Church. As one who shared the Minneapolis Congress as well, I can say that Toronto could not have happened except for Minneapolis; but I must equally say that the 1963 Congress was strengthened by every lesson Minneapolis could teach, and as well by the nine years of deeper mutual knowledge and intercourse which grew out of the earlier gathering. In size and scope, in vitality of participation (notably by the "younger" churches), in outwardness and objectivity of vision, in assurance of the greatness of the mission to which we are called—in these ways especially Toronto was a turning point in Anglican history.

It is surely too early to ask whether another such Congress should ever be undertaken. Like Assemblies of the World Council of Churches and other such gatherings, the ratio of leadership is dangerously high —there are too many who have things to say in proportion to the time and opportunity to say them, and the end is often frustration and fragmentation. This was, of course, accented by the decision—inescapable though it was—to present the "Mutual Responsibility" proposal in the midst of the highly-articulated Congress program. Inevitably there was confusion because of this, compounded because of the Congress' uncertainty as to its own nature and powers. Some of this confusion indeed persisted in the tissues of the churches for weeks afterward, providing nutriment for an interesting variety of speculations as to what had actually happened or been decided at Toronto.

But the main problem was not confusion but the degree of true dialogue possible, considering time and numbers. As I say, it is too soon to think of another Congress. Yet the questions must be asked before long as to the scope and structure of possible future meetings, having in mind the need to let informed opinion be heard and responded to, and to allow responsible decisions to grow from true dialogue. Such questions doubtless will include those of the selection and preparation of members, and of the bearing of the Congress on the life of the churches of our Communion, as well as the narrower ones of program and pattern. Attention will also doubtless be paid to the possibilities of other kinds of meetings—regional or by fields of interest—which lie ahead to be explored.

But no question or critical comment can dilute in the slightest degree the massive and unforgettable power of the Congress and its satellite meetings. There were those who feared that the summer would bring an increase in confessional self-consciousness, a renewal of Anglican narcissism, a symposium of like-minded denominational *aficionados*. This did not happen. The Congress was unmistakably a gathering of the Church of Christ within the Church of Christ, infected with the greatness of the Church and of our calling, and moved to respond with an impulse as strong as any in our history. The questions for the Anglican Communion now are what response we are equipped to make, and what changes we need in our structure to make a more adequate response possible.

Cuernavaca

Although properly overshadowed by the Congress, note should be made of yet another significant inter-Anglican conference in 1963, the Consultation on the Anglican Communion and Latin America, held in Cuernavaca, Mexico, January 20–24. Representatives of four Churches took part (the Anglican Church of Canada, the Church of England, PECUSA, and the Church of the Province of the West Indies). The Archbishop of York was the Chairman of the group, which numbered some two dozen—representatives of missionary agencies and bishops of Latin American dioceses as well as officers and metropolitans of the Churches concerned. The Consultation was assisted by a preliminary report of the study of "Anglican Opportunities in South America," commissioned by PECUSA at my request from the Bureau of Applied Social Research of Columbia University.

The report of the Consultation itself, as well as the much-larger report of the study, have now been made public and part of official Anglican planning. Attention should however be called, I think, to three significant aspects of this Consultation and its report.

First, it represented an unprecedented degree of mutual consultation and planning. We have been moving in this direction, in our Communion, for some years; and one could identify certain occasions which serve as high-water marks of inter-Anglican planning. The establishment of the Regional Councils is one such. The Nagpur Consultation in 1961 is another. At Cuernavaca, the process reached a new intensity and responsibility, marked vividly by the participation of the Archbishop of York, the Presiding Bishop and the Primate of Canada.

Second, it gave the Anglican mission in Latin America a welcome new respectability, most clearly so in the recognition which runs through the report that the vocation of our Communion in Latin America is not to be understood merely as a chaplaincy to foreigners, but as "obedience to Christ's command to preach the Gospel," whose "primary objective is the development of Latin American churches, expressive of the genius of their own countries and of the unity of the Anglican Communion."

Third, it was to a unique degree aware of the ecumenical setting and implications of Anglican life in Latin America, and therefore was drawn to think more deeply both of ecumenical relationships and duties, and also of the special tradition of Anglican life, particularly with respect to the Episcopate. Much of the central thrust of the report had to do with the new forms of diocesan life and episcopal ministry evidently required in obedience to our mission. This inescapably raised further questions about the place of the Bishop in the Church to which indeed no final answer, if there be such a thing, could be given, but which renewed a dialogue about episcopal ministry which may well prove of substantial importance in the years to come.

This dialogue was carried along a bit further, if inconclusively, in the report on "Province, Council and Diocese" prepared (although not adopted) at Huron College in July. It is possible that the forthcoming conference of the Wider Episcopal Fellowship, whose theme is to be the Episcopate, may contribute again and more representatively to this concern. But my point is merely to call attention to the concern itself and the related issues both within our Communion and in wider intercourse. We are far from a common mind, in our Communion, about an ideal form of the Episcopate. This disagreement reflects far more than merely local tradition. Indeed it illuminates the many roles the bishop plays, and has played, in the long history of his office. No bishop can do all these things, or be them. Doubtless there must be a deliberate choice and shaping of the bishop's ministry, as of the structure of the Church itself, to suit the needs of each country and culture. If this is to be done and the Episcopate understood as a living organism within the Church's life, the continuance of this dialogue is greatly to be desired.

As perhaps could have been anticipated, little attention was paid to Latin America at the Congress in Toronto. This was a disappointment to many of our Latin American companions; but it was clear that the voices of the younger nations and churches were to be heard. And this was fair enough. Not every Church can hold the gaze of our world-wide household at one time. The work of the Anglican Communion in Latin America is not neglected. Since Cuernavaca, much of the recommended program has been set in motion. Your Grace has appointed two new bishops to share the great responsibilities of our life in the southern portion of the continent. PECUSA has in parallel fashion chosen a bishop for the new jurisdiction in Colombia, to which our mission in Ecuador is to be temporarily attached. Two suffragan bishops have been chosen for Mexico. Plans are afoot for the establishment of the Brazilian dioceses in an autocephalous Brazilian province, hopefully in 1965. The Latin American dioceses of PECUSA are looking to their incorporation in a ninth province. The Churches of Australia and Canada have already assumed new responsibilities in South America. All this, I believe, is noteworthy as a mark of a new vigor and depth in the life of our Communion which for more than two centuries has borne its witness in what Lambeth 1958 called "the neglected continent."

Financial

The book-keeping year for the three inter-Anglican budgets began with an accumulated balance of £1,208, the result of special gifts and payments by churches for previous years, as well as unexpended balances. Payments on 1963 apportionment, to December 31st, were £28,092, a nearly-perfect achievement measured against the total allocation of £28,400. We may all be most grateful for this, as well as the great assistance given us by the Central Board of Finance and their secretary and staff.

Other income during 1963 came to £717. This included £40 paid on 1962 quota, sundry honoraria and fees transmitted by myself, and over-payments by churches. Thus £30,017 was available in 1963 against our needs. From this the budgets of the Archbishop in Jerusalem (£2,-740), St. Augustine's College (£12,050) and my office (£13,610), were met in full, and it was possible as well to cover much of the heavy additional cost of printing, postage, etc., incidental to the series of meetings in Canada.

I have been reluctant, as Your Grace knows, to urge any increase in my own budget. The ACMS, last summer, indeed approved an increase of £3,500 in 1964, to provide additional "Assistance." This help will be welcome, for the burden of correspondence and co-ordinating detail grows steadily; and as soon as it is clear what form this "Assistance" should take, I will very happily make the necessary appointments.

But at the same time I resisted the impulse felt by many in the Council to include in my budget a very much larger range of costs— for Regional Officers, travel funds, and the like. I am not quixotic in this. Should it be plain that a larger central operation is needed, adequately to sustain our common life, I would ask for it. But I am sure that such increases should come only when they are plainly required. I feel this way partly in respect for the many unmet needs, particularly in the less-affluent churches and societies, partly because my office is still new and in a highly-exploratory phase.

But the principal reason for my caution (and this is why I raise the issue at all) is that of the delicacy of the essential balance of responsibility within our Communion. Whatever we do, even to so small a thing as my budget, must be true to ourselves—must take account of the nature of our association. If we were a unitary world denomination, many things, including budgets, would be far simpler to plan. But the responsible, free partnership of our Communion establishes rather more complex conditions for us, under which far more depends on the voluntary action of churches and individuals themselves.

The operation of my office, in these first four years, has cost about double what has been contributed by the churches through the budget. Some of this was the initial cost of furnishing and equipping an office—presumably an expense my successor will not have to face. Some was the cost of moving my family and myself. Some was the cost of meetings, additional staff services, printing, and a host of like expenses almost impossible to calculate ahead of time. By far the greatest part was for research and special studies and projects.

These expenses were met by gifts from individuals and churches. I could not begin to express my gratitude adequately for this. No doubt it would have been sensible to include such things as the equipment of an office or moving expenses in the budget. But I am sure it would have been short-sighted to have included the much greater costs of research and the like in the annual allocation. For these things I feel we must continue to turn to the initiative and imagination of the churches and people of our Communion individually, outside the budget.

I am an American, and therefore it may not seem remarkable that my own church has been unfailingly generous in undertaking the cost of special projects time after time. I am nonetheless grateful to them. But my successor may not be able to count on such support from his church. Where will he turn? I hope he will feel he can make his needs known to every church, confident that he will meet an instant readiness on the part of his companions to offer their help in getting the common tasks done. Indeed I hope we will not wait to be asked. The peculiar privilege and vocation of the Executive Officer is to live as far ahead of where we are as he can, knowing and studying trends, trying to foresee needs, eager to excite response to needs hardly yet defined. The more we anticipate his needs and volunteer our help, the more swiftly do we move forward in mutual responsibility.

Wider Episcopal Fellowship

1963 brought a steady deepening of the ecumenical relationships known by us, currently, as "The Wider Episcopal Fellowship." Imagined by the 1930 Lambeth Conference as a "circle of visible fellowship," its first historic demonstration was seen in the Bonn Agreement of 1931, which established "a state of inter-communion" between the Church of England and the Old Catholic Churches. By the next Lambeth Conference, in 1948, similar agreements had brought the whole Anglican household into full communion with the Old Catholic Churches, and it was possible for the Conference to speak of "a larger episcopal unity" and recommend "an episcopal conference, advisory in character, for brotherly counsel and encouragement." By 1958 the group of churches so designated had considerably increased, and the Conference renewed its recommendation that a conference of this "Wider Episcopal Fellowship" be held. In April, 1964, such a conference will be held, thanks to Your Grace's initiative, in Canterbury, thus fulfilling a hope of more than thirty years' standing.

This ecumenical configuration was defined by the Lambeth Conference as those churches "possessing the historic episcopate with which churches and provinces of the Anglican Communion are in full communion or in a relation of inter-communion." At present eight churches or groups of churches are so designated—the Old Catholic Churches (including the Polish National Catholic Church in the United States), the Churches of Finland, South India, and Sweden, the Lusitanian and Spanish Reformed Episcopal Churches, the Philippine Independent Church, and the Mar Thoma Syrian Church. Increasingly, formal relationships between these Churches and Anglican provinces are in terms of the Bonn Agreement, and concordats of this type were concluded, in 1963, between the Philippine Independent Church and most of the provinces of the Anglican Communion, notably the Church of England. Notable also was the establishment of such concordats between the Church of England and the two churches of the Iberian Peninsula, for so long a peculiar care of the Church of Ireland and, latterly, of PECUSA as well.

The forthcoming conference will be deeply welcomed by the churches of our Communion. It is no dilution of that welcome to note some of the cautions and hesitations expressed by many—Anglicans as well as others—as we move into a clearer articulation of this fellowship. Some see in it the birth of a third force, ecumenically—a bloc of like-minded churches, an episcopalian super-confession, to complicate still further the ecumenical scene. Others are uncomfortable at an ecclesiastical intimacy which seems to shut out Christians with whom we have close and warm friendship within our own societies. Again, there is a measure of restlessness at what seems a unique and disproportionate emphasis on the historic episcopate. So one could continue to list the ambiguities and limitations inherent in this fellowship, as it presently exists, which are a source of concern to the churches within it as well as outside.

One would rightly distrust any easy reassurance on this score. But certain clear convictions are held, by Anglicans and others, on which a sound and reassuring perspective can be founded. One is the recognition of the incomplete and arbitrary and even accidental character of the relationships which constitute the Wider Episcopal Fellowship at this point. It is not an organization or a club; it has no structure; it has no clear definition of itself. It is no more than what its description implies—an association of churches within the Catholic Church which have special ties with Anglican provinces because they share what Anglicans hold to be essential constituent elements of the visible church. This fellowship does not pretend to be itself a church or an organization of churches. It is a fellowship which shares a peculiar intensity of relationship, and becomes thereby a partial but real pattern of unity within a far wider if less intense companionship.

Second, each of the churches involved shares fully in other relationships, outside the Fellowship. Indeed, as in the case of the Church of South India, for example, the ties it has with non-episcopal churches may be far stronger than those it shares within the Fellowship. This would be true, indeed, of Anglican provinces as well.

Third, this Fellowship has reality and power only as it is expressed in witness and service. A relationship of full communion is dangerous—if it is not impotent—as long as it remains largely theoretical. Where distance or cultural barriers or traditional alignments are allowed to make and keep this sacramental brotherhood theoretical, merely ceremonial, merely a diplomatic courtesy, we need not be astonished if the unity of the Church does not even suffer in the end. Only as *communio in sacris* yields its holy gifts of communion in the Gospel—a mission shared, a judgment accepted in common, a single witness, a life of interdependent brotherhood—is the greatness of the sacramental privilege fulfilled. When we deliberately plan our involvement with one another, moving from the altar into the world, then this partial unity may become a foretaste of the final unity in Christ for which we pray.

Because we hold these convictions, it is easy to understand the longing Anglicans feel for a deepening and strengthening of the Fellowship. We do not know what it will yield in time; we do not even know how to describe it. What we feel is that God has led us, in this growing association, closer to the discovery of a now-unknown greatness and depth in our understanding of the Church, of unity, of mission. In this, it is essential that we continue to press the implications of full communion, in developing every channel of mutual responsibility and interdependence with the other churches with whom we are so closely united. The communion we share with the Old Catholics or the Philippine Independent Church is not a different one than what Anglicans share. Therefore the summons to responsibility and interdependence must control our participation in the Wider Episcopal Fellowship. Where churches in full communion share a common country, the implications of full communion are easy to see. But our life in the Anglican Communion has taught us long ago that interdependence knows no national barriers.

Other Ecumenical Notes

No doubt the commanding event of ecumenical interest in our Anglican year, apart from the Congress itself, was the appearance of the proposals for Anglican-Methodist *rapprochement* in Britain. They are of a general type now becoming familiar in ecumenical circles, but they seem less marked by caution and protectiveness and more infused with a spirit of affirmation and inclusiveness. It is easy to see how helpful this development will be, if it leads to success, to the many other Anglican provinces engaged in the same task.

Negotiations for locally-united churches continue in Ceylon, India and Pakistan, with the possibility of successful completion in West Pakistan within a short time. So too in West Africa—in Ghana and Nigeria—where again the time horizon seems short. Conversations—not yet negotiations—are going on in many other parts of our Communion. In both Canada and Australia renewed eagerness is now felt for such conversations and in the latter continent a notable and statesmanlike document appeared during the year. Entitled "The Church—Its Nature, Function and Ordering," it is the fruit of very thorough ecumenical dialogue, in which our provinces were not directly involved but were most interested observers.

Such quests and plans are no doubt a basic characteristic of our time. Not too long ago one would have been struck, perhaps troubled, by the limited fields of tradition and allegiance so represented. Strongly "confessional" churches were not likely to contemplate easily the loss of identity which unity requires. Pentecostal bodies resisted ecumenical engagement fairly steadily. With Orthodoxy it seemed difficult to progress beyond a frontier of theological discussion. Rome remained aloof, imperial and implacable.

Because these things were so, it was easy both to welcome and fear the drive toward unity—to welcome it because it seemed to promise a balance and defense against the Roman monolith; or to fear it, if not on that ground, at least on the ground of the relative sparseness of the traditions being so brought together, and the great areas of Christian faith and practice not included.

Nothing has changed more radically, in recent years, than this sense of partiality and limitation. Most vividly felt in the Orthodox Churches, perhaps, it has also been dramatically apparent in Rome, that there is abroad in the world a new seriousness and intensity of concern for unity. And this is not limited to those churches, by any means. Great differences of conviction remain, and it would be romantic to disguise them or imagine they will swiftly yield to a new spirit. But it would be equally unrealistic to ignore the new spirit, with all its incalculable potential.

I have been impressed with these observations in the past year, particularly in their bearing on the life and witness of our Anglican churches. Sometimes we pay only lip service to unity. More often we give honest attention and even responsible leadership. But even so, there are crippling disabilities in Anglican ecumenical participation. The greatest is no doubt hidden in an Anglican excellence—our Communion is an ecumenical experiment itself, of very great importance; and we are reluctant to disturb its delicate balance or introduce disturbing new factors. But other disabilities have less exalted matrices. Our own differences at home, when held up to view in unity negotiations, often threaten to destroy our precarious inner unity. We have a strong "confessional" loyalty, all the stronger because there is no Anglican theological confession, but only rather less frank cultural and historical ones. Perhaps most acutely, our strong institutional and historical sense tends to lead us to a disastrous self-assurance, in which we come almost to the point of dealing with the Church and the Faith as if they were our property.

These are clear enough. So is it clear that in the swelling impulse toward reconciliation which now sweeps the world, there is a note of warning to us, to prepare ourselves for the ecumenical task, no longer an option. I find our need for preparation most apparent in three particulars.

First, we need to find our own unity at home. If the Anglican-Methodist proposals in Britain are defeated, one reason at least will be that our own unity was too precarious to endure the challenge and disturbance of a wider one. The proposals, with their statements of sacramental or ministerial understanding, confront a church which has not had to fight for its own unity, with decisions which threaten to fragment and divide. To say this is to pass no judgment on the Church of England. It has been the source, for uncounted millions of us, of the very liberality and comprehensiveness we love—the inclusive and generous spirit that holds together order and freedom, history and the spirit, in one frame. But the Church of England was given its unity, in its establishment, in its national identity, in parson's freehold, in endowment and custom—all of which guaranteed that men of widely-different convictions could share at least an uneasy companionship in a given institution.

Younger Anglican churches were not so equipped. The fight for inner unity was often an ever-present reality; and where this has been so, they have learned a cardinal lesson about comprehensiveness, inclusiveness, breadth in the Church. The joining of Catholic and Protestant elements in Anglican life is not a vigilant cohabitation of opposites. The reconciliation, the joining of the streams of divine revelation, is not done by parishes or parties. It is not a choice a man must make, to be, say, a Catholic or a Protestant. The Prayer Book alone should make this clear, that any Anglican must be both—must share in both traditions—must make the reconciliation and discover the unity and breadth of the Church within his own heart and life. The search for this unity and the understanding of it is an urgent part of our preparation for this age, I am convinced.

So too must we examine with new eyes the whole "confessional" issue. It is no secret that I am entirely content with our freedom from a confessional theology—we hold no other standard than the confession of the whole Church of Christ. But this nobility, as it sometimes is, can lead us to a dangerous illusion, that no confession is called for from Christians. The problem with what the younger churchmen call "confessionalism" is not that Christians confess before God, it is what they confess. The utter irrelevance to our time of so many medieval and post-medieval distinctions hardly deserves mention. What should our confession be, in the face of racial strife, of a cold and triumphant secularism, of the increasingly irrational and ungoverned use of power? It may be that a new confessionalism—one that may chafe tender Anglican shoulders—is required for this age and unity.

The third Anglican ecumenical task is the one most clearly sketched for us by "Mutual Responsibility and Interdependence in the Body of Christ." It is the task of bringing unity and mission together, of restoring a lost theological order in our life, of remembering the priority of the divine mission and its certain consequence that the Church is not ours at all, and that God is able of these stones to raise up children.

I believe that our Communion has been taught many true things by God, in history, and we have an obligation to Him and the truth to take a confident, bold, resolute part in the search for unity. I believe this search is one of the paramount duties of our age, not for the sake of unity in itself but that we may be true to the depth and glory of the Church. I share with many others the hope that we may work to make ourselves ready to take the part the sincerity of our faith requires of us. And I say all this, not to pretend to admonish your Grace or your colleagues, but simply to record what I am sure is the temper of the vast company of our companions, in this year of Grace.

Mutual Responsibility

I close with a brief account of the first months of response to the summons to "Mutual Responsibility and Interdependence in the Body of Christ." The document itself was transmitted to every church and province, and as quickly as possible, thanks to the devoted assiduity of SPCK and the Seabury Press, it was published, together with the major relevant papers, for general use.

This publication, and other communications as well, went far to untangle the confusions with which the document was first greeted, in some quarters. Chiefly it was interpreted as (a) an arbitrary dictate from higher authority, (b) a proposal for greater confessional cohesion (c) a disguised appeal for funds for missions overseas. During the later months of 1963 these misconceptions were largely dissipated. Chiefly the churches began to perceive that "response" to the manifesto would be considerably more radical and comprehensive and costly than at first understood. This perception was disconcerting as well as invigorating.

We are, I think, therefore at a critical point in this matter. Can the true size and depth and cost of the proposal be kept clear in our eyes, or will we be beguiled into making a quick and inexpensive response and so avoid the major confrontation? Much depends, I believe, on the way our churches approach their own domestic problems, for it is in their understanding of their own mission and responsibility at home that their participation in Mutual Responsibility begins.

In the United States, for example, the mission of the Church in urban and industrial life is a matter of paramount importance. Plans for a very considerable new program in this area are being made, and it is hoped that the General Convention in 1964 will launch this ambitious and costly advance. Many of my colleagues are troubled because the Mutual Responsibility matter must also be presented to the Church, and may divert attention and support from the urban frontier. Why should there be a collision here? Should not the response to the challenge of the urban mission be understood from the start as a major obedience to Mutual Responsibility? If the church in the United States can discover better ways to witness and serve in industrial society—and surely there is no more appropriate laboratory than this—and so develop new skills and strengths which can be shared with other societies and other churches, I should think this was a clear example of precisely what interdependence in the Body of Christ means.

The Church of England is now wrestling with two major proposals—the Anglican-Methodist negotiations and the Paul Report on Manpower. Again some of my colleagues are concerned at the introduction of yet a third matter, Mutual Responsibility, into an already-crowded scene. Here too, as in my own church, I am sure it would be wrong to think of Mutual Responsibility as if it were a program or a proposal in itself, competing for time and attention with other matters of immediate local concern. If the Church of England were able to find a way to end a miserable and senseless schism which has kept Anglicans and Methodists apart for nearly two hundred years, I should be inclined to think of this as a fairly substantial down-payment on Mutual Responsibility. And the same judgment, I am sure, would apply to the immensely complicated issues raised by the Paul Report.

These instances illustrate three central principles of Mutual Responsibility. First, we begin our response to the proposal where we are, as we are. Second, the obedience to mission each church shows by understanding and facing its own tasks in greater depth and more radical freedom is an essential expression of mutuality and interdependence. Third, the problems of each church are of concern to every other church.

These principles have all been represented in the few months following Toronto. The African dioceses made their first response in the form of greatly-enlarged requests for assistance in 170 projects for clerical and lay training, evangelism, the strengthening of diocesan and provincial ministry and the like. In some quarters this response was greeted with disappointment, on the ground that it was simply "asking," on a larger scale, by churches that were "asking churches" anyway. I do not doubt that the first projects, hastily-planned in many instances, are sometimes disappointing—seeming to call for little more than money, seeming to imagine little in the way of new forms of ministry. Such disappointment is sensible and fruitful, or can be, if it is the beginning of the dialogue which mutuality in planning calls for. But to be disappointed because "asking churches" try to ask more wisely and openly and prudently is seriously to misunderstand Mutual Responsibility.

Less disappointment was expressed in those cases—notably the Canadian Church—where the first response took the form of increased giving. But it would be as valid to criticize the Canadians for setting out to increase their giving as it was to criticize the Africans for proposing to increase their asking and spending. In either case, obedience begins where we are, as we are. It will be, in both cases, the second step that counts; we walk on two feet; and as "asking" becomes "giving," and vice versa, the pilgrimage will begin.

Yet even in the first stage (as if there were an order in time for these things), the two other principles I mention are illustrated. It is an essential element in mutuality that each church shall face its own tasks and nature, as part of the common life. If churches do not plan as wisely or give as generously as they ought, this is a matter of common concern, for our unity in the Body of Christ is involved. Therefore we do not wait for the more perfect response to come; we are involved in one another's struggle for a better obedience quite as much as we shall gain from one another's successes.

I am, in consequence, profoundly impressed with our present need to expand and strengthen our mutual knowledge and understanding. The fifth proposal in Mutual Responsibility may well be, at the moment, the most urgent one, as far as our corporate life is concerned— the call to "deep and deliberate involvement in one another's affairs." In his address to the Anglican Congress, Canon Waddams, as perceptive a commentator on Anglican affairs as I know, said of us that "the Anglican Communion does not display fully adult relationships between its churches," and he asked how we could hope to "make a useful contribution to Christian unity beyond our own fellowship, if we are not living Christian unity fully with our fellow-Anglicans in our own spiritual home."

Here, as in many other cases, solutions would be easier to find if our organization were different. In our case, I know of no quick panacea. Yet there are encouraging developments. One American diocese has begun the publication, on its own, of a scheme for daily intercession, based on the Anglican Cycle of Prayer, informed by brief paragraphs telling something of the diocese in question, its needs and situation. Quite independently, the Rector of St. Bride's, Fleet Street, London, has undertaken to prepare such paragraphs for every diocese. Thus in our prayers there is an impulse to express deeper mutual knowledge and interdependence.

Again it is significant that nearly every one of the numerous meetings last summer expressed the wish to find some way to maintain the mutual consultation so universally welcomed. Whether in the field of ecumenical relationships or educational affairs or Prayer Book revision or the ministry of the laity, a common element almost invariably was the planning of channels of communication through which the tides of interdependence might flow more freely.

In still another way, this search for mutuality was most deeply expressed in the directory of projects, "Mutual Responsibility in Africa: I." I think that never before in Anglican history have our churches shared needs and hopes so openly, in the light. Part of the cost of this openness, no doubt, is a new vulnerability to critical comment and perhaps hurt pride. No doubt it is also a confusing process, cutting across older, private lines of communication. But I think none of the discomforts should obscure the immense new vision of responsible brotherhood which is so movingly opened in this new phase of Anglican life.

We are, then, beginning to find our way into a new pattern of relationships, under the great impulse of the summons to Mutual Responsibility. I could not pretend to foresee what even the next few months will bring. How can the Paul Report be lodged in the prayers and brotherly concern of the Anglican Communion? How can church unity negotiations in India strengthen the conversations between our Church and the United Church in Canada? How can African dioceses share in the urban mission of PECUSA? Such questions are the present frontier and agenda of Mutual Responsibility and Interdependence in the Body of Christ.

Personal

I close this report with a double burden on my heart. One is a sense of profound thanksgiving for the unimaginable and undeserved blessings of 1963. I reported to Your Grace, a year ago, "we have now reached the point, in all our churches, where the great majority of our people can make no effective connection between the convulsive world history in which they live and the mission of Christ by Whom all things are made and saved. . . . It is not too much to say that the Anglican churches of the world need to be born again in a profound rediscovery of mission and its meaning and its cost."

When I wrote that, it was an expression as much of despair as of hope. But as I should have known, man's extremity is God's opportunity. In his mercy, He accepted our offering of perplexity and need and love and blindness, and of those things fashioned a hope—I think greater than we can yet understand, certainly greater than we deserved. I can conceive no other response to make save that of thanksgiving. The thanksgiving includes immense gratitude for particular things and particular people—for the Anglican Congress, for Cuernavaca, for the hundreds of letters and meetings and papers and speeches, for the patience of those who move faster than most of us, not least for the devotion and selflessness of my comrades in my own office and home. But thanksgiving goes beyond the particulars, to the Lord of the Church Himself, Who did not fail to give us things which for our unworthiness we dared not, and for our blindness we could not ask.

The other part of my burden is trust—I do not know what better word there should be—in the Anglican way. It was my task to address the Congress on the organization of our Communion. It was a distasteful assignment, for my thoughts do not run easily or happily in such channels. But it brought certain rewards—chiefly that of having my nose rubbed in the dilemmas, ambiguities, perplexities, inherent in any analysis of the Church's organization and structure.

There is no great difficulty in describing the Anglican Communion, as an historical organization of men and women. But the more one attempts to penetrate beneath such purely superficial description, the harder it is to be neat and clear. If there were an Anglican ministry, there would be no great problem in describing it, differentiating it from others, studying it comparatively, manipulating and molding it, and all the rest. But we claim no such ministry; we claim only the ministry of the Catholic Church as we understand it. So with the Sacraments. So with the Church itself. There is no Anglican faith, we say; there is only the faith of the undivided Church, built on the universal skeleton of Scripture and Creeds. All this is fine and characteristically Anglican, and I believe it.

But the price one pays for this freedom from restrictive definition is dilemma, ambiguity, perplexity. What does "Anglican" mean, when all historical, legal, cultural, confessional scaffolding is stripped away? What good is "full communion" when it no longer can clearly separate one company of Christians from another? What happens when an "Anglican" diocese enters a united Church? Where are the limits of "mutual responsibility and interdependence in the Body of Christ"? Is the document itself a "confessional" blood-transfusion or is it a statement about the Catholic Church?

Such questions (and they are not questions for Anglicans alone, by a long shot) reveal the dilemmas, ambiguities, perplexities. They were asked at the Congress, as they are asked wherever we talk in any depth, and they produced the characteristic frustrations. The applause of those who welcome "disappearance" is matched by the cheers of those who welcome "re-birth and continuing witness." Often the same people cheer on both sides; I sometimes do myself, and feel it entirely right to do so. This is not a moral lapse. It is a recognition of the extraordinary greatness and richness, far beyond our knowing or deserving, of the heritage of the Anglican household.

We do not know—precisely because it is the Church of God and not our toy—we do not know what God means to do with our fellowship. All we know, and I dare say all we will ever know, is that we must be true to what He has given us, and follow Him as He seems to lead us step by step. Precisely because we lack clear denominational definition, it is impossible for us to pretend to know the future shape of the Church, and build it. Precisely because we claim to have nothing of our own, it is impossible for us to make a crisp bargain with our "gifts" in exchange for others.

The Anglican tradition is simply the way this group of Christians understands the Catholic Church and the Catholic faith and tries to obey. Where this obedience will finally lead is a senseless question to ask. Even to ask it in less radical terms, as "what is the vocation of the Anglican Communion?," is, I suspect, equally senseless. The only "vocation" we can be sure of is really nothing very fancy at all—we are called to be saints, in the only way we know how, which is the Prayer Book way.

Therefore the faithfulness of Anglicans is a very modest thing indeed. It is to be true to the Gospel, to the Catholic creeds, to the continuing life of the Church, and to the real size and responsible freedom of created man, as best we can. This is what I referred to earlier as "trust." It is the quality, I believe, which helps Christians not to be afraid of the world, and to be in it but not of it. It is the quality that makes it possible for men of different minds to break the Bread of life together. It is the quality that guards us from ecumenical dogmatism and equally impels us to ecumenical action.

It makes great demands on our patience and our humility, I find. It would be nice to know where and how and why we were better than others, and how the story will come out in the end. But these are luxuries, I am sure, not for the likes of us. For us there is only the modest assurance of pilgrimage. "The Church exists to witness, to obey and to serve." This is what I mean by "trust"; and after all the excitement and discovery and eager questioning and often confusion and frustration of a climactic and exacting year, I must say that I welcome so sober and reassuring an admonition.

Respectfully submitted,
STEPHEN F. BAYNE, JR.
Executive Officer

III.

Current Inter-Anglican Organization*

Introductory

1. THE CURRENT OFFICIAL definition of the Anglican Communion was adopted by the Lambeth Conference in 1930 (Resolution 49):

> The Anglican Communion is a fellowship, within the One Holy Catholic and Apostolic Church, of those duly constituted Dioceses, Provinces or Regional Churches in communion with the See of Canterbury, which have the following characteristics in common:
>
> (a) they uphold and propagate the Catholic and Apostolic faith and order as they are generally set forth in the Book of Common Prayer as authorized in their several Churches;
>
> (b) they are particular or national Churches, and, as such, promote within each of their territories a national expression of Christian faith, life and worship; and
>
> (c) they are bound together not by a central legislative and executive authority, but by mutual loyalty sustained through the common counsel of the Bishops in conference.

2. The definition quoted, now thirty-three years old, shows some marks of wear, and of changing ecumenical and theological climate. As Prayer Book revision proceeds in the several churches, it becomes increasingly difficult to describe exactly what the phrase means, "as generally set forth," with reference to the Prayer Book. More significantly, the establishment of full communion with churches which are not "Anglican" has introduced new elements not present in 1930. However, the definition remains the official description of the Anglican Communion, set forth by its most-nearly authoritative body.

---

* A memorandum prepared for the World Council of Churches Consultation at Geneva, October 2–5, 1963.

3. There is apparently no simple answer to the questions of how a church would become, or cease to be, a member of the Anglican Communion. There is no procedure for "joining"; autocephalous churches born out of missionary or other activity of existing churches become members of the Anglican Communion when they begin their separate life. Non-"Anglican" churches (such as the Old Catholic, with which all Anglican churches are in full communion) do not "join the Anglican Communion" by such concordats. As to leaving it, the only precedent is that of the four dioceses in southern India which ceased to be constituent dioceses of the CIPBC when they entered the Church of South India. At this stage, "Anglican" status would seem to be simply a matter of historical fact, no doubt dependent on the existence of full communion, but also on other factors which have never been isolated or studied.

4. The churches included in this fellowship are (using their legal names, in the Lambeth order of precedence) the Church of England (two provinces), the Church in Wales, the Church of Ireland (two provinces), the Episcopal Church in Scotland, the Protestant Episcopal Church in the USA (eight provinces), the Anglican Church of Canada (four provinces), the Church of India, Pakistan, Burma and Ceylon, the Church of England in Australia (four provinces), the Church of the Province of New Zealand, the Church of the Province of South Africa, the Church of the Province of the West Indies, Nippon Seikokai (the Holy Catholic Church in Japan), Chung Hua Sheng Kung Hui (the Holy Catholic Church in China), the Church of the Province of West Africa, the Church of the Province of Central Africa, the Archbishopric in Jerusalem, the Church of the Province of East Africa, the Church of the Province of Uganda and Rwanda-Urundi. There are also ten extra-provincial dioceses under the metropolitical authority of the Archbishop of Canterbury. Presently there are 347 dioceses in all.

5. These eighteen churches are entirely autocephalous, in almost every case. (In two or three of the newer ones, certain ultimate rights and responsibilities are still reserved to the Archbishop of Canterbury, and thus there are some nominal limitations of autonomy.) But the churches are linked by many ties, mostly stemming from their common origin, direct or indirect, in the Church of England. Their Prayer Books still have a clear family resemblance. English is still the most commonly-used liturgical language, although the Prayer Books of the various churches are printed in 170 different languages. Most of the churches are within the Commonwealth. There are channels of "missionary" support which are still effective links between older and newer churches.

All Anglican churches tend still to lean heavily on the theological resources of the Church of England. These and the like are effective
vessels of unity within the Anglican fellowship.

6. It remains true, however, despite those deep historical and cultural links, that these churches "are bound together not by a central
legislative and executive authority, but by mutual loyalty sustained
through the common counsel of the Bishops in conference." Whatever
is done together by Anglican churches, is done through the free choice
of the churches individually. No action can be taken by "the Anglican
Communion"; it must be the action of eighteen churches. There is not
likely to be an "Anglican" point of view on most matters, but only the
points of view of the several churches. "Anglican" representation at any
meeting can only be by officers or members of particular Anglican
churches.

7. Therefore inter-Anglican organization is always determined by
the necessities of the consultative process; and all such organization reflects the fact that ultimate authority and responsibility lies in the
churches themselves, not in any central authority.

The Lambeth Conference and Its Arms

8. The "common counsel of the Bishops in conference" is expressed
principally through the Lambeth Conference, a meeting of Anglican
bishops, generally at ten-year intervals. These are informal gatherings,
now usually for five or six weeks, traditionally held at Lambeth Palace,
the London headquarters of the Archbishop of Canterbury. The first
Conference was held in 1867, at the request of bishops in Canada (and
the United States); and it set the tone and pattern followed ever since,
of a private gathering, at the Archbishop's personal invitation, at which
he is both host and president. He determines the membership by inviting the bishops he wishes, in categories he sets—either diocesan
bishops only, or all bishops, or some intermediate group. Procedure
varies little from Conference to Conference. In general the work is
done in committees on various themes, who report to and prepare resolutions for the entire Conference. Committee reports carry only the
authority of the committee itself; resolutions adopted by the Conference represent the considered view of the Conference as a whole.

9. The authority of this meeting, while considerable as expressive of
the common mind of the Anglican episcopate, is not coercive or synodical. Any action proposed by a Lambeth Conference can only be put
into effect by each church separately. A Conference may point the way
to desired actions; but the essential dynamics of the Anglican Com-

munion remain in the several churches; and the Conference retains its character as the central but informal occasion of common counsel among the bishops. These considerations are true as well of the two continuing arms of the Conference.

10. The older of these is the Lambeth Consultative Body, established in 1897 and last reconstituted in 1958. It consists, essentially, of the Primates or Presiding Bishops of the churches (or episcopal alternates designated by them) and episcopal representatives of the extra-provincial dioceses as selected by the Archbishop of Canterbury. The present membership is 23. It is "of the nature of a Continuation Committee of the Lambeth Conference," advisory to the Archbishop of Canterbury or to bishops or groups of bishops, especially in matters of faith and order, or of the Lambeth Conference itself.

11. The second arm is the Advisory Council on Missionary Strategy, established in 1948 and reconstituted in 1958. This Council consists of all Primates and Presiding Bishops and all other metropolitans (or alternates, lay or clerical, as designated by them), as well as representatives of the extra-provincial dioceses, to a total of 37. "The purpose of the Council is to enable the whole Anglican Communion to deal effectively with matters of world-wide strategy and the welfare of the whole Communion." It is, again, entirely an advisory and consultative group.

12. Meetings of both these groups have been infrequent. In August, 1963, the Consultative Body adopted a proposal for more frequent meetings of Metropolitans, at approximately two-year intervals. These meetings would include the present Consultative Body together with an additional episcopal representative from each of the Churches in Australia, Canada and the United States. The Regional Officers and selected staff advisers would also be in attendance for certain phases of these meetings.

Regional Councils and Officers

13. Since 1948, Regional Councils have been established in two areas. One is the South Pacific Council, composed of the dioceses of Melanesia and Polynesia (of the Church of New Zealand) and Carpentaria and New Guinea (of the Australian Church). The other is the Council of the Church of South East Asia, which includes the dioceses of Jesselton, Korea, Kuching, and Singapore and Malaya (all extra-provincial dioceses of Canterbury), Rangoon (a diocese of CIPBC), Hong Kong (an administratively-independent diocese of the Church of China), and the Philippines and Taiwan (two dioceses of the American Episcopal Church).

14. Councils are informal groups of dioceses (and provinces) which share a generally-common region and a sufficient involvement in one another's affairs within the life of the region, yet which have different metropolitical allegiances. Councils are not provinces or churches (although it is expected that they will become such in time, or perhaps give birth to several provinces). They are essentially inter-provincial arrangements whereby regional fellowship and planning, ecumenical action, mutual responsibility and the like can be strengthened. They may have certain quasi- or para-synodical powers, as such may be delegated to them by the parent provinces. They may include non-"Anglican" churches. Meetings of at least the bishops concerned are generally held annually. Meetings of the South East Asia Council usually include clerical and lay delegates as well, one from each diocese in each order.

15. Regional Officers were proposed by the Advisory Council in August, 1963. It is hoped that such officers will be established in these regions: Africa, Australia and New Zealand, the British Isles, India, Latin America, North America, Pakistan and the Middle East, the South Pacific, and South East Asia. Such officers are expected to fulfill three main functions. First, they will assist the churches in the region in mutual planning, ecumenical relations, communication with other churches, etc. Second, they will "represent appropriately in each region the whole life and unity of the Anglican Communion." Third, they will extend the work of the Executive Officer, both as a collegiate group meeting with him annually, and also by multiplying his availability to serve the churches.

Other Consultation

16. The "Executive Officer of the Anglican Communion" is, in fact, the executive officer of the two principal inter-Anglican bodies. But his relationship is a unique one; he is a servant of all the churches equally, and through correspondence and personal visits he maintains a continuous channel of communication and consultation, during the intervals when there are not face-to-face meetings of the various groups already described. It is his primary task to co-ordinate the activities of the several churches, to relate one with another so as to avoid duplication and strengthen mutual concern, to assist churches in evaluating new proposals, "missionary" or otherwise, to maintain general cognizance of what is going on and what needs next to be done, and to put people and agencies in touch with one another appropriately.

17. In this, he is aided by groups of "Consultants"—people, lay or

clerical, who are involved and expert in various fields such as ecumenical affairs, liturgical revision, education, and the like, appointed officially in each church. Meetings of these consultants have been held only in connection with the Anglican Congress, because of expense. But the circulation of information and correspondence goes on. This system permits a regular flow of information and ideas, and a mutual learning and consultative process to happen, unofficially and flexibly.

18. Ecumenical relationships in the Anglican Communion are maintained, almost entirely, by and through the separate churches. Seventeen of the autocephalous jurisdictions are members of the WCC (the Jerusalem Archbishopric is not regarded as possessing full autonomy, nor are the Regional Councils; and membership in the WCC is not presently open to them). The Executive Officer himself tries to maintain general liaison with ecumenical groups, especially the DWME; and as a bishop of the Episcopal Church in the USA, he is personally involved in some. But it is felt generally, within the Anglican Communion, that both the nature of the Communion itself and also the development of responsible ecumenical participation are best served by emphasizing the ecumenical obligations of the churches themselves, each in its own setting and task.

"Mutual Responsibility"

19. An important proposal, called "Mutual Responsibility and Interdependence in the Body of Christ," was issued by the Lambeth Consultative Body in August, 1963, and now is coming to each Anglican Church for appropriate response. The proposal considers the present situation and needs of the Anglican Communion and asks each church to undertake a five-fold program of immediate increased *support* of one another's projects, *study* of its own obedience to mission, *search* for its own needs as well as resources, *evaluation* of its own activities "by the test of mission and of service," and the *opening* of new channels of communication. The emphasis of this proposal, called by the Primates "the rebirth of the Anglican Communion," lies on the separate churches themselves, rather than on any central agency. As it is implemented, a new depth of inter-Anglican life will no doubt appear; but equally with this, it is felt, will come a deeper sense of mission and of ecumenical involvement at home.

20. The proposal, at present, envisages no new instrumentalities, but rather a more intensive use of the present channels of consultation and co-ordination. It was the considered opinion of the Primates

and Metropolitans that a fundamental choice of direction must be made; and in view of the traditional structure of the Anglican Communion and the needs of the separate churches themselves for full initiative and responsible freedom in their own regions and countries, it was agreed that the direction must not be toward the center but toward a deepening association of separate churches linked by the fact of full communion.

Summary

21. The present form of inter-Anglican organization remains basically as it has been stated since 1930—a fellowship of autocephalous regional and national churches linked by "full communion." The relationships between those churches are consultative and co-operative. The Lambeth Conference and other inter-Anglican bodies are advisory; they are simply ways in which churches meet and take counsel together. The decision-making processes are in the separate churches themselves. The main emphasis of recent decisions and proposals is in the direction of *intensifying* consultation, especially through more frequent meetings of representatives of the churches and regions, stressing regional development, deepening a sense of mutual responsibility, and underlining ecumenical responsibilities in the several regions and individual churches.

Part Two: Interpretations

I.

The Structure of the Anglican Communion

1. THE MODERN ANGLICAN SITUATION*

MY TASK is to talk about the contemporary scene in the life of the Anglican Communion. Let me begin with a generalization, that our present stage of life can be described as the "Anglican Communion Coming of Age." I know this is a dangerous generalization—dangerous on two grounds. First, to say that we are "coming of age" implies that we know what our maturity is going to look like; and who can pretend to know that? The second ground is that it is always perilously misleading to talk about the Church as if it were ever "young" or "old."

There is a sense, I am sure, in which human institutions do get old. Societies get old; parliaments get old; constitutional ways of doing things get old; and to some degree this is true about the Church—at least about many of the Church's institutions. But I am never sure that the Church itself, in its fullness, is ever more than one generation old. I do not think we can ever take it for granted, for one thing, as if once it is established in a nation it will be there for keeps. For another thing, the constant regeneration of the Holy Ghost—His guiding and teaching and judging work—makes the Church new in every generation, indeed in every soul. Either that, or else God abandons the Church to the death that overtakes every human institution.

Be all that as it may, I have found it helpful to myself, in trying to characterize the Anglican Communion of our time, to think of it in terms of young manhood. It is growing up into the truth about itself. It is beginning to fulfill all that was there at the beginning. It is coming to the point of making its own responsible decisions, and more

---

* Address at St. Augustine's Church Hall, Londonderry, on Friday, June 7, 1963, on the occasion of the St. Columba Celebrations.

and more exhibiting the resilience and vigor which one thinks of as the hallmarks of "coming of age."

A number of different factors lead me to think this way about our Communion. One is the now evident and swiftly-ripening fulfillment of that description of ourselves which we have used for so long. The nearest thing we have to an official definition of the Anglican Communion was that one adopted by the Lambeth Conference in 1930:

> The Anglican Communion is a fellowship, within the One Holy Catholic and Apostolic Church, of those duly constituted Dioceses, Provinces or Regional Churches in communion with the See of Canterbury, which have the following characteristics in common:
> (a) They uphold and propagate the Catholic and Apostolic faith and order as they are generally set forth in the Book of Common Prayer as authorized in their several Churches;
> (b) They are particular or national Churches, and, as such, promote within each of their territories a national expression of Christian faith, life and worship; and
> (c) They are bound together not by a central legislative and executive authority, but by mutual loyalty sustained through the common counsel of the Bishops in conference.

This familiar definition is now some thirty-three years old, and it is already beginning to show a few signs of wear. But for the most part, when it was adopted, it was more of a dream than a reality for much of the Anglican Communion. In 1930, there were close to a hundred isolated missionary dioceses, dependent on their parent churches— notably on the Church of England and the Archbishop of Canterbury. In Africa, only one of the now-five autocephalous churches was in existence. Responsible freedom was still mainly a dream in Japan and China alike, although the beginning steps had been taken for independent life.

To an outsider in 1930, the Anglican Communion would have looked like a federation of English-speaking churches, mainly on imperial soil — at least Anglo-Saxon soil — with an immense string of dependent missionary areas among those outside the magic circle of the English-speaking world. Yet despite the appearances, the dream was urgent and powerful. Whether we looked like a fellowship of self-governing churches or not, the seeds of that fellowship were already springing into life. And the next thirty years were to see an amazing fulfillment of this.

Now there are only nine of the nearly-350 Anglican dioceses which are not constituent members of national or regional churches of their own. On any Sunday in our time, the chances are that there are as many people around the world joining in the worship of the Prayer Book in non-English-speaking communities as there are those of us to whom English is the mother tongue. Our Prayer Books are printed in more than 170 languages—they are used in heaven knows how many more dialects.

In all this immense variety, the plain, persistent dream of the Anglican Communion has expressed itself. These people, of many kindreds and tongues, are gathered together in authentic, responsible churches of their own. They and their churches are not the dependent children of the Church in older and richer countries. They stand in full and equal brotherhood with us; they face their own destinies; they make common cause with their own societies and their own people; increasingly they welcome the responsibility of autonomy and are willing to pay the cost of it; and all this has meant that what was in such large measure a dream, a generation or two ago, has swiftly become a reality.

Probably it is principally because I am myself so profoundly involved in this new phase of Anglican life, that I think of it as a sign of majority and maturity. We *feel* as if we were coming of age. We may well continue to describe ourselves in terms which were current thirty years ago. What has changed is the toughness of substance which has made that definition of the Anglican Communion seem steadily more real.

The coming of age has had another effect on those old descriptions—it has made them seem somewhat out of date. I said that our classic Lambeth definition is beginning to show signs of wear. What I meant by that can be measured in two ways. First, the heart of any definition of the Anglican Communion, at the moment, is still that it is a fellowship of churches in communion with the See of Canterbury and with one another. In the early years of this century, or in the last century, when such a definition first became current, this was an adequate statement of our relationship. We were a fellowship in communion with Canterbury and one another. But when, in 1931, the concordat with the Old Catholic churches called the "Bonn Agreement" was signed, an entirely new element entered into our family life. For the first time, other-than-Anglican churches were in full communion with one another. What was then to differentiate between those churches which were clearly Anglican—the Church of Ireland, the Episcopal Church in the United States and so on—and those other churches, clearly not "Anglican" (whatever that word means), which were also in full communion with us and with one another? To this day, we have not yet come to terms with this unfamiliar, non-Anglican horizon. Two successive Lambeths have tried to cope with it, most recently in terms of what is called the "Wider Episcopal Fellowship." But the secrets and promise of this fellowship remain yet for the most part unexplored. All we know is that it has made the classic definition of our Anglican fellowship suddenly inadequate, and not at all the neat and final description we once thought we had.

There is, of course, a modification which comes into play here. In 1930, when the classic definition was adopted, one of the characteristics which was specified was that these churches in the fellowship of the Anglican Communion upheld and propagated the Catholic and Apostolic faith and order "as they are generally set forth in the Book of Common Prayer as authorized in their several churches." At the time, we probably were as tempted to find a satisfactory neatness in this Prayer Book qualification as we were in the mention of full communion. But as the years have gone on, as successive revisions of the Prayer Book have been made, it is beginning to become uncomfortably difficult to isolate that pure essence of Prayer Book Christianity which once we thought we knew so clearly.

Again, successive Lambeth Conferences have wrestled with this, but without yet reaching any final determination. It is perhaps not too difficult to describe the governing elements in Prayer Book *worship*. But one may well wonder whether the essential gifts of the Prayer Book—its most important elements—are those merely of worship. The Prayer Book is, for all of us Christians of the Anglican Communion, far more than merely a directory of worship. It is our teacher; it is the guardian of our tradition; it is the broad and noble guide to our belief and our life. And as revised Prayer Books proliferate, and as the forms of our worship change, in increasing adaptation to the needs and the condition of each of our societies, we begin to grow aware that it is not nearly as easy to define the Prayer Book as we once thought it was.

I mention these two matters because they bear a good deal on our present situation. They are part of the discomfort of growing up. If it becomes harder and harder to define the Anglican Communion, this is not necessarily a bad thing or displeasing to God. It complicates our life, no doubt; but it may even be that God is just as happy to have our life complicated a bit, as long as the Anglican Communion can only be one minor unity within the broken Body of Christ. And it may be equally good for us that we are not committed in some wooden traditional way to a single Prayer Book or a single pattern of life and work.

But only time will tell us the answers to these things. As in young manhood always, the work is yet to be done. All that has been given is the power and the freedom to do what lies at hand to be done. I think this is precisely where we are, at this point in our history.

If you do not like the image of "Coming of Age," please do not let it trouble you. I am concerned only with the facts—the immense growth of the churches of our Communion, the appearance in true and sober fact of the fellowship of self-governing churches, the reality of the inter-cultural and international life of our household, and all the other real factors that are the only ones that matter. They are the things that make the difference, in the Anglican Communion of our time.

Let me speak now of four areas where a noticeable difference may be seen. The first, of course, is that area which my own office symbolizes—the new level of inter-Anglican relationship. In actual fact, the origin of the Advisory Council on Missionary Strategy can be traced back to the Lambeth Conference of 1878. In the Encyclical Letter of that Conference, it was felt "desirable to appoint a Board of Reference, to advise upon questions brought before it either by Diocesan or Missionary Bishops or by Missionary Societies." It was urged that "the Archbishops of England and Ireland, the Bishop of London, the Primus of the Scottish Episcopal Church, the Presiding Bishop of the Protestant Episcopal Church in the United States of America, and the Bishop superintending the congregations of the American Church on the continent of Europe, and such other bishops as they may associate with themselves" should design and organize such a board of reference.

As it turned out, the Advisory Council did not come into existence until 1948, seventy years later. But it had cast a long shadow before it. Nearly a hundred years ago, it was beginning to be clear that the common life of the Anglican Communion could only be nourished and sustained on a basis of consultation. What was then only an idea now becomes daily more a reality.

The Advisory Council on Missionary Strategy (that curiously-named body) and its Executive Officer (again a curiously-named body) do not represent a central executive or administrative group. There is no way in which either the Advisory Council or myself can establish or maintain any program of our own, apart from the constituent churches of the Anglican Communion. I cannot execute anybody!

The Anglican Communion is not a monolithic world denomination. It is a fellowship of churches. And the dynamics of our life—our power and service—remain in the separate churches and the action they freely take, separately or together.

The Advisory Council is really not a group at all. It is a phase or process of consultation—a way eighteen churches have of meeting one another and exchanging knowledge and gifts. There is no way in which any one of us can refer to the Advisory Council as "them" or "they." The Advisory Council is simply "us" in consultation with one another. Its membership is entirely that determined by the churches themselves. It has no authority apart from the churches, and seeks none.

All this is by way of caution. On the positive side, what the Advisory Council represents is a completely new relationship between brother churches. Some of them are rich, some are poor. Some are numerous, some are very small minorities. Some have been established a long time, with ancient institutions and endowments, some are frail frontiers of missionary devotion.

But the fundamental axiom of our common life is that there is no church so rich that it does not need what other churches can give, and no church so small that it has nothing to give. There is no church so wise that it may not learn from others, and no church so young and untrained that it has nothing to teach. And because we take this axiom seriously, and because we are now daily more and more aware of the reality of this fellowship of churches, such meeting places as the Advisory Council become more and more important in our common life, and need to be far more articulated into the life of each of our separate churches than the Advisory Council yet is.

I am not pleading for anything here; I am simply trying to describe a stage we have now reached, in the common life of our Anglican Communion. I have all I can handle on my plate now! But I only say that I do not think we now have any option about the Advisory Council, or about any other similar expression of the depth and reality of our common life. The day has gone for good when any Anglican Church could go it alone. We are members one of another, all the more because there is no central structure with power to bind us together, because we are, in the words of the 1930 definition, "bound together not by a central legislative and executive authority, but by mutual loyalty sustained through the common counsel of the Bishops in conference." In our day there is far more to sustain that mutual loyalty than simply the Lambeth Conference. But the principle remains the same—it is mutual loyalty and the love of brothers alone which holds us together.

But together we are; we are learning how to deal with one another increasingly on a basis of receptive and loving brotherhood; we are learning to take our counsel and to submerge our differences for the sake of the unity of the fellowship. Of all these things the Advisory Council is a symbol. But the essential thing is that the consultation itself is a mark of maturity.

Let me turn now to a second area in which the growing maturity of the Anglican Communion can be seen. This is the area of ecumenical life. It is characterized by two strong currents, quite oblique to one another, in tension with one another.

Such tension is in itself, perhaps, a characteristic of young manhood. But let us examine this search for vocation a little more closely. As the number of independent national churches has increased, and more and more of our life been included in those churches, each of them has increasingly been caught up in its own local scene. It has felt the impulse, and rightly yielded to it, to identify itself more and more fully with the life of its own society. Each of these churches in particular, has become far more sensitively aware of the divided Christendom within which it lives. As its dependence on parent churches across the world has lessened, to precisely that degree it has been impelled to turn its eyes more and more to the fellow-Christians of its own region and nation.

In some parts of the Anglican Communion this awareness of disunity has moved our churches to radical concentration on unity. The most dramatic symbol of this, of course, was the disappearance of four great dioceses in India, and a half-million of our Anglican fellow-Christians, into a united church of great significance. The formation of this united church came about at the cost of the loss of traditional ties which were precious indeed to our Indian companions. But they paid the price, because local unity seemed an incomparable pearl worth any sacrifice. And one's sympathies could not but be with them in this.

South India, of course, is only the most vivid and dramatic illustration of a well-nigh universal phenomenon within the Anglican Communion. There are not many of our churches which are not seriously engaged in at least exploratory conversations looking toward local unity. In some cases, as in Nigeria or Pakistan, negotiations are very far advanced indeed. And all of this determination to achieve local unity among one's fellow-Christians in one's own nation—all of this is part of the consequence of the growing-up of the Anglican Communion. These self-governing churches, no longer living at the end of a long missionary tether, rightly turn to their own society and its needs, and are prepared to give their lives accordingly.

In almost equal measure, each of our churches is finding its place in the world-wide ecumenical movement. Every one of the eighteen Anglican churches is a constituent member of the World Council of Churches, and is represented there, in its activities and its life. Here again there is an awareness of the bitterness and cost of disunity, and of the will of God for unity, which moves powerfully in these churches, all the more as they are less dependent on stronger and richer churches of their own Anglican fellowship.

This is characteristic not only of Anglicans but of all other Christians as well, I believe. But this new sensitivity toward ecumenical involvement has in its turn awakened a contrary current—that which goes by the current slang name of "confessionalism." That word, in common usage, is used to denote a new self-consciousness of our separate ecclesiastical families in the world. Since the ecumenical movement has become a major fact in our lives, Lutherans have become more Lutheran, Methodists have become more Methodist, Anglicans have become more Anglican. There has been a notable tendency to develop world organizations of the various traditions of Christians. I do not say that the Anglican Communion has been guiltless in this respect, although it is true that we have steadfastly resisted, so far, the formation of any worldwide confessional organization, and I hope with all my heart that we shall continue to resist this. But we ourselves have become aware of a heightened sense of Anglican unity, as contrasted with a parallel sense of Lutheran unity or Roman Catholic unity or whatever.

This awareness is likely to be all the more strong where Anglicans are in a minority in a society. My own church in the United States is probably the most confessionally-minded of any of the churches of our Communion. But we are typical of probably the majority of Anglican Christians in our time, in kind if not in vehemence. All of us, in every Anglican Church, are more aware of the reality of the Anglican Communion than we were a generation or two ago. The Lambeth Conference, an Anglican Congress, my own office, the Advisory Council—all these things are symbols of heightened significance today.

This is the result of the ecumenical impact. As we have been thrown more and more into confrontation with other Christian traditions, and into the urgent search for unity, we have in the same breath tended to turn in on ourselves, to study what was distinctive about us, and to try to be more faithful to what was to be, perhaps, our own "contribution" to a united church, or at least to some less-conclusive ecumenical dialogue.

Thus, the life of our Communion, like that of every Christian family I know, has been characterized—is characterized in our time—by these two currents. It is sometimes felt that they are contrary one to another, and negative each other. I myself think of them as oblique to one another, but not necessarily nullifying one another. I am not prepared to say that it has been a bad thing for the ecumenical encounter that each of the separate families of Christians should know more clearly what their own tradition teaches them, and the treasures it contains. Nor am I prepared to believe that there is any gain to the total cause of Christian unity simply from diluting the particular unities which are the best that God has given us up to this point.

But I have some deeper questions which are in part rooted in the nature of the Anglican Communion itself. The confessional label implies that a particular group of Christians has a tradition of belief or practice of its own, which distinguishes it clearly and finally from other associations of Christians. It is difficult to find such an element within the Anglican tradition. We pretend to hold no peculiar doctrinal tradition of our own. The 39 Articles, which are still current in many of the churches of the Anglican Communion but not all, perhaps represent a "confessional" standard. But I rather think of them as a kind of monument to an attempt on our part, centuries ago, to show how far we could go in the direction of a confessional attitude without actually adopting one. In any case they are museum-pieces now, in the face of the far graver and more profoundly divisive issues which confront Christian people.

For the most part, the only symbols we have are the universal symbols of all historic Christianity—the Scriptures, the Creeds, the two dominical Sacraments. I am told by some of my colleagues that we are guilty, at least, of a "confessional" attitude toward the ministry, in our insistence on the historic episcopate. If it be confessional to hold to a common conviction about the ministry which is shared by seventy-five per cent of all Christian people, then we are confessional in this particular. But I cannot seriously take our attitude toward the ministry as being in any true sense confessional. It might be, if by the "historic episcopate" we meant some particular theory of Christian ministry. But the episcopate is a thing, an institution, far more than it is a preconceived theory.

For the essence of a "confessional" attitude lies in interpretation and limitation—in minute definition of belief, in detailed prescription of shades of meaning and sharpness of delineation—and even our worst enemy can never accuse us of any such precision of definition. What we hold to are mainly things, not words. What we hold to are the institutions of common life, not the detailed interpretations of those institutions which tend to separate one from another. I do not say that we are perfect in this, or guiltless. I do say that of all the historic companies of Christian people, the churches of the Anglican Communion are the most-nearly free from sectarian and denominational definition. And I thank God that this is so.

If there were time, I would like to develop some of the ways in which we are very guilty indeed of fomenting division among Christians. For example, there is a kind of cultural confessionalism in the Anglican Communion, which is a very great offence—as when we present our image to the world of an upper-middle-class-English-Speaking-Union-at-prayer. Even our Englishness, especially among people who have no right to it or need for it, can be an offence. We are literate to a chilly degree that sometimes destroys Christian brotherhood. And so one could continue—and I am serious about these sins of ours.

But they are not necessarily "confessional" sins. Indeed I have questioned, before this, the value of the word "confessional" at all. I feel that it is even a dangerous word when it becomes divisive, and leads us to treat our existing unities lightly. The time will come, in God's mercy, when the unity of the Church of Christ will be a visible fact. Until that time, we do well to cling to whatever partial unities we can have. If we are not faithful in little things, we may not be faithful in the great ones. And I feel this particularly about the difficult relationship of local and world-wide unity.

I must confess a disquiet at the current tendency, in some quarters, to think of unity as something essentially born locally, which may then be expanded into ever-widening circles. I do not think that the local unity of Christians in one nation or one place is anything unique by itself. Unity is indivisible. I cannot find any evidence in the New Testament that there was any difference between the local unity of Christians in one place and the universal brotherhood among whom the Apostles moved. I agree that nothing is real which is not local. A generalized Christ would be meaningless, just as a generalized spirit of unity is meaningless. But what is wrought in the incarnate Lord—so local, so particular, so individual—is nothing less than God's eternal and universal action. Christ is incarnate in man and not just in a man. He came down from heaven for all men and not a particular group of men. He accomplished a single, universal, indeed cosmic salvation. Through baptism we are brought immediately into the household of God, to be fellow-citizens with the saints. Universality pervades and infects the particular at every point. There is no progression from the particular to the universal, or the local to the general. The mode of unity is always local and immediate; the unity itself is universal and whole.

Believing this, I find any statement of unity dangerous which seems built on some necessary priority of one mode or level of unity over another. I will not accept the fact that local unity comes before world-wide unity. There is only one unity, in the universal Christ. And therefore, every expression of unity is of absolute importance, whether it be local or world-wide.

For this reason, the tension between the local unities which are sought in every part of the world, and the existing unities given us in our various world-wide Christian families is a necessary and inescapable tension, which is not to be avoided or feared, but which is rather to be pressed to its uttermost limits. The trouble with the unity given us in the Anglican Communion is not that it is a threat to ecumenical action; the trouble with it is that it has not yet become what in God's mercy it some day will become. So with any existing world-wide unity; they are not enough. But they are the best we have; and we therefore owe it to our unity in Christ to be faithful to what He has so far given.

If the world-wide unities were to hamper or paralyze the struggle for local unity, then we would really have a problem to face. But there is no evidence that this is the fact, at least in our own Communion. To the contrary, it is precisely through the support and guidance of such bodies as the Lambeth Conference that the individual churches of our Communion are encouraged and strengthened in their own ecumenical pilgrimage. There would be no gain in this respect, if the unity of the Anglican Communion were to disappear. Rather the other way—it is the modest and persistent leadership of the whole family, and its steady support, which nerves and impels small, local Anglican churches to take a fuller part in their own societies.

Yet the tension exists. I believe it is healthy; in a way I welcome it, for it is an evidence of a young man searching for his own soul; I do not fear it as long as we remember that unity itself is indivisible.

A third area in which the impact of our maturity is felt is the form and dynamic of mission. There was a time, again, when mission could have been thought of as a one-way street—a current of witness and service which flowed from older societies and their churches to younger societies. To a degree, this image of mission is still current in our time. But it is now a dangerously misleading image.

I am not at all romantic or rhapsodic about our present situation. It will be a long time before every trace of the old image is gone. But day by day there is a new spirit abroad in the world and in the Church. Older cultures, more established churches, can no longer appear in the eyes of their brothers as possessing all the answers and all the treasures. The old nationalistic swagger is gone for good. And gone with it is the sense that there is any church which has a surplus to export, and needs nothing in return.

This was the foolishness in the older image of mission. It was foolish because it presupposed that it was possible for a church or a nation to arrive at a point where they needed nothing more from outside their own society. Whether people ever actually believed this or not, I do not know. But it was a superstition which attached itself to the whole concept of mission.

But now, what is the image and role of mission and the missionary? Men and women go out from our churches, supported by our prayers and our money, not to introduce God to societies which never knew Him or them to Him Who has loved them from the beginning, but rather to take their place as servants with their younger Christian brothers in other lands. Mission is partnership; mission is brotherhood; mission is common service engaged in by men and women who are linked together in the sacraments of Christ's Church—the most intimate and radical link that can exist among men and women.

And this new sense of partnership—this new role that the missionary plays—is the product of several factors. One is certainly the new relationship between churches. The missionary going out today goes to work in another Anglican church, quite as authentic, quite as qualified, quite as complete in all its essential functions as the one he leaves. He goes because he has something to add to the witness of another church—some gift, some skill which that other church and its nation needs. But he is sent—he goes—in full expectation that he will take his place as a fellow-servant in the ranks of a companion church. And he is sent also in full expectation that there will be something coming back in return. It will not necessarily be the same thing as what is sent, for no two churches have necessarily the same gifts to give. But mission is partnership; it is common service; and it is exchange.

Even more significant, I believe, has been the vast deepening and stretching of our understanding of God's action in this world and in our history. The torment and perplexity of our time has done at least this much for our theology, that it has shaken us loose from any feeling that God is our possession or our captive, or that He Who reigns needs our patronage or our protection. We have recovered a greater understanding of God's action which we had for the moment perhaps forgotten—that God does not wait for His Church—that He leads; and it is our privilege only to follow Him. It is God who is at work in the tumult of our time. It is God who is at work in the tormented societies and the eager and searching nations of the world—God leading, God teaching, God revealing, God judging, God calling us to follow Him to where He is, that we may make Him known, and serve Him better with our brothers.

It is this renewed greatness of vision of God, coupled with the growing up of our younger churches, which has helped us so immeasurably to understand the real nature of mission, and of companionship in Christ.

Finally, the depth of full communion is coming to mean more and more to us as the Anglican Communion comes of age. I do not say that it was ever not important to us, to be in communion with Canterbury and with one another. But for a Christian of the Irish Church, for example, to feel free to worship with his brothers in the Church of England, or for an English churchman to find it natural to receive the Holy Communion in Canada or the United States, is not so astonishing a thing. We shared a common history, a common language, a common culture, a common geography. Therefore our full communion seemed only one more natural expression of unity.

As the Anglican Communion has grown, we have lost one by one all these easy natural unities. There is not any one Anglican language any more. There is not any common history that binds together a world community such as ours. There is not any single cultural unity among us. One by one all of these things—which in a way were the scaffolding which made it possible for the Anglican Communion to come into existence—have fallen away. I have no doubt that they served their purpose well in their time. If it had not been for the English language and a common Prayer Book in the beginning years of the Anglican Communion, that Communion would never have existed. But the important thing is that now they have served their purpose; and as we have come of age, they have dropped away. What is left to us now is not an easy cultural or confessional unity. What is left to us now is simply the greatest unity of all—that supernatural unity expressed and symbolized and fulfilled in the fact that we are in full communion with one another.

The most precious gifts God has given us are Holy Baptism and Holy Communion, and the saving unity with Him, and with one another in Him, of which these two sacraments teach us, and indeed which they minister to us. There is no more precious gift that Christians can give one another than a welcome to share in the deepest sacramental life of the Church. That is the significance of full communion.

And how dangerously we play with this, sometimes! We enter into concordats of full communion with other churches of other histories and other cultural backgrounds than our own, and so often this full communion is nothing more than a purely ceremonial, liturgical brotherhood, which is of little more significance to us than an example of interesting ecclesiastical statesmanship. So it is even with some of our fellow-Christians within the Anglican Communion. It is piquant and intriguing to think of our brotherhood with two million Christians in Uganda, for example. (I mention Uganda because it is the youngest Anglican brother.) But we are not likely to go there, or ever to know them. If we do go there, we are blocked from any real community with them because of language problems and cultural differences and the like. Therefore our full communion with the Church of Uganda, within the Anglican Communion, may again be nothing more than a kind of ceremonial monument.

This is the danger of full communion—that it shall be not much more than a new kind of sectarianism in the divided Church. Or again one might think of it as a treaty with some remote nation, which could exist for a hundred years and make no perceptible difference to us at all.

But how untrue such understandings would be. I say again, God has no more precious gifts for us than the two great sacraments, and the immense saving act which the sacraments mediate to us. I say again, that no church—no company of Christians—has any more precious gift to give to another than to admit them to their sacramental life, to the Font and to the Table, to the breaking of bread and the companionship which is at the heart of any church. These are not casual gifts; these are not diplomatic niceties; these are the greatest things we have to give; these are our life.

And if this be so, then how desperately important it is that we shall live up to what full communion means. We Anglicans, in our eighteen separate churches, have been admitted—quite without our deserving—into the most intimate heart of the life of all our brother churches, of every culture and race and continent in the world. This means far more than just the fact that we can find a sacramental convenience when we travel. It means far more than simply that the clergy of one church can serve in another. What it means is that we are entitled to share the sufferings of a younger church in a younger nation. What it means is that we have the privilege of a part in the life of Christians who are having a much tougher time than we do in being Christians. What it means is that we can share the witness and the hope and the promise and the task of a tiny handful of Christians, trying to bear their witness bravely in a pagan society. What it means is that we are privileged to enter into the deepest brotherhood this world affords.

Now this is the present stage of the Anglican Communion. We have lost the easy unities, which God gave us in our infancy in order to make this remarkable brotherhood possible. They have gone. We no longer need to think as children. We have now been introduced into the true brotherhood of man in Christ. It is of this that the Anglican Communion speaks. This is a mark of the maturity of our Communion, that we no longer need to huddle together in a lesser unity, given to us because we share a common history or a common language. We have been thought worthy, in God's mercy, to be admitted to the heart of unity, in the Holy Communion. This is our present situation. And our present task then is to live up to that unity.

What a difference it makes, when we look at our churches against that immense duty. If a church is to be true to the unity which has been given us, what a difference it makes in the way we look at mission. We no longer think of it as simply a gratuity that we give to the less fortunate ones, or as a bit of brotherhood to those who are in the same club with us. We understand suddenly that we are trying to work out in our life—that we must work out in our life—the cost of the implications of the common Table, and the common Bread of Life broken in brotherhood.

How it changes the relations between churches and peoples, when we perceive the unity of the Body! No longer are we impressed with our differences from them, with the advantages which wealth and historical security have given us. The struggle of the young nations of the world is our struggle. The ache and torment of the young society in Africa is our ache and torment. We are not observers of their agony—we are one with them in their agony. This is what full communion means.

Full communion means that we are not separate from the fight for unity within the Christian body, wherever it is going on. We are not put in this world to be judges of one another; we are put in this world to bear one another's burdens, and to share one another's hopes and needs. If full communion does not mean this to us, then we do not understand the nature of the Communion. But if we try to live up to the Communion which God has given us, then suddenly we discover that we are what our brothers are—that their pain is our pain—that their glory is, in a way, given to us—that their fate and ours is one—that through us all, the common life of Christ flows, like a tide of life and unity—that we are all made to drink of one spirit, as we break one bread.

This is the maturity of the Anglican Communion, at this stage of history—not that we have lived up to our full Communion, but that for the first time we are beginning to see what it really means. This is a mark of coming of age. And may God strengthen us and guide us to make that unity real, in our shattered and broken world.

2. ORGANIZING FOR ACTION*

I WROTE THE ORIGINAL DRAFT of this address last April. It was necessarily written out of convictions and hopes about the Anglican Communion which I was then praying might some day be expressed. In the last three weeks—in our meetings at Huron College, in the various decisions taken by the Advisory Council, most of all in the immensely great vision of Mutual Responsibility which the heads of our churches have held up before all our churches—flesh has been put on those bones. What was then hope has now begun to take form and substance. Therefore all my thoughts, indeed all our thoughts, need to be looked at afresh, in the light of where we are now, supremely in the light of what God is calling us to become.

I was tempted to scrap all I had written, and devote this hour to the practical questions which are in all our minds. I hope I may be able to suggest some of the answers, as far as I can see them, as we go along. But I believe it is better to stick to the principles, for they must be our guides as we improvise the new structures and relationships which lie ahead. Indeed the very first of those principles—the indispensable preliminary to anything we plan—is precisely that. The action we take in obedience to our mission—even more the way we organize ourselves for that action—must be true to ourselves, true to our nature. *How the churches of the Anglican Communion organize themselves must be determined by what we are, by the terms of our own existence.* What are those conditions for Anglican action? I believe there are at least these three.

I. The Nature of Our Fellowship

The Anglican Communion is an association, within the Catholic Church, of eighteen autocephalous regional and national churches in communion with the see of Canterbury and with one another.† This is our classic definition.

We are all aware of the ambiguities and perplexities inherent in as loose a description as this. It has become clear to us, especially in recent years, that the definition begs almost as many questions as it answers. "Full Communion" is less and less useful, as a descriptive phrase, the wider that full communion grows, even though it may be, as I believe, our most important characteristic.

There was a time when it described that association very clearly. Full communion was what Anglican churches shared; and Anglican

---

* Address to the Anglican Congress, Toronto, August 20, 1963.
† Cf. Res. 49, 1930 Lambeth Conference.

churches were those which shared in the Anglican Communion. But once we had entered into concordats of full communion with other Christian bodies which were not "Anglican," the definition began to lose its neatness. We must now try to say that the Anglican Communion is an association of "Anglican" churches which are in full communion with Canterbury and with one another. And of course this simply passes the buck to those who wish to decide what "Anglican" means! This last is one of our classic parlor-games; I do not hold out great hope of anybody winning it in the near future!

Our recourse here traditionally is to the Prayer Book. In 1930 (when last we tried to reach anything like an authoritative definition), the Prayer Book was specified as one of the necessary modifiers— (Anglican churches) "uphold and propagate the Catholic and Apostolic faith and order as they are generally set forth in the Book of Common Prayer as authorized in their several Churches." * Even as late as 1930, there was sufficient identity to our several Prayer Books to make that a meaningful qualification. But this again is fast being eroded away. With successive revisions of our Prayer Books, the time has already come when we must begin to discuss—as the bishops did in 1948, and far more thoughtfully in 1958—what the essence of the Prayer Book itself is. The time may not be too far off, I believe, when, like "Full Communion," "Prayer Book" is going to be too loose and perplexing a concept to be of much use in distinguishing ourselves from other Christians.

I cannot say that I am altogether dismayed at this prospect. I belong to a church, as does everybody else here, that has never been able to define what its membership consists of, except in terms of Baptism. There is no statutory definition of an "Episcopalian" except that he is a baptized person who comes to the Episcopal Church and pays his dues. By the same token, one is not surprised to discover an equal cloudiness in defining the Anglican Communion. I have said before that the only description which seems to me satisfactory is a very modest existential one indeed—the Anglican Communion consists of those churches which pay my salary and whose bishops get invited to the Lambeth Conference.

This perplexing lack of neatness—this cloudiness of definition—is a necessary condition of organizing for action. If we were a unitary world denomination, with a central executive and administrative structure, the tasks of organization would be relatively simple. But we are not that. If we were a body of Christians united by common doctrinal con-

---

* *Ibid.*

victions, which clearly marked us off from other Christian bodies and gave us an easy intensity of inner coherence, again our organizing tasks would be relatively simple. But we are not that.

We lack precisely these easy grounds of association. The essential juices of our nature are national and regional, not denominational, not supra-national. We rejoice, and rightly, in the free, world-wide brotherhood we share, and in the privilege of free movement and communication which full communion means. But we are eighteen churches, not one super-church. Indeed this is one of the essential elements in the Church's life as we see it, not merely an accident of Reformation history, but rooted in the New Testament itself.

And we are equally sure about our wish to remain free from any "confessional" basis of unity. From the time that there was any separate Anglican tradition at all, we have made it clear that we rejected anything that could be called a confessional standard. The only statements of the Christian faith we accept are the universal statements, the Scriptures, and the Creeds which are the guardians of the Scriptures. The only institutions we accept are those which are universal in historic Christianity, notably the two dominical Sacraments.

Even the historic episcopate—still often a sharp point of debate in negotiations for united churches—is in our eyes no more than an element in the whole and universal tradition of the Church. And it is a thing, an institution, rather than a theory. Like all historic institutions, the episcopate has been seen in many lights, and borne many interpretations. It is great enough and secure enough to be seen in many different ways; and there is room for many interpretations, as long as no one can shut out all others from the Church's life. The sting of the sectarian spirit is precisely here, that it is concerned with excluding.

All this is a familiar catechism of our virtues, no doubt. I do not recall these things for that purpose, but simply to underline one of the necessary conditions of action. *Whatever organization we have must be true to that cardinal principle of the free association of regional and national churches.* The action we are called on to take, in the first instance, is that of mutual brotherhood and support in the common tasks of the Church. God has given us this association; it is not the final association of Christians, but it is all we have now; it is put in our hands as an instrument for action. And it lays down its own requirements. If we are to help one another—if we are to share fully in our common task—it must be within the framework of this brotherhood of churches.

For nearly a hundred years, the Lambeth Conference has been our chief organ of common life. In a contracting world and a growing church we have seen that this by itself is not enough. We needed the Advisory Council, long before we had it. We needed at least some articulation of that Council's life and activity, even longer before we had an Executive Officer. But what these things stand for is neither a unitary power structure, nor a unitary confession. They stand for one thing only, the partnership of brothers freely given, in mutual loyalty to one another and to the Gospel. This is the fundamental principle of organization, which must guide us in all the particular things we plan.

The Advisory Council is a phase of brotherly consultation among equals. It is not something separate from the churches—it is the churches themselves, in more or less constant consultation with each other. It has already been proposed and agreed by the Primates and Metropolitans that they must meet far more frequently than has been the case. But this more frequent meeting only underlines the fact that steady, continuing brotherly dialogue is the essential end in view.

The Anglican Communion is not an organization by which older and stronger churches can extend their influence over younger and weaker churches. We are not interested in branch offices around the world. We care rather for a household within which many churches, representing many cultures and peoples, can take their self-reliant and buoyant place in full brotherhood, each giving and teaching, each receiving and learning. Therefore our organization must both reflect this and nourish it.

The Executive Officer is not a master of the churches, he is their servant. It is the churches who support him, who direct him in working out their common will. I do not speak of myself personally in this; I shall not hold this office for ever; I speak of any such officer. He is not an "assistant to Lambeth Palace" or to the Archbishop of Canterbury. He is an assistant to every Archbishop equally, and to every church. He is obedient to no other person or body than ourselves, collectively, in our separate churches. His work is simply and solely that of making the mutual interdependence of the Anglican Communion a little more real—as much as one man can.

All this underlines the fact that whatever organization we have must be such as to encourage to the fullest possible degree the local initiative and planning of each church. We must not only respect one another's autonomy and responsibility; we must act positively to encourage that autonomy and responsibility, and encourage initiative in every church and every region.

The proposed Regional Officers were first seen by some as threatening a new, central curial power in our Communion. Indeed they will be the precise opposite to this. I hope they will be given us by the churches they serve, your churches, supported by them as an earnest of mutual responsibility. They are to serve the churches in their area, your churches, as the Executive Officer serves them, multiplying him—each in his own region—making possible exactly the local initiative and planning of each church we seek, and strengthening the ecumenical participation of the churches—each in its own region—which is the place where all true ecumenical action is born. The only alternative to them *is* an increased structure at the center, to carry the load of our corporate life; and this is exactly what we do not want, because it would be untrue to our nature.

But in all this right emphasis on decentralization and the strengthening of regional and local responsibility in the separate churches themselves, we must take care that the tides of our life flow both ways. No church is an island unto itself. The great duties of Christians are universal duties—our witness is one, our responsibility is one, our obedience is one. And this must be reflected, too, in the planning that we do, for we are what our brothers are, and we are responsible for one another—not merely for ourselves and our witness within our own society.

II. Traveling Light

The second great condition of Anglican action is that we shall travel light—that we shall remember that we are a pilgrim people, and that a pilgrim carries with him only those things that are essential for his life. It is a characteristic mark of the Anglican tradition, at our best, that we recognize how few and how important the essential things are.

One of the vivid examples of this is what we call the "Chicago-Lambeth Quadrilateral." It is not necessary to think of the Quadrilateral as either imperishable prose or an unfailing symbol of the Christian faith. It is no more than it pretends to be—a bare statement of those elements which we regard as essential to the full life of the Church. And it is instructive to meditate on the fact that there are only four of those elements, and that they are the barest of bones. We can imagine churches without most of the things we take for granted. We can imagine them without many of the opinions we share, the vestments we wear, the prayers we say, the traditional forms and instruments of Church life as we know them. None of these seems to us essential. Only the four sparse elements are needed, in our view, and they are indispensable.

I mention this austerity because we are so often untrue to it. In a divided Church, it is very easy for us to lose our heads, and fall into the trap of thinking that our mission is to reproduce ourselves, rather than to bear witness to what God has done and is doing in this world. It is absolutely unimportant in the eyes of God how many people follow the "Anglican tradition" of belief and practice. It is of the greatest importance how many people there are who have come to know and love our Lord because of what we Anglicans have said and done.

Of course this is a ridiculous over-simplification. You cannot just be a general Christian any more than you can be a general human being. You must be somebody; you must be some kind of a Christian; and therefore inescapably you are involved in particulars—your Christian faith and life must wear a certain dress and be expressed through certain idioms and traditions of life and worship, and the like. But this is not what is in question. Rather are we confronted by a perennial problem of mortality—that of dissecting out the central things, the main things, from the unimportant and superficial things. This is as true of the Church as it is of individuals. One of the tests of intelligent Christian discipleship is precisely the ability to tell the woods from the trees, to distinguish the essential and lasting elements from those which are simply the vehicle or the dress.

The charge is often made, for example, about world fellowships of Christians, that they tend to restrict the theological freedom of the younger churches in favor of some general confessional position. I am not much impressed by this, as far as our Communion is concerned. There is no convincing evidence among our younger churches of any more confessional uniformity that the older churches know.

But I would say very seriously that we are not guiltless, simply because we do not sin in that particular way. There are other forms of confessionalism. There is a "cultural confessionalism" within the Anglican Communion (if that phrase be allowed), which can be quite as paralyzing in its erosion of the liberties of the younger church as any theological confessionalism can be. Christians in the older churches simply do not understand the enormous cultural prestige, in time past, which enveloped the missionary, whether he wanted it so or not. I do not blame the missionary for this; more often than not he was simply caught in a process far too vast and impersonal for him to see clearly himself. He did not scheme and plot to win national or cultural prestige. It was thrust on him by the history within which he lived. Indeed it is to his credit that through his teaching and example he so often helped other people to be set free from this paralysis.

But the fact is that the immense forces of cultural confessionalism, of national and racial prestige, have played their part in the development of our Communion far more dangerously than we often suspect. We have not been good in telling the woods from the trees. We have not been as sensitive as we should be in distinguishing between the essential elements of the Gospel, and the purely accidental matters of dress and worship and the form of the ministry and all the thousand and one other vestments in which the Gospel and mission of the Church are dressed.

The missionary from Great Britain or North America or Australia or anywhere else cannot help being what he is. He is necessarily the child of his own culture. All that he knows of the Gospel has come to him mediated through that culture—his nation and its tradition, its institutions, its habits and customs. But how ridiculous it is when these things are transplanted, when a new church overseas is burdened with an inheritance of an alien cultural pattern which makes no sense in terms of its own life at all. Generations of American bishops, for example, have been very badly guided in trying to pattern themselves after their older English brethren. The pattern of the English episcopate, with its immense medieval heritage, makes little sense in the American scene. By the same token, neither the British nor the American patterns are particularly relevant to the conditions of life in most of Africa, say, or India. And it is precisely here that we have not been very good in distinguishing the important from the unimportant.

It is not a case of trying to export a different product from what we have at home. We cannot do that. The only gift one nation, one culture, can make to another is the best of itself. But this kind of giving must be accompanied also by a setting-free—by a training in discrimination, a modesty and humility about one's own things, which encourages in the younger church the freedom to do its own experimenting, to develop its own institutions and its own way of doing things, without feeling that it is somehow doing violence to some imagined orthodoxy. This is the second condition of our action, that we shall travel light ourselves, and not load our brothers with burdens grievous to be borne, particularly when the burdens are as irrelevant to the Gospel as they commonly are.

III. Not An End

The third condition is that the Anglican Communion is not an end in itself. The phrase "the vocation of the Anglican Communion is to disappear" is rightly questioned, if only because it presupposes a knowledge of God's will which we may not claim to have. But the *sense* of the words—the meaning hidden in them—goes back a long time in Anglican history, at least to the great continental divide of the "Appeal to all Christian People" of the 1920 Lambeth Conference.

The phrase does not mean suicide. It does not mean a weary opening of its veins by the Anglican Communion, in some warm ecumenical bath. It does not mean the abdication of all which faithful stewardship and honest conviction have kept alive in us, during bitter and divisive years. It does not mean labelling as "sinful" every obedience to truth which differs from anybody else's obedience. It does not mean the abandonment of the great gifts God has given us in our Communion, all undeserving as we are.

It means the self-emptying we learned first in our Lord. It means the willingness, so movingly expressed by the Bishops in 1920, to abandon not our diversities, but our *separatenesses*. It means making the sacrifices required for the common fellowship, the common ministry, and the common service to the world which are the marks of the Catholic Church. It means taking the Church of the Creeds seriously. It means obedience to our given unity in Christ.

Where is such a will born? Not in a wish to save money, or pile up power, or herd together with like-minded people. The will to unity is born in nothing else than the fact of unity—the fact of the one Baptism, the one Church, the one Lord, the one Creed. At every great point in life, as at every great point in the Prayer Book, our separate churches disappear, and the one great Church is revealed before us, not as an ideal but as a fact. It is into this Church we are baptised. It is the Eucharist of this Church which we share, with Christ as our great High Priest. It is of this Church we are ministers. It is the bishopric of the one Great Shepherd and Bishop of our souls which alone can claim to be historic and universal.

This is where the ecumenical impulse is born, in the discovery of the terrible and wonderful reality of the Catholic Church. In this sense, it must be perfectly clear that the Anglican Communion is not an end in itself. Our discipleship as Anglicans, within the Anglican Communion, is simply the best way, the only way for us, in which we can take hold of the Great Church and let it be reproduced through our own faltering and passing association. We prize our Communion precisely because it points to something beyond itself. And the steady remembrance of this must be a condition of our organization for action.

Here I would turn for a moment to the summons to "Mutual Responsibility." There are those still who speak of it as "Bishop

Bayne's paper," who are incredulous when they are told that it did not exist in anybody's mind three weeks ago. But that is the fact. It was born in a hundred minds, over days of listening and hearing; and it is nobody's "paper" and nobody's "idea"; it is a high-water mark of Anglican obedience, as great as any in our history. But let us be clear as to what it means.

It means many things. Perhaps as clearly as anything it will be seen as a command to ecumenical obedience, as profound and as costly as the "Appeal to all Christian People." I say that for three reasons.

First, if Mutual Responsibility is accepted by our churches, it will put an end, once and for all, to every evil and untrue thing that "confessionalism" stands for. The central thrust of it is to set churches free from any control by others, whether it be by money or men or power or prestige. "The full communion in Christ which has been our traditional tie has suddenly taken on a totally new dimension. . . . The keynotes of our time are equality, interdependence, mutual responsibility." In a word—freedom. Freedom from beggary, freedom from condescension, freedom from cultural coercion or any kind of coercion, freedom to be full partners in the household of faith, with all the dignity and respect that partnership demands.

Second, if Mutual Responsibility is accepted by our churches, it will put the ecumenical initiative where it belongs, squarely in the responsible leadership of each church. It should not be forgotten that the same meeting of Primates and Metropolitans which adopted the summons to Mutual Responsibility, at the same session asked every church of our Communion to give its assurance that, when any Anglican province or diocese entered into a united church in its area, our support of the church's life in that area would continue, without being lessened. I do not know any way we could more strongly say, to every church of our brotherhood, that we stand solidly with them in their responsible obedience to the call of God to unity.

Third, if Mutual Responsibility is accepted by our churches, it will mean that we shall be offering ourselves, in entirely new depth, to the fulfillment of what full communion means. I say again, the only bond that holds Anglican churches together is our full communion one with another. All the other bonds, of nationality or language or culture, have served their purpose; and like scaffolding, their usefulness is past. Our "Englishness," the first Prayer Books, our common history—all these have served God well in their generation, for they made the Anglican Communion possible. Now they fall away, and a greater unity is revealed, a companionship in Christ which brings together every tongue and nation in the wonderful, frightening unity of the Bread and the Cup. There is no deeper unity given to men on earth than this. This asks everything of us, in common life, common witness, common obedience, in the sharing of one another's deepest hope and pain.

But it is not "Anglican," it is not "ours," in any limiting, possessive sense of these words. Already before us there gleams and beckons a greater unity which in our stumbling words we call a "Wider Episcopal Fellowship." This is not another denomination, another church. We do not know what it is, nor what it leads to. All we know is that we must obey it. This may be as much as God wants us to know now. But we must be true to full communion, or we will lose it. That all Christian people may be able to break the Bread together, and so share, together, equally, in His work and His love—this is our dream. God has let us, in our Anglican family, have an inkling of this in what we have now— not an association of like-minded people, not a denominational power-structure, but something much humbler yet much greater than that, the brotherhood of the Bread and the Body.

But it is not "Anglican," it is not ours; and at all costs we must be true to it. And Mutual Responsibility is now our only way to be true to this most profound ecumenical obedience.

When the Anglican Congress meets again, 25 or more of our dioceses—the heart of at least two of our churches—almost certainly will be absent. They will be absent because they will not be "Anglican" any more, in the limiting sense of that word. But it may be, if Mutual Responsibility is accepted by our churches, that this will not matter, in that we shall have passed through a door into a greater unity than even the great brotherhood we now have.

I say, in all this, "if Mutual Responsibility is accepted by our churches." It may be that we—and here I speak as a delegate and not as your servant—will want to add our support to what the heads of our churches have asked, when our churches meet to make their decision about Mutual Responsibility. If so, God be praised. But let us count the cost before we do so. Mutual Responsibility means the end, once and for all, of any confessionalism or neat denominationalism. It means the end of cautious and sometimes insincere sparring with the issue of unity. If you add your support to the summons, let it be as people who have counted the cost and will not turn back.

It would not have been difficult to sprinkle the proposal of Mutual Responsibility with ecumenical courtesies, like salt and pepper, to give it an agreeable flavor. It may indeed still be possible for "older," and wearier, churches to think of the issue of unity as an optional accessory we are graciously pleased to include in the package, at no additional cost. But unity is no option to our churches in Asia or Africa, which at this moment are seeking to lose their lives in order to find them. It is no option for dilettantes. The time for mere ecumenical respectability is gone. Therefore do not seek for conventional courtesies, ecumenical or otherwise. Mission and unity and the Bread and the Body all march together now, or they are gone for ever.

As this is true of the issue of unity, so it is of mission. The end of Anglican missionary strategy is not that there shall be more Anglicans, but that the Church of Jesus Christ shall be planted in every place. I need hardly repeat that the planting must be done by somebody, and the seed come from a particular strain. But the grand design of our mission is that we shall make God's action clear, so that in every nation men may know and love Him, and obey Him, and be free to receive His love.

Therefore the nature of our organization must be such as to let this happen. The world will not be saved by Anglicans. The world will not be saved merely because people go to church, ours or any other's. If we seem to say this to the tormented nations, this is only a measure of our failure to see that the Anglican Communion is not an end in itself. And what an impertinence it is when we fail to see that—when we seem to say to the world that their only hope is in the tepid conventions of our club.

No, the heart of mission is in God's action. He is the Creator, Who has made of one blood all nations of men to dwell on the face of the whole earth. He is the Teacher, Who leads us into truth as fast as we can go. He is the Lover, Whose unfailing remembrance of mankind keeps us all in the hollow of His hand. He is the Judge, Who strides through human history revealing the right and establishing it. The mission is His and not ours. The best we can do is to find Him at work in our world, to go to Him, to call Him by name so that He may be seen by others.

All of us have come to understand this about mission, in our time. And in understanding this, we have come to see another way in which the Anglican Communion is not an end in itself. The test of everything we plan must be the degree of its anonymity. If our organization seems to be such as to call attention to ourselves, or to perpetuate ourselves, then it is wrong. The only test we can accept for our organization is that it shall make Him clearer, and identify His action better.

These seem to me the three essential conditions for our organization for action—the nature of our fellowship, our need to travel light, and the necessity to remember that we are not an end in ourselves. These are not specifics. These are the terms on which alone we can rightly organize ourselves.

Given these three conditions of our organization, what now are the areas where our first attention must turn? I suggest, briefly, two—the area of our inter-church relationships, and that of our organization for mission.

IV. Inter-Church Relationships

We are now at something of a cross-roads in this. The supreme organ of our corporate life, of course, is the Lambeth Conference. This entirely informal episcopal houseparty has been, for nearly a century, the heart of the "common counsel of bishops" where the mutual loyalty which holds us together is born. But I wonder whether this Conference itself does not now show the strain of trying to carry a heavier burden and a different burden than it can or it should, on its present basis. It is an informal and highly personal Conference; but it is increasingly being forced or lured into another role, trembling on the brink of being a synod—of being treated as if it were a synod—without most of the necessities of synodical action.

If we wish to move from our tradition of responsible, co-operative decision by our separate churches into some more centralized way, then the Lambeth Conference very likely must accept a synodical role, and it must have a synodical constitution, through the addition of clerical and lay participants. Without those orders of the Ministry, the Conference could not speak authoritatively and decisively; indeed whenever Lambeth is now forced into even a para-synodical attitude (and this is less infrequent as the years go on) the response of the churches is likely to be increasingly negative. The Indian decisions of 1961 and 1962 are a case in point. Whatever the merits of the issues themselves, there was also an overtone of putting the bishops in their place; and I cannot say that I felt this to be improper.

If we need and want a central Anglican synod, then let us by all means have one. But it would destroy the immense usefulness of the Lambeth Conference to try to force it, in its present traditional structure, into a synodical role. For my part, feeling as I do about the free partnership of our churches, I think we gain far more than we lose by maintaining our looseness of association and our separate decision-making processes. Therefore I feel that as the Lambeth Conference develops, it will develop not as an imperfect and accidental synod, but rather in its truer terms of a profoundly moving and helpful meeting of brothers, to know one another, to take common counsel, to pray together, and so to help bear one another's burdens and share one another's witness. In this I do not doubt the need for far more preparatory study and collateral consultations as the Lambeth Conferences penetrate more deeply into the complex areas of the world's life which increasingly concern all of us. But let us not confuse or short-circuit the responsibility of every church, in its own responsible partnership, for the positive decisions on which our common life depends.

Even clearer has been our experience in recent years, which has pointed the way to new needs for consultation and new avenues to make it possible. The Advisory Council and the Lambeth Consultative Body have been our main improvisations so far. Far more frequent meetings of such a metropolitan council are now seen as a necessity; and with them, a deeper level of mutual consultation in many special areas—ecumenical, educational, communications, planning for new work and the like. The "consultant" plan, experimental for three years, now is valued generally as a step in this direction. Specific proposals have been already made in other directions by the Missionary Executives' Conference, the Advisory Council and the Lambeth Consultative Body.

All these are improvisations as we move swiftly forward into a new phase and form of our common life which none can now see in detail.

But if the responsible freedom of the "younger churches" of the Anglican Communion is to be a fact and not just a dream, there are certain further necessities of organization. One is to see to it that the younger churches have adequate financial muscles. There is little use in establishing autocephalous provinces if they do not have the power to implement their own decisions. I have spent nearly four years now in trying to encourage responsible planning on the part of our younger churches, so that the broad questions of missionary strategy can be attacked in brotherly partnership. It is clear to me that it is practically useless to develop the organs and tradition of responsible planning, if the younger churches must then still be beggars for the means with which to carry out their plans. If their free brotherhood within the Anglican Communion means anything, it means that they must have the power to make their own mistakes if need be, and certainly to plan and carry out in responsible freedom at least the essential elements of their mission within their own nations and culture.

This is not simply a case of "give us the tools and we will finish the job." The mission and life of the Church are one; and nobody can plan in a vacuum by himself. All planning is co-operative, when it comes to the Christian Church. All are involved in everyone's plans, and we stand or fall together. But the simple necessities of freedom and dignity require that all our churches be treated as brothers and not beggars.

In terms of money, one can distinguish three kinds of need. One is that of a sufficient "dowry." When a new province comes into existence, when a new church is born, an immense change is taking place. We are saying to them, in effect, that they are strong enough and mature enough to establish their own rules, define their own mission, control their own affairs, accept responsibility for their own brotherhood and for their partnership with us, take the initiative in the care of their own missionary frontiers. This respect and gift of freedom is a very precious gift in itself. But it must be accompanied by at least a minimum store of financial and institutional structure, such as to make it possible for the younger church to accept the responsibilities it gladly seeks to accept. Endowments may indeed be a mixed blessing. But building funds are not; the simple structure of provincial administration, and the means to make it possible, are not; the beginnings of an adequate pension system or the money to make possible adequate theological education are not. So one could go on, for such needs are not particularly mysterious—any church can look at itself and discover what such fundamental needs are.

"Dowry" does not mean endowment. It means the essential tools, without which a newly-independent church cannot go forward in freedom. But other needs must also be in our minds.

A second is that for loan funds—either as gifts to other churches to be administered by them, or as resources, such as some churches now have, available for use by others. Indeed such funds may themselves be a way for individuals or groups to put their own capital at work, as in the loan fund now developed by SPG within the Church of England.

A third kind of fund can also be imagined, an inter-church development fund to which all would contribute, in due proportion, and from which all would gain—a central pool of resources not in the command of any one church, but rather representing the common treasury and mission of the whole household.

The Mutual Responsibility proposal speaks of these three needs, and asks for an immediate attack on the first of them. If the new level of mutual support we ask of ourselves is given by ourselves, we shall be then able to make a start, but only a start, in providing the financial muscles freedom requires.

There are other areas of mutual responsibility, of equal importance. One is that of the composition and sponsorship of new missionary task forces. Last January, in our consultation in Latin America, there was very general agreement as to the need to re-examine our whole present practice in this respect. We all accepted the fact that every new missionary frontier must have firm rooting and sponsorship in some particular church of our Communion. But we also recognized the danger—illustrated clearly enough in Latin America itself—of identifying the mission of the Anglican Communion exclusively with one nation or culture. The life of the Church finds its embodiment in particular communities. But the Church itself, to which our full Communion bears its enduring witness, is greater than any of our national traditions or communities; and it is now an urgent necessity that our missionary task forces shall reflect this, unambiguously and with utmost power.

When a new missionary frontier is opened, our first concern must be that those who go from the other churches to launch this new companion shall be chosen with only one need in mind, that of providing the strength and the skills which that particular frontier requires. The bishop who is to be at the center of the task force, the priests and teachers and doctors who are to go with him, should come from wherever we want to draw them, to meet the needs of the society to which they go. It may be quite right to require fundamental sponsorship by some particular church or other. But it should be clear from the outset that what we are trying to establish is not a branch office of North America or Great Britain or wherever, but a new and free companionship within the Catholic Church itself. It is the whole Church that is entering into the area, not a national culture, not a partisan ecclesiastical group, not a point of view, not a particular set of techniques or traditions.

I want to make one final comment about our inter-church relationships. Our Communion is an association of churches within the Catholic Church, held together by deep bonds of unity and loyalty. But in this, our relationships with one another are not different in *kind* from those we have with other companies of Christian people. The relationships are certainly different in *intensity*; full communion is the deepest bond this world affords, where we live up to it. But it is not a wall to separate us from those with whom we are not in full communion. It is rather what lies at the heart of life for all of us, toward which we all mean to move as boldly as we can. It is the most intense symbol of the unity hidden in God's will which, some day, if we are obedient, will be fully ours.

It would be wrong for us to be disloyal to the full communion we now have, or to dilute our Anglican unity. But it would be equally wrong to act as if this unity were uniquely different from all other expressions of unity. Administratively, it may be sensible to organize our "missionary" channel separately from our ecumenical activities; but we do so at the risk of seeming to build a wall where none exists. Unity and mission run together. The brotherly help we try to give to our Anglican companions is not a different kind of help from what we try to give through Inter-Church Aid. Granted that we may not be free to do the same things in each case, the duty is still, in both cases, that of pressing our unity in Christ to its farthest possible limit.

Therefore I believe that we must organize ourselves so that all our inter-church relationships, Anglican and non-Anglican, are held as closely as possible in the same focus and the same frame of reference. This undoubtedly means taking a fresh look at both sides of our life, mission and unity. I am sure that the time has not come to abandon specifically Anglican missionary work in favor of some more diffused interdenominational mission. This would be romanticism, to imagine that separated churches can pretend to a unity abroad which they do not have, and do not even clearly intend to have, at home. We would simply be exporting bad conscience and self-deceit.

But I am equally sure that we must not keep our missionary concerns and our ecumenical concerns in separate compartments. We have passed the point of no return in this. Precisely because we are not a self-conscious denominational sect, it is impossible for us to deal with the Church, or relationships within the Church, as if some were "ours" and others were "theirs." Not in this way do we respect the mature freedom of all our brotherhood, and love the unity God has given us, and in the same breath press ceaselessly forward on the frontier of ecumenical loyalty. The Church cannot be untrue to itself. We cannot play at being the Church, and still willingly and really act like one sect among many. Unity is one and indivisible; if we are given it in our own world-wide fellowship, the other side of that is relentless obedience to unity with our neighbors.

V. Organizing Ourselves Around Mission

Finally, we must organize ourselves around our mission, at home as well as abroad. Our commanding need is to stop thinking so much about ourselves, and turn our eyes outward.

This is easy to say. It is not always easy to do. Young, small churches are almost bound to spend much of their energy worrying about their own existence—and most of our churches are small. Even the better-established churches are hard hit by the currents of life in our world, which have taken away from them both the traditional role that they have played in time past, and also the buoyancy and self-confidence which went with that role. Still again, part of the price we pay for a divided Church is that every division within the broken Body is condemned to triviality—it must spend so much of its time and thought defending its own separate identity and justifying its own separate existence; and the cost of this inward-turning, self-regarding spirit is frightening.

But these things are all human failings and sins, not some invincible tide of history. We can and we do rise above this petty introspection. And when we do, it is in large part because of the way we organize ourselves around our mission, for the sake of our mission.

The first requirement of a church's obedience to mission is mutual responsibility for its own brotherhood, accepted just as far as it is humanly possible to accept it. And if this responsibility is to be real, it must be institutionalized—it must be structured in the form of our church's government; it must be expressed in terms of our financial responsibility; it must be manifested in the membership of our governing bodies; supremely it must be expressed in the clear authority of our common life over our separate lives—parochial, diocesan, provincial. Only when brotherhood costs something is it likely to be anything more than a sentimentality.

When new provinces come into existence, for example, and do not require sacrificial mutual loyalty and responsibility, each for the other, in their constitutions, they really are not yet ready for provincial life. As I understand the church's structure, the diocesan family, gathered around the bishop, is the smallest complete unit. It is not the final unit. A province, if it has any substance at all, is qualitatively more than simply a sum of separate dioceses which take no responsibility for one another. And this is a matter of organization, of structure, of the kind of structure which irrevocably binds separate lives together into one.

But this kind of organization for brotherhood is really only a preface to mission. We do not come to the heart of the matter until we ask the question how we organize ourselves so as to turn our eyes outward. I find myself asking this question in very simple terms. Are we so organized that our center of gravity is within ourselves? Do we talk mainly to ourselves? Is our theology mainly a professional jargon or a kind of family slang? Do we mainly work so we can exist so we can go on working so we can exist so we can go on . . . ?

There are times when all the Church can do is exist. Captive churches in captive nations have to bear the only witness they can bear. Nobody questions that. But in a free society, where there is a free market in ideas, do we in fact have anything else to say than what everybody is saying anyway? Do we use our freedom for mission and leadership?

A church organized around mission is a church whose center of gravity is outside itself. And this has more to do with organization than we sometimes suspect. For example, is the training of the clergy such that we are confronted with the world, step by step as we go along, so that all we learn is learned against the steady challenge of those who do not believe it nor see any sense in it?

For example, is the budget of a church and its financial operation organized so that there is no escape from honest stewardship? So that it is impossible for a parish or a diocese to say "I have done all that is required of me"?

For example, is the deployment of the clergy organized so that there is a steady challenge and encouragement to the work of the frontier of the Church's life?

For example, is the man or woman being prepared for Confirmation helped to understand that Confirmation is not initiation into a club but ordination for a ministry? Are the laity prepared spiritually so that the mission of God in this world is the center of our lives? Are we educated theologically so that, if need be—especially if we go overseas—we can witness with power and relevance even if we are all the Church there is in that place?

For example, in the training of children for their mature discipleship, are they taught as much about the world and about people and about God in history as they are about how to conform to the Church's customs?

These are childish questions—preachers' questions—of course. But let them suggest what organization around mission means in practical terms. It means that the theological education of the Church, clergy and laity alike, must be so designed that the present action of God in history is the most important thing we know about Him, and that the obedience of the Church to the activity of God is the most important characteristic of the Church. The judgment of the world about the Church is that we are, in William Temple's phrase, "mainly concerned with religion." Very well—that is the world's judgment, and the world is stuck with it. The frightening thing is to find the Church agreeing with this, accepting this description of its function. And the root of this religiosity is in the theological education of the Church, which means basically of the clergy.

If the Church is to be organized around mission, it means that mission must be in the center of its structure, the primary thing in its budget, the first claim on its manpower and its time. The most frightening thing about the Church in our time is not its lack of prophetic passion—it is its feeling that mission is an option. How did it happen in the American Church, for example, that for so long we lagged behind the world in our concern about racial injustice? There are not many Christians in the United States today who feel anything but shame about this, that it had to be the secular forces in society which took the lead in the fight for racial justice. Why was this? It was not that we were lacking in moral earnestness, in those areas of life which seemed to us important. The fact was that we were simply not engaged in the racial conflict—this was a special mission, which was out on the periphery of the Church somewhere; and therefore we were able to avoid facing this cancerous thing which was at the very heart of American life, and is now.

And the answer to this curious blindness was not merely to have more enthusiastic and converted people. The answer was, first of all, to organize ourselves in such a way that we could not escape the conflict and the mission. It was the fact of the American Constitution and the public law which ultimately made it impossible for the American people to avoid seeing the issues. In precisely the same way, the Church needed to be confronted by the issue and by its mission, not just because of the concern of a few prophetic people but because its own structure made this confrontation inescapable. This is what organization and law can do—they cannot change people's souls, but they can help to keep us reminded of the world we live in and of our mission to it.

I have spoken of two areas in particular, theological education and racial tension, because each of them illustrates the significance of organization. In all these matters, of course, the leadership of devoted converted individuals is essential. No organization can ever be a substitute for that. But consecrated leadership itself can be stultified and wasted when there is no solid fulcrum for its leverage; and the purpose of organization—of structure and law—is to provide exactly the unyielding foundation on which conscience and moral leadership can work.

This is so with all the ingredients of the Church's life. If our theological education is largely irrelevant to the present mission of God in the world, and it is, one thing we can do is to change our curriculum and course of study so that priests are prepared to give leadership in the real situation in which the Church finds itself. If our moral witness is passionless and narrow, and it is, one thing we can do is to alter our structure so that concern for world peace, for racial tension, for social justice, for the industrial revolution is built into our central life. If overseas mission represents now only four or five per cent of our total Christian commitment, and it does, one thing we can do is to put it into the center of our attention, into the basic structure of parish and diocesan life, so that we cannot help thinking about it whenever there is money to be spent or men to be put to work. If we are not really engaged in a contest with the secular spirit in our universities or in our scientific and technical society, and we are not, one thing we can do is to put the Church into the middle of the secular society, as through the deliberate mission of Christian men in the universities and laboratories—and to bring the secular society into the Church with the deliberate inclusion of secular men and secular wisdom in our own councils.

The sum of the problem is that we are now organized so that our main energies are inescapably devoted to our own self-perpetuation. Mission is an option, reserved for those who have a special interest in social justice or individual life or overseas evangelism or whatever it may be. As long as this is so, just so long will the Church rightly seem to be a private club, existing mainly for the sake of its own members and its own mysterious and private purposes. And anything less true to Christ I cannot imagine.

But let us so organize ourselves that the first claim on our attention, on our manpower, our time, our money, is the claim of those who do not belong to us and perhaps never will—let that be done, and how swiftly the false image of the Church will be swept away. Let our commanding principle of organization be that we exist only to discover what God is now doing in His ceaseless, loving mission to the world, and to follow Him in that mission, and to make it and Him known to our brothers in creation. If every structure, every group, every law, every activity is designed and tested according to that principle, then our organization for action will be true to ourselves and true to God.

All this, and far more, is said to us in the proposal of Mutual Responsibility. Each church is asked radically to study its own obedience to mission—to study its structures, its theology, its priorities. "We need to ask whether our structures are appropriate to our world and the church as it is . . . to examine the training of laity and clergy alike, asking whether in fact God's mission is central in our teaching. . . . We need to examine our priorities, asking whether in fact we are not putting secondary needs of our own ahead of essential needs of our brothers."

If "structures" and "organization" seem alien concepts and strange words to use about the Gospel and the mission of God, let us remember that they mean simply the ways we must have, through which our obedience can be made real. Words and emotional attitudes are easy to create. The solid, soldierly obedience of men and women must be expressed in deeds, in the discipline of our orderly, purposeful life.

Therefore I end with a simple little catechism of obedience:

First, our decision-making processes: What means have we to develop and express the common will of the Church in a nation? Is the whole body of the Church, in all its orders, effectively involved in decisions? Is there an adequate flow of information? Is there preparation for decision, both in terms of information and of theological background?

Second, our financial structures: Are they such as to encourage imagination as well as duty? Are our financial objectives great enough and central enough to deserve the devoted stewardship that we ask for? Do we put the real needs of others first?

Third, our provision for theological education: Is it clear that we do believe in the unity of all truth, and apply the same rigorous standards across the board? Are we preparing ordinands for ministry in this present world; and are we equally providing adequate theological tools to the unordained, so that they can understand their own share of the ministry?

Fourth, our study and planning: Is this in fact directed mainly toward the world and mission, or merely toward strengthening our own position? Is it shared with those outside the Church? Does it make use of the skill and science of those as dedicated as we to the world's needs, but for different reasons?

Fifth, our interior discipline: Do we expect enough of ourselves, and do we expect the right things, in our preparation for discipleship? Is our devotional life and our sacramental preparation adequate and relevant to the life we actually live? Is our worship a retreat from the world or an invasion of it? Are we organized so as to show love to the world outside, and treat self-righteousness as a sin?

Sixth, our inter-church relationship: Are they such as to involve us directly and irrevocably in the life and fortune of other churches? Is our organization such as to make clear the respect and equality with which we accept the responsible freedom of other churches? Is the structure of our church's life such as to permit receiving and hearing as well as giving and teaching?

Seventh, our preparation for unity: Is our life in fact so organized that the unity of the Church in Christ and in Baptism is the underlying assumption of all that we do? Do we accept the unity of the Church across the world as a greater reality than the racial and political divisions of mankind? In our daily life, is our full communion with others a commanding reality? Is our information service adequate to teach us as much about our brother Christians as the daily paper teaches us about their politics?

These are, to me, the most important questions to ask about organization for action. I cannot help but ask them against the background of what we are, for what we are must be the necessary condition of our organization. That we must be true to ourselves is the first requirement.

But the greater requirement is that we be true to the living God, Who is not our possession but our Lord. It is He Who is acting in our world. Our action is true and right only as it obeys Him, and helps to make Him known among those who do not know Him, who do not even believe in Him. It is for their sakes that He acts—for them in their misery and their grandeur. It is for them, then, that alone we rightly organize ourselves for action.

3. AT THE CROSSROADS*

ONE OF THE QUESTIONS Anglicans ought to ask themselves, periodically, is why we are members of Anglican "churches" and not a single, worldwide "Church." This is, of course, a double-barrelled question. When you ask it, you are really asking in what sense the word "Church" can be used in the plural at all. Neither Bible nor Creed would encourage us to think of "Churches" (at least with a capital "C"), and there is something at least troubling and perhaps even a little impious in the casual pluralism of our usage.

But "churches" (with a small "c") is not quite as complicated a word —and, for the purposes of this present article at least, I use it without raising the wider implications. The fact is that we Anglicans all over the world are grouped in a "Communion," of separate churches—Church of England, Nippon Seikokai, Church of the Province of South Africa, etc., etc.—rather than in a single, centralized body. The fact is that, partly by accident, partly by design, this unique household of forty million Christians has grown up in a pattern of regional autonomy.

---

* From *Anglican World*, April 1960.

And this is a fact worth a bit of exploration, particularly in our narrowing world.

For the most part, we are members of ecclesiastical "Provinces," as they are called, meaning by that self-contained, independent (but not always self-supporting), usually national bodies. The first such to appear (outside the British Isles) was the American Church, still known officially by its curious, 18th-century title of "The Protestant Episcopal Church in the United States of America." Almost as old is the Canadian Church, now known as "The Anglican Church of Canada." Others have followed, until now there are fifteen such churches (not to mention some individual dioceses which yet belong to no province), and a sixteenth, the Church in East Africa, soon to be established. (Indeed a seventeenth will likely soon follow that.)

Some, as in Australia or New Zealand, came into existence primarily as colonial extensions of the Church at home. Others, such as the churches in China and Japan, were the result of long-range missionary effort on the part of the older churches. But in any case, the general plan of our Anglican expansion has been to lead up to the establishment of regional and national churches, fully "indigenous," fully autonomous, not at all unlike the pattern of the Commonwealth itself.

It would be pleasant to feel that this policy was solely the result of thoughtful, far-seeing strategy. It was not, at the beginning at any rate —it happened largely by accident, and was profoundly influenced by the improvisations made necessary by the American Revolution. Before there was anything much of an Anglican "strategy" overseas, there were Anglicans overseas, wrestling with the problems of what they were and how they should organize themselves. And the policy grew out of the practical necessities, for the most part, which is not a bad way for policies to grow, but not particularly a neat way. Thus it would not be quite true, even to this day, to say that there is a master plan somewhere to govern our growth. It was not until Lambeth 1948, actually, that the first steps were taken to establish the Advisory Council on Missionary Strategy, and not until Lambeth 1958 that a budget and staff (of considerable personal interest to myself) was provided, to make it possible for the Advisory Council to function.

Nevertheless, our growth has more and more followed a conscious policy of building autonomous and indigenous churches. The Anglican Communion has not wished to become a monolithic super-Church, but rather to develop into an ever-wider family of churches, each rooted in its own soil and people, each joined with its companions in a common sacramental fellowship and a deep common life. Such is the Anglican

Communion of today, a world-wide household with almost nothing of administrative structure to articulate its unity, beyond the utterly informal tie of the Lambeth Conferences and the Anglican Congresses every ten years, and the tentative and ghostly new exploration represented by my own office.

This looseness of organization has its manifest strengths, for it permits—even encourages—a healthy regionalism and a sense of local roots which are precious gifts in our increasingly standardized world. But it also has its obvious weaknesses, for our world is not very roomy any more, and time runs with dismaying swiftness. And one of the most perplexing of the weaknesses is the difficulty with which we must try to cope with areas where two or more Provinces are closely involved in a common geography and a common mission.

The Caribbean is a case in point, where two Provinces stretch side by side in a great arc across that sea. The Church of the Province of the West Indies, an autonomous church almost entirely English in its foundation and support, includes the Commonwealth countries—Antigua, Barbados, Guiana, British Honduras, Jamaica, Nassau and the Bahamas, Trinidad and the Windward Islands. Sharing the Caribbean are the American dioceses, in the French- and Spanish-speaking islands—Cuba, the Dominican Republic, Haiti, Puerto Rico, the Virgin Islands—as well as the mainland, in Central America, Mexico, and the Panama Canal Zone.

On a map, such a schizoid ecclesiastical establishment is inexcusable. As a matter of fact it is productive of some queer and painful anomalies, as in the case of a man who can make his communion where he works but not where he lives (since he lives in one province and works in the other, and the canons governing the status of people married after divorce differ quite sharply). Or again, the Anglican Communion bears one witness about Family Planning in one province, and a quite different one in the other.

But the situation is actually a lot easier than it looks, for the dioceses of the American Church are principally Spanish-speaking (or French, in Haiti), and are within the area of an inherited Spanish-Catholic tradition, while the Church of the West Indies is mainly an English-speaking body, concentrated in areas of a quite different racial and economic background. And while it clearly will be better and deeper for all concerned, when the time comes for the establishment of a single Caribbean Anglican Church, in the meanwhile the Church's work is not seriously hampered in our day-by-day concerns.

So also is it in a few other spots—on the Continent of Europe, for

example, or in certain areas of South America. But perhaps the major
and most urgent case in point is in South East Asia. That stormy corner
of Asia, ranging from Japan to India, is, by every standard, one of the
critically important and sensitive areas of our world. Here the new nationalism of our time finds turbulent expression. Here the new juices of
ancient cultures are vigorously at work. Here Communism, in its most
naked and relentless form, challenges all the easy presuppositions of a
Christian culture. Here, most sharply, the classic and powerful tide of
Chinese expansion beats on the sea-wall of the "West."

In this area, Anglican churches are at work. In India and Burma,
the Church of India, Pakistan, Burma and Ceylon speaks and acts for
us. At the other end of the arc, the non-provincial diocese of Korea and
the missions of the American Church in Taiwan and the Philippines
bear our witness. Spearheading our life among the Chinese of the Dispersion are the dioceses of Hong Kong and Singapore and Malaya—the
former officially a diocese of the Holy Catholic Church in China (but
now temporarily separated from its own Province and affiliated with
Canterbury), the latter another non-provincial missionary diocese supported in the main from England. Completing the South East Asia
complex is still one more non-provincial missionary diocese, that of
Borneo.

Thus the Churches of China, India, England and America are all
deeply involved in a common geography and a common mission. And
here the harsh necessity for a common strategy is far too clear to permit
comfortable compromise. Lambeth 1948 was aware of this; and at the
Anglican Congress in Minneapolis, in 1954, the formation of the "South
East Asia Episcopal Council" was encouraged and given such authority
and establishment as could be given. From 1954 to now, the Council
has had such corporate activity as was possible, dependent on gifts of
travel funds or the accidents of history to make meetings possible. That
activity has not been unimpressive, either, despite its difficulties. Perhaps the most significant of its fruits to date has been the holding of the
important conference of Chinese clergy in Hong Kong, in 1959, probably the first occasion for such broad consultation in Anglican history.

But the Council is only at the beginning of its life, and it bids to be
one of the most important developments in the whole broad strategy
of our Communion, as the years go on. For it points the way to a new
kind and level of relationship between independent churches—a new
kind of inter-Anglican co-operation and unity—which may show us how
we may keep all the strength of our regional and national roots and
still not be hamstrung by our independence.

The most recent meeting of the Council, a Conference which included priests and laity as well as the bishops of the area, was held in Kuching last February. The Church in Borneo, Burma, Hong Kong, Korea, the Philippines, and Malaya was represented—six dioceses with their bishops, and members of the clergy and laity. All of the diocesan bishops were English or American, but all of the assistant bishops were "national," two Chinese, one Burmese, one Filipino; all of the priests present, with the exception of one, and all of the laymen were "national."

In brief compass, two great matters and one great liturgical act summed up the five days of the meeting. The act was the consecration of the Rev. James Wong to be a bishop in the Church of God, assistant to the Bishop of Borneo. And although the act took only a small part of the time of the Conference and was not really part of the agenda of the Conference at all, it still seems, in retrospect, to sum up very much of the significance of the meeting and of all the South East Asia Council stands for. For here was a native son of China, who had lived and worked in business life in South East Asia and as far as Australia, whose life had ranged over all the diverse, rich interests and concerns of that part of the world, coming home, as it were, to take his place in the apostolate of the Church and give the leadership his experience had earned. One could not help marvelling at the way our tradition of Anglican Christianity, stemming from its roots in England so many centuries ago, had taken root across the world, in the old-new soil of the Orient, and was bearing its accustomed harvest in converted souls and disciplined lives.

The act, as it seemed to me, symbolized the massive dream for which the Council speaks. In practical terms, most of the time of the Conference was devoted to two major concerns—the question of the formation of a new Province in South East Asia, and the far vaster question of the mission of our Communion to the Chinese outside of continental China (the "Chinese Dispersion," as it is so often called).

The question of the Province affected the dioceses represented differently. Korea, only remotely related to South East Asia, was not and could hardly be expected to take any active part in such a new organization. For the time, at least, it is not clear what regional fellowship ought rightly to include Korea; here racial, political and geographical factors all work to cloud rather than clarify the picture.

The Philippines and Taiwan present a different but equally complicated picture. Anglican life in both jurisdictions is already included in another Province, that of the American Church; their clergy and laity are represented in the General Convention—the central synod—of that Church, as are the bishops in the American House of Bishops. More, the future of the Church in the Philippines seems inescapably, and rightly and happily, interwoven with that of the Philippine Independent Church, that household of more than two million Christian souls, gathered around its forty bishops, with which the Anglican churches are in daily-increasing brotherhood. Doubtless, in time, a fully autonomous Church of the Philippines is what lies ahead there.

Hong Kong has still another problem, for it is one of the constituent dioceses of the Church in China, although now grievously separated from its brotherhood. The diocese of Rangoon, now one of the Church of India, Pakistan, Burma and Ceylon, faces the unique problem of a diocese possibly soon to lose its Province and start off on its own—if the "North India" plans, looking toward the establishment of a united Church of North India in which our Anglican Church will take its full part, eventuate successfully, Burma will not be included. Thus Rangoon faces what Borneo and Singapore and Malaya already know, the peculiar isolation of a missionary diocese supported but not represented "at home," and without the deeper ties of a common provincial loyalty and life.

What will eventuate ultimately from all these tangled relationships remains to be seen. But what was voted, by the four dioceses concerned, was clear enough—it was the establishment of a "Province of South East Asia," to include at least the four dioceses most deeply concerned, Borneo, Hong Kong, Rangoon, and Singapore and Malaya. Many details must yet be faced and decided; Rangoon's membership must still await action on North India, and Hong Kong's must be to some degree conditional on its deeper tie with the Church in China. But both need and intent are clear enough now, and what remains is simply to find the way to meet the particular problems.

But perhaps the most important question, in all this matter, is of the relation of the Province-to-be with the existing Council. For the Province of South East Asia, when and as it comes into being, will still not include more than a portion of South East Asia. What it will do will be to give to its constituent dioceses a new and deeper common loyalty. But in so doing it will establish still one more autonomous Anglican church; and thus the formation of the new Province could easily increase the problems of inter-Anglican co-operation, unless the Council is equally widened and strengthened so as to become, in realistic and viable terms, a meeting-place of sister churches, competent to establish and maintain a common strategy.

Thus it was important that the four dioceses concerned, in their Declaration seeking to become a Province, should declare that they believe themselves "called by the same Holy Spirit both to continue in the common life of the Council and Conference and to proceed" in the formation of the Province. Equally was it significant that the Conference, in taking official notice of this action, expressed its belief that "this action would not reduce the significance, nor hamper the life and fellowship of the Council of the Church in South East Asia."

Do these matters seem technical or petty? If they do, I should be sorry; actually they are part of the travail of the Anglican household, seeking to keep its generous heritage of national and regional loyalties and at the same time find new means to fulfill its inner unity and meet the complex challenge of our world so terribly one and so profoundly inter-related. Nobody knows what the final answers will be; we are only at the beginning of all this, searching for a deeper unity in our diversity, seeking how to keep all the rich treasure of national and regional life and still act as one body, as the Church of Christ should act. This was the significance of the hours spent, in Kuching, in thinking so desperately seriously about Province and Council, and what we needed, and what our Lord wished.

The other matter looms much larger, at least in the world's scale of values—it was the matter of our Communion's mission and ministry to the Chinese of the Dispersion. Here I can do no more than sketch the barest outline of our concerns. Outside of continental China itself, there are some 28 million Chinese people, living in every part of the world, with the heaviest concentration in South East Asia, notably in the diocese of Singapore and Malaya. To staff our mission to them, there are about fifty Chinese priests and perhaps another fifty mission workers—a hundred people, everywhere in the world, to carry our Church's witness to Christ to these millions!

We are now facing a present deficit of thirty priests in this mission—that is to say, we need *now* thirty more Chinese priests than there are in the world just to staff our present work (and we are falling behind regularly in this for we are not preparing and ordaining enough Chinese clergymen to replace those we now have). Of what use to dream great dreams of a widened and quickened mission to these millions, if we cannot maintain what we now have? This is the first question we must face, and we tried to face it, in Kuching, beginning at the beginning with as strong and clear a call as we could make for a renewal and vast strengthening of vocation to the sacred ministry from among our own Chinese men. Whitsunday was the day we chose for special prayers and thoughts in all our South East Asia churches (and as far beyond that as the loving concern of our sister-churches would carry our need).

We begin at the beginning, with the great need for the sons of our Chinese families to offer themselves for this ministry. But we saw much further than this—we saw our need for a unified, co-ordinated long-range plan, which would cover our mission to the Chinese of the Dispersion everywhere in the world, for as far ahead as we could see. To make such a plan requires time and staff—requires money. And we had no other recourse than to ask the Advisory Council to meet our needs, with the hope that by 1963 we might be able to bring a plan back to the Advisory Council, which would make possible a thoughtful and resolute and continuing apostolate to the dispersed Chinese everywhere.

Why this special emphasis on the Chinese? Why did Lambeth 1958 set such an urgent priority on this particular salient of our Anglican mission? To answer that question rightly would take far more space than we have here. But this, at least, ought be said. The Chinese of the Dispersion are neither less dear nor more dear than anybody else, in God's sight. We do not single them out as saints or sinners, more than the rest of us. It is rather a question of the unique place they and this motherland fill in our history, I think. A great and ancient people face, in these days, an enormous test both at home and abroad. Those within China itself must cope with problems of social and political construction perhaps unparalleled in man's existence, and must make choices as far-reaching as any man has ever had to make. And their kinsmen outside of China, linked so deeply at home and yet seeking to find full rooting in their new allegiances as well, often suspected, often harried and penalized for their very strengths, often faced with loneliness and homelessness—they are a people of enormous gifts and enormous needs for the best that Christianity can give them, to enable them to make their gifts to us aright.

Most nakedly, most uncompromisingly, the strongest of worldly philosophies and the truest of God's revelation confront one another within the soul of China and her people. If we Christians do not bear our clearest witness there, we are failing to do what we ought to bring to the feet of Christ all the wisdom and power and resourcefulness of His, and our, brothers of China. Therefore, the high importance our Church places on this salient. The Chinese stand at such a cross-roads as we have not ever known before in history. Our task is to enter into that choice as boldly, as deeply, as understandingly as we can, not because of fear but because of love and of hope that somehow through our witness, marvellous new gifts may be added to the offering Christ means to make of us all, and our world.

MEMORANDUM ON THE REGIONAL COUNCIL
OF THE CHURCH OF SOUTH EAST ASIA

One of the significant developments of recent years within the Anglican Communion has been the establishment of Regional Councils. They go back, at least in principle, to the meeting of the Lambeth Conference in 1948. Two particular council organizations grew out of that discussion in 1948—the South Pacific Regional Council, and the South East Asia Council. A third, of a somewhat different type, has subsequently come into existence—the Caribbean Council (which includes, at the moment, only the American missionary jurisdiction in the Caribbean area).

The council idea is an attempt to meet the problems arising in relatively homogeneous geographical areas, where there are dioceses at work of different provincial families. The South East Asia area is the most complex, for it includes dioceses with four different metropolitical authorities and backgrounds. Yet it is in the South East Asia area that there is the strongest sense of common life and common concern. This is seen in political and economic matters quite as clearly as it is ecclesiastically. Therefore there has been a steady pressure towards deeper mutual engagement, over the dozen or so years of the Council's life.

A complicating factor in all those years has been the strong wish for the development of full and autonomous provincial status in the area. Because the geographical extent of the Council area is so vast, and the racial and political structure so complicated, it has seemed clear from the outset that no single province could ever be established which could include all the jurisdictions. This means, inescapably, that whenever provincial organization was discussed, it was felt to be somewhat divisive. In turn, the reaction against this seeming divisiveness has encouraged the exploration of the Council structure itself.

The result has been, so far, that the South East Asia Council has gone further than any other in exploring its own nature, and projecting its own possibilities. Yet this has not been felt to be an alternative to provincial organization. Indeed, every encouragement has been given at each meeting of the Council, to those dioceses which seemed most nearly ready for provincial discussion, to pursue that discussion. More than that, the Council as it is presently constituted, is specifically designed to be an inter-provincial structure, leaving room for the development of the three or four or whatever the ultimate number of provinces is to be.

Specifically, the dioceses included in the South East Asia Council are Rangoon (now part of CIPBC), Singapore and Malaya, Borneo and Korea (missionary jurisdictions under the Archbishop of Canterbury), Hong Kong (a constituent diocese of the Church of China), and the Philippines and Taiwan (American missionary dioceses).

Hong Kong regards itself as still a member of the Chinese Church, although it is for the moment administratively separate, and, until this year, had asked the Archbishop of Canterbury to be the custodian of its constitution and canons. With the new proposed constitution for the South East Asia Council, the Council will doubtless become the metropolitical authority for Hong Kong. This seems to be an acceptable proposal all around.

CIPBC has indicated its willingness to have the diocese of Rangoon leave CIPBC to become a member of a new province in South East Asia—Burma has far more in common with Malaya than it does with India, and this is accented by the unity talks in India in which Burma does not join.

The two dioceses of Singapore and Malaya, and Borneo (soon to be three, with the formation of the new diocese of Jesselton) have the greatest community of interest. This again is strongly reinforced by the move toward "greater Malaysia." But these dioceses are very closely linked historically, and are equally strongly rooted in a generally British background and orientation, more so than any of the other jurisdictions.

Korea doubtless looks to the Church of Japan as its ultimate provincial home, even though there may be long years yet before that alliance is possible.

Taiwan is a missionary diocese of the American Church, so constituted in trust for the Church of China; and the only rational plan for Taiwan—in the long run—is to think of it as a basically Chinese diocese. But this again is a very complex question, and there will not be any speedy answer to it.

In the case of the Philippines, we are probably dealing with a national church which will be, and ought to be, a province in itself. With more than 2,000,000 members of the Philippine Independent Church now bound most intimately with the 50,000 members of the Philippine Episcopal Church, it would seem that the wisest strategy is to encourage full growth and autonomy in the Philippines.

Thus we are really talking about probably four provinces, in South East Asia, and the Council must inescapably be thought out against that background. It is not a rival to provincial structure, nor an alternative to it, in the thought of the members of the Council. They have come to see it, rather, as an ad hoc organization, able to function where no provinces exist, or where several provinces co-exist, with its constitution designedly loose enough to permit almost every variation of authority, as the circumstances require.

When I first encountered the South East Asia Council, at Kuching in 1960, there still seemed to be a problem of choice between council and province. Archbishop Fisher had understandable reluctance in approving a council as a substitute for the more historic provincial structure. He tended therefore to discourage any development of the Council itself, beyond the purely conservative basis on which it was founded.

Archbishop Ramsey, on the other hand, has been receptive to the possibility of experimentation, in the Council pattern, without prejudicing the ultimate development of provinces. In Rangoon, in February 1961, the Bishops assembled in Council made this proposal:

> In our view the Council should be recognized as a new form of Episcopal Synod competent to meet the special needs of the various Dioceses, and as a consultative body, competent to formulate policy within its area. We therefore ask the Churches of the Anglican Communion through the Executive Officer whether they are prepared to extend this recognition to the CCSEA.

This request was duly submitted to the churches concerned, and formed the basis of further discussion during 1961, with the Archbishop of Canterbury, the Presiding Bishop of the American Church, the Metropolitan of Calcutta, and others.

As the result of this further consultation, the Bishops of South East Asia, meeting in Quezon City (Manila) last February, adopted a revised constitution for the Council. In this, clerical and lay representation was included (which had been one of the points made by Archbishop Ramsey). At the same time, they tried to phrase their request for authority against the existing background of needs. No two metropolitical authorities can act in the same way, or need to. It is relatively simple, for example, for the Archbishop of Canterbury to delegate this or that aspect of his provincial authority. It is not nearly as simple in the case of the American Church, where amendments to constitution and canons are required. For this reason, the South East Asia Council constitution is of a very informal and flexible kind.

Perhaps that is enough background—here is the actual constitution itself:

> We the undersigned Bishops of the Holy Catholic Church, meeting in the said Council at Cathedral Heights, Quezon City, Republic of

the Philippines on the 6th day of February in the year of our Lord, 1962, do hereby constitute a Regional Council of the Church of South East Asia; and we, being clerical and lay representatives of the dioceses of South East Asia, sitting with the Bishops, do concur in this action.

We propose that the Council shall have the following Constitution:

ARTICLE I. There shall be a Regional Council of the Church of South East Asia.

ARTICLE II. The Council shall consist of the Dioceses of Borneo, Hong Kong and Macao, Korea, the Philippines, Rangoon, Singapore and Malaya, and Taiwan. These Dioceses shall be represented by:
  a. all the Diocesan and Assistant Bishops in the Region.
  b. at least one clerical and one lay representative from each constituent Diocese, or more as determined by the Council.

ARTICLE III. The Council shall elect a Chairman from its members, who shall serve for five years and shall be eligible for re-election, and such other officers as it shall determine.

ARTICLE IV. It shall be competent for the Council to function synodically as follows:
  i. To exercise such ecclesiastical authority on behalf of the constituent dioceses as may be entrusted to it by them, and delegated to it by those Churches now exercising ecclesiastical jurisdiction in the Region. In particular the Council shall have the right:
    a. to confirm the election of Bishops in Dioceses competent to elect, where this right is not reserved to itself by another authority. When the Council is not in session, such confirmation may be given by correspondence. In any case confirmation shall require the consent of two thirds of the bishops of the Council, and the concurrent consent of two thirds of the clerical and lay representations.
    b. to act as Trustee for the Constitution and Canons of the Chung Hua Sheng Kung Hui in relation to the Diocese of Hong Kong and Macao, and to serve other Churches in a similar way at their request.
  ii. To exercise general responsibility for the Government, Discipline, Worship and Life of the Church in the Region.

ARTICLE V. It shall be within the competence of the Council to invite into its full membership any other Diocese which, with the concurrence of its ecclesiastical authority, desires such membership.

ARTICLE VI. The Council shall be competent (subject to powers expressly reserved by proper ecclesiastical authority) to determine relations of Intercommunion with any Churches not at present in Communion with its constituent dioceses, provided always that the inheritance of Truth and Grace which as a Church it has received with its Catholic Faith and Order be not thereby impaired, but rather established, strengthened and fulfilled.

ARTICLE VII. This Constitution shall become effective when approved by the Archbishop of Canterbury, the Presiding Bishop of the PECUSA and the Metropolitan of the CIPBC, and operative in the case of any constituent Diocese when approved by that Diocese. However the participation of any Diocese in any particular activity of the Council may be withheld by that Diocese until the appropriate action is taken by the ecclesiastical authority concerned.

ARTICLE VIII. Proposals to amend the Constitution shall be brought forward at a meeting of the Council. If such proposals are accepted by a simple majority of the Council, they shall then be approved by two thirds of the constituent dioceses and by the ecclesiastical authorities concerned. Such amendments shall then be ratified at a succeeding meeting of the Council by a two thirds majority of the Bishops of the Council, with the concurrent consent of two thirds of the clerical and lay representation.

ARTICLE IX. Meetings of the Council shall be held as determined by the Council, subject to the right of the Chairman (or Senior Bishop of the Council, if there be no Chairman able to act) to call meetings at his discretion. It shall be competent for the Bishops of the Council to meet at other times for mutual consultation, to initiate and consider proposals for Council action, and to act on such matters as may be delegated to them by the Council.

ARTICLE X. Council actions shall normally take the form of resolutions, which shall be effective until rescinded or amended (unless otherwise ordered). The Council is competent to establish its own financial officers and accounts, to receive and disburse funds given by its own constituent dioceses or any other source. No resolution will be held to apply to any diocese whose ecclesiastical authority has not agreed that such action is permissible.

I ought perhaps to say that all this is still under discussion by the various metropolitical authorities. Hong Kong is free, by the decision of the Church in China, to do what it wishes. The other three metropolitans have all given warm general support to these proposals, and are now exploring the various legal steps involved. There may well be modification of this or that provision of the constitution, in consequence of this.

But the general structure of the Council and its operation will doubtless remain pretty much what they now are. The Council does function, in many ways, as a regional church. Through the Council, various funds are expended (chiefly the annual gift of the American Church, of $50,000 from its "China Funds," for work among the Chinese of the Dispersion. The budget for this is drawn up by the South East Asia Council, approved by myself, and then is acted on by the American Church. In similar fashion, the budget for an executive officer for South East Asia is drawn up and supported, etc.). It is also a rudimentary planning agency, a meeting for the exchange of ideas and information, for mutual encouragement and support, and so on.

I think it is quite true to say that a constitution which would suit South East Asia would not necessarily be a blue print for other areas of the Church. Every area has its own problems, and it would be fool-hardy to imagine that we have somehow found a magical solution to them. But I grow more and more confident that something like the Council organization is needed in other areas of the world, and there-fore more and more grateful for the experimentation going on in South East Asia. How much of this constitution would be appropriate to the South Pacific area I do not know. But I think it is worth having a look at, particularly as we are increasingly involved with one another, in various common interests in the Pacific.

In sum, what the council helps to make possible is for the Church to act coherently and together in an area, even though provincial jurisdictions may cut across one another. The essence of the council plan, I suppose, is that it be so designed as not to interfere with essen-tial provincial functions and relationships, where they exist, nor to militate against the development of future provinces, but rather to permit (a) local, responsible leadership, (b) inter-provincial planning and life in a given area, and (c) a good balance of the local and regional on one hand and the wide unity of our Communion on the other.

A council is surely not a substitute for a province. In some cases it may be an incubator for provinces; in any case, it is a different kind and level of association. What modification of traditional provincial structure there might be in new provinces created in council areas, I do not know—South East Asia will doubtless be a laboratory for this. The clue at the moment, I think, is that any council maintain the utmost flexibility, thinking of itself simply as the Church in a *de facto* rather than a *de jure* association.

In the case of the South Pacific Council, I would hope that ways might be found for regular meetings, frequent enough to establish valid consultation and planning. I am sure that help will come if re-quested from the "parent" provinces to permit this to happen. It may well be that the South Pacific area is destined to become a single province in time—such would be sensible. But full provincial status involves many things which the constituent dioceses do not now have —regional homogeneity, size, capital resources, etc. In the meantime, I think all of us would be greatly aided by increased activity in the South Pacific Council. It would help particularly in major new projects of an inter-diocesan nature, such as our concerns for theological education, if partnership from other Anglican churches could be planned and sought by the Council as a whole, rather than piecemeal. I do not think of the Council as superseding the present relationships between Australia and New Zealand and their missionary dioceses. Rather I think it should supplement such relationships.

In so doing, it would ease the way, I am sure, for other churches to enter into much more responsible relationships with your dioceses than is now possible. As it is, any appeal for major participation runs the danger of seeming to say that Australia or New Zealand is not doing its job. But with a regularly functioning council, the parent provinces would themselves be involved from the start, and plans could rightly be regarded as being entirely inter-provincial from the outset.

These are general thoughts only. I hope we can develop them as time goes on. And I would hope that your council would feel, as the South East Asia Council does, that I am ready and anxious to be of any help I can in all this.

June, 1962.

To: The Bishops of the South Pacific Anglican Council

4. ACMS STRUCTURE

Introduction

IN THIS REPORT—more accurately a "working paper"—I make proposals for the next stage of development of the Advisory Council on Missionary Strategy. Although I take full and personal responsibility for the proposals, I want to acknowledge with great gratitude the counsel and help given by a number of colleagues. I cannot say that I have adopted every suggestion made to me, but each of them has been thoroughly explored and considered, and most of them, I believe, are reflected—or at least allowed for—in what follows.

To my thanks, let me add a few preliminary comments. First, these proposals are complementary to others which deal specifically with the Executive Officer's office and staff. It will be remembered that the Executive Officer is the servant of two bodies, with quite separate functions. In terms of my daily work, my time and energy is about equally divided between the two. Briefly, I have suggested the addition of two assistant officers to my staff, one to deal with ACMS affairs, the other with the general, inter-Anglican concerns which relate particularly to the Lambeth Consultative Body. This proposed enlargement of my own staff has no major bearing on the proposals which follow; it is merely a necessary step, I believe, to keep abreast of current activity.

The fact that the Executive Officer serves two bodies, and that separate groups of interests are involved, should however be kept in mind. A number of suggestions have been made, for example, which really relate to the Lambeth Consultative Body rather than the ACMS. The principle of having a single Executive Officer is, I believe, an important one, for it ensures that these two sets of interests will be kept together, in one frame of reference and one focus. But let us keep in mind that the ACMS has a particular mission and field of interest of its own, separate from although profoundly related to another broad field which is not specifically "missionary" in character.

Second, there have been—indeed there still are—some troubling misconceptions about my own office, and about the ACMS. I mention now four of these, because I think it is useful to clear away as much of the underbrush as possible before we tackle the main issues. The first has to do with the "authority" or "power" of the ACMS and its Executive Officer. As I wrote to Archbishop Fisher in 1959, when we were exploring all this, it is essential, in my view, that the Executive Officer have no constitutional or coercive authority. (This would apply also, I believe, to the ACMS, as a general principle.) My experience has confirmed me in this feeling that the usefulness of the Executive Officer's ministry is in large part derived precisely from the fact that he has no coercive authority. What was desired by the bishops at Lambeth, 1958, was a ministry that would excite co-operative response from our churches, establish communication, promote corporate action, remind all the separate parts of our Communion of our common life and its needs and opportunities. A structure of power and responsibility would only get in the way of this. These same thoughts apply to the ACMS, as its very title indicates. I shall have more to say about power a bit later on.

A second misapprehension is related to this—it has to do with money. I repeat again what I have said several times before, that I believe it would be a serious hindrance to the main purpose of my office if it were to be involved in either the raising or spending of missionary funds. I will return to this theme again, on the positive side.

Then, third, there has been a tendency to think of the ACMS as a means by which something is going to be done for somebody else. Those churches traditionally in a "sending" posture have been, understandably and inescapably, affected by this. Not everyone is yet aware, for example, that the ACMS *includes* the Church of England, and is not a non-English counterpart to the Overseas Council. The Church of England, of course, is assumed to be as fully and completely a part of the ACMS as any other Anglican church. But this misconception is not restricted to England, or the "sending" churches as a whole. The younger churches of our Communion have equally been tempted to think of the ACMS as a means whereby something is going to be done for them. At times, this has even been narrowed down to a feeling that the ACMS was, fundamentally, a way to gain greater American participation. Doubtless greater participation by PECUSA and other churches is highly desirable; but I need not point out that such misconceptions are untrue to the nature of the ACMS, and could be quite destructive of its fundamental purposes, if they were to linger.

Finally (and no doubt in large part because membership of the ACMS is by churches), there has been a measure of apprehension lest it represent a decision by the Anglican Communion against the "society" principle of missionary support. I have tried to make my own position on this perfectly clear; every church of our Communion must, and does, make its own decision in this matter, and arranges its affairs accordingly. Missionary societies, like boards or departments, exist to serve the church, not their own ends. Churches determine policy and strategy; how these are to be implemented is for each church to say; and to me, as Executive Officer, or the ACMS, there cannot be any one right way.

So much by way of clearing the ground. Now I should like to speak about the four main principles which seem to me to be the determining elements in any planning for the ACMS.

I: Principles

First, the ACMS cannot be understood except as an expression of the unity of the Anglican Communion. The nature of our Anglican unity, as all of us recognize, is unique. We are not a world church or a world denomination. We are not a confessional body. We are not an international or supra-national organization. So one could continue fencing off misunderstandings. What are we?

We are, in the familiar phrases of the 1930 Lambeth Conference (Res. 49)

> . . . Fellowship, within the One Holy Catholic and Apostolic Church, of those duly constituted Dioceses, Provinces or Regional Churches in communion with the See of Canterbury, which have the following characteristics in common:

(a) they uphold and propagate the Catholic and Apostolic faith and order as they are generally set forth in the Book of Common Prayer as authorized in their several Churches;

(b) they are particular or national Churches, and, as such, promote within each of their territories a national expression of Christian faith, life and worship; and

(c) they are bound together not by a central legislative and executive authority, but by mutual loyalty sustained through the common counsel of the Bishops in conference.

The Encyclical Letter of the same year uses these vivid words: "This Communion is a commonwealth of Churches without a central constitution: it is a federation without a federal government. It has come into existence without any deliberate policy. . . ." And Archbishop Temple wrote a superb gloss on those words when, in his Primary Visitation Charge as Archbishop of York, he spoke about our Communion having been "guided by the Holy Spirit, as we believe—though it has never at any moment been consciously decided—to go forward in a unity which relies absolutely and completely on the mutual loyalty of the several parts. There is no other bond." (I am indebted to Canon Max Warren for this quotation from Temple.)

It grows indeed progressively more difficult to define the Anglican Communion because of the ever-widening circle of full communion which has knit together with us Christians of other historical backgrounds than our own. We find this in itself not unpleasing. For we are a federation of churches; and therefore our unity is both deeper and more delicate than can be given any simple cultural or confessional or structural expression. It is nonetheless real for all of that; but it requires constant and careful examination of all that we do together, to be sure that what we do is appropriate to our free association, our full communion, and our unity in diversity.

This is the positive side of what I said before about power. Whatever we do must be done—if we are to be true to ourselves—by the initiative of the separate churches. The principle of delegated authority, of responsibility committed to some central, inter-church body, is always a dangerous one for us. I do not say that we should never accept that principle. I only say that the slower way, of winning the free and eager consent of the brotherhood, is almost always the desirable way for us. Thus the Executive Officer, in my opinion, should not become either agent or victim of a power structure. This has nothing to do with his title, which derives simply from the fact that he is the person designated to carry out whatever his two corporate employers decide. But it is a determining factor in the nature of his work, and equally so in that of the ACMS.

Second, the ACMS is more accurately understood as a process of continuous consultation than as an executive or administrative body. The word "Advisory" is of course the key here. The ACMS itself, as well as the earlier committees and movements which led to it, was born out of an urgent sense of need for such consultation as would make it possible for us better to share one another's burdens. The emphasis lay, and lies, on *consultation.*

There may well be common projects which ought be undertaken by the ACMS or some other central body; indeed, I am sure there should be such, and that we shall progressively explore them. But the fundamental purpose of the ACMS is not to administer, but to consult—to bring churches together, to evaluate priorities, to learn from one another and share with one another, to explore, advise, recommend courses of action which our separate churches and their various agencies can then undertake.

Thus, in our planning, we are bound to look hardest at this process of consultation. At the moment, such consultation is very difficult, and must necessarily be carried out, for the most part, through my own correspondence and personal visits. This is clearly not satisfactory; all that one can say about it is that it was the only possible beginning. But I am sure that the basic test of any proposal for the ACMS must be whether or not it furthers consultation, primarily (but not exclusively) among the Anglican churches.

Third, Anglican consultation must always be entirely mutual, and in full and responsible partnership. No two Anglican churches are alike, nor are their cultures. It would be foolish to try to equate them. But it would be equally foolish to think of some as "sending" or "giving," and others as "receiving." I am sure this point does not need much elaboration. Each Anglican church has resources; each has needs. Each has something to teach; each has something to learn. Each should give what it has; each stands to gain by what others give.

I am sure that this is the right perspective within which to view the ACMS. It is a difficult principle to fulfill. Much of what the ACMS— and my own office—has to deal with are certain kinds of needs, for personnel and materiel, which are for the most part needs of certain churches which other churches can meet. But we have surely grown out of this conception of mission as a one-way street. One of the most critically important matters before us, at this stage in history, is precisely to ask what younger churches have to give to older ones, and to find the ways in which the church which feels that it has nothing to give can discover what in fact it does have to give. The charge of "confessionalism," so often levelled against the older churches of the West, is frequently, I suspect, only a disguise for confusion and uncertainty within younger churches as to their own contribution to the life of the Body. To end this uncertainty, and to find ways for the buoyant and resilient participation of all our churches in our common life, is a matter of very great urgency indeed.

Therefore, any proposals for the ACMS must reflect a sense of complete brotherhood, and of eagerness to give and receive according as each has resources and needs.

Finally, relationships between churches are "total" relationships. The bond which unites us is that of "full communion." If this has any more than a merely ceremonial meaning, it signifies that we are fully involved with one another, within the unity of Christ's Body; that we share one another's full life and fortune and mission; that we are fully committed to one another, in every aspect of life.

Within our Communion, at this stage, we are not well organized, to express this broad and mutual commitment. It finds its fullest expression at a Lambeth Conference, I suppose, or at an Anglican Congress. In the time between such summits, we tend to divide our relationships into two categories—those which are technically "missionary," which are the concern of the ACMS, and those more broadly inter-Anglican in character, which fall to the Lambeth Consultative Body. As I noted above, I think it is important that the Executive Officer be fully responsible and related to both these bodies. In fact this is so; and thus I am obliged to be constantly reminded of this breadth of total relationship.

The time may come when we shall want to reconsider the fundamental structure of both the ACMS and the Lambeth Consultative Body, and raise the question as to whether the two ought not really to become one body. I am not entirely persuaded that they should; and in any case, this is not a decision which can be contemplated in these present proposals. But the principle of unity which underlies the question is an important one, and has its bearing on our thought about the ACMS.

Inter-church relationships can never be limited simply to questions of recruiting and supporting missionaries, or meeting financial needs. The ACMS must be, by the very nature of these relationships, concerned with far more than these matters. Every element of common life—exchange, communication, literature, technical skills—must be part of the business of the ACMS; and our organization and procedures must reflect this breadth.

Those seem to me to be the four cardinal principles which must determine our practical proposals. They are not the only ones, I am sure; but I am sure that they are the critical and decisive ones. Now let me turn to consider the practical necessities.

II: Practical Necessities

Let me now list what seem to me the six most important practical necessities which must be met, if the foregoing principles are to be effectively realized.

First, there must be clear access to the decision-making elements in each of the churches. In our present structure, this is met in part by the provision that the ACMS itself shall be composed of the Metropolitans of the Anglican Communion, or their appointed deputies. This guarantees consultation at the highest level, and the maximum amount of responsibility in that consultation. There are clearly very great practical difficulties, however, if we are to look for more extensive consultation. Metropolitans cannot be expected to meet frequently, nor to be able to devote the time and energy required to technical matters. But if a technical group is added to our structure, then we must think carefully about the relationship of that group to the responsible, decision-making bodies. This necessity will have its bearing on the practical proposals I shall make.

Second, our planning procedures must be such as to nourish and develop the dialogue and partnership implicit in consultation. All planning, in my thought, ought to be as fully shared as possible. This means not simply co-operative planning between two churches, say, who are engaged in a common task. The whole of our Communion is involved in what each of us does; and this means that, as far as possible, planning should be shared with all and understood by all. This present meeting is the first real opportunity we have had, in my time, to do this, although in more limited terms, the Cuernavaca Consultation, and the Latin American Report, gave us some experience. We need a great deal of thought and experiment in this area. The suggestion is often made that a central planning agency is the way for us to do this. I am not myself sure that this is so—largely because I resist centralization, but also because I think there is still so much to be learned about the very process of planning itself. But this is a necessity to be met.

Third, relationships between any central officer or body and the churches themselves must be direct, strong and clear. At present, my official relationships are always with the Primates and Metropolitans themselves. I have a very carefully organized list of correspondents, and a full protocol of relationships, within which I work. This is as it should be. But it does not meet the needs of an effective, group consultative process. This point has been raised by nearly every adviser, and it is an important one. What is at stake here is not simply clear and good relationships with churches. It is rather relationships with a region and a culture which are at stake, for the sake of understanding and planning.

Fourth, for effective consultation we require far more information than is now available. This is involved, of course, in the two preceding necessities. But it is worth being set out as a point in itself. One reason why we know so little about one another is that we have almost no useful channels of communication. But a deeper reason is that we often do not know very much about ourselves, and therefore have relatively little to communicate. Therefore there is a notable importance to study, both self-study and also common study; and our structure and procedures should encourage this and make it possible.

Fifth, communication is the lifeblood of the Anglican Communion. By "communication" I mean many things, of course. First, the circulation of ideas and information through the written word. I have begun some simple experiments in this, as in the establishment of "consultants" or in the circulation of "Exchange" and "Compasrose." But these are only beginnings, and need themselves to be re-studied, as well as new possibilities explored. But communication also means letters, personal visits, books, visual aids, meetings, and a host of other instruments.

Sixth, there must be meetings, at intervals appropriate to each level of corporate life. I am entirely sympathetic with the overloaded calendars of our times. I am also aware of the expense involved, whenever any meeting is planned of an inter-Anglican nature. There is no novelty about these difficulties, nor are they an answer to anything, in themselves. We must be prepared to expect, pay for, and reserve ourselves for sufficient opportunities for that appropriate consultation needed to express and fulfill our unity.

Those seem to me to be the six practical necessities which must be met by any proposals, if the proposals are to be responsive to our fundamental principles. Now let me turn, finally, to the practical proposals themselves which I hope will inform our discussion.

III: Specific Proposals

1. *Executive Officer:* I have, in a separate paper, urged that this office be continued (with any desired change in title); that the principle of a single officer responsible for both ACMS and Lambeth Consultative

Body be maintained; that he be given two principal assistants, respectively for missionary affairs and general inter-Anglican and ecumenical affairs; and that this office continue to be supported proportionately by all the churches of the Anglican Communion.

2. *ACMS:* This Council, consisting now of 37 members, is established by the Lambeth Conference, and presumably no change in its structure can be effected until the next meeting of the Conference. In substance, it includes the Metropolitans of the Anglican Communion. However, a study of its structure, and the basis of representation, and its relationship to the Lambeth Consultative Body, might well be continued, with a view to making specific proposals to the next Lambeth Conference.

3. *Executive Group:* It is clear to me that we need a smaller, but responsible, group which could meet at least at intervals of 18–24 months. I envisage such a group as between 7 and 12 members in size; appointed by the Advisory Council (probably through the Chairman or the Executive Officer); not necessarily representative of particular churches; chosen to represent general aspects and ministries of the church rather than areas or special interests; lay or clerical in character, as required. Such a group would be subordinate to the Advisory Council and advisory to the Executive Officer. Their primary function would be consultation. They would all be people of other interests and responsibilities, so that this duty was an additional, part-time one. Their function would be to plan research, advise about the development and assignment of responsibilities, have cognizance and oversight of new missionary experiments, and in general to serve as a working party for the ACMS. They would need travel expenses, and doubtless some other allowances for special projects.

4. *Regional Officers:* I am sure of the necessity for at least five regional officers, whose function it would be to represent the Executive Officer and the ACMS in those areas where the planning and development of new and critical missionary work was in the forefront. In my view, such officers are needed now in (a) Latin America, (b) East Asia, (c) the South Pacific, (d) Africa and (e) India and the Middle East. This would be the minimum number required. These men would be extensions of the Executive Officer in the field, responsible to him for the planning and execution of projects, for general liaison and communication with the areas concerned, and as a group of companions, indeed of alter egos, to him in general. At a minimum, they should be devoted at least half-time to this duty, although it is possible that each of them might also serve some other purpose in his area. Their salary, allow-

ances, and travel expenses should be enough to permit them not to be an undue charge on the church of their locality, and to permit at least an annual conference with the Executive Officer.

5. *Consultants:* I think this system is worth continued exploration. I am not satisfied that we are yet eliciting the correct appointments, in every case. But it seems to me essential to establish a group in every Anglican church, primarily for advisory and consultative purposes, and to keep in touch with one another. This group could be as large as the churches provide, and it need not meet save perhaps at times—at a Lambeth Conference or an Anglican Congress—when the household is generally gathered anyway.

6. *Costs:* Clearly, the Executive Officer and his immediate staff should be a proportionate charge on all the churches of our Communion. The same argument, I believe, should apply to the costs of the regional officers, although it would not seem inappropriate to suggest that some of them, at least, might be supported by particular churches or societies, as the case might be. The expenses of the executive group could perhaps be borne by separate churches again, depending on who they were. My principle is to keep any central budgets as small as possible, because every central budget, proportionately divided, becomes a charge on every church, many of which cannot really afford it without subsidy. But there should be enough of a central budget to guarantee that the work is done, and that there is no uncertainty about lines of responsibility and communication.

7. *Responsibility:* The basic channel of responsibility and authority, in the Anglican Communion, is to the agreed collective action of our constituent churches. In this present case, that collective authority is represented by the ACMS. I am responsible to it; and therefore, in everything that I do as the Executive Officer, I am responsible to the 18 churches. I believe that the regional officers should be, in the first instance, related directly to the Executive Officer, since they are essentially extensions of him. As Executive Officer, he is also Executive Officer of his executive group, for they are an extension of the ACMS.

8. *Planning:* I am not convinced yet that we need a central planning agency. What we do need is to do our own experimenting, church by church—indeed greatly to extend it—and to maintain constant exchange and communication in this area.

9. *Study Programs:* It is essential, if the corporate life and witness of our Communion is to be maintained, that there be concerted, planned common study of the central problems the churches face in nearly all societies. Examples of such would be the Church and Urban Society,

the Family and Marriage Discipline, Religious Freedom and the like. Such programs for study should be planned so as to engage as many churches as possible; they should be developed by the ACMS in conjunction with available research and planning facilities as our churches provide; they should be, as far as possible, directed toward the needs and program of the next Lambeth Conference; they should be planned with careful consideration of the place and role of St. Augustine's College, Canterbury, St. George's College, Jerusalem, and other potential centers for study and research.

10. *Communication:* I am reluctantly obliged to feel that there must be added, in the Executive Officer's structure, some simple but effective scheme for disseminating information to provincial and diocesan periodicals, to boards, departments, societies, and to the churches generally. This would not duplicate existing information agencies. Doubtless they would be used far more than they are. But there is need to provide additional services to them, in order to be sure that current and sensible information is circulated.

11. *Central Funds:* As indicated above, I am sure that neither the ACMS nor the Executive Officer should be in a position of responsibility for administering missionary or other funds, beyond what are needed for the operation itself. On the other hand, it is abundantly clear that we need a very great enlargement of the capital funds available for the development of younger churches and new frontiers. A separate paper will discuss these funds. Suffice it to say here that, if there is to be inter-Anglican action in this respect, I believe that a separate administrative body should be established for this purpose.

12. *Ecumenical relationships:* The danger of any inter-Anglican ministry is that it may be interpreted as "confessionalism," or the establishment of a world denomination, or the like. Such a development would be quite untrue to our own Anglican nature, and a disservice to ecumenical life. Our ecumenical relations should remain basically the responsibility and function of each individual church. It is, however, inescapable that the ACMS and its officers will be involved, appropriately, with ecumenical agencies. In such matters as missionary planning and consultation, this is highly desirable. It is essential, I am sure, that in the sphere of action, the dynamics of the Anglican Communion remain where they are—in the constituent churches.

STEPHEN F. BAYNE, JR.

II.

The Life of the Anglican Communion

5. WITNESS, MISSION, UNITY*

THIS IS TRULY a "day which the Lord hath made," and I rejoice at the honor of being part of it. Many messages have come and will come to you from your brother Churches within the Anglican household—most of all from the Archbishop of Canterbury, who is the center of our Anglican unity. I would only want to say to you that there is none, among all the millions of our brotherhood, who would not wish to say to you the Lord be with you, and pray that He Who is the Way may guide you boldly and steadily in the Way. Now, in fullest and most responsible freedom, this Church takes its place among its brothers, to give and teach and comfort and share with all that a vigorous and powerful nation has at its command. May God give you confidence and boldness in this new life. This is the thankful and brotherly prayer of every Anglican the world around.

For myself, I can wish no better thing for this Synod and your Church than the profound and disturbing and ennobling words of Christ to the disciples, "Ye have not chosen me, but I have chosen you and ordained you, that ye should go and bring forth fruit, and that your fruit should remain" (John 15:16).

They occur in the Gospel for St. Barnabas' Day, the day on which I was myself ordained priest and then consecrated bishop; and they have been a steadfast guide to me for many years. By them our Lord puts all our concerns as churchmen into their right order, for He reminds us that the Church is not ours but His; that the initiative in

---

* Sermon preached at the First Synod of the Church of England in Australia, St. Andrew's Cathedral, Sydney, N.S.W., May 8, 1962.

salvation is His; that Mission is His; that the Ministry is His; that the life and witness of the Church and her essential strength, her teachings, her love, her power and grace—all are His, and not ours at all.

How easy it is for us to forget this! We of the clergy forget it, engrossed as we are in the duties and cares of our ministry—and suddenly we awaken and find that we have been trapped into acting as if we were the masters of His saving Body and the merchants of His love; and then we are ashamed indeed, but still there lingers a fear that if we do not protect Christ from His enemies and even His friends, He will be defenseless; and then first thing we know, we are up to our old tricks again, using the Church, using the Bible which is at the heart of the Church, to support what *we* think right, not content to be chosen and sent by Him.

The laity forget it, for to us in the laity, the Church seems always to be something which depends for its very existence on our loyal support and participation. Indeed, to all of us, there is a little sense of grievance in our response to His words "Ye have not chosen me." We *have* chosen Him. In the midst of an unbelieving and skeptical world, who but we have chosen Him in our devotion to Him and the Church? We have given up many things to make that choice and to it we have given our loyalty and our hearts—what does He mean that we have not chosen Him?

So we *have* given much. But always it has been given in response to His choice. No priest is a priest very long before he understands this about his own vocation—that what seemed to him to be his own choice was really only an answer, long-delayed and only imperfectly given, to a call that began when he was born. And does any layman, when he thinks deeply about his own life, not marvel at the way God has been leading him over long years, leading him in his life and his job, leading him, it may be, to love and marriage and children, leading him in his discipleship? And only dimly and slowly do we come at length to see the choice was God's at the first and God's all the way through—that He had brought us into existence as an act of His love, had richly blessed us and guarded us and given us all we needed to be what He created us to be! "Ye have not chosen me, but I have chosen you and ordained you . . ."

This is the depth of Christian life, to know the priority of God and to accept His choice of us and obediently and gladly to follow. And it is precisely this which I wish most for the Church of Australia, at this gigantic door which now opens before you. It is a door into a new land, where landmarks are unfamiliar, where you do not know the way. There will be many temptations to retreat, or to find good reason for not entering what lies ahead. But I pray that the constant remembrance of God's choice may strengthen and arm you, that the Church may go forward in peace and unity and obedience.

What will the future ask of the Church in Australia? I think three great qualities. First, powerful and relevant witness to Christ, in the soul of the nation. Second, deep and costly brotherhood in mission with the nations and churches with which we share the narrow world. Third, unity within our own household and nation. *Witness, Mission, Unity* . . . these are the gifts.

Not one of these qualities comes except as the choice and gift of Christ. We do not choose them: He chooses us and gives us what we need to accept His choice.

How else can we bear witness to Him, in all the perplexities of our society, except that we let Him lead us and we confidently follow Him? If the choice is not His, then all we seem to offer, all we can offer to our nation is ourselves. And people caught in all the compromises and confusions of a secularized society need more than a mirror of themselves to save them. And the basic question about the Church in our time is whether it *is* anything more than a mirror of society, a mirror in a valuable antique frame, no doubt, but still telling us only what we ourselves already know.

A church or a people who feel that *they* have chosen Christ are in danger of feeling that they possess Him. But He will not be possessed. He will not be patronized by anybody. He will slip out of our grasp, and leave us alone with ourselves, talking to ourselves, talking about ourselves, talking with increasing shallowness and hopelessness about ourselves, until the world outside wonders what possible good this silly club with its mysterious language could bring.

I am sure that Australia does not need any more religious clubs. Australia needs what my own nation needs, or any nation needs—it needs to learn how to be master of its possessions. People say about your nation what they say about mine, that we are "materialistic." And what they usually mean is that we spend much time with the things of this earth—growing and mining and making and building and buying and selling. Very well, let this be said. We are both nations determined to build a society which is fit for big, free people, a society with decency and dignity and liberty in its tissues; and you do not build a society like that out of words or sermons or wistful longings—you build it out of the created things of the earth, the material things. When men and women are engaged in such a task, what they need is to be helped to keep some sense of proportion and direction about their task, so they do not get trapped in their work and captured and possessed by their possessions.

When we are trapped like that, then we are "materialistic," we become a people who cannot see beyond the endless cycle of making and buying and selling and consuming, who even do not believe that there *is* anything beyond that endless cycle. Only the perpendicular vision of God will save us from this—the continual reminder of God and His judgment. And this is the Church's witness and her task, to be the soul and conscience of a nation.

If the Church is to be this, then she must do two things. First, she must talk about real problems—exactly the problems of a "material" society. Second, she must bring to that society a wisdom greater than her own. If she talks about God as if He spent most of His life in church, and was unconcerned with what man must spend most of his life being concerned with, she is no use to a society like ours. Nor is she any good for us if she only tells us, in sanctified terms, what we already know. Christ is not a clergyman who needs to be sheltered from the facts of life. He stands ever in the midst of the world of men and women at work, and says to us "I have chosen you." He is the worker; He is in the work; it was by Him that all these things were made; He is no stranger to our struggle for a decent society. But to set justice in it, to bring order to it and make room in it for the great hopes and dreams of men—this is His chief business. And therefore it is ours, because He has chosen us.

As with our witness, so with Mission. The Church has no mission of its own. All we can have by ourselves is a club or a debating society; and our only hope, left to ourselves, is to win as many members for our own club and away from other clubs as we can. And whatever this is, it is not Mission.

Mission belongs to God. The Mission was His from the beginning; it is His; it will always be His. He has His purposes from the foundation of the world, and He means to fulfill them; and the only part the Church has in this is obedience—a share in the eternal and life-giving obedience of the Son of God. "Ye have not chosen me, but I have chosen you . . ."

If we fail in obedience, if we do not follow Christ in His ceaseless mission and invasion of the world, we will not defeat God, we will only defeat ourselves. God is able of these stones to raise up children unto Abraham. Isaiah said that God "shaves with a hired razor." And the most terrible judgment on the Church comes when God leaves us to our own devices because He is tired of waiting for our obedience—leaves us to be the domestic chaplains to a comfortable secular world—and goes Himself into the wilderness of human need and injustice and pain.

This judgment does come on churches and on nations, when they forget that God is in command, that He does the choosing. Therefore, the first question churchmen must ask themselves about their mission is not where we would like to go or what we would like to say, in order to perpetuate our own image—the first question is where God is going and what He is saying and doing. The first requirement of mission, in other words, is to read the signs of the times, to discern as best we can the meaning and direction of the history through which we are living.

And here one thing must be said at once. Australia stands today in the heart of all the turbulent history of the Pacific world and of Southeast Asia. Neither her national destiny nor the mission of her church can be found by turning eyes and thoughts backward nor away from this region. It is exactly in *this* confused arena of conflicting purposes and agonizing needs that both the nation and the church stand. And God is likewise at work in this same arena—creating, revealing, redeeming, judging. What is He doing? What are His purposes in this time, in this place? This is the question which will determine mission for the Australian Church, in the first instance.

It is easy to oversimplify both the question and the answer. Precisely because Southeast Asia is the present frontier of the sharpest conflict between two vigorous and aggressive ideologies, it is tempting to interpret the Church's mission in those terms alone—to see the confrontation merely as one of "Christianity and Communism" or to interpret the Church's mission simply as one of supporting the Western democratic states in their fight for survival. I do not question that duty. There is no more imperative political necessity in our time than the unity of the great democratic powers in the Pacific world.

But this does not define the mission of the Church. It only defines the world within which God is at work. Mission goes beyond frontiers precisely as God does. He is not the property of the Western democratic nations. We are His property, if our religious professions mean anything. Therefore our mission always crosses the passing political frontiers, into the far more perplexing area where political alignments are still being debated, where the primary questions are not whose side one chooses, but hunger and sickness and the need for work fit for men to do and a life fit for the children of God to live.

New nations crowding to be born, needing every skill and encouragement older brothers can give them, needing most of all the love and hope God holds out to them—these are our neighbors, and here is where our mission begins for it is here that God is at work.

But mission does not end here, for the world is one and very narrow, and there is no nation anywhere, even our own, which does not need to know that God is at work in it, and how He works. But always, at home or abroad, the heart of mission is our obedience to Him Whose mission it is. If we ever let ourselves conceive of our mission as a way of extending *our* influence, or spreading some pet point of view of our own, then we are not the Church but the very opposite of the Church—we are people pretending that God is our captive. What is it He has chosen us to say and be, in our world, among our brothers?

And where will the gift of unity come from, except from Him? As this nation has moved steadily forward into unity, trustingly putting aside old fears and ignorances that once divided it, so does it call—so does God call—this Church to a new unity within itself and with its nation. The great dream of one Church, single and whole, which shall be in truth the church of a nation, is the determining dream and inheritance of Anglicans everywhere in the world. It is our supreme inheritance from our mother Church of England; it has found its way in the hearts and lives of millions of Anglicans in every continent and race the world around; it is the dream which lies behind the new constitution and the new, responsible national identity we celebrate so thankfully today; it is the dream which drives us relentlessly forward into the profound ecumenical engagement with our fellow Christians in this land as in every land.

But unity is not made by constitutions. All that a constitution can do is make unity possible. If the gift itself is to come—if unity is to be achieved—it must be *chosen* and born in the wills of brothers who have compacted together to share their whole life, at any cost, come what may, and who will not be any longer divided. What the constitution accomplishes is up to the church whose creature it is.

And the hunger and fierce determination to win this deeper unity is the gift of the Lord again, to those who will accept it. Unity is not an armistice devised by men; it is not a vacuum of convictions; it is not a smooth porridge composed of things nobody cares about very much; it is not a grudging agreement to abide by common decisions as long as they do not cost very much. Unity comes not from shallow people thinking alike but from free people acting together. The constitution makes that action possible. No constitution can supply the *will* to act together; that will is the response we make to Christ's choice of us.

How often the Church has been torn apart by opinions, by honest convictions, with conscientious men ranged on either side, feeling that even at the cost of brotherhood, what each sees to be right must be maintained inviolate. And how often afterwards, when we look back on that history, we see how wide of the mark both sides were and how terribly irrelevant and petty the whole division was! But we do not come to this wisdom by simply abdicating our convictions. Rather we are led to it by the Lord who gently guides and teaches us as we are prepared to be quiet and to be taught, and prepared at all costs to keep the brotherhood inviolate.

For example, four hundred years ago the Church was profoundly torn by such words as Sacrifice, Offering, Priesthood. Because sinful men had abused them and what they stand for, others—no less sinful, no less honest in their convictions—stood against them, and our fore-fathers had to take sides, and they did, and the Prayer Book to this day bears the marks of that division, so careful as it is to leave room at the Lord's Table for men on both sides.

I suppose that now, in our time, we can think of this ancient and almost-forgotten quarrel with amazement that once it was so bitter. What has happened over the years? Have those who stood for minis-terial, offering priesthood finally been ejected, defeated? Have those who fought for the unique and unrepeatable sacrifice of Christ been ejected, defeated?

No such thing. What has happened is that God, through the Church's unwavering will to stay together, through her quiet, obedient study of the Scriptures, has led both sides to see that neither was right, in full perspective—to see that both had been talking as if Christ were dead, or absent from His Church—to see that both sides had forgotten that He was still in command, choosing whom He would to speak and act for Him, as He intended that they should.

The Sacrifice was indeed once offered, by Him. It could never be offered again, by any earthly priest. But when we remembered this, we also remembered that He was the only Priest the Church had ever had; that His Offering was an act of His, not of ours; that the Sacrifice was not something buried in antiquity but an eternal fact about Christ, which endured as long as He endured, which had to be accepted and fulfilled in every soul to the end of time, if God was not Himself to be defeated by His creation. And suddenly, with the renewed sight and thought of Christ, the Lord of the Church, the differences and tensions melted away.

The evangelical, so rightly insistent that Christ was not the victim of an earthly priesthood, and the catholic, so rightly insistent that Christ was not a captive of time but rather the creator and master of it—both suddenly came to see how foolishly they had forgotten His priority in all this and how much they had needed gently and lovingly to be recalled to it; and unity came to the Church because it had remembered Him and His choosing, and put Him first again. And He led us and leads us, by the Spirit, into all truth, as we are ready to accept His choosing and find our peace and unity in Him. But the will for that comes from Him, not from any easy compromise of ours.

So it will ever be with us. We must make our own choices, for we are creatures of time and space and not dolls to be manipulated by God. But when we make our choices, we will—if we are ready to—see that really He is doing the choosing all the time. We will choose our officers and make our laws and write our liturgies. But unity will not come because we choose safe men, or write custard liturgies or laws which offend nobody because they really say nothing and cost nothing. Unity will only come when we bring all our separate convictions together in a common obedience to Him who is the Lord and the Minister—the only Minister—of the Church, who chooses us all unworthy as we are.

If He is not the Primate of this Church, then there is no primacy that matters and no center around which the brotherhood can gather. If He is not the Shepherd, then there is no episcopate. If He is not the Priest, then there is no Word and no Sacrament. But precisely because He is all these, then there is order and offering and the Word. He governs, He is the Shepherd, He is the obedient Minister and Servant, and He chooses us to go this way with Him, and only in Him; and only if we are obedient to His choosing, is there peace and unity for us.

6. ESTABLISHMENT*

I CANNOT IMAGINE anything less important than my views about the establishment or disestablishment of the Church of England, so I will not display them. I am not sure I have any, as a matter of fact, as far as the main issue goes. But I have opinions about all kinds of related issues, even as most Anglicans.

* From *Anglican World,* Jan.-Feb. 1963.

Like most Anglicans, I belong to a church which owes its existence to the Church of England and has drawn its central attitudes, ideas, feeling (as well as its very life) from that mother church. Therefore I am what I am in part because the Church of England is what it is (or was what it was). On the other hand, like most Anglicans, I belong to a church which is not established, not the state church nor the national church of a country. Only in England does this unique relationship exist. The seventeen other churches of our Communion, old and young, large and small, are all private and voluntary associations, taking their unprivileged place in their plural religious societies. Therefore, as a child of a younger church, I look at establishment from outside it. And from this double vantage point, some things can be seen which I think are worth seeing.

Let me take three of the central issues of church life—its leadership, its unity, its mission to its own society. First, leadership: In the Church of England, the choice of its leadership is in the hands of the Queen, acting through her Prime Minister. Archbishops and bishops and most other major ecclesiastical figures are selected, essentially, by the political leader of the country. To some—within as well as outside of the Church of England—this seems monstrous. They say that no matter how logical the system may once have been, in days when the membership of church and state were virtually identical, it makes no sense now. How much better it is, they say, when the church can choose its own leaders, acting through its own synods, determining its own fundamental directions through the officers it wishes to select.

It is a platitude, of course, to say that the system is illogical but that it works. It does work, as generations of superb leadership can testify. But an outsider can say, fairly and modestly, that like any other system, it works within its own conditions. Given certain values, purposes, needs, aims, a system "works" in proportion as it meets those desired or necessary ends. But they are not necessarily the only ends.

I remember my own bishoping vividly and with great thanksgiving. Anything less like the appointment of an English bishop I cannot imagine. I was elected, as are all American bishops, by the clergy and laity of the diocese, in an open meeting, chosen from among half a dozen nominees—chosen in fact, without my permission or even knowledge—and confronted by the arbitrary decision of a democratic assembly. I doubt if any one of the fourscore priests or two hundred-odd laymen and women who chose me knew as much about me as would be known about my English opposite number, nor was there much of the dispassionate statesmanship which can function so thoughtfully in the

English scene. The rank and file of a diocese are not statesmen, nor passionless; they may indeed be very limited in their information and evaluation.

Can this system be defended as so much more logical than the British one? I doubt it. But it works, within its own conditions. For the needs, the values, the ends to be served are doubtless quite different from those in England, and are better served in the American scene, in the American way. All the tangible and intangible qualities of the episcopate in America—its intimacy with the family of a small diocese, the responsible and personal partnership, the sense of a common lot and a common household—all these both determine and grow out of the American conditions. It would be impossible for a diocesan bishop in the Church of England to have anything like the same relationship with his great numbers of clergy and lay people as is taken for granted of an American bishop. And contrariwise, when an American bishop tries to act like an English bishop, he simply sounds stuffy.

This is not at all to compare bishops, or the ideal of the episcopate. The episcopate itself is not at stake. I am talking about the particular form of the ministry of the bishop, which is different in different cultures, and requires different instrumentalities. If the Church of England wanted American-type bishops (which I am sure they do not) they would have to establish about three times as many dioceses or more; they would have to develop a whole tradition of diocesan synodical life; they would have to train an entire generation of clergy and lay people into an entirely new relationship with their bishop; they would have, in other words, substantially to change the whole picture of the episcopate and the church with which they are familiar. And precisely as great a convulsion would be necessary on the American side, if a corresponding change were sought.

Again I say, I am neither making a comparison nor pleading for or against such a change. I am simply saying, to the protagonist of disestablishment as the source of all blessing, that he must have much more than mere disestablishment to get what he wants. On the other side, those who have establishment had better learn to appreciate what they do have. Neither establishment nor disestablishment alone really gets to the heart of the matter. It is the whole setting and pattern of the church, particularly of the episcopate, which is at stake. And these things are not put on and off like an overcoat.

A second issue, and one which I have written about before, is that of the unity of the church. The Church of England, alone among the churches of the Anglican Communion, has its unity given to it. That unity is given from outside. It is given by the establishment of the church, by the formal identity of the church and the nation. The Church of England does not need to be held together by the voluntary loyalty of its members. It is not held together by their support or their attendance or their contributions. It is held together by the law of the land, and by the land itself.

This is not an unmixed blessing. But it has succeeded in giving to the Church of England—and in turn, to all the rest of the churches of our Communion—an extraordinary liberality of spirit and gentleness of mind, which tolerates wide differences of opinion and variations in theological outlook, within the working unity of the Catholic church of the land. To me at any rate, this is one of the most precious of all gifts. And I rejoice to find it transplanted—transplanted to North America, to Japan, to Central Africa, to Brazil, to any other part of the world you can mention. It was given to the Church of England, because of its hopes and necessities as a national church, to discover a profound secret of unity—that the unity of the church does not consist of people thinking alike but in people acting together.

For all this I give the most devout thanks, along with a very great multitude of others. But it is also instructive to look at the other side of this. I said that the Church of England alone does not have to fight for its own unity. Every other Anglican church does. In the younger churches, there is nothing which can give us unity except our own voluntary determination to achieve it. Where the Church of England can exist, tolerating the most extraordinary extremes of partisan thought and expression, no other Anglican church can. We younger churchmen have had to learn, by sometimes bitter experience, that the unity of Anglicanism is not simply an accidental, geographical collocation of parishes or outrageously different opinions. True Anglican unity is not a geographical accident, nor is it a legal requirement.

True unity is found only within the soul of an individual Christian himself. He is the one who must know and accept and love the great gifts of both the Catholic and continuous life of the Church, and also its reformed, inquiring, protesting, sometimes even rebellious inheritance. He must accept and welcome these tensions; he must live out his discipleship within them. The battlefield is not between dioceses or parishes. The battlefield is in the soul of the individual worshipper. The Prayer Book is the same for all men. There is one priesthood and one sacramental structure, which all must share. No man can opt out of the Prayer Book or pick and choose from it, with all its marvellous and delicate balance of the full spectrum of many centuries of Christian experience.

I have written about this before, because it is one of the major instances of the necessity for humble and brotherly dialogue within the Anglican Communion. At the moment, I want simply to point a moral again—that neither establishment nor disestablishment really has much to do with this issue now. Establishment originally created the conditions which produced an insight into unity of the greatest possible consequence. Disestablishment cannot now destroy that insight. Our Anglican understanding of unity has long since outgrown the historical accident which first produced it. Now it stands on its own feet, and no mere change of circumstance will either create it or destroy it. It must be sought for itself, and fought for itself, and won for itself alone.

Finally, let me think a bit about the third issue—that of the church's mission to its own society. Here I think the younger churches of the Anglican Communion envy the establishment of the Church of England with all their hearts. There is no other Anglican church in the world which has the same responsible relationship with its own nation as has the Church of England. Establishment gives to the nation a solid rooting in the Christian tradition. Establishment gives to the church a responsibility to the nation which it cannot escape. Establishment builds into the lives of generations of people in England—enemies of the church as well as friends of it—the blessing of a constant, watchful, loving concern which is unparalleled anywhere else in the Anglican Communion.

It is all very well to say that the Church of England often does not live up to this, nor does the nation either. You cannot wave away the all-too-solid facts of the lack of money and the lack of men which make the responsibility of the Church of England almost more than any church could possibly bear. Despite those limitations, the fact remains that there is not a foot of land in England which is not the direct, constitutional responsibility of a priest; there is not a person in England, no matter what his faith or lack of faith, who is not a charge on the responsibility of the congregation and its pastor; there is not a question which confronts any community in England, which has its proper Christian implications, which is outside the scope of concern and of response by the church.

It is perhaps needless to point out that this quality of national responsibility is bred into all of us who are even the remotest children of the Church of England. Even in secularized America a "parish" is still a geographical term, and when a man is instituted into a parish, he must accept the cure of souls for a whole community. But actually this is in large part a fiction, and we know it. Indeed the problem of all the younger Anglican churches is how to maintain any sense of responsibility to the whole community, when in point of fact we minister only to a tiny fraction of the community. In a secularized, pluralistic culture, it is well-nigh impossible for the priest or the people to think of themselves as anything except a private religious club—an association of like-minded people, who come together for their peculiar forms of worship. This does not weaken loyalty to the church as an institution; indeed it strengthens it; but it often strengthens this loyalty at the expense of any deep relevance to the community of which the church is a fraction.

This is a particular problem of the younger Anglican churches. It would be a sorry day if the Church of England were ever to have to face the same problem. For one of the great glories of the Church of England is that it is so little concerned with "religion" in the narrow sense, and is so profoundly concerned with the life of all the people, outside of the church as well as within it. This is a privilege none of the rest of us can share.

Do I need to point out the accompanying dangers? Just as the younger churches, in their life as minorities, run the danger of becoming mere sects, run the danger of "religiosity," so does an established church run the danger of simply accepting the privilege, and doing nothing about it. I do not need nor pretend to stir the conscience of the Church of England on this subject. The danger of accepting the privilege which is the other side of responsibility, while denying the duties that go with it, is too obvious to need mentioning.

Would this be affected by establishment or disestablishment? Clearly it would be, at least in the loss of an officially-privileged position. Neither I nor anybody else would be sorry to see the privileges go, if the responsibilities could remain. For it is the obligations which matter, that responsible partnership between church and state which has meant so much, and means so much, within the life of the British people.

In the final analysis the Church of England has the right—indeed it is under the necessity that commands every Christian—to be free. If this freedom requires disestablishment, then I have no doubt that disestablishment will come. But if it comes, there will be lost a precious requirement of relevance and responsibility which to me, at any rate, is a glorious gift. Perhaps the fact of establishment does have a primary significance here. There may be no other way to bind the church in responsible ministry to a nation except this.

I am not certain that this is so. I have the idea that other Anglican churches have found other ways in which to nourish a similar sense of social responsibility. I cannot say that the situations are identical. I cannot say that it is as easy for a Christian in one of the younger Anglican churches to have the same sense of responsibility as a Christian citizen, as does his English brother. There may indeed be gains on the other side—gains in sharpness of understanding and a clearer memory of the great parables of the yeast and the salt and the light. But to make this comparison is either idle or mischievous. Of these things no man can judge.

All any of us can see is that the establishment of the Church of England has meant obligation—responsibility as well as privilege. The question is not simply one of abandoning privileges. There is far more involved than that. I have no doubt that the Church of England would be quite as competent to cope with disestablishment as any other Anglican church. This is not the point. The point is that there is much more than the mere legal fact of establishment or disestablishment at stake. There is a whole complex of attitudes and commitments at stake. And it behooves all thoughtful and loving Christians in our Communion to keep all these greater things in their minds, when they are tempted to pass quick judgments, one way or the other, about an established church.

I do not know that I have any more wisdom than that on this most-complicated question. I know that establishmentarians and disestablishmentarians alike had better quit thinking about either solution as if it were a panacea. I also know that all of us, no matter which kind of church we belong to, need to stop trying to take credit for history. Nobody earns his history; nobody deserves the blessings history gives him. Nobody can take credit for the church he belongs to. It was there for him; it will live long after he has gone. Nobody is good enough to be an Anglican, really. All the blessings that have come to us through our Anglican tradition—all the history that has given us the churches we serve—all this is the most un-earned and un-deserved treasure I know.

The best we can do, I believe, is try to live up to what we have, and to move in our hearts and lives as we think God is moving in history and in the Church. Who knows what form and pattern of the Church God holds in His will for those who come after us? What lessons there are still to be learned about the ministry, about unity, about mission! The Anglican Communion itself, in all its immense variety of form and culture, is not yet big enough to show us all that the Church is and is to be.

If we are ever to learn those lessons—even catch the faintest glimpse of what is to come—we will need to remember how to be humble in the face of history, and eager for what is yet unrevealed, and true to the light that we have, and gentle and loving in our companionship along the way.

7. YOKED TOGETHER*

"The Protestant Episcopal Church in the United States of America" was the title chosen, in 1789, when the Anglican clergy and laity in the United States finally completed the organization of their church. It still remains the legal title of the American Church, quaintly cumbersome though it be, and it is a monument to several not-unimportant matters in church history. For one thing, it served as a reasonably adequate description—at least in the 18th century—of the principal difference between the Anglican tradition and other traditions. As respected most of non-Roman Christianity, we clung to the Episcopate. As respected most other Episcopal churches, we shared fully in the major Reformation impulses. Thus both qualifying words played a useful descriptive role.

More significantly, it was the first time, I think—at least in Anglicanism—to devise a particular name, a denomination, for the Church. "The Church of England" had sufficed up until then, as it still does in England. No need to say what church or differentiate it from other Christian bodies; it was enough simply to refer to it as The Church. But in the new republic, where no church could claim to be "the" church and none could be established as a national church, it was felt to be needful to give some description to what was peculiar or characteristic of the Anglicans in contrast, say, to the nascent Methodist Church or the Roman Church or whatever. For better and worse, the fact of a pluralistic society had to be openly faced, a society composed of minorities, a society in which the Church must exist in the form of voluntary religious associations, of sects and denominations competitive or at least sharply contrasted with one another, of private organizations none of which could claim any official tie with the secular, national government.

Of course this did not mean, nor does it now mean, that the new nation was anti-religious. In some states, as in New Hampshire for example, churches remained established until well into the 19th

---

* From *Anglican World*, Aug.-Sept. 1961.

century. To this day countless vestiges remain in American life—chaplains in the armed forces or the legislature, the use of the Bible in the inauguration of the President, the quotation from the Psalms on American coins and bills—of the Christian cocoon from which the nation came. Even at the time, although formal church allegiance was true of only a minority of the colonists, two-thirds of the signers of the Declaration of Independence were Anglicans; and the Episcopal Church has played a powerful part in American life ever since, as have other religious bodies as well.

But the United States was, in its origin, a then-unique experiment in a state free from any official attachment to any church; and the church in the United States consequently and equally grew up in a new situation and mood. Free from official establishment, it had all the privileges (and ran all the dangers) of being a private society—it could organize itself and arrange its discipline and worship as it chose (and it could also disdain any responsibility for the nation's life and limit itself to that most barren and profitless ecclesiastical exercise, talking solely about "religion"). The laws of the nation protected it and sheltered it, but enforced no privilege—therefore it had to fight for whatever influence it might gain in national affairs (and do this in rivalry with other religious societies, so that often the national good seemed to matter less than temporary advantage over another sect). It was utterly dependent on its own people's resources and generosity for its support. It had to improvise (and was free to improvise) to meet the unprecedented problems of the frontier.

In the case of the Anglicans particularly, all these new conditions and tasks were complicated by the ancient roots of our life in England; the American Anglican stood on the frontiers of a new and puzzling society, yet was deeply tied to the traditional ways of the mother church, ways often preposterously unsuited to the needs of the new society. To some degree Episcopalians in the United States still are caught in this difficulty (as well as enriched by the historic continuity tied up with it). But in the early years of the American Church's life, the difficulties often clearly outweighed the enrichments; it is doubtful if any church, in any age, was less prepared to cope with the frontier than the American Church was in the 19th century, and the religious history of the United States will bear the marks of this in all the years to come.

Yet, the American Church has discovered a genuine and positive vocation of its own, and responded to it with a substantial measure of true obedience. It is not my part to defend American Anglicanism; I am a product of it and of course I would be proud of its peculiar gifts; but the point of my writing is not to defend but only briefly to describe. And in this I should lay stress on three elements in the life of the American Church which are characteristically "American," influenced and indeed excited by the circumstances under which this oldest child of the Church of England came into its separate existence. Each is, I suppose, a matter of degree rather than an innovation. Yet the degree is what so profoundly influences the pattern of American Anglicanism, and in turn has contributed to some extent to the whole life of our Communion.

One is the sense of being a minority, a voluntary association of a group of people among many such associations. To hark back to my first paragraph, this is reflected in the necessity to choose a name for the Church. No American church is in any other case; all alike share this perplexity and situation. Therefore the question of *identity* looms large to all American Christians. This is accented by the fact of diverse national origins, which fact played an immense part in years past, still does to a lesser degree now, in the stratification of American religious life. The Scottish immigrant was inescapably Presbyterian, the Irish and Italian were Roman Catholic, the Scandinavian was a Lutheran, and so on; and while these generalizations were far from completely true, they still sharpened greatly the whole question of identity.

And who were the Episcopalians? Clearly they were the offspring of the English colonists, the root stock of beginning America. Even as late as my own boyhood, such labelling was taken for granted. In parts of the United States, fifty years ago, it was not at all uncommon to speak of the Episcopal Church as "the English Church." And while this matter of social or cultural or racial identity was important enough, what is far more important is the persistent pressure toward doctrinal identity, again characteristic of all American Christianity and of Episcopalians as well. We constantly tremble on the verge of becoming a sect (if by "sect" you mean, as I do, a club of people who think alike in even small things). No Anglican church could ever become a sect and remain Anglican, for the nature of our Anglican identity and unity does not lie and cannot ever lie in identity of belief—we are one not because we think alike but because we act together, because we join in the same sacraments and prayers, because we share the same Prayer Book in each church. But such a loose unity of action is most difficult to maintain in a competitive, pluralistic religious society. Therefore there is a constant pressure on American Anglicans to define their beliefs more sharply, and to clarify points of difference with other bodies, to ask and answer the question "what are the distinctive beliefs of the Episcopal Church?"

No other Anglican church, I think, has moved anything like as far as the Episcopal Church in this direction. It would still be impossible, within the Church of England, to produce books such as the American "Church's Teaching Series" which not only pretend to but succeed in being used in parishes representing the entire gamut of churchmanship, and in teaching what the church's position is, in distinction from the teaching of this or that school of thought within the church. In no other Anglican church, I think, is there less consciousness of or respect for partisan differences of opinion. This is both a strength and a weakness—a strength because unity within the household can mean both unity and strength in our witness—weakness because it is so easy to achieve doctrinal identity if you do not ask any very deep questions nor expect any very important answers.

If the weaknesses and dangers can be avoided, I should fully welcome the strengths, and I do, for I am sure that the necessities of Christian witness in our world call for clear and united doctrine. We Anglicans cannot afford the luxury of pretending that beliefs do not matter; the easy days are gone, when you could take it genially for granted that everybody was sort of generally Christian in the basic things and therefore we could and should tolerate the widest diversity of theological expression. But the peril is great, of reducing Christian doctrine to puerile insignificance for the sake of getting everybody to say the same thing. And if we cannot afford not to take Christian belief seriously, no more can we afford to deal with it as if it were no more than a few childish phrases and definitions. This is the peril implicit in the search for identity, and the American Church is not free from it.

Nevertheless, I should set all this down as one of the significant elements in the life of the Episcopal Church—this whole element of the clarification and unification of belief in the search for identity. Indeed I should think it potentially one of the American Church's major contributions to the Anglican treasury.

Second, I mention the somewhat parallel element of wholeness, of corporate and single and united action. The Episcopal Church is the despair of many other Anglicans precisely because we operate so much as a whole. And this wholeness, basically, is built on loyalty to the Church, not to a person or group or ideology. Priests and bishops take their ordination vows not to a metropolitan, in the classic tradition, but they "promise conformity and obedience to the Doctrine, Discipline, and Worship of the Protestant Episcopal Church in the United States of America." It is doubtless true that the upshot of this is a level of obedience and unity quite as great as that in any other Anglican church. Nevertheless, there is a significance to the object to which the obedience is given—it is the whole life of the Church to which we promise to conform, not simply the incarnation of the Church in any individual bishop or archbishop.

I should not want to over-emphasize this difference. Some do, foolishly, and suppose that there is some essential lawlessness or Presbyterianism or other grievous sin about the American clergy not present among their brothers! There is not; we feel exactly the same way toward our bishops and our metropolitans as anybody else does. But there *is* a difference, and it is in the sense of the wholeness and singleness of the church's life over and above any person or diocesan individuality.

The supremacy of the General Convention, the American Church's supreme legislature, is a unique and determining expression of this. Although it meets only every three years, and then for a brief two weeks, its authority is immense. The constitution and canons of the church are in its keeping, and the missionary program and budget— indeed the whole operation of a nation-wide church for the ensuing three years—is decided by it, it takes precedence over any regional or diocesan interest, its decisions direct and bind the day-by-day leadership of the Presiding Bishop and the National Council (which are the continuing executive and administrative agencies of the church).

I know how often this is misunderstood by other Anglicans, for many appeals for men and money, ultimately come to my desk, often accompanied by resentment at what is felt the refusal of the American Church to respond to them until they are endorsed, approved and accepted by the central body of the church itself. Or again, many other Anglicans are confused by the way American overseas missionary dioceses are so closely identified with their parent church, almost as if they intended to be "American" instead of African or Asian or whatever. In both cases, the element of wholeness, of the single life of the church, is what is really involved. It is the settled policy of the American Church that mission is not an option, that it is part of the normal full life of every churchman and every congregation. Therefore missionary policy and budgets are concerns of the whole church, not of private groups of devoted people. Similarly, the overseas missionary diocese is held to be a constituent part of the church. Its bishop sits with all his brothers in the House of Bishops; its clergy and laity have their proportionate share in the General Convention and other central church bodies; and until the time comes for such a diocese to take its place in a new province, as in Japan or China, it remains in the fullest sense part of the whole and single life of the church from which it sprang.

These are instances of a very wide philosophy of church life. The philosophy arose, no doubt, from the exigencies of a new church in a new land. In church as well as nation, the issue of wholeness had to be worked out; and alike in both cases, the end was a vast strengthening of the sense of unity and corporate singleness of purpose. Again, it is a philosophy not without its dangers—dangers of the stifling of originality and ingenuity, of the loss of individual or regional self-reliance, of the adoption of compromise decisions for the sake of peace, of the lessening of goals in an endeavor to avoid delay or dissent.

But the vast majority of American Episcopalians, I am sure, prefer to run the risk of the dangers for the sake of the concentrated effort which is the prize. What is needed, so many of my countrymen feel, is not to weaken the policy of central and united work but to add to it the myriad other ways in which buoyant individual and local intitiative can be expressed.

At all events I think it is true that the American Church operates with a higher degree of single purpose and united action than any other in our Anglican family. Although there are eight "Provinces" in the continental United States, they are in no sense separate regional jurisdictions; they have tended not to develop into more than neighborly associations of church people, for discussion and edification. Decisions are taken on a national basis; the church in America perhaps is more of a national organization than any other Anglican body, in action at any rate; and this, with all its perils, probably remains a major contribution of the United States in the world-wide Anglican dialogue.

The third prime element, I think, is that of the full and responsible participation of the laity in the government and management of the church. Again, this is partially due to the peculiar situation of the church in colonial America and the young Republic. Institutions, officers, agencies, traditions which existed in mature power in the Church of England were simply absent from the American frontier. There were not even bishops until 1784, which meant that for nearly 180 years the church in America had had to improvise its life in the absence of even its most central figure. The colonial clergy were either missionaries from England or were trained and ordained only at the great cost of trans-Atlantic travel. There was no settled authority to deal with the vexing questions of clergy discipline or parochial responsibility. Endowments were sparse or non-existent. Colonial governors assumed ordinary jurisdiction, often in a vacuum. And in all this difficult time, it was only the laity of the church who could be a stable and continuing factor.

Thus, the "Vestry" became, in the American Church, the unique and powerful body it is, a "mixed" body indeed, with the Rector always a member and president, but still a responsible group of the lay parishioners who hold title to the property as trustees for the congregation and share responsibility for both temporalities and spiritualities in the parish. Thus it was that the vestry, as representatives of the congregation, became the group responsible for choosing and inviting the priest to the ministry of the parish. True, he had and has "parson's freehold"; nevertheless there grew up a tradition of the marriage of priest and people in a parish, of responsible partnership of each with the other, which is probably unmatched in any other system of clergy appointment.

Thus it was that when bishops were possible, the custom was established of their election by the diocese—almost universally by the laity and clergy of a diocese, voting separately but obliged to make a common choice. This procedure strikes many of my English friends with horror, and I do not say it is a flawless system by any means. There are grave problems whenever the government of the church is exposed too freely to the democratic process. But these are not the only dangers church government faces; and one must choose what dangers he prefers, I suppose.

Thus it was that the central synod of the church, the General Convention, as well as the conventions of the several dioceses, are again mixed bodies, with clergy and laity equally sharing in the rule of the church. In the General Convention, the bishops meet separately in their own House; and there must be agreement between the bishops, collectively, and the clerical and lay deputies. Thus the American Church is by no means a church dominated or controlled by the laity. But no more is it a clerical preserve, tolerating the laity—a tragic malformation cherished by the medieval mind, but completely inappropriate to our times.

This is not at all to say that the American laymen is in any sense better than he ought to be, or wiser or more responsible than his African or Indian or South American or British cousin. It is simply to say that he grows up in a tradition of responsible participation, which attracts and holds his best gifts and most powerful leadership. It is notorious that the American Church grows very largely through adult conversions—in my thirteen years as a diocesan bishop, there was no year in which I did not confirm more adults than children, even though my diocese was a nursery of considerable size. Such a flood of adult converts presents extraordinary and continuing problems, and taxes the teaching ministry of the church to the utmost. But it is perhaps chiefly significant as underlining the way in which a responsible lay ministry makes its appeal to men and women who are seeking to find a satisfying level of participation in the life of the Church.

Once again, there are dangers. There is no magic which prevents an uninformed layman in a position of power from making a dangerous nuisance of himself, any more than there is any miraculous grace of order which prevents an ignorant priest from the same fault. In a society as drenched in worldly values as American society is, there is a constant danger of the dilution and secularizing of the Church's witness. There is the danger of the parsonification of the laity, or the laicizing of the clergy. There are countless dangers, as anyone can see.

But surely, in the full and healthy life of Christ's body, the cure for these dangers is not less partnership of clergy and laity, but more. It is precisely the challenge which each offers to the other, when they are yoked together in the Church's government and life, which sharpens and purifies witness and deepens understanding. This, at any rate, has been the characteristic experience of the American Church—an experience won not without pain, but not without profit either.

Let me conclude by saying again that I have chosen three particular points of emphasis, areas in which the church in America has largely been forced, by the circumstances of its birth and growth, to do a good deal of experimenting. It would be utterly wrong to suppose that the experience of the American Church alone or of any other Anglican church alone, can be a final word. The essence of our Anglican life is that we learn or can learn from one another, all the more in the deep interchange and conversation which has become so notable in recent years.

8. PRAYER BOOK REVISION*

ONE OF MY PECULIAR OCCUPATIONAL HAZARDS is that of being exposed to all our different Anglican Prayer Books, as I go to and fro in the earth.

---

* From *The Living Church,* May 21, 1961.

Being an American, the Prayer Book I know best is that of the Episcopal Church; and left to my own devices, I would simply command that every Anglican province adopt it forthwith, since it is probably used in heaven anyway. (Note: this remark is not intended to be taken with utter seriousness.) Living for the most part in London, as we now do, my family and I have grown accustomed to the 1662 Book of Common Prayer, with its rich and sometimes perplexing variations, additions and subtractions. As to most Americans, the Holy Communion liturgy in the 1662 Book seems to me curiously bob-tailed. One has the feeling that the Holy Communion is received in the middle of the Prayer of Consecration, not as the summit and conclusion of it. And one must make all sorts of minor accommodations, as with the Prayer of Humble Access said before the Consecration, which requires a quite vivid devotional adjustment. (But here I can remember the pre-1928 American Book, which followed the same order.) But one quickly grows accustomed to such differences, even finds them enhancing and invigorating. And what chiefly concerns me at the moment is the way—despite the differences and through the differences —the Prayer Book is recognizably a bond of unity among all our provinces.

How deeply does the Anglican Communion owe its unity to the Prayer Book? How deeply should it? The Committee on the Prayer Book of the 1958 Lambeth Conference dealt with those questions somewhat provocatively. The report pointed out that Anglican unity really existed "because we are a federation of Provinces and Dioceses of the One, Holy, Catholic, and Apostolic church, each being served and governed by a Catholic and Apostolic ministry, and each believing the Catholic faith. These are the fundamental reasons for our unity." Then the Committee went on to speak of a unity "at a less profound level," derived from our sharing a common history and tradition, of which the Prayer Book in its various forms was probably "the most powerful symbol." Doubtless this lesser unity is an aid to the common life of the churches of our Communion, but it is hardly essential to that unity.

All this is surely sensible and wise. But it does not help us immediately in dealing with the pressing problems of Prayer Book revision. And these problems are pressing, in many parts of our fellowship. The Church of England perhaps is most aware of the need for revision. Although it has met the necessities of legal paralysis with courageous liberty, the result has been a confusing variety of rites, which cannot— so the Lambeth Committee thought—be felt to be an ideal solution.

But the desire for revision is not born simply in discontent with old rites. It is a product of the flood of new liturgical knowledge and understanding, in the face of societies radically different from that in which the Prayer Book was originally written. And it is found in every part of our Communion, to some degree at least. The latest major revision is that of the Canadian Church, completed in 1959. The Japanese Church similarly has only recently prepared an extensive revision. And such proposals are in the air wherever one goes.

In revision, how closely are we bound to follow a normative liturgical pattern? Is there any such pattern? I think the answer to the second question is easier than to the first. There is a normative pattern of Prayer Book worship now, with the exception of the Holy Communion service. We do not read the same psalms or lessons, necessarily, on the same day; in some cases we have alternative collects, epistles and gospels; but there would be no confusion in moving from one province to another, when it came to Matins or Evensong, or to Holy Baptism or Ordination. Such differences as exist are minor ones; the great patterns of congregational partnership and of a balanced form of public, vernacular worship are identical.

Only in the Holy Communion service is there a substantial variation. There are two great families of rites. Some liturgies—as those of Scotland, America, South Africa, India and Japan—stem in general directly from the first Prayer Book of 1549 in their form. Others—those of England, Wales, Ireland, Australia and New Zealand—follow the order of the post-Elizabethan-settlement Book as finally adopted in 1662.

This variation between the two rites is more than merely a verbal one. It reflects a profound theological dispute about the Eucharistic sacrifice which was bitter indeed, in the tug of war of the Reformation. But little in history has changed more radically than this once-basic disagreement. Both sides have learned immeasurably over the years— learned about each other—learned new perspectives on the Reformation itself—learned more about the actual teaching of God in Holy Scripture. Now the historic argument seems almost a museum-piece. Indeed, the Lambeth Committee felt that "as the result of new knowledge gained from Biblical and liturgical studies the time has come to claim that controversies about the Eucharistic Sacrifice can be laid aside . . . and the way prepared for the making of a liturgy in God's good time which will in its essential structure win its way throughout the whole Anglican Communion."

But, if this be so, the first question must then be asked, as to how

closely we are bound to find and follow such a normative liturgy. I
know I do not have a single answer satisfactory to myself, here. Ideally,
yes; I should like nothing more than to be able to go anywhere in the
world, and follow the same words and actions in the same order, in
whatever language and culture. But the important thing is not liturgical identity, in word and form. Such identity could be no more than
a cultural fashion—a sort of club ritual—and any such shallow uniformity might stifle the very creative freedom all of us long to have in our
various churches.

The important thing is not that the words be identical, but that
what they express be held in common. Why should words written for
16th century Englishmen or 18th century Americans, say, necessarily
be the words 20th century Malayans must use? I am not arguing
against a single, universal, Anglican Prayer Book. I am only saying
that it would not be the answer to every problem at all. It is far more
important that there be agreement as to the Eucharistic liturgy—the
acts we are to do, the things we are to ask God to do, the understanding of what our Lord Himself is doing.

I think this is what the Lambeth Committee was pleading for,
when they asked that a "Committee representative of all parts of our
Communion . . . be asked to work toward the production of an outline
of the structure of the Holy Communion service." Presumably such
an outline could then serve to guide Prayer Book revision in every
part of our Communion. The Committee recognized that there would
be difficulties in such a plan. Of course there would, for it would
require a re-examination in great depth of inherited patterns of
Eucharistic worship and devotion which could not help but be chal-
lenging and even painful at times. Yet it is hard to imagine any
corporate exercise within our household which would bring greater
blessings, in new understanding both of one another and also of the
great common act on which our unity as a Communion is based. And
the end result would not be a victory for one rite or the other. It
would be, it should be, a new formulation which would include what
both rites, in their beginnings, were seeking to preserve and teach.

It is to be hoped that such a central group may soon begin to
function. For what they would be doing, I think, would not be at all
a mere bit of denominational tidying-up. True, they would be leading
the whole of our Communion to a more united worship than what we
now have. But precisely because the Eucharist is not ours, but His Who
is the Lord of the whole Church, such ways as we find to reconcile and
heal old divisions and establish a more profound brotherhood in the

liturgy, would be gifts to the whole body of Christians of every allegiance, everywhere. This is the secret of all Prayer Book revision, I think. As long as we seek it merely for our own convenience, unity, intellectual satisfaction or whatever, we are bound to miss the point. It is only as we understand liturgy as an obedience to Christ and a doing of His truth, that our worship is purified of narrowness and provincialism. It is more than a form of words that gives unity to the Anglican Communion.

9. OUR PARTICULAR TREASURE*

AT A MEETING a while ago, I found myself in the position of being the only Anglican in a group of Christians who mainly did not use set forms of prayer, and who were assaulting me slightly about our dependence on "book prayers." I will tell you what I said in defense of the Prayer Book; then I would like to express some other thoughts that came to me in the course of our conversation.

I said four things. First, that the use of the Prayer Book is an immense liberation for us from the tyranny of the individual or of fashion. It does not matter whether we have gifted clergymen or not, as far as our corporate worship is concerned. Our prayers do not depend on our pastor's skill or depth or holiness. We are guaranteed a full, rich, balanced liturgical life no matter what his abilities or limitations. Equally are we free from the tyranny of fashion, for there are fashions in theology and in prayer, and there is no time—just as there is no man—free from its peculiarities and eccentricities. But the Prayer Book ranges back and forth across the centuries, drawing from every treasure in the long life of the Church. These treasures are given to us, and no man, no school of thought, can take them away from us.

Secondly, I said that the Prayer Book is a major tool of unity for us. This thought comes as a surprise, sometimes, to people of other traditions who are over-impressed with the wide variations in Anglican life and practice. They are mildly astonished to discover that two congregations grotesquely different in the ecclesiastical costumes or the ceremonial habits they are accustomed to, nevertheless use the same rite, the same words. Yet, indeed, this is one of the deepest secrets of unity—that we pray together and do the great acts of worship together no matter how exotic our differences in dress and mode of worship. It may be, as some say, that we Anglicans think too much of

* From *The Living Church*, May 26, 1963.

uniformity, and so stifle liturgical experiment and growth. I am not so persuaded, myself. But if we are over-sensitive, that is a good fault in our fragmented Christianity where there is so little that unifies.

Then, thirdly, I said that the Prayer Book is our great teacher. Lacking elaborate catechisms or detailed statements of what Anglicans believe—for that matter lacking anything much that could be called specifically "Anglican beliefs" anyway—we are taught our Bible and our faith and the outlines of the Christian life mainly by our prayers and services. When somebody says to us, "What is the Anglican faith?" our best answer, usually, is to thrust a Prayer Book in his hand and say, "Read that. If you can say those prayers and join in those acts, then come along with us." Of course, the Bible is the supreme master of our doctrine. But the Prayer Book is so steeped in Scripture, so compounded of Scripture, that much of the time it is only a kind of liturgical Bible class, teaching us what Holy Scripture means in the corporate life of Christian people.

But it goes further than this because it also takes us—in the Collects, for example—through the whole range of Christian history and experience. During Lent, for instance, we use some Collects which have been said by Christians certainly since the fourth century, some written in the sixteenth century, some (in the American Prayer Book) written in the twentieth. How different the Church was, and the life of Christians, in those different times. Yet the continuing life of the Church persists; each generation has its own bits of wisdom and experience to bring to the common life of the household; and all this is opened to us and taught us in our prayers, which is the way doctrine is best born and tested anyway. The Prayer Book is the guardian of the living tradition for us. It is one of the chief ways in which the Holy Spirit guides us into truth.

Finally, I said that the Prayer Book is our best watchman of the supernatural and the holy. No matter how the world swamps us and captures the Church, there is always, in this book, an unfailing reminder of the eternal. How often we are recalled to our true nature and the truth of the Gospel by the prayers we hear and say. They make us uncomfortable, indeed, as when we devote hours at some meeting to discussing how we are going to save the Church or the world or ourselves, and then close by saying, "O God, forasmuch as without thee we are not able to please thee . . ." and we are cut down to size again, and restored to some decent perspective before God.

These are blessings that are given us by our Prayer Book, and I am sure they are at least some of the right things to point to, when

Anglicans are questioned about our peculiar institution. But while I was saying those things, I thought of the perils which come along with the blessings; that the gift of the Prayer Book has often made us careless of our preaching of the Word; that the prayers can be so rattled off or gargled or muttered, as to be unintelligible physically and spiritually; and that the very availability of such glorious common prayers can enervate our concern for private prayer and spontaneous prayer.

Those are thoughts we often share, and rightly. Do we then go on to look at deeper and more subtle perils? That the very language itself of the Prayer Book is becoming a dead language, so that we are slowly but surely returning to where we were before the 16th century? That the beauty of the Prayer Book prose can become not a vessel for prayer but a formula which imprisons prayer and even presumes to imprison God? That all the violent, astonishing, explosive action of God in our history can be entombed in familiar words, so that we think the essential doctrine of the Church is an it and not a He? That we shall not be taught by the prayers, but rather think that we possess them?

Is there any safe middle point here, where we can keep the blessings of the Prayer Book and avoid the perils? I think the answer is no—at least as far as any fixed point is concerned. The greater the gift, the greater the danger. If we are to gain so greatly from the Prayer Book, we really need a special set of devotions and disciplines to help us use it aright. We also need another set of devotions and disciplines to help us understand Prayer Book revision for what it is, an exercise in obedience to the living God and not (a) an attempt to be more "relevant" to a culture which we will serve very much better by a little more "irrelevance," (b) an essay in antiquarianism, or (c) an attempt to brighten up worship in the hope of recapturing some of the mystified worldlings to whom we should have preached better in the days when they went to church.

We might even helpfully develop a bit more humility in parading the Prayer Book before those luckless ones who do not have it. I do not envy them the lack of it. But I wish we preached as well as we prayed, and I wish we prayed with as much first-hand wrestling with God as some of our brothers who cannot nimbly pluck a collect out of their pockets. God did not idly give us the Prayer Book because we are deserving children. In His wisdom, He entrusted us with this particular treasure (as He did others with other gifts). It is an uncomfortable trust and treasure as well as a precious one. That is what I really meant to say to my brothers, that day.

III.

The Anglican Communion and Mission

The Meaning and Cost of Mission

10. FOUR NOTES OF MISSION*

IT HAS BEEN many years since the Anglican Communion has felt so deeply the urgency of mission. It is an unfamiliar mood, really, in which our Church finds itself today—unfamiliar, I should think, for more than a hundred years.

There are many marks of this. First, the Overseas Mission Society itself is a mark of this new awareness. An excitement bears a fruit, and the fruit is in the form of dedicated people who can direct excitement. This is precisely the function of this unique body in the life of our Church, indeed in the life of our whole Communion. But other signs are not lacking. That profound stirring within the Church which gave rise to the Committee of Conference on Overseas Missions, the Gray Committee, so-called, is one. The report of that committee has had and is having a profound influence on the structure and life of the Church and will have such influence increasingly. This also is a measure of our awareness of mission. The warmth with which the establishment of the office which I have the honor to hold was met in our Church—the warmth with which our Church greeted the establishment for the first time of inter-Anglican planning—is another sign.

And so it goes. A profound wave of awareness of mission is a characteristic of the Church in our time. Of course, it is a product

---

* Address at annual meeting of the Overseas Mission Society, Philadelphia, January 1961; from *The Living Church*, February 19, 1961.

of the unease of our times, of our growing awareness of the challenges to the Christian Faith and to Christian mission everywhere in the world.

In the midst of this new seriousness and excitement about mission, I want to talk about four notes of mission in our time, four conditions under which mission must be seen. Each of the four has its danger. Each of the four has its greatness.

I. The first note is the changing character of the missionary himself. To most of us of my time, the missionary was a rather vaguely defined figure, a man or woman sent like largesse from the surplus at home to live in a kind of theological extra-territoriality somewhere else. He went, or she went, to live in China or Japan, not, of course, as the natives live—those picturesque people whom one saw in the pages of the *National Geographic Magazine*. He went to live in a kind of compound, a kind of Little America out of which he reached to do something to those natives. Missionaries were queer people and many of them obviously could not have done very well at home, but it was awfully good that they were abroad.

Of course, I am talking about myself and my ignorance—I am not talking about what missionaries were really like. There was, one must admit, some truth in this picture. It was very hard for the missionary of the 19th century not to live in the 19th century world, and the 19th century world was a world in which the West was successful. It was a world in which the West was victorious. It was a world in which the West had all the answers. And when the missionary went he was expected to have the religious answers of the West just as the man who sold Singer sewing machines or whatever was expected to have the industrial answers of the West.

We cannot blame the 19th century for being the 19th century The missionary represented his culture and he spoke out of it and for it.

In those days we did not see what was happening in the world; we did not understand that people would not obediently stay children all the rest of their lives. We did not understand that you cannot go into a primitive society and talk about brotherhood and liberty and equality and not be heard. We never really counted on being heard. We never really believed that we would be heard save in the narrow confines of church membership. But we were heard and one of the consequences was that the world was turned upside down for us.

In the 20th century it is not the victorious and successful Christian West which knows all the answers; the Christian West itself is now being examined thoughtfully and somberly tested. We are tempted to say, "Well, then, the time for the missionary has passed; the time has gone by when men and women can go from the West into Africa, Asia, or South America." It may be true that the time is rapidly passing when ostensibly Christian witnesses can go. The doors are closing—they have not closed, they will not all close, they will not close this year, but they are closing. It is increasingly difficult now for Christian men and women, ordained or not ordained, to move freely into other nations and set up their ecclesiastical shops. But men and women will always be going from one nation to another, and they will be going on many errands. And as the time comes when it may be difficult or impossible to send the officially religious missionary, it may be that we shall then look with new eyes on the opportunity and vocation of the man or woman who goes not because he is a Christian missionary but because he is in military life or diplomatic life or because he is in business, or a student abroad, or an exchange professor. It may be that we and they will look at their lives a little differently, that we will recapture something that we have lost of the ministry and witness of the laity. In discovering this we shall be rediscovering the essence of the missionary.

The danger is that we shall fail to see that we are on the threshold of what may be the greatest missionary era the Church has ever known because of the vastly increased interchange of persons in an increasing number and swelling strength everywhere in the world. It is not as easy as it once seemed to become one with the people to whom you go, and we need to look with very careful eyes at the ways in which we train our priests and our lay people when they go abroad. But the great gift is there. It is the gift of persons, of those who care for people for people's sake as Christ does.

Now this vocation is not closing, and those who can fill it and will fill it are everywhere. Our need is to look with more thoughtful and more reverent eyes at the life and witness of the man in the secular job, the businessman and the consular agent and the Air Force man and the student who goes abroad, and to ask the question: Whom are we going to receive in exchange for him?

The great gift of the missionary of the 19th century and other centuries was that he established a sense of a larger world, and as he went to the Orient, to Africa, he opened a door for people so that they came into some living contact with a larger society and a larger world than the one they knew. But the gift of persons is a two-way street and the opening of the door is something that needs being done not merely

from West to East but from East to West. The time has long since come
when we must think of these gifts in terms of exchange in which both
give and both receive.

II. The second condition, the second note of mission in the world
of today is that when we are talking about overseas missions, we are
really talking about inter-church relationships. Some churches have
gone a long way in recognizing this new situation, our own included.
The report of the Gray Committee quite rightly stressed the fact that
we have reached the point in which we must learn to look at our overseas commitments not in terms of largesse from home but in terms of
comradeship, church-to-church.

This is a very attractive thing to talk about, but it is not quite so
easy to establish. It is certainly the Anglican ideal that we shall establish, as rapidly as possible, autonomous, independent Provinces. It is
not our ideal that we shall somehow build up ecclesiastical empires
of our own. We are not concerned with establishing some sort of
American sphere of influence, nor in building some great world-wide
power structure. We are concerned with the establishment of independent churches. The consequence of this is that we must increasingly learn to think in terms of inter-church relationship. When we
give aid to missionary work we shall not simply be giving aid to those
who are ours. Rather we shall be giving aid to the sister church, which
runs its own affairs and does its own responsible planning.

We have come a little way in this and indeed it is my job or half
of it to see that this happens more and more and more. In 1963, God
willing, when we may have the first realistic and full-dress meeting of
the Advisory Council on Missionary Strategy, of which I have the honor
to be the executive officer, we will have material enough so that we can
make some brotherly church decisions and not merely proceed on our
own as separate churches using their own money to support their own
people in "missionary districts."

But there will be a danger to this. The danger will be that we shall
lose the very precious sense of personal involvement. One often hears
the American Church criticized because we have our own unique
relationship with our missionary districts. We are accused of keeping
them in infancy too long. But I know this, that our American system
at a certain phase gains enormously because it binds the overseas
missionary district very close to the family at home, and the bishops,
and priests, and the lay people from the overseas district play their
part at home in the life of the great Church. They are not merely

orphan districts but a part of the life of the whole Church. It may be that we hold on to them too long. It may be that we are tempted through pride or because we are human to build up a little empire here or there; but for a time it is a good and nourishing thing, provided that at the end it looks always to the establishment of responsible and mature freedom, so that we can come into full relationship with our sister churches. The danger is that we shall lose the intimacy of *direct* relationship, and this is a danger that we must meet whether it be through companion dioceses or some other means.

We must meet the danger but we must never forget the glorious opportunity of the mature, responsible relationship, church-to-church. No Christian wants to have another Christian thanking him for a favor. Anglican churches want to deal with one another in terms of what each has to give and in terms of what each needs, and this is the ideal of the life of our household.

God keep us from ever again having an American sphere of influence, or an American diocese, or an English diocese, or an SPG diocese, or a CMS diocese, or a Canadian mission. We have grown up out of that, in God's mercy. Within the wholeness of the Church our part as a little family in that great household is to greet in brotherly manner other families in the household, not asking what their history is or where they got their name or what their background is, but only what they need and what they have to give us, and asking of ourselves only what we have to give and what we need. When we reach that point of brotherly dialogue, then the Anglican Communion will become a reality instead of the somewhat sentimental and gossamer thing it is now.

III. But you cannot talk about inter-church relationships, important as they are, without coming to the third note or condition of mission which is that of the overwhelming sense of mission and of brotherhood and unity within which every Christian must work. Canon Warren quoted somebody who said to him, when he was preparing some lectures, that he hoped Canon Warren would give a lecture about the theological significance of Bishop Bayne. Canon Warren has been around the world since and I have not heard whether he has done this—I hope that he will. I have done it, not publicly, a good many times because I know the force and sting of the question, and I know how deeply I have got in honesty to search my own heart to find the theological significance of my work.

It could be that the theological significance of an Anglican executive officer is that the Anglicans are going to have as good a club as anybody else. It could be that the theological significance of setting up an office and a staff for our Communion is that the Anglicans want to have for themselves a confessional unity as strong as that of the Methodists, or the Lutherans, or the Baptists; that we have felt the lack of this and that we want to be just as modern and tough as anybody else. If this were the theological significance of Bishop Bayne, then it would be a tragedy that Bishop Bayne had ever been born.

We do not really care to fracture the One, Holy, Catholic Church in order to assert our own Anglican existence. There is no true child of the Prayer Book who does not say thoughtfully, week in and week out, that he believes in the One, Holy, Catholic, and Apostolic Church. And to us this is not a misty phrase; this is the overwhelming reality under which we live. This is the Church.

Do you ever stop to reflect how hard it is to define exactly what an Episcopalian is? We are wrestling with the word "Anglican" at the moment and we Americans use it a little bit uneasily because we do not quite know what else to call ourselves. It seems sort of *infra dig* to refer to the Archbishop of Canterbury as an Episcopalian, so we say, all right, then he is an Anglican. And therefore there must be Anglicans and the Anglican Communion is something we know about, and it does not really mean High Church. It does mean, well, everybody who uses the Prayer Book—and then we go on trying to define it. Don't! That way lies madness. There is no way to define the Anglican Communion. I have tried it. Take it from me, it cannot be defined.

I have more than half a suspicion that this is the way that God intended it. I do not think He intended us to find some satisfying definition. I do not think He intended us to find any basis for our own life short of the only basis there is, which is that in our Baptism we become members of the One, Holy, Catholic, and Apostolic Church. This is the only unity, this is the only Church you can define, the only Church you do not have to qualify or explain. This is the only Church that really exists, according to the Prayer Book and according to our own Faith. It is against that background that we must look at our confessional unities.

When I say this about the one Church I say it as a child of the Anglican household. I have never been anything else in my life, nor my family before me. This has given me everything that I am and everything that I have. I believe with all my heart in the witness of the Anglican tradition and the Anglican family. It is all I care about that I shall serve its best interests. But I know that the time will come when we must disappear because God does not mean us to be Anglicans but only to be Christians.

The Church has four notes and not one, and I know that there is more at stake than merely its unity. I take it for granted that we all understand this, but still the drive toward the establishment of the unity of the Church in every possible place—this is an urgent obligation on those who believe in the mission of the Church. There is a danger in this.

The danger is that for the sake of one unity we shall lose another and a greater one, that in establishing local unity in Africa, India, or somewhere else, we shall suddenly wake up to the fact that we have somehow cut the bond of the unity of the world-wide Church which once we had. The Anglican Communion is a real node of unity within the Catholic and Christian life. And if sometime that node is to disappear, it will only be because we have been restored to that unity from which we came. The theological significance of the Anglican Communion is that it shall work and pray unceasingly for that day to come, and in the meantime bear its proper trust and witness in a divided and shattered world. Now, mission has got to be seen within that condition. We cannot separate mission and the ecumenical task.

IV. And last of all, the final condition, the final note about mission is that basically mission is not about things that we do as much as it is about what we are. The mission of the Church is not, first of all, to do something but to be something.

In our world, broken and divided by the barriers between nations, it is very hard sometimes for us to do very much. The one weakness of the Gray report, to my way of thinking, is that it tended to bid us be ashamed because of how little we had done without asking that we be ashamed for how shallow we were. I am not sure that measuring how little we can do or have done means too much because in our world it may be very difficult for us to do things.

I go in the Orient or to Africa, and look at the great benefactions of time past when it was possible for great hospitals and universities and school systems to be built out of the munificence of churches. This kind of thing cannot happen any more in many parts of the world. We cannot give these things; we cannot send vast numbers of people; we cannot overawe and impress with our riches. Therefore, we are being forced back on being something, and the essence of being something is in the little cluster of ideas which is the only precious and irreplaceable treasure at the heart of the Christian body.

It may well be that we can no longer be so extravagantly munificent abroad because it may teach us to look a little more deeply at what our own life reflects, to assay the strength and purity of those ideas on which our life at home is built. There was a time when the West could work off its bad conscience in its missionary munificence, but that time is no more. One result of this is that we learn to look at ourselves and at the clarity of our own witness, that we see that the imperative thing about the mission of the Church is the ideas which are communicated, together with the life of the family expressing those ideas.

The one thing which the Church alone can give to an empty world is the fruitful group of ideas out of which the new world can build the institutions it needs.

This is where the conflict between Christianity and the other religions of the world, and notably between Christianity and the religion of secularism, suddenly becomes very bitter and sharp. When you go to Southeast Asia it does not take a very perceptive person to be discouraged about the confrontation of Christianity and Communism, because Christianity seems sometimes almost intellectually bankrupt in meeting the problems of a new society struggling into existence. All too often the mission of the churches has been a mission in which men talked idly about religion when all around them were people who were eager to know how you organized a society so that there was justice and a job for people. The missionary talked about "religion," but there were far more subtle and more thoughtful people who were talking about over-population, and about the right handling of natural resources, and about the dignity of nationalism, and about how you leapfrog from the Stone Age into the middle of the 20th century in one generation.

Now, Christianity is built on the ideas on which alone a just society can be built, but God save us if we do not communicate these ideas. This is precisely the point about being. We do not communicate these ideas very clearly because we are not very clear about them at home. We live in a mature society, but a youthful and healthy society is still trying to discover how it puts what it knows to work. Therefore, the danger of the time in which we live, a time which asks so much of our ideas, is that we shall fall back on the inheritance of time past because we have no capacity to imagine new forms, because we do not really know the ideas which have been at work in that society.

That is the danger, but the opportunity comes with it. There was a very somber note about many of the comments at the inauguration of the new President, and about how dark a time it was. I dare say it is dark enough for those who do not know any better, for those who do not believe that God has anything to do with history, for those who do not have any faith, but I do not think for Christians it is dark. God in history is stripping off the non-essentials of the Church's mission and bidding us again look at the simplicities. The mission of the Church is to organize itself around these simple words and ideas which are the irreplaceable treasure and gift of God.

So it may be that with all of the excitement—the good and nourishing and welcome excitement—about the mission of the Church that our Communion is experiencing, there may also be a new simplicity and austerity about us. It may be that we will discover that it does not much matter how much money you have, or how many buildings you have, or how many men you can send abroad if they do not have very much to say when they get there.

The mission is God's, not ours. He is the One who is at work out there. We go out to meet Him. We go out to encounter our blessed Lord, creating and sustaining and loving and forgiving and inspiring and dying and being born again among the people of the world who do not know His name, who would even spit His name out of their mouths.

Underneath all of the conditions of it and the hopes of it, underneath all the wisdom that you or I could bring to it, is the great simple truth that all this is His and not ours, that the mission is His because the world is His, the people are His, and the love is His. The pain and the search and the torment and the itch of a new society being born is God at work. The new knowledge that flickers and flames into fire in these societies is His. And such grace and wisdom as men come to know, however they come to know it, is His. He is at work there and the mission of redeeming and fulfilling is His. And to us, less than the least of all saints, is this grace given that we are privileged to go where He is and for a minute to stand by His side.

11. FOLLOWING IS MISSION*

THE PRESIDING BISHOP last Sunday night gave us the watchword for the Convention. It is "obedience"—obedience to Christ's call, obedience to Christ's sending of us, penitent and thankful obedience to all that God has done and is doing and will unfailingly do. This is mission.

I make all this my own tonight, with all my heart. But it is the

---

* Address at Missionary Mass Meeting of the 60th General Convention, Cobo Hall Arena, Detroit, Friday, September 22, 1961.

obedient *following* of Christ which is in my mind. Obedience means, first of all, that we follow Him. His unforgettable command, spoken time and again, was "follow me." He saw Simon Peter and Andrew his brother, and He said "follow me." He found Philip and said to him "follow me." And so it was with James and John; and so with the others. . . . "Whosoever will come after me, let him deny himself, and take up his cross and follow me." And so with us; every one of us who has knelt before the bishop at Confirmation has faced the question "do you promise to follow Jesus Christ?"; and we have answered that we do; and we mean it.

It is *following* which is the commanding form of our obedience. It is *following* which is mission.

1. *We follow Him in His love of this world and its people.* Mr. Khrushchev waxed theological the other day, in his interview with Mr. Salzberger of *The New York Times.* Mr. Khrushchev said that his cosmonauts had established that there was no heaven—they had hunted for it but it was not to be found. Mr. Khrushchev said that he did not think many Christians really believed in heaven anyway, because they did not seem any more anxious to get there than anybody else, and if heaven was really all it was cracked up to be, they should want to go there at once. Mr. Khrushchev was in a very comical mood.

I think that God will have news for Mr. Khrushchev presently. It will not be comical, although I hope it will be merciful. But Mr. Khrushchev should not wait for this; Mr. Khrushchev should look at his own people, and ask the 25 million Christians among them why they do not take the easy way out, and set themselves free from the ache and anguish of trying to live a free man's life in a society which has no room for such big people. Mr. Khrushchev should look at the history of which he is a child, and ask about the millions more of Christians and Jews and Muslims and all the others to whom heaven is very real, who did choose heaven and death because it was the only witness left to them to make. Mr. Khrushchev should take a long look at the very movement itself which gives him the power he has—he should look at the hope of justice and the dream of dignity which is the soul of Europe, which was the gift of Christian faith to mankind, which stayed in the hearts of men even in prison and in torture, which burst out like fire whenever the wind of the spirit could get through to it to feed it, which raged across half the world in a gigantic convulsion that carried the likes of him into power with it—that hope and dream that "earth might be fair and all her people one," which gave to the Russian Revolution such honor and pathos as it has, which is the same strong wind of change blowing everywhere in the world. Mr. Khrushchev should look long at this hope, because it is a legacy to him from twenty centuries of people who have believed in heaven, who still believe in it, but who follow their Lord who loved *this* world and its people and loved them to the end, loved them more even than the easy way out. Mr. Khrushchev should not forget these people because he is living on inherited wealth, and it will not last forever.

It may be that Marxism itself is a Christian heresy. I think it is. But what is infinitely more important is that we understand the immense upheaval of our times and the incessant and sometimes pitiless and always impatient grasping for power everywhere in the world, for what these things are. These are not evil spirits from outer space. They are not mysterious goblins sent to make western Europeans and Americans uncomfortable. For generations, for centuries, men and women have gone forth into the world and talked about Jesus and about His Church—they have followed Him as He told them to—and other men and women have heard what He said about the real size of humanity in God's eyes, and about the love of God, and about how God's children ought to treat one another and every man. They heard these things and they have believed them.

Many times they have heard them without knowing who said them first. Many times they believe them without knowing why they believe them, like the bankrupt Mr. Khrushchev, who goes on stupidly repeating words of hope and justice without knowing what gives those words any meaning. But always, at the heart of all this vast unrest, are men and women who have heard what the followers of Christ said, what Christ said, and who now turn to us, the followers, and ask why we do not go along with them.

This is an uncomfortable time to be alive. But there is no mystery about some of the discomfort, at any rate. We should never have sent the missionaries if we did not expect the people would believe them. But we did send them, and they were heard; and all our history, with its glorious heritage of beauty and gentleness and the hard clean lines of scientific truth—all this is the tangled consequence of following. We cannot follow Him in His love without cost. If we would follow at all, we must be prepared to go where He went, to love as He loved, to accept the pain and the stupidities and the sin and the perplexities and the anguish of people fighting their way to a better stake in the world than anything they have ever had before.

It is to this that He has called us to follow Him—into precisely all the discomforts of a world wrestling with unfairness and wrestling with hopes almost too great for men to understand. And the first obedience of the missionary Church is to accept this, knowing that He has gone this way. If the Church, at home or abroad, does not understand this elemental love of mankind, we do not understand mission. Our first obedience is to share that love, not to peddle theories or theologies or to win people to join our club or to try to make the new nations of the world safe for us to manage.

In Africa today, there are some ten or eleven million children in primary and elementary schools. Seven out of every eight of those children are in Christian schools. These are the children who will have to pay the cost of the new Africa and who will determine what the new land will be. If they are to be what Christ in His love wants them to be, they must have wise and expert and dedicated teachers, and they must have buildings fit for the new life into which they are coming. This is still a primary charge on the Church—or to say it in a better way, the Church still has the privilege of speaking and acting for the love of Christ in teaching His children. There is not very much time left. And the need is very great. It is a need for men and women willing to go and teach, with almost no privileges or comforts—hundreds of men and women. It is equally a need for generous and unstinted capital funds, for the money that national and international resources cannot supply. This task, in our time, is on us. And it is against that need that we in our Church must measure what we spend on ourselves, and what our young men and women do with their lives. It is the simple question, "do we mean to follow Him in His love of this world and its people?"

2. *Second, the Christ we follow "made Himself of no reputation, and took upon Him the form of a servant. . . . He humbled Himself, and became obedient unto death. . . ."* This is the self-emptying, the hiddenness of Christ. Most of the men around Christ knew everything about Him except who He was. They knew His teaching, they knew His power, they knew what His hands were like laid on a man's eyes or holding a piece of bread, they knew what He looked like when He was stripped and flogged. But they did not know who He was.

This was His choice, for the Father's will was all that mattered. The truth must be spoken, the love must be poured out, the healing strength must be given, the offering made, the light must shine . . . and He must be the means by which all this is done. Therefore it is not His title that matters, but what He does and says. He took upon Him the form of a servant. This emptied, hidden, humble Servant—this is the One we follow.

There is one question Bishop Gray's Committee of Conference on Overseas Mission did not ask. I do not fault them for not asking it; they could not really have asked it, for I suppose that even the world itself could not contain the books to answer it. That question is, what do we have to say to these people if we go there? If we do send missionaries to them what have they to give? What is it we want them to do and to be—how should they change—what is our message?

I am afraid that to some, the message is no more than a foolish wish that these people would please become middle-class Americans as soon as possible. This would be a solution to the world's aches! If 600 million Chinese would only go away, and if we could find 600 million middle-class Americans to take their places and sell electric typewriters to one another, this would be a mission easy to understand. But it is unlikely.

But this is precisely the present bankruptcy of America far, far too often. We do not know what else to say to these people than what we say to ourselves—that the world was comfortable once, but it is not comfortable anymore; that our amiable security is threatened by people who will not any longer stay content with what they once had; that we had better dig a hole and crawl into it and pull it in after us, and hope that somehow, some miracle will take away the ache of the times.

Church people do not say this, at least most do not. But there are some who seem to. Maybe because I live so much away from America nowadays, I am more conscious than I used to be of what America seems to be trying to do to Christ's Church. Not all America, not you here tonight. But do you know what I mean when I say that many Americans seem to be trying to tame Christ? It is not so hard to do, at least the attempt is not hard. You start by talking about "tolerance," a very beautiful word which means carrying something—it means helping to carry somebody else's load. But what is meant by this far too often is not anything very beautiful; what is meant is indifference—"I will not mind what you say or do because I do not care about these things myself and I don't think you really do either."

That is indifference, not tolerance. And with indifference comes a second step, a rule that no conviction—particularly no private religious conviction—be permitted to enter a controversial area. And "controversial" means any area of life where there is any difference of opinion. Therefore it must not be suggested that God has any concern or any connection with our laws or our taxes or our foreign policy or our civil liberties or our television or our advertising. . . . He must be content with what we label as "religion," that is to say, soft custardy generalities against certain sins, sins about which there can be no argument at all.

The Church then becomes the religious club, decorated with appropriate medieval or early English pageantry, organized to do some indefinable good to the community. The Gospel—at least the non-controversial parts of it—should be taught to children. Clergymen should make brief, pleasant, non-controversial addresses to like-minded people. Short selections from the Bible, cleaned up a bit to suit a family occasion, may be used to give a religious tone to the club meetings. Christ is generally to be approved as long as He supports the status quo. The Church—and this is the ultimate blasphemy—is to be tolerated as long as it is good for society, for society's stability and for the maintenance of public order.

This is the ultimate blasphemy, to presume to tolerate Christ and His Church because they will keep our society comfortable, because they are "good" for American society. It is a blasphemy uttered by the world. It is a blasphemy accepted all too often by the Church.

The Church is not good for this society, or for any society man could possibly devise. The Church is the Divine Society, which works like yeast in any earthly community to purify it and to change it. God will not be tolerated by anybody. He will not be made a domestic chaplain for America or for anybody else.

Yet this is exactly what we seem to say. This captive Christianity, this castrated Christianity which masquerades as the Gospel—this *is* the Gospel to countless men and women who have never really heard the Gospel at all in the Church or outside it. How often all the Church seems to do is hold up a mirror to the world in which it lives. And in that mirror men see only what they are, not what God made them to be. The wastefulness of our society is no better-looking in such a mirror. The deliberate dirtiness which defiles American life under the excuse of freedom—this is just as dirty in the mirror. The fear of America lest our richness be taken away, the mental laziness of us, the abuse of God's created gifts, the playing fast-and-loose with the promises of marriage, the slippery way we make ends justify means . . . if all the Church does is hold a mirror up to society, then we see in Church only the reflection of what we now are, sanctified by Gothic arches and Tudor prose. And this is not mission.

I know how fantastically untrue such a caricature is to America. America was not born out of non-controversial religious indifference. Everything that we hold dear—every gift that we have received ourselves or made to the world, of self-restraint and ordinary decency and truth and the sublime certainty that man is bigger than any state that can ever be devised—all these things came not from pleasant people who wanted to get along, but from people who above all other things were trying to follow Christ into a new kind of country altogether.

Let us be perfectly clear about this. An American man or woman abroad, whether formally a "missionary" or not, is an American. He cannot change his spots. He is a child of this culture. He has gained all he has from the incredibly rich gifts of this nation and its life.

Yet he must learn slowly, painfully, to set himself free from this Americanism so that he can say what the secret of this Americanism is. The American way of life—our opulence, our skills, our restraints, our easy habits—this is no use to Asia.

When children go to sleep hungry, when men sit up half the night trying to learn to read so that they can devise a good constitution for their new nation, it is not any good to tell them that they should have been born Americans.

The mission of the Church overseas shares that humility, that emptiness, or else it is not mission at all. This is equally true of the Church's mission at home. To follow Christ means to be anonymous, to be nobody and to be everybody. In lands overseas or at home, it means that the American lays his life alongside the life of his brother, content to make himself one with the people among whom he lives as far as that may be. He remains an American perforce, for he must be somebody, and he is the child of a certain culture, and that is the only culture which will ever be his. Yet it is the grace of the incarnate God given to man both to be limitless particular, and in that particular individuality to belong to every person and every culture. Christ is within cultures, over against cultures, above cultures, all in one. And all this is part of following.

St. Matthew was one to whom Jesus said "Follow me." The Epistle for St. Matthew's Day, yesterday, has these words: "We preach not ourselves, but Christ Jesus the Lord; and ourselves your servants for Jesus' sake. For God, who commanded the light to shine out of darkness, hath shined in our hearts, to give the light of the knowledge of the glory of God in the face of Jesus Christ." This is a way of talking about the humble self-emptying of the Christian, who preaches not himself "but Christ Jesus the Lord; and ourselves your servants for Jesus' sake." It is a way of talking about the humble self-emptying of Christ whose work it was to let the knowledge of the glory of God shine through Him.

You know that now I spend my life with the needs of our Anglican mission overseas. I know how many priests and medical people are needed in a place called Simmangang. I know that an Australian bishop is now short eight men on his frontier. I know that a task group of twelve is needed in Pakistan. I know that one of the great missionary societies of England is seeking for fifty men to fill present vacancies in the dioceses that society serves.

I know these needs in terms of money. I know them in terms of the needs of our American responsibilities. I know them in terms of the ministry open to every American businessman or soldier or diplomat or tourist who goes overseas.

I have now on my desk in London appeals for 300 men and women, priests and lay people, to come to share the life and the work of our brother churches in the Anglican Communion. I hope we may find such volunteers. They would be welcomed. But if they go, they must be prepared to become part of the church and the people where they go, not Americans enjoying extra-territorial privileges. This means lower salaries, it means working under the direction of the national clergy of that country, it means becoming part, lock, stock and barrel, of the life of another Anglican church within another nation. There would be no point in offering one's self for this ministry unless one were willing to accept the emptying, willing to set himself free from the particular and the individual, so that he might preach Christ Jesus the Lord.

3. *Finally, we follow Christ where He is now at work.* If following Him were simply a matter of remembering Him over the 2,000 years, then following could very easily become nothing but sentimentality. But Christ is not a good dead man. He is the Lord which was and is and is to come. Therefore we need not be surprised to find Him already at His loving work long before we get there. We follow Him into our own world and our own history. God reigns, now. Christ ministers and offers and loves, now.

I said that God was not an American. This hardly needed saying. Perhaps it does not need saying either that He is not an Episcopalian. Nor is He a Christian. He is not our possession. He is not the chaplain of our group. He does not spend all His time at church services. He is not defeated when we fail Him. He is not shut out of human history by people who do not believe in Him or who are disobedient to Him. We do not lead God around at the end of a rope.

We follow Him in Christ Jesus. For wherever mankind is—working, sleeping, eating, making love, dying, believing, hoping, imagining . . . wherever mankind is, He is already there. The missionary goes overseas and he is not surprised to find that Christ is already there. Perhaps He is there under His own name. Perhaps He is there hidden in the crowds of our flesh and blood. He is there in love, for whoever gives a cup of cold water to anyone in His name is giving it to Him. He is there in judgment, in the midst of war and division and perplexity. He is there on the Cross of history, offered and being offered day by day in all the sin and the blind fumbling of humanity. He is there renewing that offering every moment of every day, not just on the altar, but in the world. Do you think God is not able to use whom He will for what purpose He chooses? The Assyrians were not the first nor were they the last people who unknowingly served God's purposes. The historians of the Chinese People's Republic would do well to read Isaiah carefully, all he said about the razors and the axes and the brooms God uses.

So would American interpreters. So would missionaries at home and abroad. So would the Church. The image of panicky uncertainty which America so often shows to the rest of the world is chiefly born in the fact that people do not read their Bibles aright. We act as if we have to keep God in business, to protect Him from his enemies, even to protect Him from hearing what people are saying about Him. Brothers, it is not necessary to be solicitous about God. He is able to take care of Himself. Our job is to follow Him, so that we may find Him in the very midst of our own history.

Creator, Brother, Judge, Redeemer . . . He is at work in this world in all the gentle, loving anonymity of Christ. It is the privilege of the Christian to follow Him and to find Him, and to identify Him in the world, and to take our stand by His side wherever we find Him.

To follow Christ in His love of this world and these people—to follow Him in His humility as the hidden servant—to follow Him as He goes about His work in our world—this is the form of Christian obedience, and this is mission. Mission is not simply making more Episcopalians, although in this divided world it is impossible to get away from the labels—a man must be something. But the end of mission is not that there shall be more in our club, but that more and more may follow Jesus Christ. Mission is not a romantic career for clergy and laity seeking some exotic life somewhere else in the world. Mission is not a disguised way of exporting the American way of life. Mission is obedience. That is to say, *mission is following.*

I believe with all my heart that our Church wants to follow Christ just this way. Half our trouble is that we do not understand that this following is mission. The other half is that we have never dared to believe in mission enough to hurt.

When sensitive, thoughtful, faithful people spend more on one dinner at General Convention than the average communicant gives in a year to the work of our Church overseas, this is not because we are in-

sane or selfish; it is because we have not understood what mission is—
that it is what Christ is doing, first, and then our following. When le-
gions of young men and women grow up and grow old and die without
ever having faced the call of Christ to follow Him, this is not cowardice,
it is that we have never had the courage as a Church to take the living
Christ seriously.

If we are going to accept a new challenge to our obedience, it can
only be in the toughest terms of what it will cost. You may not follow
Christ with what is left over when the world gets through with you, in
life or money.

Well, I leave it there with you. I want 500 young men and women to
offer themselves for this obedience. But I do not want them tomorrow;
I want them six months from now, a year from now, when they have
weighed the costs of this and of their willingness to be nobody, and go
where Christ has gone and where He is waiting. I want the men and
women of this church to give at least as much to others as they spend
on themselves, to look realistically at what the new, young churches
need if they are going to give to their societies what Christ is waiting for
for them to give.

Why do I say "I want"? What matters is that *He* wants these things.
Now, as it ever was, He asks of us what He gave of Himself, everything.
All this is what it means to follow Christ. He never said it would be
easy. I do not think we really expect it to be easy. But I do not know
any greater thing that can come to any man than to have Christ say to
him, Come, Follow. And this is exactly what He is saying to us, this
very night.

12. CHOSEN FOR MISSION*

I GIVE YOU TWO TEXTS. Really they are the same text, one in the future
tense, one in the present. The first is from the First Lesson read to us
this afternoon, in which the prophet Isaiah looks forward to God's
choosing of His servants; the second is found in the prayers which
close this service, from St. John's Gospel, in which our Lord fulfills
the choosing.

Isaiah 49:7:
Thus saith the Lord, the Redeemer of Israel, and his Holy One, to
him whom man despiseth, to him whom the nation abhorreth, to a

---

* Address at The Missionary Festival Service, Monday, May 28, 1962, at the Cathedral Church of St. Michael, Coventry.

servant of rulers, Kings shall see and arise, princes also shall worship, because of the Lord that is faithful, and the Holy One of Israel, *and he shall choose thee.*

St. John 15:16:

Ye have not chosen me, but *I have chosen you,* and ordained you, that ye should go and bring forth fruit, and that your fruit should remain: that whatsoever ye shall ask of the Father in my name, he may give it you.

We come this day to give thanks for the Mission of the Church and for all those who have freely spent themselves in the service of God's Kingdom, and who do so spend themselves. Indeed it is essential that we come together for this purpose at the very outset of the life of this great building. For if there is not obedience to mission in this place and pouring out from it, then it will be no more than a museum or a mirror of our own complacency. So let there be this obedience in all our hearts, and in the daily ministry of this cathedral—obedience to God's choice of us, obedience to mission.

What is it that we give thanks for, in a missionary festival? For one thing, it is the men and women who serve the mission of the Church overseas and at home. For another, it is the new churches and the new Christians born of their witness. For another, it is the great company of all God's saints who from the beginning have laid up treasures for us, treasures which have come to us without our deserving, without even our awareness.

But each of these points beyond itself to something greater than itself. Without God there is no mission. There are heroic men and women to be sure, and there is a Christian memory and flavor in the culture, and there are churches. But there is no mission without God. For mission is God's, and not ours. "Thus saith the Lord to a servant of rulers . . . the Lord is faithful, and He shall choose thee." "Jesus said to His disciples 'Ye have not chosen me, but I have chosen you.' "

Always the initiative, the choosing, is God's. The most we can hope to do is to obey and follow Him. Mission is God's action, first of all. It is God who as an act of love and out of His measureless love calls this creation into being and us with it. It is God who gives a touch of His own reality to our time and space—gives as much of reality as time and space can hold. It is God who lovingly draws existence to Him step by step. It is God who reveals Himself in us, and then to us, as fast as we are able to receive Him and understand Him. It is God who judges us and even lets us understand and accept judgment. It is God who overrules our sins and ignorances in history, and makes fresh starts possible.

It is God who invades our separateness and comes inside our own manhood. It is God who fulfills our humanity and our society. It is God who chose us in the womb, and gave us all that we are and have. It is God who never fails to know and love even the least of His creatures, even when we forget them.

It is God who takes the initiative; the mission is God's; the creating and redeeming and fulfilling work is God's. Where in all this is there any cause for self-congratulation? Our thanksgiving is to Him and for Him, for all mission is His, and He has chosen us, His creatures, to hear and obey and follow. Our only choice is to obey. Here is where missionary thanksgiving is born.

Anything less than this would be destructive of the very heart of mission. And it is, when we forget it. For example it is terribly easy, in a divided church and a religiously divided world, for us to mistake church extension for mission—to think of the job of missionary as that of winning more members for our club, of extending the number of our churches and dioceses and institutions and the people who belong to them as fast and far as we can.

I know how the spread of the Anglican Communion has excited our thankful interest in these latter years. We can count Anglican Christians in the scores of millions, in eighteen self-governing churches on every continent, including clergy and lay people of every race and color under the sun. But all this means nothing or worse than nothing, if it is not of God's choosing. There are too many cheap reasons for being an Anglican to let us suffer under any illusion about this. If there were no God, there would still be a hunger in the world for a religion of stately and humane form, shared by the best people and in the center of the world's best liberal tradition. And all that saves us from such homesick, antiquarian ceremonies is the certainty that God is at the heart of all we do.

The Prayer Book is not just classic English prose—it is a solemn language fit for grown men and women to use toward God. The religion of the Prayer Book is not merely part of the English countryside—it is the best way free people have found to answer to the acts of God. God is not the chaplain of the English-speaking peoples of the world. He is not our possession.

And missionaries do not go out into the world to introduce the world to God or He to it. He is already there; He has been there from the beginning; He is standing waist deep in history, calling us to join Him. For the mission is His and not ours. We are not talking about church extension or making more Anglicans, when we give thanks for the mission of the Church. We are talking about God's action and the mission He has undertaken from the beginning.

Therefore a thanksgiving for mission begins with God; and it is a thanksgiving for Him and to Him, for His great love. Perforce that love is expressed in the history of the creation. Therefore the first key to our obedience in mission is not to be found by asking what would be advantageous for us or for our churches, but by asking what God is doing now in history. This is the root missionary question, on which all missionary strategy depends.

It is the ministry of the missionary to join God at work in His world—to find Him and join Him and call Him by His right name, so that He may be identified by those who do not know Him or even believe in Him. Therefore the root question is what God is doing now, in our history, in our world.

The work of the missionary is not done in churches alone, because God does not spend much of His time in churches. I do not scorn worship when I say this. It is in church, in worship, that we can come most directly face to face with God, in His presence. Therefore church is a place to come to; but it is also a place to leave, having seen what God and life are really like, having renewed our obedience once again. For He is principally at work in the world, in the stormy times in which we live—revealing, judging, guiding, always loving, always busy with the needs and hopes of His children. And it is there that we shall find Him, and watch and imitate what He is doing, so that we may know what we should be doing in order to identify Him in the eyes of the world.

The second key to our obedience is that we shall understand that mission is one and whole, and not something for others—for "them." The great glory of the missionary explosion of the nineteenth century was at the same time its great danger, that it was sustained far too much by a sense of noblesse oblige, even of condescension. I give thanks with all my heart for the immense obedience to mission which England above all other nations showed in time past. But always there was the subtle danger of thinking of all this as something for export only.

And in our time the danger is even greater, for now we run the risk of adding the cold war to our condescension, and of redoubling our concern for mission because it will not only relieve our conscience but it may also weaken our enemy. The cold war is a fact; it is the controlling political fact of our time; and it sets the stage for mission overseas just as it does for any action anybody takes in our history. But it does no more than that. It defines the world within which God is at work, but it does not define His work. And if we take it otherwise than this, then we run the risk of forgetting that He is also at work in us and among us, and that the task of finding Him and identifying Him in our own society is sometimes even harder to do than it is in the far more vivid changes of the new societies of the world.

Mission is one and whole, in every nation; and therefore the search for unity is inescapably bound up with obedience to mission. Precisely because there is one God and one history within which He acts, therefore all alike are under the same judgment. We are what our brothers are. One judgment, one hope, one fate, one glory—this is the underlying secret of humanity. And if the Church in its obedience to its mission—at home as well as overseas—does not remember that terrible and over-ruling unity, and act on it, then we have no right to use the word "church" to describe our various societies for the discussion of theology.

The third key follows the second—that mission involves us in something to be received as well as something to be given. Something received from God, first of all. People from younger nations and younger churches, like Americans, like myself, are moved to say something to British churchmen. We envy you your ancient, lovely churches and your long history of Christian faith. But we also cannot help seeing what you sometimes cannot see, that these ancient churches can be the curse as well as the glory of this land. They may be a curse not just because they are small and expensive to keep up. Actually they are about the least expensive museums anybody could ask for. But they are a curse because they are all done, all completed; they were done long ago, before anybody can remember; we had nothing to do with them nor with what produced them; and therefore we run the deadly risk of thinking that God's work is done among us (or mostly done), and we lose the giant expectancy which is the heart of true religion. God is not old. The Gospel is not an inheritance. It lies always in the future. It is always something yet to be received.

It would be better if church buildings were magically built for one generation alone, so that every generation had to face its own vocation. This cathedral may awaken a thousand sleeping hopes and eagernesses in England because it is something we have made; it must answer for the faith of this time and the expectancy of this time as to what we have to receive from God. Some of what we receive is expressed in the beauty and imagination of this church. But what is it our society needs to receive from Him, through His Church if it may be, or in spite of His Church if it must be?

And what shall we receive from our fellow Christians in other lands, to whom we send so much? It is a necessity of mission in our time that we shall never send anything or anybody without realizing that we have needs equally, and must therefore ask in the same breath what we need to receive in return. What has Africa to bring to us? It may be that we shall receive from them a renewal of our sense of duty to the Church. It may be that they have to teach us what the cost of any industrial society is, and how the Church should meet that cost, and not merely note it and build around it.

Indeed this is the core of the Anglican Communion, and its potential greatness, that it shall be more and more a meeting place of Christians, giving and receiving as each has needs and abilities, that we may the better manifest the full communion which is our prize. And if such exchange means a new modesty and humility on the part of older churches, it must also be said that it will bring a deepening of mission and an awakening of faith for which older churches long.

Indeed we shall receive from more than other Christians. God has never been without His witnesses, and He shaves with a hired razor. And the discerning of His teaching and His work even among those who know Him not, who would spit His name out of their mouths, all this is part of mission.

The fourth key of mission in our time is that we must let go of our gifts. They are not ours but God's. His is the mission. We may not even call what we do "mission." The most we can do is make an offering toward God's mission. Therefore if it is a true offering, we must be prepared to let it go into His hands, to use as He will.

If we build schools, we build them not to advertise Anglican generosity but because a new society needs schools. If we establish hospitals, we do so not because we want to buy baptisms with beds, but because God can use our hands to heal. If we send men and women, they go to spend themselves in the building of a new society, they go to lay their hearts and lives alongside the life of a new nation, not to stake out a claim on behalf of older societies. If we export ideas, we send them as free gifts, not asking for any gratitude, least of all not asking that these talents, these ideas, be returned to us in docile conformity, but hoping only that they may be set to work fermenting and exploding into life in a new culture as they did with us.

Our gifts, our people, are not ours. Missionary societies and churches cannot do God a favor. They cannot initiate mission or terminate it. We can only obey it, by offering whatever we are or have to the following of God in His steady, ceaseless invasion of the world He makes and loves. And it is of the nature of an offering that it ceases to be ours. We must let go of our gifts.

These are the four keys of mission of the obedience we want to give to God's mission. Mission is a discerning of God's whole action in the world. Mission is single and indivisible. Mission means receiving and giving. Mission requires that we let go of our gifts.

These are the great keys to mission in our time. And running through all of them, and penetrating and sweetening them, is the one cardinal truth—that God does the choosing. It is for this that we give thanks, for the initiative He takes from the beginning, and the consequent obedience of all those loving and dutiful spirits in whose debt we stand. May God give us such grace to hear and obey and follow. May He give us such a knowledge of Himself that we can never mistake His action for the prosperity of our church, or lose sight of the greatness of His work in the world.

Blessed be God, who has chosen His servants and given them the honor of following. Blessed be God, who has of His own love chosen and called and sent us. Blessed be God, in His unfailing, seeking, invading, choosing love for us, and for the grace He has given us to hear and obey and follow. This is our thanksgiving.

13. THE COST OF MISSION*

THE CHANCES are enormously against your ever having heard of Spokan Garry. Some who, like myself, have lived in the Pacific Northwest of the United States (known locally and accurately as "God's country"), will recognize his name, perhaps because of the city which, like Garry, shared the name of the Indian tribe whose country it was. But they will bear with me if I write a little about his life, for it illustrates two of the basic problems of the Church's mission (whether at home or overseas). And I ought to add that one of the reasons I write about him is that I have just read an excellent and moving biography of him by the Reverend Canon Thomas E. Jessett (*Chief Spokan Garry;* T. S. Dennison & Co., Inc., 1960).

Garry was born in 1811, a son of the chief of the Middle Spokanes— the "salmon trout people"—born into a perplexing new world for the Indians, for Garry's life spanned the era of white settlement in the Northwest. As a boy he came to know the white man, the "King George" men from Canada to the north, and the "Bostons," from the mysterious land to the east. When he was fourteen one of the "King George men," a Hudson's Bay governor, took the initiative in bringing

---

* From *The Living Church,* January 22, 1961.

Garry and another Indian boy to what is now Winnipeg, to the mission school on the Red River conducted by the Church Missionary Society. For four years he studied there, in company with perhaps thirty others, and returned to the Spokanes in 1829, to begin a long life as a leader, "a chief," starting a school and teaching his people what he knew of the Christian religion—daily prayers, the Decalogue, Bible reading and so on.

There were others like him, for it was settled CMS policy to train Indian boys for this ministry, and Garry was only one of six educated and sent back to the Northwestern tribes, to the Nez Perces, Kootenays and Cayuses as well as the Spokanes. Little is known of the others; but Garry lived a long life and the influences of his teaching remained. Bonneville and Wyeth, early "Boston men" exploring the Northwest, wrote of the strangely Christian character of the Indian worship they encountered; and the first missionaries, in 1836 and thereabouts, discovered that basic Christian teaching was already familiar to the Indians in the area.

Garry's first experiment as teacher and evangelist lasted only a few years. American missionaries, both Protestant and Roman Catholic, began a desultory work in the Northwest, which introduced religious division within the tribes. But what was far more significant was the fifty years of conflict between the Indians and the white settlers— years of mounting ignorance and distrust, of faithlessness, of exploitation and war, which ended only with the virtual elimination of the Indians as tribal units. Garry remained a leader of his people through all those difficult years, and the history of the troubled time is lighted steadily by his moderation and his forlorn attempts to find a way for just dealings and responsible partnership. But the times were not apt for such relationships, and Garry's best mediation came to nothing. As Canon Jessett says, Garry himself "lived too long"; he died in 1892 in poverty, with few to honor his years of leadership. But he has a window in Spokane Cathedral now.

The irresistible, irrevocable tide of white settlement was flooding in, and the Indian had no defender. He was simply in the way. Even the missionary was not able to help, even when he understood the problem; and in Garry's case there were no missionaries. Not until 1884 did the first clergyman of his church come to Garry's country; and he was an enemy, or at best a confused ignoramus.

Now what is the moral of all this sad little story? It is not merely to point out the iniquities of the white man *vis-à-vis* the American Indian or any other aboriginal people. American settlers had no monopoly on such iniquities. The story illustrates two recurring dangers the Church faces in her mission. First, we are in danger of failing to be the bridge between cultures, between peoples, that Our Lord intended us to be. He who is man's peace, "who hath made both one, and hath broken down the middle wall of partition between us," is often badly served and obeyed by His Church. The American Church of the nineteenth century, beginning to awaken to the somewhat romantic challenge of the Far East, in many ways failed to see its duty at home. There were magnificent exceptions—Kemper, Whipple, Breck, Hare . . . and our mission to the Indians is still a major part of the American Church's life. But still all two frequently we fail to be the reconciling force which could bridge the gulf between cultures. To "evangelize the Indian" meant, much of the time, to do something to "them" rather than to "us." It meant to persuade the Indian to accept peaceably the end of his way of life and the loss of his own country, rather than to win him and the white settler alike to a new partnership which alone could justify the conquest.

This first danger is not unrelated to the second, which is our perennial danger of sending a boy to do a man's work, and not being prepared to finish what we start. Our Lord has some rather thoughtful words about this, when He speaks of a man building a tower or a king making war, and not counting the cost before he starts. There was nothing wrong with the plan of the "King George" missionaries to train Indian lads at their school. What was wrong was that they were not prepared to carry through what they began. They were not ready to stay with it, and bring it to the harvest. The story of Spokan Garry is only one of innumerable instances of this, of eager beginnings which petered out in the end because we really did not mean business and were not prepared to pay the cost.

This is, of course, part of what "missionary strategy" means. There are some who do not like the word—I do not myself, for that matter, but I do not know a better. But whatever word we use, the essence of the Church's mission, our "strategy," is to decide what we must do in obedience to Him, and then give it all we have. And there is a recurring danger—that we shall simply nervously pick at our mission, instead of following through to the end.

I would hate to know how many places there are in the Anglican Communion, where we are simply carrying on a holding operation—where our work is launched, but where we utterly fail to develop and exploit it, and carry it through. We have a curious Anglican habit of sending men alone, all too often, and giving them ten or sixty or whatever stations to cover and then, because we are able to maintain a skeleton of church services, to account the work as being done. Or we train a handful of converts and then are obliged to leave them mainly to their own devices; and heaven knows they are faithful; but what began as a mission ends as a club or a family association. Or we project new missionary frontiers, and then send a team of two or three to begin what needs twenty to do if it is to be done at all. I agree that it is better to light one candle than to curse the dark, and I have nothing but praise and thanksgiving for the devoted men and women who carry on these impossible holding operations. But this is not true to Our Lord, when we fail to count the cost. Whatever is worth doing is worth doing well—this is a maxim for the Church as well as for the worldly-wise. This is "missionary strategy," for that matter. And I pray that never again, in our Anglican life, will we fail to count the cost.

14. TAKING COMMUNISM SERIOUSLY*

This article is written on Christmas Day, in Iceland. Nobody will like it very much; but I must add, such pessimism has nothing to do with Christmas or Iceland, actually. I am glad to report that the Feast of the Nativity survives very nicely in the wintry dark—in fact, there is a sort of added authenticity to thoughts about the Light that lighteth every man, when there is so little of the lesser sun, and the three of us are having a most cheery visit to this NATO base, baptizing and confirming and sharing the bread of life with American airmen and British Embassy staff and Icelandic friends and all sorts of people.

No, my pessimism arises from the concern in my heart at the moment with the confrontation of Communism and Christianity. What brings me to Iceland is the collateral duty (and privilege) I have with respect to the United States Armed Forces in Europe, whose father-in-God I try to be as best I can, considering other roles and duties. The tiny, proud nation of Iceland is a member of NATO, and the American armed services make the military contribution in behalf of Iceland (which has no military establishment). It is not the easiest of all relationships, clearly; and there are doubtless moments when both parties cordially wish it did not exist. But for the most part it is accepted by both as part of the inescapable cost of defending the historic civilization from the danger of military attrition from the Communist world.

---

* From *Anglican World,* February-March, 1961.

This is why these men are here, and we with them. Otherwise we could all be at home with our families. As it is, the whole of my Christmas reflection has been conditioned by the cold war and, far more, by the stern and implacable frontier between the Christian faith and the Communist. This frontier runs all around the world, of course. It is far more evident and far more sensitive in other places than doughty little Iceland. Southeast Asia, for example, is a frontier of the highest priority in the strategy of both sides; so is Africa; so is Latin America. So, for that matter, should be the mind and will of every man and woman alive; but there are certain geographical frontiers which grip our thoughts at once.

One has only to trace on a map the vast crescent of Southeast Asia, with the aggressive salient thrusting its way from China into gentle and fertile lands, to be seized at once with the sense of frontier, and of the clear urgency of that frontier and our duty to man it and guard it with the best we have. Here is the heaviest concentration of the Chinese of the dispersion, for instance—that talented and resourceful people who were so deeply in the thought of the bishops at Lambeth 1958, on whom so much depends of leadership and development —and they are a frontier people par excellence.

But Southeast Asia is only one of many areas where one sees the confrontation of Communism and Christianity in such vivid and urgent terms. This confrontation is one of the determining facts of our history and it is no wonder that many millions examine the Church with thoughtful care, for the Church must be the champion of our civilization in that encounter. How many there are who make their judgment about the Church on this basis, like the gentleman I talked with a month or so ago, who told me that "the Catholic Church was the only one which took Communism seriously," and he thought he would join it. Disregarding the fact that he had "joined the Catholic Church" some forty years before when he had been duly baptized in his parish church in England, and disregarding also that the Roman Catholic Church outside of the United States seems to be not nearly as monolithic in respect of Communism as is sometimes supposed, the gentleman's comment was still the kind of remark which illustrates a depth of concern shared by very many thoughtful companions. And if it were true that the Roman Church, or any church, had some special copyright on taking Communion seriously, that would be a fact of major significance.

It is not true, of course. The challenge of Communism is to any church and all Christian belief—to all working belief in God of any tradition or description. But it is a very complex challenge—and this is where Christians are so often confused, and sometimes even facing the wrong way at the critical time. For example, there is an easy confusion between what is called "Communism" and what is in fact the historic drive of the numerous and powerful Russian nation toward a major share in the political and economic and intellectual life of the world. It was not Lenin who introduced aggressive expansionism into Russian life. The Soviet Government is walking in quite familiar footsteps in this; and it is of great importance that this be steadily understood. Otherwise our response to it will be the wrong one.

Or again, it is necessary to distinguish between the theoretical Communism of the doctrinaire mind and the practical politics of the work-a-day world. The Roman Catholic in Italy who is a staunch supporter of the Communist Party, or the Orthodox Christian in Russia who gives unhesitating allegiance to his country and its government, could very easily be labelled as a "Communist," and so he is. But Communism is something quite different to him than to the theoretician who writes the textbooks or the newspaper columns or whatever. To recognize this is not to be "soft" on Communism—it is to be accurate in defining where the enemy is, and what he is.

Still again, it is absurdly easy to say that the answer to Communism is to get people to join the Christian club as if there were some magic about Christian ceremonial or Christian formularies which automatically supplies the intellectual and social response needed. It will not be by merely reading the Thirty-Nine Articles or the Rosary that the attack of Communism will be turned away. The Roman Catholic Cathedral in Shanghai, I think it is, rejoices in a statue of Our Lord at one end of the reception hall and of General Mao at the other, which (if it is anything more than a rather naive patriotism) is suggestive of the case with which such superficial ceremonial accommodation can be had, as well as of the meaninglessness of the process which underlies it.

Well, one could go on . . . the point is that what is called "Communism" is a very complex thing indeed, and requires very careful dissection and analysis. This is not to say that we must back away from trying to answer it. It is rather to say that we must be sure that our answer is an answer to the untrue and subhuman heart of Communism and not to something else, on the fringe. It is perfectly right that Christians should have their witnesses in Africa or Southeast Asia or wherever, in the face of militant Communism. But it is of consummate importance that they bear their witness for Christ, and not merely for

the settled world they grew up in. It would be a tragedy if missionaries to the dispersed Chinese, for example, were betrayed into seeming
to be merely outposts of Western political policy in Asia, or if missionaries in Africa were to seem to be spokesmen for some status quo or
other. Christianity is revolution; it is the most radical of all revolu-
tions; it breeds revolution. But it must speak in its own terms, and not
those of some particular national policy or social structure.

Communism, as Charles West deeply observes (in "Communism
and the Theologians"), is not the revolution it purports to be. The
revolution is seen in resurgent nationalism, in rebellion against economic exploitation, in a demand for educational opportunity, in an
unswerving insistence on what Mr. Nehru called "the fourth freedom;
freedom from contempt," in all restless boiling up of once submerged
people.

> Communism claims to organize this revolution and give it direction
> and meaning. But the revolution is bigger than Communism . . . and
> the need for Christians who know the meaning of repentance, and
> who are free for endless experiments in new creation or service, will
> not soon be exhausted.

Christianity is revolution, for it is Christ alone who selflessly enters
into and bears the restless pain of the world. Christianity is revolution,
for it alone can give fundamental answers to the root problems of
human relationships, of inter-racial justice, of social and economic
organization, of power and freedom, of the ultimate meaning of life.
But it must speak for itself and for the revolution. Thus it must be
prepared to cut loose from mere nationalism, however civilized, and
from any confusion with merely traditional social patterns, however
deeply they may have been rooted in Christian faith, in time past.
It is the task of Christian witness to help to discover the new forms
and relationships which the immature, emerging societies require; and
this calls for a degree of inventiveness and of identification with the
new societies which we do not always show. Chiefly it calls for a willingness to immerse ourselves in the life and problems of those new
societies and make common cause with them, rather than to seem to
deal with them with long tongs, as if they were radioactive. And if
these generalities are to be fulfilled, it means taking chances in a way
safe, conventional churchmanship dislikes—taking chances with a
wider ministry of the laity, with a greater thrust in education, with a
fuller status for indigenous leadership, with a willingness to be involved in "secular problems" infinitely more deeply than we are accustomed to.

In short, it presupposes a change within Christianity so great as to be a revolution in itself. Whether we are free enough and concerned enough to accept this change is another question—our feet are so heavy with the clay of inherited respectability and timidity, when we should be ready to walk swiftly with Our Lord and our companions. But the first step is to watch where He goes, and see the people to whom He goes, and their hopes and needs and pain. Communism gives unspeakably bad answers to the problems of mankind. But it does move unerringly toward the real problems, or some of them, and in this respect it has something to teach Christianity. But He moves even more swiftly and surely. The question is whether we are prepared to go where He goes, and to accept the fact that He is already there when we get there. Indeed, this is the ultimate humiliation of the missionary, to discover that he is never the first one to preach the Gospel. But this is another story.

15. TELSTAR AND THE BODY*

THIS BEGINS as a sort of Anglo-American reflection, I am afraid, and perhaps it will not seem to make sense to readers elsewhere in the Anglican Communion. But I think it really does conceal a general point. It is about Telstar, the astonishing new satellite on which we can bounce various messages across vast reaches of the world's surface.

We stayed up late in our house to watch the inaugural program, a while ago. The satellite was hoisted into orbit satisfactorily, and after about five trips, there was to be an attempt to carom a television program from Maine to the two stations in Cornwall and Brittany. Ultimately it came out all right, as everybody knows, and there was even a return of compliments from France and Britain. As I write, the exchange seems not to have been entirely without stress and at least a breath of competitive international spirit. But this will settle down, no doubt. The great event itself was undeniable and clear; it was a most significant technical step forward; it will pave the way in very short order for an astonishing increase in international communications; once the bugs are out of it, it will permit immense new ranges of common experience; and it is one more miracle which a poor clod like myself cannot even understand.

I am old enough to remember sitting up half the night twiddling what we called a "cat's whisker" on a crystal set, hoping to get Sche-

---

* From *The Living Church*, July 29, 1962.

nectady (which was all of 150 miles away) and maybe hear a band playing or even the time signals. Now I sit up half the night watching somebody else twiddle an invisible finger of energy no bigger than a pencil, hoping to intercept a ball 600 miles out in space, traveling at some incredible velocity. And I cannot understand one any better than the other. So still another burden of helpless and ignorant wonder is added to the load of it most of us carry anyway, in our technological society. However, that is another story.

During the build-up for the first try at catching the satellite, our British television commentator filled the time with various interesting and sensible speculations. What would this marvelous new thing make possible? What television programs would come across the Atlantic, from North America to Britain? What would be sent back, indeed? So we looked at various bits of film. Some excellent Lapland reindeer, I remember, figured in the dialogue, for one thing. But being an American, I was particularly interested in what our commentator had selected to illustrate the probable U.S.A. component of this exchange.

I was not altogether surprised, I am sorry to say. One clip was of a housing speculator at Cape Kennedy. Another was of the successor to the Twist, as seen in a Harlem night club. (I am afraid that some assume that attendance at such galas is the standard evening entertainment of American families, who take the kids and have supper out at various picturesque *boites* such as the one illustrated.) Then there was a round or two of prize fighting. Finally, we were taken to a large university campus where we learned all about how high-school girls in the United States are taught how to twirl batons and be drum-majorettes or "pep girls." (It seemed again to be assumed that American universities—when they are not occupied in training people how to loft satellites into space—devote their buildings and energies mainly to such intellectual arcana as baton-twirling.) So we had an interesting half-hour of cultural exploration of American life, to prepare us for the miracle about to happen, and what would follow it.

If I took a somewhat dim view of the picture of the United States which was presented, it was not defensiveness. Because of my job, I happen to know more about both the United States and Great Britain than such a silly performance could either teach me or disguise. I know that I must brace myself, whenever I hear the word "American," for what is coming; so often, alas, it will be a distasteful and marginal revelation of some foolishness in the United States, and it does not seem to occur to the revealer that maybe Americans feel just the same way as he does about it. (May I at once add that I brace myself equally at home, when some dim wit starts to describe British life in terms of the Changing of the Guard, the Empire, British coffee, a nationalized Church supported by taxes, etc.)

I know that it was not ignorance which prompted the selection of scenes from American life, nor was it simply a sneer. Americans, like anybody else who lives abroad, know how complicated the problem of international understanding is, and how it is confused by questions of prestige, jealousy, insecurity, and all the pulling and hauling of international and intercultural rivalry. If the American image abroad excites the kind of smooth mockery which it often does, let no American, least of all an Anglophile like myself, put this down merely to ignorance or dislike. It is no more than the echo of our own voice, just as the offensive image of the British abroad reflects a similar impression of arrogance or ignorance. This is where the problem of understanding begins; you have said very little when you have simply described the impact of one culture upon another; you have really only defined the problem.

The important facts, the other night, were not the shallowness or the mockery. The important facts—the essential facts—were the shining sphere sailing through the night, and the immense and ingenious labor of men on two continents who could open such a great door of understanding. The important facts were the clean brilliance of Englishmen who could concoct television in the first place, of Americans who could get the satellite off the ground, of Russians with their more powerful engines, who could have gotten the satellite ever higher, if only they would come out from their cellar and join the human race.

Still more, there were the people on both continents—the anonymous people behind the images, trapped in the images—who are wrestling with the problems symbolized by Telstar. It would not be difficult, for example, to pick a few films of British life which could be as unfair as the ones shown from the United States. A dim but nimble American wit might have thought to introduce Great Britain to America by showing the recent Nazi rally in Trafalgar Square for a starter, followed by some shots of British Army life in a German village pub at 2 a.m., and then ending with a study of a rumble in some neighborhood dance hall in north London. But what sense would there be in this kind of comparative sneering? The only things which matter are the people behind the images, who have to cope with precisely the problems our civilization poses, including the problem of technology that runs so far ahead of even the best and brightest of us, including the crazy excesses and folly of a free society and a ridiculously rich and generous technology.

This is the essential problem of communication, not merely the exchanging of images, favorable or unfavorable. It is perfectly true—indeed, it is fatuous to say so—that every new development in communications like Telstar, poses problems to the technicians and the agencies and the nations involved. These are matters for the sparring of negotiators, and the arrangements of technicians.

But who is going to worry about the people behind the images? Who is concerned with the communication between the people themselves, who are at the heart of the pain and the wonder of their own cultures? I do not honestly know that there is any other communication agency at that level except the Church. Where else can a door be opened between the plain people of Great Britain (or France, or Japan, or Malaya, or Bolivia, or . . .) and the plain people of America, whereby each may understand something of the struggle and hope and fear and agony of the other? For to understand people, and to enter into the secret of their lives, is something which requires infinitely more than technical gimmicks. It requires imagination and humility—that imagination which is love in action, and that humility which is born in a sense of our common creation and our common hope and our common judgment. And these are the commodities with which apparently only the Church deals.

I do not intend to suggest that we should have ecclesiastical Telstars, or ask the nations of the world to provide more adequate religious programs for television broadcasting to satisfy angry Anglicans. The gimmicks we have, and what they make possible—movies, television programs, pictures and words, and all the rest—these are simply the thermometers of culture and politics at any given time, and the tools. The task of the Church lies behind these or beyond them. The concern of the Church is nothing less than the unity of mankind under God. To speak for this unity and to claim it, to express it in every possible way, to judge all that our nations do in terms of this unity, to apply the unity as a standard of life for all of our separate cultures and civilizations—this is the Church's business. And our own Anglican household has a significant part of this glorious ministry to carry.

Of course there are responsibilities here for the television authorities, the political leaders, the various tycoons and nannies who must sift what we shall see and hear. They do not underestimate these responsibilities, in the main. The question is whether the vast brotherhood of small men and women, who know that they neither deserve nor understand the power they wield nor are wise nor good enough to master it easily, is to discover itself across the world. The question is not how silly Americans can sometimes be (or British or Lebanese or Chinese or Filipinos or . . .); this is easy enough to document. The question is how one people can enter into another people's confusion and discontent and hope to see not the folly but the pain behind it, not the confusion but the search and the hope and the sense of judgment and the fight for responsible freedom which surges like blood through the universal arteries of humanity. This question is the heart of "telecommunication"; and I wish that the Church were better at asking it and seeking an answer to it, for in truth I think it is our principal business on earth.

The Indigenous Church

16. A PROVINCE IS BORN*

"THE CHURCH of the Province of Uganda and Rwanda-Urundi" was born Sunday morning, April 16th. At least that was the day it began its official career as the eighteenth independent Anglican church, launched with the prayers of the Archbishop of Canterbury who formally relinquished his direct responsibility and jurisdiction to the new Archbishop, and the bishops and clergy and faithful laity of the eight dioceses in the new Province.

This eighteenth member of the brotherhood of the Anglican Communion includes nearly a million-and-a-half Christians in the Protectorate of Uganda, that rich, green, high country at the head waters of the Nile. A century ago, Christianity was unknown there—unknown save perhaps through the hostile mind of the slaver, plying his dreadful trade in the gloom of the forest or across the baking open country. Eighty years ago the first Anglican bishop of the area was martyred. Indeed the whole early history of the Church in Uganda was nourished and lighted by the dark flame of martyrdom, for the Christian inherited the shame of the slaver; far more, he stood, as he must always stand, for an immeasurable threat to an existing way of life; and the price of both inheritance and threat was a great one.

But it was a deep and joyful experience to be a spectator at so climactic an event in the life of the Church. For one thing, it meant that every diocese of our Church in Africa except one, was now included in a self-governing, indigenous church. (The one exception,

---

* From *The Living Church,* June 11, 1961.

of course, is Liberia—still a part of the American Church). For another thing, it was the fifth and final time for Archbishop Fisher to officiate at such an occasion. How deeply he will be remembered for the tireless way in which he has worked to lead missionary dioceses into the mature and responsible freedom of which provincial status speaks! I could not help comparing, somewhat ruefully, the birth of the Province of Uganda with that of my own American Church! Things were not done quite as simply or as cordially in 1776 and thereabouts. There were tea parties on both occasions, but of a somewhat different character, as I remember them. There was no Archbishop of Canterbury present when the Protestant Episcopal Church in the United States of America came into existence—in point of fact, Archbishop Fisher's predecessor had some difficulty in quite placing what had happened, and the routines were by no means as well rehearsed in the 18th century as they are now.

But what happened was the same, in sober truth. In both cases, the devotion of pioneer missionaries had led to the establishment of the Church. The seed had been planted, and nourished by the love and faithfulness and imagination of countless people. And in God's good time, what had been a very frail seedling found its maturity and its strength.

Three pairs of thoughts keep recurring to me about these provinces. One has to do with the phrase we use, so often, about them—"younger churches." So they are; the history of the Church in Uganda covers barely three generations of Christians; and like any other of the newer provinces, traditions and institutions and resources all are at the barest minimum. One keeps reaching for things which are not there—habits of mind and customs and inherited attitudes as well as buildings and money and staff.

Young indeed these provinces are, and lacking in much of the self-reliance and resourcefulness which only time can bring them. But it must also be said that Christianity is never particularly old or young. In the most important respects, Christianity is never more than one soul deep. Wherever the Church is—whether in a parish church fifteen hundred years old, or the soul of a first generation African convert— the Church is the same. Old cultures have something to say to young cultures, and vice versa; but the voice of the Church within those cultures is as fresh and true one side as the other. This is a counsel to all of us who are members of "older churches," to take "younger churches" a good bit more seriously than we sometimes do.

My second reflection has to do with the nature of a province itself.

It is settled and universal Anglican policy, in the founding of missionary dioceses, that as soon as possible, those dioceses be included in regional and national churches—churches completely self-governing, completely indigenous, developing within their own cultures in responsible freedom. As early as the second Lambeth Conference in 1878, this principle was accepted as the agreed and settled policy.

Indeed it would be hard to imagine any other policy within the Christian Church. Yet with this profound agreement, there arises also a question. It would be so easy to feel that the job was done when a new province was created, to dust off our hands, spiritually, and turn to some other interest. The truth is that not every problem is solved when a new province is founded. It is completely right that the Church should become autonomous, and rooted in its own soil. But this by no means carries with it the assurance that the new church has all it will ever need to obey Christ's mission fully and effectively. I do not know any province of the Anglican Communion which is complete unto itself, and has nothing to receive from others, to say nothing of what it has to give. These new provinces still have every need for strength and encouragement and counsel and brotherhood. So have the older provinces. I can speak of my own American Church, for it is my own from birth. The American Church is the oldest Anglican Province outside the British Isles; it has been rooted in American life ever since there was any American life, since 1607; it has grown up with its nation and shares in all the vigor and resources of its nation. But it would be a very shallow and empty-headed Episcopalian who did not know how much the American Church has to learn and gain from its sister provinces—in theological education, in the rediscovery of mission, in the purification of our own inner life, in the wisdom and encouragement of our brethren.

I would be bold to say that precisely these same things are true of every Anglican province. A province is simply not an end in itself; just as a diocese, although it is the basic unit of the Church, cannot find its own fulfillment except within the brotherhood of a province, just so do provinces look beyond themselves for an ever-wider household within which their life can be perfected. Let us not fall into the trap of feeling that every objective of missionary work has been accomplished when a new province is born. What has changed may be no more than the terms of the mission. A new maturity, a new responsible brotherliness, a new church-to-church relationship has been established. But the obligation of the unity of the Church remains.

Finally, what of the part these new provinces play in the unity of the Anglican family? Here again I have two somewhat oblique thoughts. The Anglican Communion, in our classic definition, is a "fellowship within the One, Holy, Catholic, and Apostolic Church, of those duly constituted dioceses, provinces, or regional Churches in communion with the See of Canterbury." When a new province is created, one more free brother is added to this company. And it is hard for us, as we rejoice in this, not to feel a measure of pride that our family is growing larger and the list longer and the maturity and national rootedness of Anglicanism deeper.

Gratitude is something we have a perfect right to, in such a case. But pride is a two-edged sword. For what we really may be saying is not that we rejoice in the fact that the Church has become planted deeply and securely in the soil of a nation, but rather rejoicing that the imperium of the Anglican Communion has been extended. And when we let ourselves get in the mood of pride at what looks like an enhancement of imperial power or prestige, then we need to remember that it is the Church of Jesus Christ that we are talking about, and not a club or an ecclesiastical empire.

The fact that our mission is to build independent regional and national churches as swiftly as we can means also that we must expect and welcome every consequence of that independence—most of all, the involvement of the new church in the life of the Christian community as a whole. Side-by-side with the establishment of a new province comes the inescapable challenge of the ecumenical encounter. We have been hearing much, lately, about the "disappearance of the Anglican Communion." Where this means a fuller and deeper unity within the Church of Christ, no one can question this disappearance. This is part of our vocation, to work and pray tirelessly for the day when we can add our gifts and strengths to the common life of the whole Body of Christ. And nowhere is the pressure toward this deeper unity more strong and insistent than in the areas of the new provinces. Therefore with every thanksgiving for the launching of a new church there must also, and equally, come a sober expectancy that this new church there must face the implications of its own independent life. The mission of the Church leads to responsible freedom; but responsible freedom inescapably leads to a new and deeper confrontation of the ecumenical issues.

Our salvation here is to remember that it is with the Church of Christ that we are dealing, not with a possession of our own. If it is our privilege to be used by Christ in his mission, and so to pave the way toward the enlargement of His Church, we must be content to let the Church be His, obedient to His mission of unity as well as to His mission within our own Anglican household. I do not need to say how much the unity of the Anglican family means to me, or how deeply I share every right and good hope for its increasing strength and widening unity everywhere in the world. All I am saying is that we all need to remember, as I need very much to remember, that it is the One, Holy, Catholic, and Apostolic Church of which we are thinking, in all our proper rejoicing when a province is born.

17. EAST AND WEST*

THIS IS WRITTEN from New Delhi, where the Assembly of the World Council of Churches is in its early days, still at the stage of being bombarded with words by assorted theological howitzers, not yet settled down to full dialogue. The Anglican delegates are all present and on duty, I am glad to report. One more Anglican Church, that of Uganda, has been admitted to membership, so there are three more delegates from our flock to add to the about-80 Anglicans among the 650-odd delegates here. We sit separately, by nationalities and churches, among our companions of other traditions. There is not any Anglican "bloc" or confessional organization—I sit as one of the 13 delegates from the Episcopal Church in the USA, which astonishes some who look for me among the Church of England's lambs or on some lonely eminence of my own.

But it is not of Anglicans I want to write, but of East and West. Quite properly and movingly, most of the speakers thus far have been from Asia, and have underlined the necessity of "de-Westernizing" the Church and its teaching if it is to take deep and fruitful root in Asian soil. The preacher at the opening service, for example, the Rev. U Ba Hmyin of Burma, asked, "Is it possible to make the radical break from purely Western ways of thought, to do in Asia what first-century Christians did in the Greek world . . . ? We need the contribution of Oriental modes of apprehension based on primitive Christianity of Hebraic origin." Or, again, Dr. Paul Devanandan of India said, "We need a Church which is truly indigenous, and witnesses who think and speak and behave like those whom they address."

Who would not whole-heartedly agree? Certainly every North American would understand something of this need and wish for a "truly indigenous" church. My own church was, of course, the child

---

*From *The Living Church*, December 10, 1961.

of imperialist colonialism; not for 182 years were we permitted an indigenous episcopate. The fight to throw over the thrall of foreign rule and influence was a bitter one, and for generations we were dominated by an alien culture. But in God's good time we developed an indigenous ministry and church. Our American bishops and clergy are now mainly natives, and we have at least begun to develop American forms and patterns for the preaching of the Gospel and the ministering of the life of the Church. So in a tiny way we can share in this widespread thirst for new and more natural forms of thought and teaching.

So, too, I may presume to offer some sagacious counsel on this subject. Three thoughts occur to me. One is that it is always dangerously easy to be among the struggling minority, among the "younger" churches (to use a silly bit of jargon, as if the Church were ever anything but continuous with the Incarnation if it is the Church at all). The danger lies in the temptation to rest in an attitude of protest—to dwell on the need for restatement and reformulation and not go on from there to do some restating and reformulating. I think we "Westerners" are sometimes more anxious for indigenization than our non-Western companions are. Like the policeman in *The Pirates of Penzance* (a Western cultural phenomenon, alas), our brethren cry, "Forward on the foe," but they do not go. I do not say that it is so now, but it could easily become so, that the cry for cultural and theological independence would become simply a fixed slogan. You do not "indigenize" Christianity simply by changing words here and there, or wearing different costumes. I know, because we Americans have been through that mill, and tried it, and discovered that real indigenization calls for an understanding and penetration of one's own culture which is deep and costly and difficult and slow. The American Church is only in the early stages of this process, even 350 years after its beginning (1607, in Jamestown, not those Johnny-come-latelys in Massachusetts). So my first bit of sagacity for the indigenizers is to get cracking, and particularly in the most delicate and complex task of getting inside their own culture and imagining what our Lord is presently up to in that culture and then going to find Him and take their stand by His side. He is the only truly indigenous Minister there is.

Second, we need to ask just how much of the Christian apparatus is "Western" anyway. Certainly the Bible is not; the Bible is far more alien to England or America than it is to India. I cannot walk in a Delhi street five minutes before I have seen every important type of Biblical character and situation. I know that they are also and equally present in a New York street, but they have to be discovered there. They are not indigenous to the West; they are Eastern, and the Bible as a whole is Eastern. And so are the Creeds. Such odd bits of Greek thought-forms as are in the Creeds only remind us that Greek philosophy is again not "Western"—it was a product of the exciting, jostling traffic in ideas born in the fecund countries east of the Bosphorus at a time when the West was still wandering among the trees. But for the most part, the Creeds are simply war-songs for the simple, so they can cry together in a few phrases what the Bible teaches about the great acts God has done and is doing and will do.

Is nothing then "Western"? Well, yes, many things. Church government, for one, is full of Western and largely medieval eccentricities. It is certainly not characteristic of Biblical culture for the Church to be run by the clergy; this is a Westernism. So is the lord-bishop (here I must tread delicately—I hasten to say for British readers *et al.* that there is no hidden agenda here and no bolshevist attack on the nobility; all I say is that the medieval form of the episcopate is not the only one). So is the catechism, at least in some of its forms. So are the 39 Articles. So is a Bach chorale, or the Tudor dress of bishops, or the long monologue of the Communion service in the Prayer Book—and so one could go on. There are many such, often unsuspected, often most subtle. And the identification of these is a task for the most painstaking and expert research. How to dissect out the Westernisms in the relationship of church and state in a new Asian nation, for example, or in the preaching of the one God to people who have believed in Him under various aliases for a longer time and with greater assiduity than anything the West can boast?

Finally, the whole matter of translation, of de-Westernizing, is not simply a matter of exchanging new words for old. There are no words in any language adequate to express or communicate the deep things of God. Christianity never has found a vocabulary or a philosophy equal to this task. What we have done is to take words and ideas where we found them, and then to stretch and twist and remold them until they could serve our purposes with at least minimum adequacy. "Person" is such a word, for instance—we have taken and used this word in three languages. It was not big enough in any of the languages to do the job, but it was the best word we could find to communicate even a fragment of the intense and glorious selfhood of the Lord Jesus and at the same time be true to the immense action of God expressed in Him. So we borrowed it, crammed it full of a meaning it did not originally bear, sent it forth with an image and superscription on it which gave it an exchange value for the needs of the Christian community, indeed even far beyond that community. "Freedom" is another such word, "grace" is yet another, and so they go.

The only point I am making is that this is going to be true always, with any language or culture or philosophy. Yang and Yin, or the profound solitude of Eastern techniques of meditation, or the depths of non-violence or whatever—none of these will prove any more commodious a vessel for Christian truth than our poor, limited Western words have done. Christians have always had to put new wine into old wine-skins. There was no help for it, when it came to words and institutions, and there never will be any help for it. In our time we have used the forms and the ideas of many cultures, and we will continue to do so, just as our Lord used the bread and wine which was at hand. But the important thing is not the words or the customs or the institutions or the habits of mind; the important thing is what we do with them. Bishop or vestment or theological statement or form of worship or church constitution or hymn or whatever it is, none of these is anything in itself. Simply to change them will accomplish nothing. It will only be the unchanging life and faith of Christ's people, poured into these narrow bottles until they fill them and overflow and cascade in immeasurable richness to bless the lives of our brothers, that will accomplish the "de-Westernizing" we seek. And it may be, at that point that we shall discover that in Christ there is no East or West. But that is another story.

Let none of these thoughts suggest I am against indigenization. As an indigenous clergyman, much concerned with the problem of translating Christian truth into the indigenous language of the West, I welcome allies in non-Western areas, particularly if they are concerned to translate and communicate Christian truth and not simply to domesticate it. The truth is that we are all, East and West alike, perplexed as to how to translate the acts of God into the terms of this mortal creation. There would be an indigenization worth seeing! The curious thing is that that greater translation happened quite simply and easily and almost unnoticed at the time, when the Word was made flesh and dwelt among us.

18. "STRANGERS AND FOREIGNERS"*

THIS WHOLE BUSINESS of "indigenous leadership" is perplexing, I find. When I hear the phrase on the lips of churchmen from the newer

---

* From *The Living Church*, July 15, 1962.

churches of the world, I know what it stands for, and I agree whole-heartedly. God means for His Church to stand on its feet in every land; and one of the prime marks of that sturdy rooting is that the leadership of the Church in each place shall be of that place and its people. The purpose of the missionary—indeed his first purpose—is to cause this to happen. Older churches do not want ecclesiastical colonies or dependencies; they pray that they may be enabled by God's grace to have a part in planting everywhere in the world free, national, Catholic Churches, whole and single in each region and manned by that region's flesh and blood. Certainly this is our Anglican dream, and we are not alone in it.

Therefore we echo warmly the hope of the newer churches, that their affairs may be in their own hands, that they may be free to develop their own spirit and cultural tradition, make their own gifts to the ecumenical life of Christians, take their own part through their own clergy and laity in the world-wide dialogue of the Church—in a word, their hope for "indigenous leadership."

But I find myself (and this is the perplexing part) always a bit uncomfortable at this point. For one thing, this stress on indigenous leadership is sometimes taken as a farewell to missionaries; and I do not believe the time will ever come or ought ever come when the missionary should disappear. Mission is not something that belongs only to the infancy or poverty of the Church, nor is it something we owe to "them" (whoever they may be). Mission is a "note" of the Church fully as central and as Catholic as the four traditional notes—One, Holy, Catholic, Apostolic. I dare say it would have found its way into the creeds, too, along with the classic four, if there had been any quarrel about it. Indeed, I wish it had, for, in the familiar phrase (I do not know who coined it, actually), "the Church exists by mission as fire exists by burning." The time will never come when mission and missionaries cease.

The form of mission and the relationships contained and expressed in mission change radically, as they should. No church is so rich that it can condescendingly spill over its surplus on the deserving poor, and no church is so poor or weak that it has nothing to say to its older brothers. Mission to one another as well as mission to the world is the life-blood of the Church; mission and the missionary remain; and any system of indigenous life and leadership will and must and does make room for this.

But I go on in my reflection. The bishop who was my pastor for much of my life, who made me deacon and ordained me priest, was not an indigenous American bishop—he was an Englishman. The bishop who gave me, together with all American churchmen, the imperishable ecumenical dreams we have was not indigenous to the United States—he was a Canadian. The peerless Anglican poet of our time who has glorified English life and letters for a generation is not an indigenous English writer—he is an American. And so I go on, thinking of those who have given me the great gifts in my life, and one after another turns out to be a "foreigner," an "expatriate."

You may boggle at this point and say that I am choosing easy examples from the tight little Atlantic community—Manning, Brent, Eliot. So I am, for these lessons are clear and direct. God intends us to learn, and He starts us off with easy lessons. I grant that there is a vast difference between an American heading an Oxford college, say, or an Englishman teaching theology in the United States, and a Japanese heading a race-relations unit in the American Church or an African choosing candidates for a British missionary society. Yet these more difficult things happen, too (to our great enrichment), and they turn out in the end to be not at all different in kind from those easier transplants between more cousinly cultures. All that happens is that we grow bolder and more confident as we learn.

But the main point is the harsh and unforgivable impoverishment of life which would be the cost of any inflexible rule of indigenous leadership. No church, no nation, no culture is sufficient unto itself. We need the strength and the wisdom of the stranger who comes to us and makes our life and our cause his own.

And at that point I realize that there is a third truth to be remembered, that the strength and wisdom come to us from the expatriate, the foreigner, only because of love, only because he does make our life and cause his own. Again, I know that this is easy to do across the absurd puddle of the Atlantic. It is not remarkable that Hughell Fosbroke, a child of England, became the wise and disturbing leader of American theological education that he did, or that Paul Elmer More, an American born and bred, should have been the supremely luminous interpreter of the Anglican spirit he was. The love that rejoices in a common life of faith and culture, in men like that, is perhaps not as surprising as the love that has spoken uncounted times in men and women who have identified themselves with alien cultures and hostile peoples, and who have yet succeeded in laying their hearts and lives alongside those of strangers and so broken down a middle wall of partition between us.

This is, no doubt, a more costly love, that leads a man or a woman to bury himself in a life which is not remotely his own, which never can be his own. But costly though it be, it is not infrequently met. I think of those I have encountered in my wanderings who, like the great Expatriate, made themselves of no reputation, and took upon them the form of a servant. They can never be anything save foreigners. Yet their foreignness is so used by love that it uniquely and profoundly enriches the life of their adopted country. A man in Japan once made a speech to me about their need for indigenous church leadership. Then I asked him about X and Y, who were expatriates. His eyes widened and he said, "Oh we don't think of them as foreigners—they are really one of us."

So it is, and so may it often and happily be. I do not suggest in any sense that we abandon the drive toward indigenous leadership. Indeed much of my life and thought now is devoted to strengthening that leadership in our Anglican family. All I mean to say is that it is not as simple as it looks. Heaven is the only place where I am entirely sure of the sufficiency of indigenous leadership. The wide earth comes second only to that; yet even this wide earth's indigenous leadership turned out to be insufficient. Certainly I should not want to see any lesser gates shut against the free movement of ideas and persons. But the secret, as we learned in the Incarnation, is the love—the love that is content to be anonymous and to lose itself in the life and pain of others. Given this, I would pray that we all, in every nation, would eagerly welcome the guest, the stranger, who loves us enough to want to make our life his own, knowing that it never could be, yet living that way among us in humble brotherhood.

Strategy and Structure

19. MISSIONARY STRATEGY*

I MUST BEGIN by saying what all of us will doubtless feel before we are done reading, that the Anglican Communion is very far from having a single and united missionary strategy. There are many disheartening passages in what follows—disheartening not so much in the size and burden of the task before us, as in the fact that there is so little common effort and common understanding of what each part of our Communion faces. Churches, provinces, even individual dioceses seem

* From *Pan-Anglican,* Spring 1961.

so isolated from one another and from the whole body. They are by
no means ignorant of their mission or its importance and cost, but one
wishes for them some cheering sense that they are part of a very great
household, and that all the strength and intercession and loyalty of
that world-wide family is on their side.

I should be untrue to myself, and to the facts, if I emphasized what
is disheartening at the expense of what is so gloriously encouraging—
the enormous work now being done, the resolute new sense of mission
which stirs in so many parts of our Church, perhaps most of all the
eagerness for corporate, inter-Anglican thought and planning. This
last is, to me, most moving and encouraging. It is so partly because
my own new life and ministry is a product of it. It is so, infinitely more
significantly, because of the new age of Anglican mission and witness
which glows and brightens ahead of us.

But the heartening and disheartening elements must be taken
together. It would be folly to imagine that a new spirit is to be born
in our church life without disturbing and jostling old ways and old
habits of mind. Those who dream easily of a realistic and virile missionary strategy had better measure well the vast distance we have
to go to reach that goal, and the hard work that it will require. And
I think, first of all, we need to examine the very idea of "missionary
strategy" itself, and what it will cost, and how we may hope to build it.

"Strategy" is a dirty word to quite a lot of people. I read, awhile
ago, a very brisk little article by a churchwoman, in which she had
some sharp words on this subject. She described the Church (presumably the Church of England, but I do not know that she was too particular) as "far too often . . . a pompous old windbag, neurotically
busy, increasingly fussy with her 'image' . . . increasingly interested
less in love than in the nasty calculating thing called 'missionary strategy.' " Then she continued, "Any self respecting agnostic hearing the
word 'strategy' would, I should hope, start to run, and I, for one,
would lend him my running spikes any day. Christ knew nothing of
strategy in this sense, and it is, literally, a damned disgrace for His
followers to approach His children in such over-weening presump-
tion." *

Since at least one third of my present job is to be the Executive
Officer of the Advisory Council on Missionary Strategy, I was not
entirely unmoved by this. Granted that at the moment there is not a
great deal of inter-Anglican strategy for me to execute, it is still my

* *The Spectator*, September 16, 1960.

mission to help develop it. Granted also that the word "strategy" has a non-ecclesiastical ring, and I do not particularly like it myself, it is still a bit hard to be told that it is a "damned disgrace" for us to use it. I do not think it is at all. In fact, we have it on the best authority I know, that rather the contrary is true. Our Lord was speaking of nothing else than discipleship when He bade us apply to ourselves the lesson of the king who, "going to make war against another king, sitteth not down first, and consulteth whether he be able with ten thousand to meet him that cometh against him with twenty thousand." (St. Luke 14:31.) This consultation is the essential strategic preliminary; the weighing of needs against resources and the decision about objectives is the fundamental strategic process; and the whole art of waging a successful war against an enemy clearly seen and worth the fight is strategy itself. Christ taught us that we must so deal with our obedience to Him. And it would be either a cowardly or an incredibly sentimental Christian who was not willing to apply the same rigorous and realistic test to every part of his discipleship.

I am frank to say that I have no patience with people who talk in generalities about "love" or "faith" or "holiness" or whatever, and then refuse to put these things into practice, in any way that matters. And this is precisely the danger we run when we are afraid of "strategy," for the word means nothing else except the putting of something into practice. Strategy is the process of reducing a vague and general aim to specific objectives and possible steps—it is the process of using our strength in the best way we know how—it is the process of seeing where the fight lies, and what we ought to try to win, and how we can best win it. And if these things do not matter to Christians trying to obey the Lord Who sends us into a real fight in a real world, then the Gospel words do not mean anything at all, and we might as well retreat into the kind of acid and self-centered pietism I instanced above.

No, I do not particularly like the word "strategy," but I like what it means; and I am utterly convinced that the Anglican Communion needs and longs for exactly the thoughtful weighing of our mission and our objectives and our resources which the word signifies. And we need this and hope for it on a truly world-wide scale. This was the conviction of the Lambeth Conference, at any rate, in making their own the trenchant words of their Committee on Progress in the Anglican Communion:

> Dispersed throughout the world and working under every conceivable condition, (the Anglican Communion's) growth tends to a frag-

mentation of its efforts and a failure to reap the full benefit of its resources. It needs to be reminded in all its parts that no one lives to himself, and that as a body with a common life the whole is always something greater than the sum of those parts. In the context of the modern world with its pressures, competing systems, rival philosophies, and expanding frontiers of knowledge, the need for consultation is of paramount importance.

If the responsibilities of a world-wide Communion are to be grasped and its resources mobilized, fuller expression must be given to four vital principles of corporate life—co-ordination, co-operation, consolidation, cohesion.

Our Communion has not had very much of those four principles, especially in our specifically missionary life. There are obvious reasons for this. One is the nature of our history. The Anglican Communion came into existence with about as little deliberate planning as can be imagined. Church people left England and went to North America and took their church with them; and the church back home was not lacking in provision for its children, but it was the adventurousness of the children that told the story, rather than the missionary zeal of the mother church. Not until the first daughter churches in North America had actually been established on their own—not until the great missionary outburst of the 19th century—was the overseas mission of the Church of England taken seriously. Then indeed it bore a glorious harvest of dedicated men and women and of new national churches founded everywhere in the world. But we were and are marked by our history; it is not yet natural to us to think in terms of a united resolution and plan.

Another reason lies in the very looseness of our federation itself. This is, doubtless, a source of strength as well as weakness. We Anglicans are wedded to the national principle—to the principle that the Church should not play at being a super-state, but should rather be deeply and richly rooted in the soil of its own country and people. This principle is rightly held precious by us; and it would be as nearly inconceivable as it would be wrong for us to abandon it in favor of some world-wide ecclesiastical power structure.

But the principle has its dangers, which are those of isolation, of provincialism, of division and narrowness, which breed weakness and disunity, and which dissipate strength and defeat our essential unity and our mission. These dangers threaten now more and more ominously, the more our world shrinks and we are forced into a new realization of our interdependence. The world of the 19th century was, by contrast, a roomy, easy-going world, with ample time and scope for adventure and for experiment. But there is no room left, and no time, in our world; we are deeply bound together, so that it is hard to say where one national interest ends and another begins; and while we rightly cleave to our independence in our separate churches, we are also deeply aware of our need to think and choose and act together. This, we come to see, is not at all a surrender of our traditional freedom, but rather an intelligent and far-seeing use of it.

A third reason may be found in the highly voluntary character of much of our missionary initiative and support, especially in the mother Church of England and her missionary societies. I think most of us would accept whole-heartedly the words of the 1958 Lambeth Report:

> Missionary societies came into existence to recall the Church of England to a task which had been neglected: indeed, many Provinces of the Anglican Communion would not have come into being, had it not been for their work. They have done and are doing a missionary task as handmaids of the Church.

I would only point out, in this connection, what Lambeth also pointed out, that "any plan by which the societies would be drawn into even closer co-operation should be welcomed." This is actually happening in a remarkable way, as the contribution from England will illuminate. But it is important to recognize in the principle of these voluntary societies, one of the reasons why there has been as little co-ordinated strategic thinking as there has been.

And the same voluntary principle has served, with the parallel principles of the autonomous national church, to create the curious Anglican missionary profile in many areas of the world. Americans ask, "Why is there so little Episcopalian missionary work in Africa?" English people wonder at the fact that two, quite separate Anglican churches are both at work in the Caribbean. An Anglican looks almost in vain for a priest or a mission of his church in Indonesia or the Congo or many parts of South America. In Japan there are (or were) "American" areas, and likewise "SPG" areas or "Canadian" or "CMS"— as if there were no single Anglican life at all.

This is what I mean by our curious missionary profile. It is the result of having no long-range plan in such things. For all the vigor and imagination our voluntary system gave us, it also cost us much, in terms of neglected areas or partisan feelings or even division within our own ranks. Indeed there are still places where it is hard to believe that two Anglican churches are still in the same household—indeed, where two missionary traditions seem almost to be hostile one to another.

But this is passing, more swiftly than anyone really knows. And with the passing comes a new sense of the Church, the Church of Christ as He is known and worshipped and followed by the children of the Prayer Book. And this new sense of the Church, a sober, urgent sense of the unity of our life and our mission, is what gives such buoyant vitality to our present search for a new missionary strategy.

How is this to be found? The central agency—indeed the only agency we have in this search—is the Advisory Council on Missionary Strategy. This body, composed of the heads of all our 17 Anglican Churches (or their deputies), came into being officially following the 1948 Lambeth Conference. It had only the most shadowy existence in the ten years following, and was extensively redesigned and implemented by Lambeth 1958, chiefly through the adoption of a new organization and new terms of reference, by the appointment of an executive officer, and by the establishment of a modest working budget. All this is entirely voluntary, of course; I do not know that the Council officially exists at all, and I have not the faintest idea what job security I have. Nevertheless, the establishment and purpose of the Advisory Council is whole-heartedly shared by every one of our Anglican churches; in theory at least, there is not one of our forty million fellow churchmen who does not have a share in its support; and all our hopes for what the Council may do for our common life are very high.

The Council, of course, can only recommend to the churches it represents matters for them to consider and decide for themselves. Yet the Council is so deeply representative of all our separate churches that I am sure we are likely to take its recommendations seriously. What might such recommendations be? How would they be arrived at?

My own thoughts are very simple ones, at least as to procedure. The Council is a collective body, therefore it must meet. But there is not much use in its meeting until there is adequate material for consideration and decision. Therefore my initial task must be to prepare for the Council the material it will need to make the recommendations it should.

I imagine that the first target date for the Council's next meeting would be in August of 1963, when so great a part of our Anglican family will be gathered together in Toronto, for the next Anglican Congress. This means that for the next thirty months or so, my energies must go into assembling the data—the studies and surveys, the background material, the statistics and all the rest of it—which will make it possible for the Council to take intelligent and far-seeing action. The areas needing such study and decision were in large part laid down by the 1958 Lambeth itself. Geographically, five areas were specially mentioned by the Conference—the new African townships. South America, the "Chinese of the Dispersion," the highlands of New Guinea, and the Middle East. This was not intended to be an exhaustive list, by any means; it was meant only to underline the areas which the bishops at Lambeth felt were of particular and immediate concern.

Other areas as well seem quite clearly to need special thought. It seems, for example, hopelessly unrealistic to expect the Church of England to sustain the vast and increasing missionary frontier in Africa, with little more than token support from other Anglican churches. Yet it is easier to imagine such redistribution of a load than it is to plan it; to plan wisely for better sharing is a matter requiring our deepest and most thoughtful insights.

Our whole Pacific frontier equally bids us to thoughtful appraisal—our church in Japan occupies one of the most critical social and political sectors our world knows; and the comradeship we all feel for that extraordinarily devoted little church needs to find far broader and more far-seeing fulfillment than what we now know.

These are some of the areas where, very likely, our common planning ought to begin. If all goes well, the first long, thoughtful meeting of the Advisory Council, in 1963, will result in practical decisions which will then come to the constituent churches of our Communion for discussion and action. Thus may be born at least the beginnings of a unified, inter-Anglican missionary strategy.

I have underlined in the following pages, some points which I think are of particular concern in the development of an Anglican strategy, such as the question of missionary societies or central organization, the urgent need of provincial and inter-provincial study, the question of the redistribution of present commitments.

Our dialogue does not touch significantly on a number of other questions which also must eventually figure in our common thought. I mention some of them now merely to indicate the areas where further conversation is needed. What is to be the future development of such regional groups, inter-provincial groups, as the South East Asia Council, for example? It seems clear to me that we are in great need—in such areas as the Caribbean or Africa—of a device which will foster a healthy regionalism in consultation and planning, in some way which will not over-ride present provincial boundaries. The South East Asia Council does this admirably at the moment. What is the real value of such councils, and where and how should they be developed or changed?

Another whole group of questions revolve around the practical difficulties of the "inter-change of persons" so vital to our common life. Questions of salary, pension, jurisdiction—questions of education and preparation—questions of relationships between nationals and foreigners—questions of the training of the laity—all these, quite practical and doubtless quite susceptible of solution, given the will, are still perplexing ones when it comes to strategy.

Still a third group of questions arise on the frontier of our Communion with the ecumenical movement. National church union schemes, ecumenical study programs, the very existence of the ecumenical movement itself, all introduce radical new factors into our strategic thinking, about which we have a constant need to think aloud.

Yet again, there is little in this present dialogue bearing on our Anglican, Christian encounter with the non-Christian religions. Strategy is not merely a matter of men and money—it is, perhaps far more, a matter of ideas. The strategy of the Church is never geographical or statistical. Like the loaves and fishes, our task is to put into the hands of God the insignificant things of the world, which are quite enough, in His providence, to meet the world's needs. Often we seem to forget this. Yet, in the end, it is the cardinal truth about strategy. What are we to say? What has the Church to say—what ideas, what new words, what new insight into human relationships and the value and destiny of human life have we to contribute to the eager restless searching of our time? These are the basic strategic questions, really, seen most sharply when asked against the background of the ardent religions of the world, or the resurgent nationalism or racialism we confront.

20. SOCIETY OR CHURCH*

THERE ARE, in the Anglican Communion, two main ways in which we give our missionary support. One is the missionary society; the other is the missionary department or board. One is a voluntary group within a church; the other is a function or division of the Church as a whole. The Church of England is organized entirely on the society principle; the American or the Canadian Church use the other system. Some, like the Churches of Australia or New Zealand, have a mixture of both.

I am not going to argue which system is right! Undoubtedly there is no "right" system. The great missionary societies were born—chiefly to meet the needs of the infant American Church, as it happened— within an established church, a fully national church, a heavily-en-

---

* From *The Living Church*, March 24, 1963.

dowed church, as a way for groups of especially-concerned people to express their concern. After years of attempting to transplant the British system into North America, into a church which was itself a voluntary society, not established, not "national," not endowed, it came to be accepted that societies did not meet North American needs, and another system, in which the whole Church was regarded as a single missionary society, involving every churchman, came into existence. To try to judge which is the right principle is like trying to pass a moral judgment on a British winter or Hudson Bay.

It is proper, I think, and helpful to note the excellences of each method. To me, an American, certain unique gifts of the society principle stand out. One is a precious sense of responsibility, personal responsibility. The loyal supporter of a missionary society knows that the work of a certain bishop or even a certain missionary depends on him. He gives directly to it, if he chooses to; he knows about the diocese, that mission; he prays for the work and the workers; he very likely knows some of them personally; he is himself involved, in prayer as well as in his stewardship, with the particular sector of the Church's mission with which he has identified himself.

Another gift of the society principle is that it encourages missionary education. Not only because of the element of personal responsibility but also because the society's work depends so much on informed membership, there must be steady attention paid to the endless process of communication between the society's work overseas and its membership at home. Pictures, the printed word, personal visits—every medium of communication is brought into play so that those who support and pray for the Church's mission shall know what it is they are working for.

A third gift is that of flexibility. When large new projects are planned, or an unforeseen need arises, the society has a resilient and responsive group to which an appeal can be made. "Our" mission is threatened or "our" mission can take a great step forward, and the society can appeal to that responsible, personal concern and find strength quickly to meet opportunity or need.

Finally, I might mention a certain vividness of understanding of mission, a depth in awareness of the centrality of missionary obedience in the life of a Christian, which is a gift of the society principle. A conscientious supporter of a society's work is, by that very personal commitment itself, accepting obedience to Christ's mission as part of his personal discipleship. And this spiritual yeast of commitment at the heart of the Church is an admonition and an example to be envied.

To be fair, there are also certain special gifts and strengths from the other alternative, the "Church principle" of missionary obedience. One is the reminder that mission is not an option for the "missionary-minded" churchman alone, but part of the universal duty of all Christians. In the American Church, for example, the church's program includes overseas missions as well as every other activity of the church as a whole, and the cost of that program is apportioned to every diocese, and then to every congregation in due course, and so finally to the conscientious stewardship of every individual. Thus, the individual cannot limit his support simply to certain sectors of the budget which strike his fancy.

Another excellence to be noted is the unity given to missionary work by the fact that it is an act of the whole Church. The missionary dioceses of the American Church are constituent parts of the Church—their bishops, clergy, and laity are members of the General Convention, the supreme governing body of the Church; their needs and hopes are part of the total concern of the whole Church; their witness represents not the interest of a group within the Church but of every member of the Church, at home and abroad.

Third, there is a gain from the inclusion of missionary work in the same budget, the same frame of reference, that includes everything the Church does. This helps to force on the Church, a steady, helpful reminder of the single mission, abroad and at home, which is the heart of the Church's life. Still again, I might mention the unity of direction and support which the Church principle encourages. The whole strength of a church stands behind its missionary decisions, and this can give a welcome degree of certainty and of stability, especially to precarious missionary frontiers.

Neither system completely lacks what the other has, of course. Nor is either system without its drawbacks. I am more familiar, probably, with the weaknesses of the unified Church principle because I grew up within it and know it intimately. It is rare in the American Church, for example, to find anything like the same depth of responsible, personal concern and identification with overseas missions as one finds in the Church of England. This lack of personal identification is a by-product—no doubt undesired and unnecessary—of the impersonal budget method by which the unity of the Church system is preserved.

Again, the central administration of a church's whole life can unintentionally work to weaken missionary education. In the overseas budget of the American Church, for instance, practically nothing is set aside for missionary education. There is no need for the Overseas

Department to promote support for itself. Promotion and education are concerned with the whole program of the Church, not mission alone; they are the responsibility of other Departments. The result tends to be a lack of specific attention to missionary concerns and to the development of personal knowledge and identification with overseas work.

Again, any budget, anywhere, is an invitation to parsimony. When any church under heaven reduces its work to a money total, money to be raised by apportionment, that work inescapably looks like a tax, feels like a tax, and therefore cries out to be reduced. It is perfectly true that this same comment would apply to the voluntary society, if its funds were raised in a similar way. But the principle of offering, of stewardship, of giving because of one's own need to obey and give, is infinitely stronger in the society system than in the central, unitary plan, and as long as that is so, those who follow the Church principle are likely always to have their generosity stifled and their creative freedom paralyzed.

With respect to the society principle, I like least of all its tendency to divide witness and to perpetuate differences. Recently I commented on the question of Anglican unity-in-diversity. I could have illustrated the point from missionary history, notably from the clashes of conviction that, in days gone by, bred societies devoted to "Evangelical" principles or "Catholic" principles or whatever kind of principles. Ardent defenders of the society system plead the inclusiveness of Anglicanism, and the place of the voluntary society as a way of expressing this inclusiveness. I am not particularly impressed by this, precisely because the tensions within Anglicanism—the tensions, say, between "Evangelical" and "Catholic" elements—are not options for groups or parishes or societies to choose. They are tensions built into the very heart of the Church, into the Prayer Book, into the life of the individual clergyman or layman himself. The precise point of the Prayer Book is that it is both fully Catholic and fully Reformed all the way through. There are not two priesthoods or two kinds of sacraments or two Churches.

Believing this, I do not like any system which seems to present alternative versions of Anglicanism, or which keeps Anglicans themselves from facing the issue of unity. There may well have been times when the freedom of a society to witness to certain Anglican principles was essential to the Church's wholeness. But we have all too often exported our domestic problems into nations which knew nothing of them and needed to know nothing of them, and thereby we have unwittingly perpetuated disunity. I thank God that this is now largely a matter of history, not of present missionary activity. But the danger remains.

I might add a second question I have about the society principle, that it tends to perpetuate antique stereotypes of mission and the missionary, partly because he and his work are thought of as something outside the normal range of the Church's life and responsibility, and partly because of the very important element of personal identification itself. This is too complicated a subject for analysis here. Any appeal for support for anything depends on stereotypes, and stereotypes are usually antique. The Marxist ideal of the happy worker-peasant or the figure of the artist-intellectual is as much of an antique as the classic picture of the missionary teaching happy natives how to say their prayers under a palm tree. Both are probably inescapable as public relations devices. But to anyone who feels about mission that it is not an option but a duty, an over-dependence on personal or individual identification seems to run the danger of sentimentality.

But I do not mean to draw out these impressions and comparisons. I began by saying that I thought it was impossible to judge one system over against another. I feel that quite strongly. Such judgments would be unimportant and irrelevant. What matters, I think, is that each system shall learn from the other—add to its own excellences those good things which the other system makes possible. I cannot say what I think the missionary societies could learn, or ought to learn, from the churches organized in a different way. I have already indicated some of the things I think can be learned from the society principle.

I would covet for American church people precisely the sense of responsible identification and commitment which they so often long to have and do not have. Equally I would covet for the Church in America an infinitely greater knowledge of the mission of the Church overseas than what is now possible. Most of all, I long to see an end to the burial of overseas missions in the huge impersonality of a dollar budget. My American colleagues have heard me on this subject before, and I shall not dilate on it. In any case, I am speaking only as one more American, even if I have had a rare opportunity to see both missionary systems at work.

But the only point I want to make is that, if we are to learn from one another, there must be dialogue—which in turn implies a willingness to study and listen. I am sure that such dialogue will be found when the churches of our Communion meet in Canada this coming summer. This is one of the principal reasons for such a meeting.

However, as we engage in the dialogue, I would pray that we would all bring to it an understanding that there is no final orthodoxy in such matters to be required or defended. The immense, single mission itself is the only thing which matters. How we channel our obedience is a matter of constant thought and amendment; no method is perfect; no obedience is complete; we can never safely say that we have done all that is required of us. Let the greatness of mission itself cleanse and deepen our dialogue—I am sure this is the prayer with which all conversation within the Anglican Communion must begin.

21. THE STRETCH IN BETWEEN*

A WHILE AGO I wrote about the differences between the two main ways we have, in our Communion, of supporting overseas missions—the "society" principle and the "Church" principle, as one might call them. (Both words are somewhat misleading, actually, because societies serve the Church, and the Church is simply a single society, and I should be just as happy to call them "System A" and "System B," if anybody knew what I was talking about.) At all events, writing that article got me thinking about another of these sets of variations within our Communion, those clustering around the relationship of the young missionary diocese to the Church which gave it birth and to the future Church into which it will grow.

The beginning of missionary work is always the same. It is born in the obedience and devotion of existing Christians in existing churches. The end of missionary work is always the same. It is the planting of the Church in a new soil, a new culture, so that it takes root prepared and ready to live its own life, expressing its own genius, making its own responsible decisions. It is the stretch in between the beginning and the end which taxes our wisdom and our humility, and invites continuing and patient experiment.

This middle stretch is a difficult one. It involves the Church, both the older and the newer, in countless practical decisions, stage by stage. Control over funds and property, the assignment of the clergy, liturgical originality, canons and government—it is around such issues that the discomforts and misunderstandings in missionary history gather. On the part of the newer church, there is a constant and wholly justifiable longing for that responsible freedom which is the mark of matur-

---

* From *The Living Church*, April 14, 1963.

ity. On the part of the older church, there is an equally understandable reluctance to have the young church lose too soon the experience and wisdom which an older church undoubtedly has.

Sometimes, as now, this inevitable tension between older and newer churches is complicated by yeasty political and social factors. The church in the emerging new societies of the world, quite understandably, feels a heightened thrust toward liberty and maturity. What is so often called "confessionalism," in the ecclesiastical slang of our time—meaning unfair control of a young church from outside or unjustified influence over it—has its roots deep in this multiplied thrust.

What we do not often enough see is that all this is a problem in Christian unity. It is not simply a matter of finding appropriate and wise ways to transfer power and control. These are the practical issues, indeed, and they must be met. But the deeper question involved is how to establish and maintain, at every stage, the fullest possible expression of the ultimate unity of Christ's Body, in ways which are appropriate to whatever stage we have reached.

In general we have followed one of two paths, in dealing with this problem of unity in Anglican history. In one case, we have thought of the infant missionary diocese as essentially separate from the sponsoring church, at least administratively, from the outset. It is, of course, nourished and supported by the older church. The missionary societies or boards or whatever they are accept full responsibility for its life. Through them the sponsoring church gives its strength and leadership to build the younger church. But it is clear from the beginning that the younger diocese is on its own. Its horizon is its own nation and its own people. It has little part in the life of any larger unit than itself, at the beginning. Its bishop is alone (save for his personal relationships with other bishops and with his metropolitan, of course). Usually its bishop is a missionary sent out to it, in the early stages. Even after an indigenous clergy is fully developed, the selection of its bishop is usually in the hands of a remote authority. In all these ways, the young diocese is on its own from the beginning, with only the most limited bridge to its sponsoring church—a bridge composed of missionaries, for the most part, who come and go from a mysterious, largely unknown, remote and foreign church.

I contrast with this another pathway, also familiar in Anglican life. Here the new diocese is from the outset part of the sponsoring church. Its bishops are members of the parent episcopal synod; representatives of its clergy and laity, in many cases, share in the government of the parent church; indeed, it may be in every way a constituent diocese of the parent church even though separated by very great distances. American church people, for example, might well marvel more than they do at the presence in their General Convention of bishops and clerical and lay deputies from the Philippines or Brazil or Africa. And so might the Australian or Canadian or New Zealand churchmen find his organic partnership with younger churches remarkable. All this has the effect of giving to the young church a sense of participation in a far wider whole. It establishes a certain level of unity; it gives to the young diocese a representative share in its own government; it may even give that diocese the right to join in determining its own support; it strengthens the bridge between the younger and the older church.

This second pathway can lead to strange anomalies, sometimes. It is strange, for instance, to call an African or an Asian diocese an "American" diocese. It is strange to have the government of a new church, in its own indigenous culture, still controlled by constitutions and canons developed for an older church, in an entirely different culture. It is strange to have the indigenous, national bishops of a new diocese chosen by a house of bishops, most of whom may never have seen the new church nor its society. An even greater danger is probably that of an excessive paternalism. Precisely because the young diocese is so securely set in equal partnership with other dioceses in the mother church, there doubtless is a tendency to prolong that relationship unduly, perhaps so far as to build a spiritual wall around the young church so that it remains foreign even among its own people and in its own culture.

Of course this pathway is not alone in its dangers. The other has its anomalies and dangers, too—doubtless at different stages, and in different ways. From what little knowledge I have, I think I can see weaknesses pretty equally in both systems. I do not mean that the weaknesses, the problems, are equal; they come at different points and in response to different situations. What I am really saying, I suppose, is that I think neither system is a perfect system. If there is a danger of paternalism on one hand, there is a danger of isolation and loneliness on the other. If in one system a diocese is constitutionally closely identified with the parent church, there may also be on the other side an identification all the more powerful because it is personal or cultural rather than constitutional, because it is through others rather than through the responsible participation of the national people themselves. If it seems strange to have an "American" diocese in the Philippines, for example, it is no less strange to find a "CMS" or "SPG" or "UMCA" church somewhere else. It is no more odd, really, to have an

African bishop elected by the American House of Bishops than it is to have an Asian bishop appointed by the Archbishop of Canterbury.

I make no judgment between these two systems. I can see losses and gains on both sides, and I honestly would find it impossible to say that either one is correct, at all stages of growth and under all conditions. What I am getting at, of course, is that this is another instance where dialogue is needed—where every Anglican church needs to teach every other, and learn from every other. Some churches have got to learn how to let go of their younger partners sooner. Others have got to learn how to give their younger partners more mature experience and training.

I myself like the American way of doing things, in the early stages of missionary life, because I think it gives the new church a deeper sense of unity at the start, and gives it that sense through the participation of the young diocese in the whole life of the American Church from the very beginning. I like having the bishops of the Church in non-American cultures and societies sharing in the community of bishops with me. I like having Asian or African priests and lay people sharing in the budget and government of the Episcopal Church. I think it is good for both the young church and the older one to share a common life, from the start.

But I can also see that it is essential to build into such a system a clear and progressive path toward that full independence which lies at the end of the road. If I may quote the American system again, a major weakness in it is that there is really no intermediate stage between infancy and maturity. The passage from the status of missionary diocese to that of autonomous province is taken in one convulsive step, and I myself believe this to be a weakness.

By contrast, the other system tends to give the new church a very much slower start. Its only window into a large church is through the expatriate missionary; its unity with the wider Church is likely to be restricted to national identity or missionary dependence; it runs the risk of a persistent infantilism; it tends to discourage the development of self-reliance and buoyant indigenous leadership. Yet I must equally say that the passage of such dioceses from their missionary beginning to the full autonomy of an indigenous province can be a lot faster and more aggressive than under the other system. Precisely because the American missionary diocese is a member of a Province from its birth, there is not nearly the eagerness for the development of the indigenous, regional Province that one finds in dioceses nourished under the other system.

We begin at the same place. We end at the same place. Our questions are the important, practical questions of the stretch in between the beginning and the end. And with the growing intensity of inter-Anglican life—with the growing interdependence there is within the Anglican Communion—there is a steadily greater need for us to take common counsel, to learn from one another, to experiment together, and to find successively wiser solutions, God willing, to our common problems. I do not know of any more urgent ecclesiastical task in our time than that of finding better ways to nourish responsible leadership in the younger churches, and to do it without violating the essential unity of the world-wide family of the Church. This is, I say again, the real point behind all these thoughts and questions.

I hope I will be forgiven for burdening readers with what may seem to be merely technical problems. I do not think they are merely technical. I believe so profoundly in the unity of the Church across the world, that I think all the aches and pains of the relationships between older and younger churches are really only the surface indications of a profound and imperative concern. And I close with what I have found a most moving insight into all this, luminously expressed for me by Bishop Newbigin [Church of South India]. Speaking of precisely these problems, he asks the question, "Have we allowed the work of missions to become assimilated to the processes of Western cultural invasion, so that we have made of it an affair in which we were responsible for directing a process of teaching and training for the so-called younger churches until in our judgment they were ready for responsibility?"

He goes on to comment, "What does not seem to have been noticed is that the question does not seem to arise at all in the biblical situation. There is no period in which the Church is independent. From the very beginning every one of these young churches, with all its manifold weaknesses and even scandalous sins, is treated as simply the Body of Christ in that place, the dwelling place of the Holy Spirit, and, therefore, as being not independent and not dependent but always and from the very beginning in a position of reciprocal inter-dependence with the other members in the Body of Christ."

If this vision of unity and interdependence be true, and I believe it is with all my heart, then our question must be, how shall we better organize ourselves so that just such interdependence, just such unity, is clear before our eyes at every stage? This is a question for Anglicans, and I think an urgent one.

22. LATIN AMERICAN MISSION*

"THE NEGLECTED CONTINENT"—that was the phrase used by the bishops at Lambeth 1958 to characterize Anglican attitudes toward South America. The phrase could have been applied to all of Latin America, for that matter; and it could also have been applied to others than Anglicans. The Roman Catholic Church, which can claim at least the nominal allegiance of 80% of Latin America, has used the same phrase to describe its own attitude toward this vast area and its people. I remember the scorn with which a Roman Catholic friend greeted my comment about "a Catholic culture" (when I wrote once about Latin America)—a "pre-Catholic culture," he said, "is the most that could be claimed; and if we cannot find the 30,000 priests we need to serve our empty parishes, we shall not have the right to claim even that."

Well, Rome must speak and act for themselves, and they are doing so. I can speak only of ourselves; and the "neglect" Lambeth spoke of is true enough to hurt. It is partly ignorance. The recent statement from the Consultation on the Anglican Communion and Latin America reminded us that Anglican churches have been at work in this area for two centuries; and I dare say that fact came as a surprise to most Anglicans. So would a knowledge of the scope of present Anglican life in Latin America come as a surprise. British people perhaps know of the Diocese in Argentina or of the work of the South American Missionary Society in Chile or in the Chaco. Americans may have heard of our church in Cuba or Panama or Puerto Rico. But in contrast to our intense interest in Africa or Asia, most of us have only the sketchiest knowledge of Latin America.

Yet nearly half of the missionary budget of the American Church is spent in Latin American fields. The Church in Brazil—now three dioceses and soon to be four, God willing—very likely will be the next Anglican province to begin its autonomous life as an entirely national Portuguese-speaking church. Eight dioceses of the American Church (apart from Brazil) bear our witness in Latin America, six of them with Spanish as their official language and one with French (Haiti). Eight dioceses of the Church of the West Indies share the common life of the Caribbean, three of them responsible for work on the Spanish-speaking mainland.

Some of these jurisdictions are of comparatively recent missionary origin. Some, like Haiti or Mexico, began a century and more ago as independent national churches, later coming into full partnership in

* From *The Living Church*, February 24, 1963.

the Anglican Communion. Some are now entirely or almost entirely national in staff. Some still consist extensively of chaplaincies to English-speaking communities. What binds them all together is the obedience of which the Cuernavaca Consultation spoke: "In obedience to the Divine Commission, we have been ministering for nearly two centuries in Latin America in the name of the Lord. Today, in response to a fresh prompting of the Holy Spirit, we are renewing our dedication to this ministry, on a larger scale in the face of drastic and dynamic changes in Latin America, through which the Lord of the whole earth is as ever working out His purposes."

It is ignorance, in part, that has led to much Anglican "neglect" of so great a sector of our corporate life. But much more has entered into it, of course—for instance a feeling that Latin America was already an "evangelised" territory; a sense that it was a backwater in history by comparison with, say, Africa; a view of it as an appendage of North America, or of older, European Latin cultures. None of these is true. Perhaps ten per cent of Latin Americans (I quote Roman Catholic sources here) are practicing Catholics and another three per cent are working Christians of other allegiances. The inherited monolithic culture, based on at least a remotely Catholic world-view (I still call it a "Catholic culture" in spite of my Jesuit friend's admonition), is fast being pulverized by the hammer-blows of secularism. Latin America is now perhaps the most alluring prize in the eyes of Communism. For all its profound economic and political ties with Europe and North America, Latin America now leads its own life and makes its own decisions. There is no excuse any more for Anglican neglect, or anybody's neglect, of this immense and powerful land.

The Lambeth comment, of course, led to the Consultation in Mexico, a few weeks ago. Two dozen bishops, theologians and missionary leaders met for four days with the Archbishop of York as chairman. The primates of the Canadian and American churches, bishops or delegates of two West Indian and five Latin American dioceses, and representatives of the missionary departments and societies of England and North America composed the group. We met in one of the boys' hostels of the Diocese of Mexico, a land where any religious instruction in schools is forbidden and where therefore the Church must develop its own unique agencies for teaching the Faith.

The Consultation heard first the preliminary findings of a study of four South American societies, commissioned by the American Church from Columbia University's Bureau of Applied Social Research. This study in itself was a remarkable development which sought to apply the best help of contemporary social science to the strategic questions of the Church's mission. Addresses were then made by men long in the field in Latin America. We discussed a number of practical problems of jurisdiction, the forms of new work, the broadening of the base of support and prayer, etc. We finally drafted a report for the Advisory Council on Missionary Strategy to consider at its summit meeting in Canada next August. And running through all these matters was a thrilling sense of brotherly engagement among our different Anglican churches. At every stage the common interdependence of us all was the ruling consideration. "Our primary objective," we said, "is the development of Latin American churches, expressive of the genius of their own countries and of the unity of the Anglican Communion, and ministering alike to the needs of their societies and the wider brotherhood of the world community." Again, "The whole Anglican Communion is responsible for offering itself to the whole world, expressing concern for the whole man, in the whole of society."

Yet these phrases have a hollow ring in the face of the paucity of Anglican energies and resources now being devoted to this mission. And no consultation, nor the Advisory Council itself, can change this. The dynamics of the Anglican Communion lie in its constituent churches and their people; and until our hearts and consciences are stirred, our response will still be sleepy.

What is the answer to this? More knowledge, certainly, of our current Anglican activity there. A clearer and more contemporary understanding of Latin America itself, so long remote to Europeans, and patronized familiarly by North Americans. An appreciation of the dignity and stability of life in these republics, so profoundly rooted in Western civilization yet so expressive of their own unique history. An awareness of the secular-scientific revolution which brings with it great blessings and great perplexities, and will end—is now ending—the majestic certainties of a culture rooted for four centuries in unquestioned Christian tradition.

These gifts we need, if we are to see Latin America as it is, and respond in obedience to our mission there. Perhaps most of all, it is in Latin America that the ecumenical realities and necessities press most urgently. Any mission in Latin America is a mission within a nominally Christian land. It is not "proselytism"—Anglicans would not welcome or support deliberate subversion of Christians. It is, as in our own plural Christian societies in Europe or North America or Australia, a witness to Christian life and faith in company with others and in preparation for a unity which is to come. Non-Roman churches are strongly established in many Latin American countries, and we Anglicans have a brotherly obligation to work with them toward unity, to the limit of our power and conscience, precisely as we do in London or Toronto or Sydney or New York. So do we have a parallel obligation to the church of the majority.

If we have nothing to say to the Roman Catholic Church—if there is no validity to Anglican witness as contrasted with Roman Catholic witness—then we have no business anywhere. But I do not believe that the dialogue of the English Reformation is completed. Nor do I believe that, in a divided Church, any church is complete, lacking nothing. We need, as the Consultation said, "to stand alongside our fellow Christians in order to face with them both the perplexities and opportunities which confront us."

It would be utterly wrong, I am sure, to think of our Latin American mission as directed against the Roman Catholic Church. If they, at times, seem to un-church us or regard us as outside the brotherhood of the faith, I hope that we are not guilty of the same wrong. Our unity with all Christians in Holy Baptism is far too great and basic a unity to be forgotten in the heat of controversy. I think that most Anglicans, when a circle is drawn which excludes us from fellowship, draw the wider circle of Baptism which includes us all. And it is within this wider circle that the mission in Latin America must stand.

There was a most moving episode, in the course of the Consultation, which I must record. The (Roman Catholic) Bishop of Cuernavaca thoughtfully invited us to visit his cathedral—a 16th century church, now being reconstructed and adorned in most remarkable liturgical simplicity. He himself met us and guided us around, then led us next door for tea with him. After a pleasant visit, when we rose to go, he asked us to wait while he prayed with us for unity. So we did, saying the Our Father with him, then following in his prayer that we all might once again live together in one Father's house. Then he blessed us. Then he asked, because of our brotherhood, that we bless him. And after a moment's wonder, one of us did give him and his people a blessing.

No doubt this is not a characteristic relationship among Christians, in Latin America or anywhere else. No doubt there are not many churches where the Holy Bible is "reserved" along with the holy oils and the Blessed Sacrament, as it is in Cuernavaca. No doubt there are not many churches whose main, west doors are blocked by a huge sunken font, confronting us with inescapable unity as are those in this ancient cathedral. I am not romantic about this experience alone, in the terrible balance of intolerance in the world.

All I say is that unity is there to be found, by those who speak the truth in love, who try to see together what God is doing in our history, and try to obey the one Lord in as great brotherly love as we can offer. In that discovery of unity I am certain that the life and witness of the Church in Latin America may play a decisive part. Clearly, at any rate, the ecumenical dimension must be paramount in Latin America, in shaping our mission and our obedience.

One final reminiscence . . . the ancient frescoes on the walls of Cuernavaca Cathedral, now being uncovered after generations hidden under elaborate adornment, were of the Nagasaki martyrs, that band of two-score Christians put to death in Japan in the first Roman Catholic mission there centuries ago. I could not help thinking of the untutored Indians who, generation after generation, knelt in prayer and saw around them the reminder of other Christians, in an infinitely remote land, who shared one faith and hope and glory, with courage and singleness of heart. I wish we knew as much of the needs and pain of other nations, and of the task of other Christians, as those new Christians of old Mexico must have known. Perhaps if we did, we might be moved to a deeper concern and more loving obedience. At all events, it is precisely those two gifts of God, expressed in profound and tireless brotherhood, which must be the marks of our mission in Latin America.

23. THE NEEDS OF THE ANGLICAN COMMUNION TODAY*

THREE TOWERING NEEDS mark the Anglican Communion today. The first is for the imagination which will help us take seriously the needs of others, especially the younger churches. A generation ago, we might have said "more money for missions." To say that now would put the emphasis entirely on the wrong foot. The money is desperately needed; but to seek money by itself is a mistake we have made far too long. The reason why money is a problem is not that we lack it. The reason is a bankruptcy of imagination, which has paralyzed our ability to see and respond to the needs of Christians in the younger nations.

Therefore I do not speak of money first. Our faithful missionaries over all the years have planted the Church on every continent. The Christian people are there. Their needs for schools, churches, theological colleges—all these are there. But our younger brothers will lose

---

* From the *Canadian Churchman*, June 1963.

most of what they have now, and the lives of devoted priests and lay people will have been wasted, if we do not fulfill in brotherhood what was begun in loving obedience, to give our younger churches the muscles, the resources, to carry on what was so wonderfully planted. An African friend writes that "every year I have spent in Africa, the fear has been growing that this magnificent achievement of Anglican missionary work should fade away unnoticed by the rest of the Church, and I believe this is now an immediate threat."

I see no point in simply beating people over the head because we do not "give more for missions." It is true that we spend only a tiny fraction of our churches' income on anybody but ourselves. You can say this in picturesque ways. A friend tells me that the members of the Church of England spend more on birdseed each year than on overseas missions. Another friend tells me that if all the Episcopalians in the United States lost their jobs, went on relief, and then tithed their unemployment compensation, the income of the Episcopal Church would increase by 50%!

Maybe these things are so. If they are, the trouble is not that people are selfish. The trouble is that we cannot imagine the simple needs of under-developed countries and churches. If we could—if we North Americans could imagine what it would be like to be as hard-pressed as we were a hundred years ago, with as much to do and as little to do it with, and to be that under-developed in the world of 1963 instead of 1863—we would never lack the funds to do what must be done. Therefore, our first need is the imagination and the knowledge which would help us to take the needs of others seriously.

The second need is to develop and strengthen our ties with other Christians across the world. This is not simply a question of better communications, although it is that—it is ridiculous for Western Christians to know as much as we do about the political problems of Southeast Asia, say, and as little as we do about the Church in Southeast Asia and its struggle and brave witness.

But our ties with other Christians are not simply a matter of information. They are a matter of the partnership we express with other Christians, the common tasks we undertake together, the thousand ways in which our unity in Christ and in the Church takes precedence over our political and racial divisions. We need to plan together, in brotherly equality. We of the older and more established churches need to learn how to receive as well as give—we need to learn how to hear what the younger churches say, and to respect the dignity of their responsible freedom. Because the great missionary effort of the 19th century was so profoundly a "Western" movement, we in our time have grown up all lop-sided in our understanding of the Church. In the Anglican Communion this is particularly vital, because our whole system is that of establishing a fellowship of independent regional churches, in free association with one another. Precisely because we are not a huge, monolithic, international body, we need to learn how to develop the brotherly exchange and intercourse which is the lifeblood of our body. God does not give us unity for nothing—either we express it and fulfill it or we may lose it.

Finally, all Anglican churches, in every part of the world, need to recover a lost sense of mission, at home as well as abroad. Because Christianity is divided, we all of us spend a ridiculous proportion of our energy in trying to understand and justify our differences from other Christians. I do not say those differences are unimportant, but I do say that no church is an end to itself. Our job is not merely to make our own association stronger. Our first duty is to remember that God loved the world long before we existed—that mission is God's act, first of all, which we are privileged to follow.

When we recover this true sense of God's priority, then we may be saved from being simply private, self-regarding clubs of religiously-minded people. This is our peculiar problem in countries where there are many Christians, to remember that the Church is not an end in itself; the Church is the company of those who are called to follow Christ.

This following is not just a pious devotional attitude. To follow Christ is something one does with mind and will as well as heart. What is Christ's will about the racial problems of our time? What is Christ's judgment on our international tensions? What is Christ doing about our industrial societies, which seem to have no other purpose except that we shall have more possessions for ourselves?

I do not pretend that there are easy Christian answers to such questions as these. But we will not get any answers until we ask the questions. And to ask the right questions of our society depends on our seeking the questions God is asking. God is not the possession of the churches. God is not just a clergyman, concerned with whether we go to church or not, or support Him or not, or even believe in Him or not. God is before the churches; we need Him—He does not need us to protect Him or keep Him in business. When this ancient sense of the sureness and greatness of God is ours again, then the churches may be able to capture their lost greatness again.

IV.

The Anglican Communion and Unity

Anglican Unity

24. "DISCERNING THE LORD'S BODY"*

I LIVE A DOUBLE LIFE, these days, and therefore I bring you a double greeting. First, as a minister-general of the Anglican Communion—as a kind of universal suffragan to 340 diocesan bishops—I greet you in Christ, in the name of all our Anglican household. The Church of Canada has been second to no other Anglican church—not even my own—in giving your love and imagination and support to what my office stands for. This is the first chance I have had to say so, and I do it with all my heart.

Second, I am a citizen of the United States and a bishop of that church. Therefore I greet you as a neighbor, knowing all the tensions and strains, all the cost of the co-existence of two free peoples side by side in this narrowing continent. The three thousand unarmed miles of our common frontier is a fact of immense significance. But we are not deceived by that into thinking that all our brotherly tasks are behind us or that we can take our friendship for granted. Indeed we cannot. In the Church no doubt we have a depth of brotherhood and of common life which the world may not have, and I rejoice at that, and greet you again in the Body of Christ. But there is work for us still to do, if the peace and unity of mankind is to be rightly served by Christians.

---

* Sermon preached at the opening service of the General Synod of the Anglican Church of Canada, Kingston, Ontario, August 22, 1962.

I take for a text four significant words from I Corinthians. St. Paul is writing about the Lord's Supper, and the disunity the little church in Corinth faces when they gather to celebrate it. He says this about those who violate the brotherhood: "He that eateth and drinketh unworthily, eateth and drinketh damnation to himself, not *discerning the Lord's body*" (I Cor. 11:29). It is the last four words which I suggest, "discerning the Lord's body." This is the test of worthiness to St. Paul; this is the standard of judgment. Where the selfish and thoughtless have failed is in this, that they have not seen what it was which gathered at the Communion and celebrated it and shared it. It was the Lord's Body, but they did not see that at all; they saw only their friends and their neighbors and their enemies and the strangers on the fringe; they saw only their own positions and their own needs; and because of this—because they failed to see the Body—they ate and drank damnation to themselves.

Those four words—"discerning the Lord's body"—those words come to mind because it is only on the basis of the Body that I can be here today. Because of the Lord's Body, because of the brotherhood shared in full communion, because your church and mine recognize and accept a unity in the Lord's Body which is greater than any division in the world—only because of these things can I be here, could the Anglican Communion exist, could the profound unity between Canadian and American Christians be expressed, as thank God it is expressed, in the warm fellowship of our two churches.

The fact of the full communion of our Anglican family—the fact of the Lord's Body which we try to discern and obey everywhere in the world—this is the only essential unity the Anglican Communion has. It is one of the commanding ecumenical facts. *Indeed the most urgent single task before Anglicans in our times is to discern this Body for what it really is*—to see it and to obey it. This is what I want to say to you.

I want to speak of this, on one hand, against the background of our Canadian-American tensions. I have lived nearly all my life close enough to our common boundary so that Canada was always a living reality to me. Part of my family was Canadian. My parish church in New York had given Canada its first bishop. For nearly thirteen years I was bishop of a diocese more closely involved in the common history of our two nations than any other. And all that has taught me important things. It has taught me how alike we are, and how different. It has taught me how easy it is to take one another for granted, and how dangerous that is. It has taught me the inevitability of our tensions, and the folly of them. It would be an absurdity for anyone to suppose that we could wave away our differences with a cheery greeting. We are two separate nations, in many ways incompatible with one another. The power of money, the power of mass communications, the power of military capacity—these are not jokes for Rotary Clubs. These are the way things are. And so is it true that our international lives are different. Canada is a member of what may be a unique federation in history. What the future holds for the Commonwealth is not for me even to guess; but the extraordinary present fact of it is no illusion, nor is the privilege Canada has of sharing in a world community in which my own country may not share.

These are sober realities. They could easily become points of acute pain and even hostility. I can think of no greater blow to the free world than serious division between our two countries. But the way to avoid that unimaginable bitterness is not just to make agreeable noises at each other over an occasional luncheon table.

Nor is the way to be found by projecting more attractive images of ourselves to each other. This whole contemporary excitement about "images" is the greatest illusion I know. It is perfectly clear what people mean when they talk about images. I think I know what some of the American images are (and I learn more, day by day). I know what the images of some other nations are. These are not hard to see.

But it is not the image which matters in the end, and it is not a new image which heals. It is what lies behind the image.

I have been watching Telstar perform recently, and very interesting it is too, and profoundly impressive as a demonstration of man's technical skill. But it is a cheat and a liar, Telstar is, when it is used simply for nations to hurl their images at each other; and that is precisely what we have had so far. With the best will in the world (and I do not doubt that will) an image can only sharpen the problems in the end; for images are simply non-military missiles, which tell us nothing except what the intention of the other really is.

It is what lies behind the image—it is the people, the small people, the helpless people, who are caught up in all the vast technical world they cannot even understand, much less control—it is those men and women in the tragic glory of our century who matter. An image of America is meaningless. The question that matters is, Who are the Americans and what are they like, struggling for meaning and decency and to find their way through the swamp of our history. And no projection of images will answer that question. It takes something more than that. It takes the patient, loving brotherhood of people who will not give up until they can get inside their neighbor's life and see what he sees and hope for what he hopes and grieve for his pain. If there is not this much imagination to serve our friendship, then the friendship is a cheap thing indeed and hardly worth fighting for.

I believe it is worth fighting for. If Americans and Canadians, sharing so deeply in the greatest patrimony this world holds, cannot establish between them the profound brotherhood which is the only hope of our world, then the whole cause is lost. The problems we face are the universal problems. If they cannot be met with penetrating and patient understanding here, then there is no hope for anybody anywhere. And the answer is not to try to "sell" the United States to Canada, or Canada to the United States. The answer is not images designed to convince others of the way we think they should see us. The answer is to discover our common humanity, to discover the people as they are, and bear with one another and talk with one another and listen to the unspoken words that come from one another's hearts and souls.

And I think this is a primary task for the Church. I do not say that the Church must do the nation's work. But our churches are the souls of our nations. And it is our job to lead in this, not just to follow. With us of the Anglican Communion, this task takes a uniquely deep form. It takes the form St. Paul saw in it, when he called it "discerning the Lord's body." For this Body, gathered here this morning, gathered week by week in ten thousand parish churches, does not stop in those churches. There are not *many* bodies in *many* cities. There is one Body, one Lord, who walks with His immense strides over every middle wall of partition between us, who brings us all together by baptism into His Body so that when we celebrate His Supper it is not just those we see who share it with us. Angels and archangels share it; but millions upon millions of lesser ones share it too. And if we, huddled together on this continent, cannot discern that Body, then we are only playing at Church.

Let the Body be real to us. Let it speak and teach and admonish us. Let it break down distrust and ignorance and prejudice, and lead us both to see that peace is more than a refusal to fight, that unity is more than just a sullen determination to buy a bad bargain. The unity of the Lord's Body, that unity which our churches of Canada and the United States share, is the ultimate statement of what unity means—a sober, patient, loving willingness to bear one another's burdens, to share one another's pain, to stake our lives on each other, to think and pray and work together that all mankind may be one. This is the task and the glory that full communion lays on our national churches.

But I may not end there. The full communion our two churches share is only a fraction of the immense unity which holds our whole Anglican household together, and more still of other heritages. And the duty to discern that world-wide Body is no less commanding and no less urgent.

There was a time when the unity of the Anglican Communion was easy to see. We were churches of English-speaking people, of a common culture, with a common Prayer Book, sharing the same temperament and history, largely linked together by a common political structure. How swiftly, one by one, all those unities have withered away! It is hard now to define the Anglican Communion. I do not know any other way to do it, actually, than in very existential terms indeed—it consists of those churches whose bishops are invited to the Lambeth Conference. An even more modest and existential definition might be that it consists of those churches which are asked to support the Anglican Executive Officer!

And I think we must honestly say that this cloudiness of definition pleases us. The more we have lost the easy unities of culture and language and race and tradition, the more we have been driven back to fundamentals. The only fundamental unity, the only essential unity we have is that of full communion. And all this forces us back to the realization that our unity is not only not cultural—it is not denominational or confessional.

We have no particular theological statement of our own to fence us off from other Christians. We have no international power structure which forces our younger churches to conform to some alien pattern of life. We have no central executive power. We have no uniform Prayer Book. We have no common language. We have no laws which limit the freedom of any church to decide its life as it will. We have no ecclesiastical colonies. We have no "Anglican" religion. We have no test of membership save that of Baptism itself. We have nothing to hold us together except the one essential unity given us in our full communion. And even this is not limited to Anglican churches, for we share in the table of other churches as well, in increasing number.

Nor will we be satisfied until there is nothing left which can be called Anglican at all. For we think that God makes it hard to define what is "Anglican" primarily because He does not care that the Anglican Communion should be an eternal fact. The Anglican Communion, in our eyes, is only a particular fragment of that full communion which must some day hold all Christians together. We are an accidental historical configuration, which came into existence by God's providence

to bear our witness in a divided Church. But we should disappear and
we are disappearing as those divisions are healed.

So it has happened in South India. So was it the wish of the bishops
at Lambeth that it might happen in Ceylon (a wish not fully shared,
at the moment, by the clergy and laity of every Anglican church). So
was it our wish, and is it, that the same disappearance might be possible in other places, where plans for united churches are developed
which contain what surely are the essential elements and organs of full
church life—the Holy Scriptures, the Catholic Creeds, the two Gospel
sacraments, and an undoubted ministry whose credentials can meet
every test of antiquity and universality. And I cannot honestly imagine
any lesser basis of unity than these four things.

But God forbid that we should end here, with ourselves. I said at
the beginning as I do now, that the most urgent single task before our
Anglican churches today is to see our full communion for what it is,
in all its greatness and all its cost and all its immense and fathomless
meaning. To discern the Lord's Body—this is our task now everywhere
in the world.

What is it that we are doing here this morning? Is this an Anglican
service of worship? Is this some tribal rite of Anglo-Saxons? Is it some
kind of spiritual cafeteria, with each of us coming to take what he needs
and wants for his lonely refreshment? Is it some kind of pageant for
like-minded people to share, for their own comfort? You know it is
none of these things. Here, now, He comes—to teach us, to forgive us,
to receive what little we can bring and add it to His limitless and perfect offering, to let us take our little place within His eternal priesthood, to bring us out of our separateness and loneliness into His
company, to feed us in brotherhood with His life poured out for us.

There is no unity greater than this. There is no brotherhood more
deep, more wonderful, than this we share at this moment. Here, together, in absolute humility and obedience, we speak His words and
our hands obey His hands, and He comes, to receive our most secret
selves and join them all and fulfill them all in His perfect self.

But what is the final meaning of this unity? What is its significance
once we leave this altar? What does it do, what does it cost, how does
it change us, how does it deepen our brotherhood outside this place?
How do Christians discern the Lord's Body out in the world, where
we are torn apart by nationalism and race and poverty and fear and
all of the ache and misery of mankind? Those are the questions for
Christians.

If full communion means really nothing more than a kind of ceremonial courtesy, to be trotted out for state occasions, it is not the Lord's Body which we are seeing, but only a kind of childish sacramental statesmanship. If this communion is only a gate by which you separate one kind of Christian from another, then it is an insult to the Cross. Let the Body teach us how to bear one another's burdens; let it teach us about the common humanity which breathes and hopes and fears and suffers and rejoices in every place in every race of man. The whole world is with us at this altar. That is the meaning of the Body. But the Body needs to be seen for what it is everywhere—not here alone, but wherever men live and work and love and pray and die.

Christian Unity starts with full communion, and goes on from there to the very limit of brotherhood. We have only begun the discovery of unity when we can share in the sacrament.

Mission starts with the communion, and goes on from there to the very limit of the witnessing fellowship. We have only begun our obedience when we join at the altar.

Evangelism starts at the communion, with His eternal priesthood opened to be shared and fulfilled in our wills and lives; and it goes on from there until a man's whole life, and all of every man's life, is conformed to Christ's priesthood. We have only begun our witness when we make it in the Liturgy.

To press the meaning of full communion to its farthest limits in unity and mission and evangelism—this is what it is for us to discern the Lord's Body. And this is our task, we to whom the Body has begun to be real in this sacramental fellowship. We know enough to know that it is Christ who is celebrating this Eucharist, not any man. We know enough to know that it is humanity which is being offered here and sacrificed, not a little money or a few prayers of a handful of people. We know enough to know that this service is not just a rehearsal of a lovely pageant, but this is God redeeming the world. This is where we first see and understand the Lord's Body. Then God grant that we do not forget what we have seen and done here, but that He may lift our eyes until we see His Body in the uttermost parts of the earth.

25. AN EXERCISE IN BROTHERHOOD*

THE ANGLICAN COMMUNION is not a "confession" nor a super-church nor a world-wide denominational power-structure. It is, in the familiar words of the 1930 Lambeth Conference, "a fellowship, within the One

---

* From *Anglican World*, October-November 1960.

Holy Catholic and Apostolic Church, of those duly constituted Dioceses, Provinces or Regional Churches, in communion with the See of Canterbury." Although this definition now needs re-phrasing (since there are more and more churches in communion with Canterbury, such as the Old Catholics, which are not "Anglican"), it still enshrines the two central words of our brotherhood—"fellowship" and "communion."

A "confession," one may suppose, is a group of Christians and churches bound together by doctrinal statements which at once identify their unity and differentiate them from other Christians and churches. This is precisely what is lacking in the Anglican Communion—the only primary theological statements we hold are those which are common to all Christians and all churches, the Creeds and the Scriptures from which the Creeds grow. In fact, it is most difficult to tell what defines a member of an Anglican church except that he goes to that church—neither Baptism nor Confirmation makes us Anglicans, nor do we need pass some theological test to count ourselves members. Anglicanism lacks denominational neatness and doctrinal tidiness, which makes it the despair of its tidy-minded adherents as well as of the indefatigable ecumenical book-keepers who are in duty bound to try to classify it.

Even more is this the case with "denominationalism." Except to lawyers and census-takers, a denomination or a sect is probably best seen as a sort of "non-U" version of a confession, a do-it-yourself confession, whose unity is perhaps founded more on property and institutions and organizations, or on custom and tradition, rather than on some deeper theological inheritance. And little of this applies to our hopelessly uncentralized Communion.

But this is only playing with words—the two great, serious words we use about ourselves are "fellowship" and "communion," and I would like to expand each of them a little. "Fellowship" implies what is a distinguishing mark of both the Anglican and the Orthodox churches, whose genius is to establish not massive monolithic world structures, but rather the maximum of local and regional and national autonomy. The 1948 Lambeth Report describes this in a rather moving paragraph:

> The Anglican Communion today is like a river that is made up of streams, each of which passes through a different country, each with a colour drawn from the soil through which it passes, each giving its best to the full strength of the river, flowing toward that ocean symbolic of a larger comity when the Anglican Communion itself will

once again become part of a reunited Christendom. No one stream is superior to another. The glory of each is its contribution to this river which, while being enriched by all, enriches all the countries of the world wheresoever it flows.

This dream is only possible where there is full and mature freedom among brothers in a household, and this is part of the Anglican tradition. The correlative of this responsible freedom is what the word "communion" describes. What gives unity to the Anglican churches and people is not institutions or catechisms or laws. It is the fact that we break the Bread of Life together, in full and unquestioning acceptance of one another. Our unity lies not in our thinking alike but in our acting together, most of all in the supreme Christian acts of the offering and the breaking and the sharing the Body. These acts, the summit and the epitome of Christian fellowship, are what matter most to us, I think. The Holy Communion is the unique test of fellowship and the means of it and the image of it and the crown of it.

To label our communion as "Anglican" is to use a descriptive word which one day, please God, will be only of historical interest. At the moment, "Anglican" describes a certain node of unity within the broken Christian body—a swirl in the stream of Christian history—and it is a true and honest and useful word which tells of the reasons why there is a "communion," and of the common heritage and tradition which engenders our fellowship and makes our unity a recognizable and useful instrument in God's hands. But it will pass and die, some day; already it is insufficient, for, as one network grows of our fellowship with churches which are not "Anglican," that wider unity presses the limits of a narrow word, and one day will break it into fragments. But "communion" will remain always, for it is the heartbeat of the Body of Christ.

Now this is not intended to be just an essay on words. It prefaces what I want to say about a complex exercise in fellowship and communion which goes by the short names of "North India" or "Ceylon." The situation is this:

One of the churches of our fellowship, the Church of India, Pakistan, Burma and Ceylon (called CIPBC, generally) has participated over a period of years in negotiations looking toward a union of churches in northern India and Pakistan, and in Ceylon. The North India-Pakistan "Plan" embraces seven principal bodies, the Ceylon "Scheme" five. In both cases a very wide spectrum of ecclesiastical background is included, ranging through traditions as diverse as those of Baptists and Anglicans. The Plan and the Scheme are not identical, but the end in view in every case is the coming together of these now separate bodies, to form United Churches, in the three areas.

The Negotiating Committees have done all they feel they can do in planning; and they have now asked the churches involved to say yes or no to what is proposed. Our own companion CIPBC has agreed to make this choice, at the next meeting of its General Council, in 1963, and has asked each of its dioceses to vote on the matter in the meantime. It has also—and this is the point of what I am writing—asked each of the other Anglican churches a cardinal question, "Will you be willing to enter into relations of full communion with the prospective United Churches from their inauguration?"

Thus, in an effort to answer this question from CIPBC, during the months ahead there will be very wide discussion of "North India" and "Ceylon" in all our churches. I have had a particular duty in this regard, to edit a book containing all the relevant material for the widest possible circulation everywhere in our Communion. The point of the book is to put into the hands of as many people as possible all of the official documents on which our answer to the question of the CIPBC must be based. All this material will be discussed and debated; there will be much talk of "The Bringing Together of the Episcopates" and "The Unification of the Ministry"; Confirmation and "anomalies" in relations with other churches and the meaning of "membership" and a host of other questions will be in many minds and on not a few tongues.

Why? If the CIPBC is a sovereign and independent province, as Anglicans say it is, why should it be any of our concern what they do? Why should the counsel of the Lambeth Conference have been sought, in 1958? Why should the CIPBC say that they will not try to give their answer to their fellow-Christians in India until the Anglicans in England and Australia and Canada and Japan and South Africa and the United States and everywhere else outside of India have said what we would or would not do?

The answers to these questions revolve entirely around the two words "fellowship" and "communion." If the Anglican Communion were a centralized denomination or a unified hierarchical structure, the decision would probably not belong to CIPBC at all, but would be made at Lambeth or Canterbury or wherever the heart of the power-structure was to be found. But because this is not our nature—because the CIPBC is not a fraction, but a brother in the household—the CIPBC does two things at once. Maturely and responsibly, it seeks its full obedience to the leading of God within its own country and among its own people, seeks to know and follow its true vocation as the church of the Anglican Communion in India should do; but it does this as a partner in the fellowship of the family. And since the crowning mark of that family, that fellowship, is our companionship in the Blessed Sacrament, our communion, the critical question must be the one which is asked, "Will you be in communion with us when we cease to be 'Anglicans' and lose our separate identity in a new and wider fellowship?"

It is not at all a matter of the CIPBC asking us to make up its mind for it. That would be an abdication of the responsibility of a free church. But what we say will matter to them; it will enter into their decision most deeply and costingly; and therefore we share their choice with them, not as judges or critics, but as people who have shared the whole of the Gospel with them and all the richness of our own tradition, and by God's mercy hope to continue that fellowship.

For the relationship, this gossamer bond of free fellowship within a single and whole communion, is one of the most precious things on earth. It is compounded of amazingly insubstantial things—the memory of a shared history, a common store of ideas, a hope of responsible freedom, the companionship of people of every race at the one altar. The relationship itself is a bond of honor and of love, not of law or institution. It all sounds so unreal and so unworldly; and it is the latter, really. But it may turn out in the end to have a durability the things of this world do not have. Even more, it may open the way to a free association far wider than anything any of us now know.

So be it, if it be God's will. No Anglican would wish for any other goal for our Communion than that it should, in Lambeth's words, "flow toward that ocean symbolic of a larger comity when the Anglican Communion itself will once again become part of a reunited Christendom." In the meanwhile, the fellowship and the communion are ours, and richly true, and deeply nourishing. Thank God for them, and bear them in your mind and heart when the North India questions are asked.

26. UNITY AND TRADITION*

PROBABLY the best way to think of my work is as a ministry of unity— unity expressed in ways appropriate to the nature of the Anglican Communion. This is not a different unity than what all churches seek; it is not a special kind of unity; it is simply unity in Christ, expressed

---

* From *The Living Church*, February 3, 1963.

with the intensity of full communion among Christians who share a very large number of things in common. But it must be expressed in ways appropriate to what we are and the tradition and spirit we share.

For example, uniformity in liturgical detail would not befit an international family of self-governing churches. Again, a centralized administrative structure would defeat our hopes for healthy regional and national responsibility. Yet again, no statement of the Christian faith less inclusive and universal than the Nicene Creed could ever be accepted as a common Anglican confession. The 39 Articles, indeed, were an attempt to show how broadly the Church of England could extend toward confessional points of view without actually holding one, but the Articles do not enjoy universal acceptance in the Anglican family despite even this theological generosity.

So one could continue, for many bases and expressions of Anglican unity have been known and explored and found wanting. The profound national sense uniquely true of the mother Church of England has played a great part in time past, and is still a significant factor. Thirteen of the eighteen Anglican churches are rooted in Commonwealth countries, and certainly we are still largely an English-speaking household (although by no means Anglo-Saxon, if I understand what that means). Indeed it was not until 1850 or thereabouts that full communion was established with the church in the United States. Until that time clergymen of the American Church, like those of the Episcopal Church in Scotland, were not permitted to officiate in England; and in both cases, national considerations played the decisive part.

To this day "Crockford's," that singular arbiter of the "U" and "non-U" in things Anglican, lists the American Church in a sort of limbo behind suffragan bishops, ex-prime ministers, advertisements for communion wines, etc. (although still casting a wistful imperial cloak over the Jerusalem Archbishopric, South Africa and the Hong Kong diocese of the Church of China).

All this simply reflects our experience with still another level or expression of unity—that of national identity. And while Anglican unity has long since outgrown that tie, it has bequeathed to us a great gift, that of a sense of profound identification of a church with its nation and people. This sense is in the bloodstream of every Anglican church; it helps to save us from sectarianism and religiosity; it establishes among us a sturdy independence; it is or can be full of good things.

But by the same token, on the other side, almost all of Anglicanism must wrestle with the problem of its own identity and unity. The

Church of England alone, because of its establishment as a national church, has its unity given to it. Every other Anglican church must accept the role of sect or denomination, and must therefore fight for its identity, its mission in its nation, and especially its own interior unity. In England, the widest extremes of "Catholic" and "Protestant" are at least tolerable, because at least a measure of unity is already given the church, and does not depend on the voluntary cooperation of people of different opinions.

No other Anglican church enjoys that luxury. We of the younger churches have had to learn how to contain "Catholic" and "Protestant" within one voluntary body, one diocese, one parish, indeed one soul. We have had to learn (and I am more thankful for this than I can say) that the co-existence in one church of the two great Christian spirits—symbolized as "Catholic" and "Protestant"—is not after the manner of a Neapolitan ice or a pousse-café, but rather after the manner of an arduous, costly, humble spiritual pilgrimage, a creaturely struggle for depth and wholeness, a struggle within the spirit of every Anglican. No one of us, priest or layman, can opt out of either the Catholicism or the Protestantism given us by our Prayer Books. We must come to terms with both spirits, in one flesh. Otherwise we will have no unity at all in our churches, or no depth.

There are dangers, clearly, in this fight for interior unity—dangers of accepting the role of sect or denomination, and thereby losing the great inheritance of the English Reformation. But it is also true that it is not accidental that so often the most perceptive understanding of the Anglican tradition is found in non-English writers (or those with long experience outside of England). It is not mere American bumptiousness which leads me to say that of all who have written on the Anglican spirit, in modern times, the American philosopher, Paul Elmer Moore, was by all odds the most sensitive. Like all of us in the younger churches, he had to fight to understand and establish the identity, the mission, the unity of his church, and in that fight there are unforgettable lessons to learn, lessons not similarly forced on our English brethren.

Now, what am I writing about? Unity—Anglican unity. These reflections are not aimless ones. There are appropriate expressions of unity which are not confessional or national. As usual I am writing on a plane, having just shared a quarterly meeting of the American Church's National Council. Included in the routine business of the Overseas Department was the provision of funds to pay the salary of an Australian priest to work in Viet Nam, various arrangements about an American priest now working in India, whose salary is paid by the Scottish Episcopal Church, and a 50/50 partnership plan with the Canadian Church whereby both churches join in providing a needed administrative assistant for a third church in Africa.

These are three small instances of a very wide field of inter-Anglican co-operation, entirely appropriate as an expression of our unity. For they speak, small as they are, of a partnership based on nothing less than full communion. It is not cultural unity or doctrinal identity or ecclesiastical uniformity or administrative centrality which speaks in such things. It is nothing less than that complete trust in one another, within the single love of God, whose outward expression is that we break the Bread of Life together in mutual, brotherly acceptance.

Indeed this full communion extends beyond what could be called "Anglican." For example, at that same meeting, other routine actions were taken to provide clergy of the Philippine Independent Church to minister to Anglicans in Hawaii, for the support of British nationals in an institution of the Church of South India, and for literature for theological education in the Spanish Reformed Episcopal Church. Again, these are tiny instances, which could be duplicated widely in other Anglican churches, of what full communion means, expressed in brotherly love. And if we Anglicans grow confused sometimes as to what is "Anglican" and what is not, it may be that God is just as well pleased.

Any basis of unity, any expression of unity, short of that full brotherhood in Christ in which we share one another's needs and strengths without regard to culture or nationality or theological opinion or practice, is imperfect and doomed to pass as we grow up in Christ. This is why I speak so often of "disappearance" as the vocation of the Anglican Communion. It would never be enough, because it would never be true to the unity Christ gives us in Baptism and the Holy Communion, for us to stop short of complete involvement in one another's lives. Simply to go on endlessly in parallel lines, with an occasional bridge of ceremonial inter-communion, would deny us— does deny us—exactly the assurance of common life, common hope, common fate, common salvation which is the central mark of unity in Christ. One of the heartbreaks in Anglican history is that when the young church in America needed so much encouragement and strength, it could not be given them because of national walls which now rightly seem absurd. How different the history of the United States might have been, had the unity of the Anglican Communion been a working fact two hundred years ago.

Well, regret is profitless except as it teaches a lesson. The lesson is that there is one Lord and one Gospel and one salvation, and therefore one Church; and to the farthest limits possible to us, it is our duty to live up to that given unity. For the time being, there is a particular intensity of unity possible to us in the Anglican family and those other churches allied to us in full communion. We shall not rest content with this; but it would be both sin and disaster not to press it and express it with all our imagination and power, not because we happen to like one another or share common cultural gifts or preserve in our churches many elements of a common heritage, but because we may not keep even what unity and witness we have unless we live up to it.

It must be expressed, this unity, in ways appropriate to our Anglican tradition. As far as I can see, the Incarnate Lord, in all His terrible and wonderful anonymity, is the heart of our "tradition." He came, at a certain time and place, to become the glorious power that broke down every middle wall of partition between us and to make us one in Him. No less a healing, hurting brushing-aside of unimportant differences and divisions will suffice for us. May He teach us how to be true to Him and to one another in Him!

The Wider Episcopal Fellowship

27. THE EPISCOPATE*

1 CORINTHIANS 4:9.

> For I think that God hath set forth us the apostles last, as it were appointed to death: for we were made a spectacle unto the world, and to angels, and to men. We are fools for Christ's sake, but ye are wise . . .

I have a double pleasure in sharing this service tonight. For one thing, this is the first time—of what I hope will be many—for me to visit the Scottish Church as your Anglican Executive Officer. It is a curiously un-churchly and cumbersome title for what is really a very churchly and very simple ministry. The title simply means that all of our Anglican household the world around—forty million of us gathered in 330 dioceses—have said to one bishop, "You must leave your

---

* Sermon preached at the annual meeting of the Representative Church Council of the Scottish Episcopal Church, St. Paul's Cathedral, Dundee, Tuesday, May 17, 1960.

own flock and the concerns of one diocese so that you may be free to think and speak and act for all of us, to express our common life and our common witness."

For what binds our Anglican brotherhood together is far greater and far more enduring than the national and traditional differences between and among our fifteen separate churches. Indeed, we are far more one church than a federation of churches. At least, this is the faith and the hope this new ministry symbolizes. In it, I come to Scotland not as a visiting American, but as a servant and a member of your church—indeed your employee, for your church, like all the others, carries a share of the cost of this work. This is not only a matter of £.s.d. (though it is that), but equally in the cost of your church and to every Anglican church of making the sacrifices which are inescapable if we are to move forward in common action.

In another sense, I rejoice that I am an American, for the currents of brotherly intercourse between the Scottish and the American Churches are uniquely deep. I do not need to recite our history—from you did our American Communion Service come, and for nearly two centuries now we have shared the deepest things of the Spirit. Together we have stood steadfastly by the episcopate, together we pioneered in the Anglican world in giving to the laity a fully responsible place in the church's councils; together we commit ourselves to that high adventure, "Evangelical Truth and Apostolic Order," the motto now of your church as it was the standard of the heroic bishop of New York, John Henry Hobart, more than a century ago.

Most of all, of course, the American Church owes to Scotland the historic episcopate. When our mother Church of England could not find the way through the thicket of legalities, it was three Scottish bishops who gave to Bishop Seabury and his church the central gift of Apostolic Order. Thus forever there must be a unique bond between us, and a thankful and humble piety in the heart of any American pilgrim, such as myself.

Now it is about that central gift of the episcopate that I mean to preach tonight, not theoretically, not with reference to any individual bishop, but the episcopate as it is in itself. To both our churches—indeed equally to every Anglican church—the ministry of the Bishop is the heart of true Church Order. We have clung to this in hard times; we have built our life around it; we are willing even to be called the "Bishops' Church," the "Episcopal Church"—willing and even proud.

As a result, we need always to be sure that we are as wise and apostolic in our understanding of the episcopate as we are devoted in our loyalty to it. *And here we Episcopalians run a twin danger—the danger of claiming too much for the historic episcopate, and the danger of claiming too little.*

I think we all have been reminded of the first danger, particularly in times when we are specially concerned about the unity of the Church. I remember being struck with this in 1946, when our American Church came to a decisive point in our conversations with Presbyterians in the United States. In truth, I think neither church really wanted unity enough to pay anything of any consequence for it: I do not think it would be fair to blame anybody more than anybody else for this—as so often happens, the members of both churches were sadly out of touch with the leaders actually doing the negotiating. But the point of my memory is only this, that it was strange to see, on our side, how the idea of the episcopate became almost a fetish with us, so much so that we seemed to be saying to the Presbyterians that the *only* thing the Church needed for its fulfillment was to have bishops, and without them the Church could not exist at all.

Mind you, I am completely committed to our Lambeth Quadrilateral in this. There is no doubt in my mind as to the necessity for a single, universally-acknowledged ministry in any united Church; and only the historic episcopate can possibly claim to be that. Indeed, I would go further than many, perhaps most, in the ferocity of my convictions about this.

For example, lately it has been fashionable to play with various "esses"—various senses of the Latin word "to be"—asking whether the Catholic episcopate was of the *esse* or the *bene esse* or the *plene esse* of the Church. As far as I understand these words, they are intended to distinguish between thinking that you *had* to have bishops to have the Church at all, or that it is *better* for the Church to have bishops, or that the Church is not really *complete* if it does not have bishops.

For the life of me, I cannot see any possible substance to these alternatives. I cannot imagine how you could have a "better" Church one way than another, or how you could "improve" the Church or make it somehow more complete. It is God's Church, and He has made it, and He makes it what He will, through the dying of His dear Son. Our honor is simply to be permitted to have part in it, and to obey as best we can what He has ordained. Therefore it seems unbearably man-centered to talk in these comparative terms.

I cannot seriously imagine the Church of Christ existing in various

strengths, like the different proofs of whiskey in the American market!
—to say that you get more of the Church with 2,000-year-old distilled
bishops than you do with the more watery presbyters seems to me
playing like children with God's truth.

If it is good for the fullness of the Church's life that we have Catholic
Episcopal Order, then we are really saying that this order is of the
esse of the Church's life. It is quite inconceivable that God should
ever be content, or wills us to be content, with anything less than the
wholeness of His Church; the man who admits the episcopate at all,
must admit it the whole way. *The real question here is how seriously
we take God's action in history.* If He has led His Church to the episcopate, and established it as the pattern for the Church's unity and
continuity, then that must be the governing consideration. If, on the
other hand, the development of the Catholic episcopate is purely an
accident of cultural history or whatever, then nobody could say that
it is "necessary" or even "good," for that matter, for it would be im-
pertinent for man to decide what is "good" for God's Church. This is
the real choice, I think. Our problem is to answer the question "Has
God led the Church to this?" rather than to find some agile phrase
which will let everybody play as he wills with what he thinks would
be expedient for the Church's life.

At any rate, this is the way I understand these things. What is
necessary for the being of the Church is what is good for the Church
and fulfills it—the *esse* grows out of the *bene esse* and the *plene
esse*. For myself, I am confident that the episcopate is of the *esse* of
the Church—is necessary for the Church—precisely because it is for
the Church's good and fullness, precisely because it is God's will for
His Church and not merely an accidental development of history. But
the minute I say this, I have also said that the historic episcopate is
God's and not ours, that it is part of His providing care for His Church,
and that therefore I do not need nervously to keep on proclaiming it
at every turn, as though it would disappear if we did not continually
resuscitate it with the vehemence of our convictions.

I believe with all my heart that the episcopate is of the *esse* of the
Church. So do I believe that the preaching of the Word is of the *esse*
of the Church. So do I believe that the full sacramental life is necessary
to the Church. So do I believe that a total and complete commitment
to evangelism is necessary to the Church. So do I believe about charity,
and penitence, and apostolic zeal, and the witness and graces of the
Christian life. The Church does not fully and rightly exist without all
these things, for God wills them all for His true and perfect Body, and

without any one of them, the Body is to that degree imperfect. Our mistake—even our sin—when we Episcopalians forget that the Church is God's and not ours, is that we then seem to make episcopacy an end in itself and to say that it is the only indispensable characteristic. When we forget that all this is God's doing and God's will, then all we have to fall back on are our pronouncements about the episcopate and our commitment to it, and the search for the truth and fullness of the Church's life dwindles until it is no more than a shouting match between human opinions.

This is what I mean by saying that we claim too much for the episcopate. Paradoxically, it is only those who claim the most who do not claim too much—it is only those who believe that the episcopate is of God's providence and therefore is of the very nature of the Church itself who can then be content to accept that there are also other things which belong to the Church's nature, and that they all need to be humbly remembered and humbly sought. Remember that the Church is always in God's hands, and He is able to accomplish His will and His work despite all our failures. The Church exists as He makes it. We cannot make it or unmake it. We have only to obey as best we know how, and pray that in our obedience, something of the true nature of the Church may shine through. He is the Lord of the Church; we are in danger of thinking of Him as our prisoner. This is the danger of claiming too much for the episcopate. We need always to remember that God "is able of these stones to raise up children unto Abraham."

The greater danger is that we shall claim too little. We do this in various ways. We do it, for example, when we mold the episcopate into a purely administrative form, or overload the bishops, or suffer them to overload themselves with administrative detail. The war-time phrase "Is your journey really necessary?" ought to be adapted for bishops—"Is this meeting necessary?" When the ministry of the bishop is seen simply as an executive office, we are claiming far too little for it.

So are we when we deprive the bishop of the support and counsel he needs, and make him, or let him make himself an autocrat. That church is governed best which has the most responsible and widest possible sharing of decisions. Anglicanism—and here I would feel that your church and my own are to some degree exempt from this criticism—has a curious weakness in this respect. Once the disciplined hierarchical structure of the medieval Church was dissolved in the Reformation, we had the chance to grow into a far more adult and responsible partnership between clergy and laity. But this has been a very slow business; what has often developed instead has been a kind of "diocesanism," a sort of large scale parochialism, which was a purely Anglican contribution to Church Order and not a very good one either —a spirit which seemed almost to resent any judgment save the bishop's, and to treat all other members of the Church except him as children. How wonderfully this is changing, as we move more and more into a real acceptance of the corporate character of the Church, really hearing what St. Paul said about the Body with its single, interdependent, common life. But to make 300-odd petty diocesan papacies out of our Anglican family is to claim far too little for the episcopate.

Still a third example comes to mind—what I call the "Queen Bee" theory of the episcopate. The queen bee, I am told, is an object of great importance in the hive. Nourished and comforted by all the workers, she moves in somewhat plethoric splendor from cell to cell, laying eggs as rapidly as possible for the perpetuation of the hive. The comparison of this with a certain theory of the episcopate is thought-provoking. I have caught myself, at times, surrounded by buzzing hordes of presbyters, reasonably comforted and fanned by the devoted laity, moving in stately progress from ordination to ordination, or confirmation to confirmation, laying my ecclesiastical eggs, wondering whether this apostolate of the bishop were really anything more than the well-nourished captivity of the abbess of a hive. To claim for the episcopate nothing more than the reproductive function of the Church is again to claim far too little.

I think we puzzle our non-Episcopalian friends a good deal by these antics of ours. They wonder why, if we set such store by the episcopate, we let it come to so little in the end. They wonder why we waste an office which we say we prize so highly, in doing jobs the laity could do far better, or in splendid ecclesiastical pageantry which often says little or nothing to the needs of this harsh world. Many of us share this wonder, to tell the truth, and long for a new and fresh and deeper look at all these things.

A curious little fragment in the report of the 1958 Lambeth Conference was a recommendation that we move toward what we called a "Wider Episcopal Fellowship." I think we really had no clear idea about what we meant. For one thing, it was confused with our somewhat sentimental feelings about the ex-Anglican bishops who went forth from us into the new united churches. The Lambeth Conference has many faces, and one of them is that of pure friendship; and it is natural that we should be concerned with keeping such friendship fresh and dear. But a far deeper thing was being born, in our talk of this "Wider Fellowship," far deeper and far more enduring than merely personal friendship.

Little by little, as the ecumenical network grows, our Anglican churches are entering into responsible relationship with other non-Anglican, episcopal churches. The old Catholics, the Polish National Church, the little churches in Spain and Portugal, the Swedes, the new churches in India and Ceylon . . . the number is increasing Just ten days ago, the great Philippine Independent Church—a body of two million communicants gathered around their forty bishops—proposed without one dissenting voice that they enter into full communion with all our Anglican household.

Little by little, a fellowship of free, primitive, Catholic churches is coming into being. It is not an "Anglican" fellowship. Indeed, to some degree, as in India, it is born out of the dying of our Anglican body, in any case, it is something quite apart from it. It is a brotherhood of Christians of widely-varying traditions, who have maintained the essential structure of Catholic order, who find themselves involved more and more with one another. This is the "Wider Episcopal Fellowship" of which Lambeth spoke.

I long for the day, not too far distant now, I think, when a conference of bishops and theologians of all these traditions, including our own, can meet to think together about what episcopacy means—not Anglican episcopacy, not South Indian nor Filipino nor Polish—but the episcopate in itself. Each of us shall have something to give to this exchange, but infinitely more to learn. For out of it—out of the interchange of our differing national patterns—out of the various theological traditions we represent—could come a life-giving return to first principles, which would help keep us all from claiming too little for the episcopate.

If I had the making of such a conference, I should want to start where St. Paul leaves us, in the text I gave you at the beginning. "For I think that God hath set forth us the apostles last, as it were appointed to death . . ." I should hope that we might somehow empty ourselves and our idea of the episcopate from all the inherited pettiness and clap-trap, and see it as nearly as we can, in the terms of the apostolate at the beginning.

One thing we should surely learn is that we need to raise our sights as to just whose apostolate we are talking about. If, when we are speaking of the episcopate, we are speaking only of a power and position arrogated by men for the governance of the Church, then such a text would have little to say to us. If the episcopate is of man's design, and a power to be seized and used by men, however responsibly and wisely, then it is mockery to speak of bishops as "men appointed to death" and "made a spectacle unto the world." We might be appointed to death and we might be spectacles, but it would be for our own sins, and not because God so ordained it! If it be Christ's Bishopric which the Church shares and of which I speak, then it is a totally different matter.

Lately, in our conversations with non-episcopal churches, we have begun to talk about "episcope," "oversight," as a principle which is expressed, in various ways in different churches—expressed, for example, in a presbytery or even in a congregational meeting. I think no one word nor any one idea is going magically to solve our ecumenical problems. Nonetheless, I think this is a helpful new start, for it forces us to think afresh about what "episcope," "oversight," means. And it reminds us of the one commanding truth in all this—that there is only one Bishop, really, and one Shepherd and one Priest and one Governor of the Church, and that is Christ.

It is His "Episcope" which alone is good and alone matters. His Bishopric of the Church is the only one that counts—it is the only episcopate there is. As in His high priesthood, either He moves and acts within His body, or else all we do is blasphemy. There is an "episcope" expressed in the Church; it is His; and therefore every member of the Body shares in it. When the Presbyterian says to us that his presbytery is the organ through which the episcope of the Church is exercised, we may not altogether quarrel with this. We had better not, for if there were anything in the Church—presbytery, laity or whatever—which did not share in the single Bishopric of Christ, it would be a tragic deformation of the Church. If He, the great Bishop and Shepherd, is not acting through the priesthood and the laity, in their separate orders, as much as through the bishops, then we are hopelessly lost.

And this may be the most tragic instance of our expecting too little, claiming too little—to imagine that His great apostolate could somehow be limited to, contained within the minds and acts of isolated men scattered here and there throughout the Church. If such a thing could happen—if a single man, however brilliant, however good, were to be thought somehow to be able exclusively to reproduce the episcopate of the Lord—then we should be guilty either of a human pretension and pride beyond endurance, or else of so belittling the work of Christ the Bishop, that we should rightly be a laughing-stock for the whole world.

This is the real point of such a body as this Representative Church Council. The presence of laity and clergy with the bishops in consultation about the day-by-day life of the Church—this is no mere act of condescension on the part of the bishops. If it were, I think I know enough about the thrawn, the stubborn angularity of both clergy and laity to predict that only a handful—and they the wrong handful—would be here! I belong to a church which has been long accustomed to the full participation of the laity in our diocesan life and in our national life. This does not mean to anybody that some act of grace is involved in this; the laity and the clergy share in the single work of Christ in His Church in every way and at every level, not because they are nice clergy or specially wise laymen, but because they are members of His one Body and therefore share by right in every part of the life of that Body.

This does not say that therefore we do not need individual bishops, to be the voice and hands and heart to express all this finally in acts. This is a different question, to be answered on its own merits; and I have no doubt myself but that God has led the Church to the answer long since. But the episcopate of Christ is the enormous central reality; this must be faced in its own immense terms, and the whole life and structure of the Church examined against that background, before we can hope to raise our ecumenical discourse above the level of mere quarrelling about history.

Therefore, brethren, we Episcopalians need above all to make sure that our Episcopalianism is not in words only, but works itself out in every part and tissue of our body. If to be an Episcopalian—in Scotland or America or whatever—means only that we have central officers called bishops, this would be to claim far too little for the episcopate, no matter how good our title deeds might be. It is precisely at this point that our non-episcopal friends most rightly question our pretensions. They say, and they are quite right to say, that if all episcopacy means is a sort of antiseptic prelacy—a prelacy shorn indeed of the financial advantages it once had, but otherwise unchanged—then they want none of it, for it seems to be of man only, and not of God.

If the apostolate comes last of all, destined to death and willing to be made a spectacle for the sake of the flock—if the apostolate is of God's ordinance and is the final and all-inclusive way of speaking about what Christ is doing through His Church in the world—then we are claiming what alone is right for us to claim about the episcopate.

Is this to claim too much? If it were power or glory or privilege, it would be. But what it is is a claim for all of us in the body of the Church, to selflessness and obedience and emptiness of worldly pretension. What it means is not that we shall have more lordliness and mastery over Christ's Body, but that there shall be an infinitely greater comradeship within the Body. What it means is the steadily deeper and richer partnership of us all, in all our differing orders, in the Bishopric of Christ. It means a new and united brotherhood—what I as an American might call an ever-more democratic brotherhood—which will bind the Church into a deeper seriousness about our task, and a new sense of our common sharing of that task.

We claim too much for the episcopate when we seem to make it the only important part of the Church's life. We claim too little for it when we deal with it as if it were the specialized job of a few exotic individuals. We only claim it aright when we remember that there is but one flock and one Shepherd, remember that He goes wherever He wills to lead His flock, remember that He is the only Bishop, who has chosen us all in His Body to fulfill His apostolate, in humility, in modesty, in steady willingness to let Him fulfill His death in us, in united obedience to His will to make us spectacles in the world's eyes, in order that the weak may be made strong.

We Episcopalians do not take the episcopate seriously enough—that is the size of it—or else we take it far too seriously, as an earthly pretension. Our salvation is to see Him in all we do—to see His hands in ordination—to hear His voice in our common councils—to watch His loving gentleness with suffering mankind as He leads them—and then see our life together, in His Body, as the working out in history of Him who was the Sent One, and who then sends us to be, together, what He is and what He means to be.

28. CONCORDATS AND COMPANIONSHIP*

ONE OF THE SHARPEST charges against us Anglicans (not always unfair, either) is that we do not take our own claims seriously. What is meant by this may be one of several things. For example, a few weeks ago, a disquieted friend worried with me about how we seem, in our more timid moments, to seek to bolster the "catholicity" of the Prayer Book by decorating our worship with an assortment of archaeological curiosities or nineteenth-century Mediterranean exotica. I am not one to criticize the true enriching of worship in any way; what I refer to here is a lurking suspicion that the Prayer Book alone is not quite valid, and needs this or that to qualify. No amount of green paint will bring a dead tree to life. If the Prayer Book and its rites and teaching is not in itself a full Catholic book, then our whole cause is lost. But we do not always act in accordance with such sturdy confidence, I am sure.

* From *Anglican World*, June-July 1961.

This article is not about the Prayer Book, but about quite a different matter, yet one also illustrating our need to be sure that we do take our claims and beliefs seriously, and act on them. I want to write about what the Lambeth Conference calls "The Wider Episcopal Fellowship." Specifically, I am thinking about our valiant little sister churches in Spain and Portugal, the Spanish Reformed Episcopal Church and the Lusitanian Church. Not long ago I had the privilege of making visits to them both, primarily in relation to the Concordats of full Communion, which the Episcopal Church in the United States has proposed to establish with them, as with the Philippine Independent Church.

All three of these churches, like the Old Catholic churches, are bodies of Christian people, holding to the historic faith and order of Catholic doctrine, yet rejecting decisively the abuses and distortions of that heritage within the Roman Church, and sharing in many ways the primitive, biblical, free and national emphasis of Anglican tradition. None of them is an "Anglican" church, even though there has been deep and loving comradeship between them all and members of the Anglican Communion. Bishop Binsted and his colleagues and successor in the (American) Philippine Episcopal Church have given warm support to the Philippine Independent Church for nearly twenty years; and that great Church has moved, thanks to God, into an abiding comradeship with the Episcopal Church which will, I pray, lead in short order to the fullest brotherhood with all our Anglican family. In the case of Spain and Portugal alike, the Church of Ireland has been their notable friend and sponsor for nearly a century. Yet in no case could it be said that they are "Anglican"—they are independent, national, reformed Catholic churches, growing out of their own soil, worshipping in their own language and idiom, developing their own spirituality, giving leadership to their own nations in their own way, fulfilling a vocation precisely parallel to that to which Anglican churches also seek to be obedient, yet in their own terms.

What is currently being proposed in the American Church is the establishment of formal and public agreements (Concordats) with them, establishing for all to see and know what is already true in fact, that each recognizes the catholicity and independence of the other, and maintains its own, that each agrees to admit members of the other to participate in the Sacraments, that each believes the other to hold all the essentials of the Christian Faith (but does not necessarily accept all doctrinal opinions, sacramental devotion, or liturgical practice characteristic of the other). It is a formality in all these cases, I should think, for in fact such a mutual confidence has governed our life for many years.

The Lusitanian Church of Portugal began its separate history in 1867, when a Spanish priest, of the American Episcopal Church, began to preach in Portuguese, in Lisbon. In 1871, the first service of the Spanish Church was held in Seville. In 1880, the Lusitanian Church was formally organized, with three congregations, under the leadership of Bishop Riley of Mexico.

Certainly from that day on, the life of both churches was a concern to many Anglicans, especially to the Church of Ireland. Successive Archbishops of Dublin and Armagh—most notably Plunket and Gregg—visited them frequently, to confirm and ordain and to counsel the faithful clergy and laity. Prayer Books were adopted, closely following Anglican patterns, but containing significant elements drawn from the Braga and Mozarabic rites—classic liturgies of Spain and Portugal. A bishop was even consecrated for Spain, by Irish bishops, in 1894, and for more than twenty years Bishop Cabrera led his church with great power.

After the Second World War, relations with the two churches began to assume a new stature and importance. In 1956, a second bishop was consecrated for Spain, Bishop Molina, at the hands of the Bishops of Meath, Minnesota and Northern Indiana. In 1958, Bishop Fiandor was consecrated for the Lusitanian Church by the Bishops of Southwestern Brazil and Meath, and by Bishop Nash, then Bishop-in-charge of the American churches in Europe. On Bishop Fiandor's retirement in 1960, Dr. Luis Pereira was elected to succeed him and, God willing, soon will be consecrated to that office.

It is clear enough, from this skeleton history, how intimately the life of these two churches has been interwoven with the Anglican Communion. Yet it must be said again that they are not creatures of Anglican inspiration and initiative. It has been the honor of Anglicans to be able to befriend them and to do for them what we could, for we saw in them, as in the Philippine Church as well, the same vocation to responsible freedom within the Body of Christ as that which gave birth to our own churches. Yet they stand on their own feet, and obey their own genius.

What these Concordats will do is only add the security and dignity of public acknowledgment to what God has already led us to see in fraternal partnerships. As such, the Concordats will be welcomed on all sides. But they also, at the same time, will underline once again the need for Anglicans to think deeply and seriously about "The Wider

Episcopal Fellowship"—and this brings me back to the point I started with.

Thanks to God's providence, the essential seeds of the Church as we know them have been planted in those lands—the historic episcopate, the primitive and scriptural faith, the sacraments, the full and unfettered Bible. Those seeds have taken root and grown and borne fruit. Now we are being called on to recognize what God has done, and see how what is "ours" is really not ours at all, but His, to do with us what He wills. All too often, we deal with the historic, constitutional episcopate or with reformed catholic faith and life as if they were Anglican possessions, not really to be found anywhere but on our own soil. We do not really believe in them as the universal gifts they are— we act (or seem to act) as though they were only valid within our own tradition and nation, and that elsewhere some other principles were true and effective. Sometimes, Heaven help us, we seem even to act as pure relativists, as if the Roman Catholic principles are true in some areas, like Spain or South America, yet untrue in England or America—as if one doctrine were true in Java or Scandinavia, and a different one in Ceylon or South Africa.

Any such timidity about our own convictions is utterly untrue and unworthy of us. From the Lambeth Appeal of 1920—the first, great proclamation in our time of the essential unity of the Church—we have held before the world and before ourselves "the vision . . . of a Church, genuinely Catholic, loyal to all truth, and gathering into its fellowship all 'who profess and call themselves Christians,' within whose visible unity all the treasures of faith and order, bequeathed as a heritage by the past to the present, shall be possessed in common, and made serviceable to the whole Body of Christ. Within this unity Christian Communions now separated from one another would retain much that has long been distinctive in their methods of worship and service. It is through a rich diversity of life and devotion that the unity of the whole fellowship will be fulfilled."

The key to that unity, we have said, lies in "the wholehearted acceptance" of:

The Holy Scriptures, as the record of God's revelation of Himself to man, and as being the rule and ultimate standard of faith; and the Creed commonly called Nicene, as the sufficient statement of the Christian faith, and either it or the Apostles' Creed as the baptismal confession of belief:

The divinely instituted Sacraments of Baptism and the Holy Communion, as expressing for all the corporate life of the whole fellowship in and with Christ:

A ministry acknowledged by every part of the Church as possessing
not only the inward call of the Spirit, but also the commission of
Christ and the authority of the whole body.

The only basis on which we can say that is that these four essentials
are God's and not ours. Because they are God's we need not worry
about them or seek to limit them; we need only do whatever we can to
plant and nourish them, and God will take care of the increase. And
this is precisely what has been happening, in many parts of the world.
And to recognize that, and to move freely and wholeheartedly into the
brotherhood built on that foundation, is to enter "The Wider Episcopal Fellowship" (which is a sort of Lambeth jargon for the unity of
the Church).

I grant it is not always a simple step, to enter into that fellowship.
It involves us, at times, in anomalies which nobody likes, as when we
seem to tolerate two bishops exercising jurisdiction in one place (as
in America, where bishops of the Polish National Church work side-by-
side with Anglican bishops), or to establish separate jurisdictions for
different languages or cultural groups (as in Europe, where English
and American chaplaincies co-exist with national churches with which
we are in communion). And it is complicated by the fact that, particularly in Spain and Portugal, the Roman Catholic Church is established
as the official and historic Church of the land.

The little Reformed Episcopal Church in Spain is most sharply
limited by this, and the Lusitanian Church only a little less so. One
need not expect to find one of Bishop Molina's churches easily, for no
cross may adorn the building or even a sign board identify it; the
clergy may wear clerical dress only indoors, not in the streets; and no
congregation in Spain may exist very long without fearing a visit from
the police, and very possibly, a padlock. (As I write this, one of the
churches in Spain has just been closed and its priest imprisoned, for
reasons which do not have to be given and doubtless will not be.)

And the social and personal penalties are costly ones. A young man
being confirmed in the Spanish or Lusitanian Church knows well that
by this act he is irrevocably closing doors to a possible career in government service or the army or professional life. In this respect, his
plight is not markedly different, in fact, from that of his Christian
brother in Russia. In Spain, particularly, the Roman Church has been
dominated, in the words of a distinguished Spanish Catholic intellectual, by the purely negative ideal "of preserving Spain from all contact
with the pernicious modern world, keeping her at a safe distance from
its errors and, as much as possible, remote, immobile, inaccessible and

insulated from the passage of time." This climate is changing, and changing more swiftly than is often realized; but it is still a powerful force molding the witness and life of any free Christian group within such a society.

But to this must be added all the other complexities of witness within a Catholic culture. No Anglican is entirely comfortable in such a situation, for he recognizes a brother—estranged, no doubt, and mistaken, but still of one blood—in any Christian anywhere, and as much in his Roman companion as any other. Yet he also knows that he must be true to his own lights, that he has a truth he must bear witness to himself, that he has something to say to his brother as well as something to learn.

And this is still further complicated by political considerations—by treaty rights or the exigencies of a cold war. Relationships can become most tangled indeed. Parenthetically, I may say that the Church of England has no monopoly on such problems. By some mysterious protocol, for example, Bishop Molina may not be invited to visit the American forces in Madrid, to confirm or celebrate the Holy Communion, but instead an American bishop must be imported to do this. The Wider Episcopal Fellowship is by no means an easy path to follow!

But underneath all these awkwardnesses and limitations, the clear fact of the fellowship remains. In England or America, the ways are open now for friends of those churches to express their support and brotherhood. The proposed Concordats will make that brotherhood clear for all to see. But far more, the Concordats—like those now in effect with the Old Catholic churches—will be a door into a new depth of unity altogether, in which our Anglican unity finds a place and to which it has contributed very much, but still a unity greater and deeper than one built simply on a single historical tradition.

What can such a wider unity be and do and express? Only God can tell us, as we move into it, and grasp it and explore it. But He may not tell us anything about it as long as we look on it simply as a theoretical exercise in ecclesiastical politics, or as a sort of charm to wear on our watch chains. We shall only learn what is hidden in it in proportion as we commit ourselves to the great Godly institutions—Creed, Sacraments, Episcopate, Scripture—as universal gifts of Christ's Church and not merely as Anglican peculiarities.

In proportion as we do yield to that assurance, we shall cease being nervous about these things, as if they were treasures we had to protect or else they would disappear. Much more, we would begin to discover an immense and unexpected richness in the life of the Church. When we meet and work and worship and witness with our brethren in every land, who hold with us all the essential gifts, yet find expression for those gifts in their own quite different cultural and national settings, then the nature of our unity will for the first time become clear. Only then will "The Wider Episcopal Fellowship" become more than a name or a convenient way of tidying up peculiar ecclesiastical relationships. Only then will the true wealth and vitality of the one body, living out its life in many languages and many temperaments and many histories, become clear to us. May that day come soon; and I pray that not because I am a luke-warm Anglican or an impatient ecumeniac but because both the diversity and unity of God's creation must somehow find its full expression in the diversity and unity of His Church, if either that Church or humanity is to survive at all.

29. A WIDER FELLOWSHIP*

As proposals are made, in various parts of the world, for new local unities of Christians (as in India, U.S.A., Nigeria, Malaya, etc., etc.), a parallel question immediately arises as to what happens to the unities we now have. It would be a deceitful bargain if we were to gain one unity—a local or national one—at the cost of another, perhaps even a world-wide one. And this is precisely the sharp question which all Anglicans must face when we try to enter wholeheartedly and sympathetically into these proposals. Is the new fellowship truly a wider one, or merely another one?

Any such plan necessarily involves the disappearance of a portion of the Anglican Communion. In South India, for example, four Anglican dioceses and half a million Anglican Christians left our Communion, to be henceforth outside it (though hopefully in full communion with it). What is to be substituted for the churches of our Communion, as they disappear? What will take the place of the unity we now have? Imperfect and partial though it be, the present unity of the Anglican Communion is a fact; it is a tough and enduring reality, based on all the central gifts of faith and order, and bringing together Christians of every race and culture in a true family life. It is a working unity, as strong and true as any this world affords; it is a unity incredibly rich in promise to broken humanity; and no man in his senses will lightly lose it or bargain with it.

It is all very well to rhapsodize about our Anglican "vocation to

* From *The Living Church*, April 23, 1961.

disappear," to lose our life in a new and larger life which may more than make up for what we shall have lost. I believe with all my heart in that vocation; and I have done my share of rhapsodizing, too. But all such venturesome visions of the greater Church that is to be, could become the most irresponsible day-dreaming, if we who share the vision and the hope did not count the cost of it, and did not take the patient steps required to make the greater dream come true.

What cost? What steps? The cost, broadly stated, would be the loss of that intangible yet precious reality contained in our Anglican fellow-ship, at least in so far as that fellowship depends on our being separate from others. And much of it now does depend on such separation. Who can understand the texture of the "Anglican tradition" without equally understanding how it has come into existence largely because it was something other Christians did not have, or could not have?

In most societies in the world, Anglicans are a minority. We have clung to the Prayer Book and to episcopacy where most of our fellow citizens have not; we have insisted on a vernacular liturgy and the supremacy of Holy Scripture and the place of the laity in the Church's government and a thousand other matters where the current of our societies was setting against us; we have built a tradition of humane and liberal thought, and of a profoundly sacramental way of life, in the face of often calculated and bitter hostility to these things. And in all this, our life has been continually refreshed by the streams of con-verts who come into our fellowship precisely because of these differences.

All this is simple history, and its final meaning will only be seen in what we do with our history. Nonetheless, it is a fact that now, in our divided Church and divided society, the separateness and the dif-ferences play an immense part in deepening our common Anglican life. And if we are to enter into new, united churches, part of the cost of that unity will be the loss of the privilege of being "separate."

I forbear laboring the obvious, or reminding anybody who the "separated" people were, in the New Testament. All I say is that a lot of Anglican self-consciousness cannot help but depend on precisely the quality of being different; and that therefore any measurable move-ment toward unity must take this into account, being prepared to abandon it in favor of a vastly greater alternative.

And at this point, my second question comes into play. What steps ought we of the Anglican Communion to take to make the great vision come true? At the moment, I stress one in particular—that is, to make a beginning at what Lambeth called "The Wider Episcopal Fellow-ship." I think that neither in 1948 nor 1958 did we know fully what we meant by this phrase. This is nobody's fault; the fact is that the phrase and the Fellowship ultimately refer really to nothing else than the fully-united Church for which all Christians hope, that "fellowship with one another through one baptism into Him" as the 1960 report of the Faith and Order Commission of the WCC described it, "holding the one apostolic faith, preaching the one Gospel and breaking the one bread, and having a corporate life reaching out in witness and service to all." That fellowship in any place, the report goes on, must be united "with the whole Christian fellowship in all places and all ages in such wise that ministry and members are acknowledged by all, and that all can act and speak together as occasion requires for the tasks to which God calls the Church."

So great and almost unimaginable a unity is not very easy to talk about. Yet it is precisely this which is the jewel at the heart of Lambeth's modest phrases about the fellowship which ought now to unite "episcopal churches within the Catholic Church," and of Lambeth's hope that a conference of the bishops of those churches with which we are in some relation of full communion or intercommunion might be called in the not-too-distant future. The family of those churches is not now more than a foretaste of what some day may be. Yet even now it includes such a wide variety of traditions and relationships as the Old Catholic Church or the Polish National Church of fully European and American background, the Church of South India from the great subcontinent of India, or the Philippine Independent Church, so uniquely a product of Asian national development.

The danger of such a fellowship is that it should seek to become a super-confession, a "third force" as between Protestantism on the one hand and the Roman Church on the other. This is a danger that the Church at any stage on the ecumenical road cannot avoid. But what binds this fellowship together is precisely that constellation of gifts which both Lambeth and Faith and Order alike hold to be essential to the full life of the Church—the two universal sacraments, the apostolic faith, the whole and single gospel, as revealed in the Holy Scripture, and the universal ministry, of laity and clergy alike, which is accepted by all as the means for a more perfect service.

The "Lambeth Quadrilateral" proposes this constellation of gifts, in a now familiar and classic formulation. The Faith and Order paragraph I quote speaks of these same things in more general phrases. Yet both alike are attempts to state the bony structure of unity; and this structure does now exist, in limited compass, within "The Wider Episcopal Fellowship."

Of course it is not the only unity we know or should know. Not until there is not one Christian outside it, could such a unity be complete. And God has opened to us all, in ecumenical life, many levels of unity and many partial fellowships, which must in time be brought to fullness. But for the moment, this "Wider Episcopal Fellowship" is in our hands; it is a present reality which seems to open the way to a greater unity than what we now know; and it is a step to be taken, on the long road to the fully-united Church which all of us long to see, in obedience to our Lord's prayer.

Confessionalism

30. WORLD CONFESSIONALISM AND THE ECUMENICAL MOVEMENT*

I AM EXTREMELY GRATEFUL for the invitation to share in an important ecumenical conversation. I should like to propose three questions, for my part, without pretending to be, in any way, a spokesman for the Anglican Communion. They are real questions, in my mind, and not disguised affirmations, and they are in the background of most informed Anglican thought in this area.

First, is the word "confession," as it is currently used, a useful and communicating word? I am inclined to doubt it. The word is of most honorable origin, and may still refer to a cardinal Christian attitude of disciplined loyalty to the Gospel. But of late years it has been increasingly used to denote a bundle of relationships and attitudes— I think too large a bundle for any such word to hold without spilling over; it has become charged with various resentments and defensivenesses; and it shows some signs, at least, of being used to suggest an ecclesiological category into which very diverse patterns of church organization must somehow be made to fit. For all these reasons, I hope that the word and its derivatives may disappear.

I think this is true even of the highly-antiseptic definition arrived at by the discussion in April. At that time "confessional bodies" was understood to mean "the organization which represent families of churches," families sharing, "not only the general tradition . . . common to all churches, but also specific traditions which have grown out of the spiritual crises in the history of the Church." Such families also

---

* From *Lutheran World,* January 1963.

were said "to desire to render witness to specific convictions of doctrinal or ecclesiological character which they consider essential for the
life of the whole Church of Christ." Even this more eirenic definition
suffers from the difficulty of trying to say so many different things.
Indeed it seems so broad a definition that it is hard to imagine any
configuration of churches in our world which would not be a "confession," if it existed in any wider unit than a local or at most a
national one. For that matter the WCC itself would be a "confessional organization" in this definition, at least when seen from the
point of view of a non-member body.

I do not propose a substitute, for I think there is none. My question
therefore really is, would it not engender far more fruitful dialogue if
the *specific* issues and tensions were dissected out for discussion separately? These problems are real and most urgent; they call for the best
thought of Christians; but such thought cannot be given them, I think,
until they are isolated from the general misery called "confessionalism." I do not underrate that general misery. The ache and tangle
so labelled is real enough, heaven knows. But I am myself persuaded
that there is not much more use in trying to treat "confessionalism"
than there would be in a doctor trying to treat "sickness." Therefore
I think it would be more fruitful to deal with at least the major specific
problems themselves, in detail.

Certain of these stresses and difficulties seem to me, as an Anglican,
the radical ones. One is certainly the question of particular statements
of the Christian faith as developed and used by groups of Christians,
especially when those statements are exported and imposed or required
as part of the theological furniture of "younger" churches. In a strict
sense, I think there is no universal Anglican confessional statement.
The 39 Articles of Religion are the closest we come to a specifically
Anglican statement of the Christian faith. While in many ways it is
true that these Articles were written to show how close the Church of
England could come to particular confessional attitudes without adopting one itself, the fact remains that the Articles do "witness to specific
convictions of doctrinal or ecclesiological character" (in the words of
the April definition). To the degree that these Articles have been imposed on the younger churches of the Anglican Communion, there
would be a real sting to the charge of "confessionalism" as denoting
theological narrowness or exclusiveness within the Anglican family.

Mercifully the 39 Articles have not been generally so imposed nor
accepted. But is the Nicene Creed "confessional"? If so, is there anything save the Holy Scriptures themselves which may rightly be made

a basis of unity among Christian people? If the Holy Scriptures alone may be so used, what authority are they to be assigned, and what interpretation given of their history, language, etc.? Is there to be any consensus of agreement in all this that may not be regarded as imposing a "Western" or "confessional" thought-form or whatever on the younger churches of Asia? Is there any validity to the process of theological exploration and statement, and if so, what?

The point at issue here is that of the minimum theological statement required as a basis for visible Christian unity. The Anglican attitude, generally, is a median one in this area—we tend to distrust any "Anglican" statement of the Christian faith and to dislike any attempt to fence any Christian in or out of the life of the Church on the basis of a particular statement. The 39 Articles represent one problem for us in this area, admittedly (although it would be a sharper one if they were "required" of the younger churches of the Anglican Communion, or of other churches in unity negotiations). But Anglicans do have certain statements which they regard as fully authoritative, and essential as a basis of unity—namely the Holy Scriptures and the Catholic Creeds. Therefore from the Anglican point of view, ecumenical enquiry into the whole question of the validity and authority of particular statements of the Christian faith (beginning with the authority of the Holy Scriptures, and the Creeds as summaries of the Biblical revelation) is and would be of great significance. What is suggested is not a theoretical study but rather the discussion together, by "younger" and "older" churches, of the place in the ecumenical problem of any "statement" of the Christian faith (including the Holy Scriptures)—of its validity, authority, and particularly, of the bearing such statement, however broad, ought to have on the fulfillment of unity.

Again, "confessionalism" is often a way of referring to arbitrary or unfair procedures in the relationships of older with younger churches, especially "missionary" relationships. While in the Anglican Communion virtually all the eighteen separate churches are entirely self-determining, all too often the granting of this provincial autonomy has not been accompanied by a corresponding freedom from dependence on missionary funds, particularly for capital purposes. While I should not myself question the continuing place of the foreign missionary in inter-church relationships, it seems to me a persistent infantilism to require younger churches to continue to appeal to older ones for building funds, pension funds and all the other capital tools which should have been supplied them at the outset of their autocephalous life. I do not know the situation of other Christian bodies in this respect; but it would be helpful to the Anglican churches to explore this whole area of continuing dependence.

Again, "confessionalism" is often a way of referring to certain cultural attitudes—so-called "non-theological factors" which still call for fuller exploration than they have so far been given. In the case of the Anglican Communion there is a cultural confessionalism still strong in certain areas, which in fact limits freedom of action unfairly and substitutes a sub-Christian basis of unity. This is manifested, for example, where there is still strong attachment to British or American roots and affiliations. Such cultural dependence needs to be clearly distinguished, of course, from the natural historical ties which are the inescapable channels of the Church's mission. The Christian in the younger church will rightly welcome the insights into Christian life and thought which have come to him from other churches and nations; but similar acceptance should not be expected from him of the particular social habits, cultural traditions, political alignments, etc., which so often seem inseparable from the greater gifts. An ecumenical enquiry into these factors would bring a wholesome liberation to older and younger churches alike.

I have cited these three areas as illustrative of my feeling that we will gain by dealing with specific inter-church tensions separately, and in their own peculiar settings, rather than under what seems a meaningless general head.

Second, what is the bearing of our disquiet about "confessionalism" on the deeper question of the unity we seek? I reiterate that my views are only those of one Christian of the Anglican Communion. Yet I know that it is around this second question that the self-examination of many responsible Anglicans chiefly centers. This is so because the unity of the Anglican Communion is itself such a problem to us. In the first place, the self-identification of each separate Anglican church is quite unclear. That is to say, no church of the Anglican Communion has any very neat test of what constitutes "membership" in it. Any baptized person is a member of the Church. Presumably what makes him an "Anglican" is that he chooses to attend that particular congregation and identifies himself with it by supporting its work, etc. It is required, as a matter of general discipline, that he be confirmed by a bishop before being admitted officially to the Holy Communion, but the bishop need not be an "Anglican" bishop, nor is confirmation regarded as "becoming an Anglican." Certain particular rights may be reserved to those who are confirmed communicants, or who attend regularly or make regular contributions to the Church's work, etc. The criteria for establishing those rights are practical (i.e., attendance and participation) and moral (i.e., he is not excommunicated; and the grounds for excommunication are broad and usually only those of open and knowing defiance of the more generally-accepted Christian moral teachings). In general, then, the membership of a particular Anglican church is very poorly defined, and tends to grow very vaporous indeed at the fringes. This presents statistical and administrative difficulties, but on the whole Anglicans are well content with this for we feel—along with most other Christians, no doubt—that God is well content that fences between the separate companies of Christian people be as indistinct as possible, and that there be no eternal clarity about any particular Christian company in itself.

This same haziness characterizes the Anglican Communion as a whole. This Communion consists of eighteen separate national or regional churches, almost all of which are entirely free of any control by any other church (save for a right of ultimate appeal to Canterbury or to the corporate judgment of the Anglican Communion in a few cases). There is no central administrative structure within the Anglican Communion. There is no such thing as an "Anglican" in any general sense—one can only be a member of a particular church of the Anglican Communion. There is no possibility of common action by the Anglican Communion as a whole; all that can happen is that separate Anglican churches shall agree to certain common actions, which they must do individually and voluntarily. The only fundamental bond of unity among them is the fact that they are in full communion with the See of Canterbury and with one another. That is, the lay members of any of these churches are generally at once and without question admissible to full and equivalent participation in the life of any of the others, and the clergy of each may likewise minister in any of the others. (Each of these rights is subject to routine disciplinary control on the part of each church, of course).

The only definition of the Anglican Communion which can approximate an "official" one is that adopted by the Lambeth Conference in 1930:

> The Anglican Communion is a fellowship, within the One Holy Catholic and Apostolic Church, of those duly constituted Dioceses, Provinces or Regional Churches in communion with the See of Canterbury, which have the following characteristics in common:
> (a) They uphold and propagate the Catholic and Apostolic faith and order as they are generally set forth in the Book of Common Prayer as authorised in their several Churches;

(b) they are particular or national Churches, and, as such, promote within each of their territories a national expression of Christian faith, life and worship; and

(c) they are bound together not by a central legislative and executive authority, but by mutual loyalty sustained through the common counsel of the Bishops in conference.

This definition now is becoming anachronistic notably in sub-paragraph (a). This is so, first because the Prayer Books of the churches tend to grow more dissimilar as revision proceeds and national liturgical experiments proliferate. Second, there is a growing number of churches which are in full communion with the See of Canterbury and other Anglican churches, yet which are not "Anglican" in the traditional, historical sense. This "Wider Episcopal Fellowship," as the 1958 Lambeth Conference referred to it, is a node of increasingly thoughtful attention among Anglicans for many reasons. One reason is that it underlines the loose and transitory character of the Anglican Communion itself, and makes unsatisfactory even such a recent statement as the one I quoted from the 1930 Lambeth Conference. Probably the only satisfactory definition of the Anglican Communion at the moment would be a purely existential one—that it consists of those churches whose bishops are invited to Lambeth Conferences.

This uncertainty of definition reflects a far deeper uncertainty within the Anglican Communion. There was a time when there were many bonds of unity among us—language, British descent, a recognizable common Prayer Book, etc. One by one all these unities have been taken away from us. The Anglican Communion is no longer a fundamentally English-speaking fellowship; it is no longer definable as the Church of the Empire or the Commonwealth (although the maverick Americans, Japanese, *et al.,* always make this a less-than-satisfactory level of unity); the Prayer Book is no longer a comforting universal. This last point, indeed, is the present center of considerable disquiet on the part of many Anglican bishops, as witness the significant passages in the report of the 1958 Lambeth Conference (too long to quote, but interested readers will find some revealing Anglican self-examination in the report of Committee III of 1958 Lambeth, especially pages 2.78–2.94).

Thus the Anglican Communion is being forced back to fundamentals, and to a realization that its only permanent bond of unity is that of full communion—a bond increasingly shared by other than "Anglican" churches (whatever that rare essence of "Anglicanism" may be). This realization is not unpleasing, in the main, for Anglicans do not, as a matter of policy, regard the Anglican Communion as an eternal fact, but rather only as an accidental historical configuration, which came into existence as part of the general violation of visible unity in the West and which will and should disappear as those divisions are healed. Thus the Anglican Communion by its very nature (and I intend no comparison here with any other family of Christians) is driven relentlessly into ecumenical action, when it is true to itself.

The "disappearance" which I mentioned above has already occurred in South India. It was the wish of the bishops at Lambeth that this same "disappearance" might happen at once in Ceylon as well (a wish not fully shared, at the moment, by the clergy and laity of every Anglican church). Similarly, it was our wish that the same "disappearance" might be possible in other places, where plans for united churches were developed which contained what Anglicans regard as the essential elements and organs of full church life—the Holy Scriptures, the Catholic Creeds, the "historic" ministry and the two necessary sacraments.

I have already intimated that the requirement of these four characteristics—at least of some of them—ought to be the subject of further ecumenical study. But a different question is involved, for Anglicans, at this point. We do not suppose that full communion is in itself the final form of Christian unity. There must clearly be far more sharing of the common life and needs, and far more involvement in one another's lives, than what, after all, may be simply a ceremonial brotherhood trotted out for special occasions. But full communion is an essential element in unity; and most Anglicans would feel, I think, that we have not even begun a serious approach to Christian unity until we have reached full communion.

Therefore, we would feel that the full communion now shared by the churches of the Anglican Communion and others as well is not one which can be helpfully categorized as merely an Anglican or "confessional" unity, but should be approached as a question basic to the nature of the Church itself. Thus the "Lambeth Quadrilateral" is, in Anglican eyes, not a "confessional" position or gift or witness. No doubt other Christians could or would say the same about a particular statement of the Christian faith, or conviction about polity. It may even be that the World Council of Churches would say the same of the Toronto statement about the Churches, which perhaps also could be characterized as a "confessional" position. Let this be so; it only underlines my first question about the validity of the confessional concept in itself.

I know that it will promptly and rightly be said that the preceding paragraph could be interpreted as nothing more than Anglican exclusiveness or arrogance. So it may be, for I am a sinful man. But let me at once say that Anglicans do not seek to be excused from the debate about "confessionalism" on this ground. We recognize how powerfully historical and cultural forces can use even a valid and universal statement for their own purposes; and it is certainly true that a position even as relatively free from particular, "Anglican" traditions and limitations as the Lambeth Quadrilateral or the "Appeal to All Christian People" of 1920 Lambeth, can be used as an excuse for precisely the arrogance and insincerity in ecumenical life which has often justly been laid at Anglican doorsteps.

I say that in all sincerity, and as one who has been driven unwillingly into ecumenical encounter over the years because of my own profound belief in the principles of the Quadrilateral. But I should also say that the nature of Anglican unity should not be dismissed merely as a "confessional" position, or as loyalty to a denominational family or tradition. It is, I am convinced, a profoundly significant clue to the nature of the unity we seek, a clue forced on Anglicans, in all our stupidity, by the accidents of history in the first place, and which we are coming to discern only slowly and with pain. Our English roots have planted deeply within us the principle of the national Church. They have also endowed us with a certain constellation of attitudes and liberties which are often abused, and for which we take no credit. These inheritances have been transplanted into a family of churches in every continent, representing every major culture in the world, a family now constitutionally bound together by little else than our full communion (I do not forget the cultural confessionalism, the missionary infantilism and the rest, which are potent but certainly unworthy and sub-Christian imitations of unity). This Communion must not be judged by our failures as individual Anglicans, but by its validity as an ecumenical fact in itself, an existing, visible unity in a divided Church. Therefore I feel that the enquiry into "confessionalism" must not be thought of as the examination of an alternative to or a rival of the ecumenical goal itself, but rather as a real achievement of true unity, however partial, and in its full relevance to and bearing on the nature of the unity we seek.

Finally, to what degree does world confessionalism provide a wholesome balance to local unities? I was privileged to share infinitesimally in the drafting of the original Faith and Order statement on "Churchly Unity" (which after considerable amendment and development was adopted in the report of the Committee on Unity at New Delhi). I remember the uneasiness I felt and expressed at that time at what seemed a certain over-emphasis on local unity at the expense of wider unities, or, perhaps more directly, a mistaken sense of logical priority in these unities. The unity we seek (in the New Delhi phrasing) is seen "as all in each place . . . are brought by the Holy Spirit into one fully committed fellowship . . . and who at the same time are united with the whole Christian fellowship in all places and all ages," etc. (The New Delhi Report, pp. 116 ff.) It was an uneasiness on my part and nothing more, at what was a cloud no bigger than a man's hand (and perhaps not even a cloud)—at what seemed a tendency to think of unity as something essentially born locally, which must then be extended into ever-widening circles.

Indeed I am not accusing the statement of being tendentious. In its final form, the statement links the universal fellowship with the local in a clear attempt to provide for the wider as well as the more immediate manifestation of unity. But there still remains the suggestion that the local unity is the primary one. I think this is a mistaken sense, and potentially dangerous.

I say this not doubting that the action of God in the Incarnation is clearly particular and local, nor that the Church of the New Testament is likewise local. Indeed this is the necessary condition of Incarnation, I should suppose, and of Christian unity as well. Nothing is real which is not local. A generalized Christ would be meaningless, just as a generalized spirit of unity is meaningless. But it is God's eternal and universal action which is wrought in the Incarnate Lord; it is in man and not just in a man that He is incarnate; it is for all men and not a particular group of men that He came down from heaven; it is a single, universal, indeed cosmic salvation which is accomplished; and through Baptism we are brought immediately into the household of God, to be fellow citizens with the saints. Universality pervades and infects the particular at every point. There is no progression from the particular to the universal, or the local to the general. The mode of God's action in time and space is always particular and arbitrary and localized; the action itself is universal and eternal. The mode of unity is always local and immediate; the unity itself is universal and whole.

Believing this, I find danger in any statement of unity which seems built on a necessary priority of one unity—one mode or level of unity—over the other. I do not at all question the absolute necessity for visible unity "of all in each place." But this is absolutely inseparable from the unity in all places and all ages which has been given us in Baptism and in the Body. Therefore the ecumenical task, at all times and in every case, is a double one.

This double task takes a particular form in our time. The Church in the nations and societies which are just now coming into self-conscious independence is rightly highly sensitive to its duty to express the particular genius of its own cultures and traditions. This sensitivity is accented, in many cases, by the facts that the Church represents a small minority of the population, that it often lacks the articulate traditions of the Church in older societies, that it feels itself swamped by the cultural privilege and power of the Church in its majority situations, that it feels itself to be on the frontier of mission in a way unknown to most Christians, and so on. For myself (and doubtless for most other Christians) this self-consciousness is warmly welcome. Indeed a great and happy part of my present task is that of finding ways to elicit precisely such a response from the "younger" churches for whom I work.

Inescapably and rightly this response is profoundly linked with the ecumenical movement—with a vigorous pressure toward a united Church within the nations and regions themselves. Anglicans, because of the strongly national character of our tradition, are particularly receptive to this and concerned for it. The danger I feel is that in this (entirely true and moving) struggle for local unity it will be forgotten that the unity of the Church is universal and indivisible, that it is not composed of the multiplication of local unities or the extension of them, that there is no local unity which is not simultaneously universal and which does not at once establish claim of the unity of Christ's Church and his Lordship over all human divisions and separations, and the loyalties born out of them.

I dislike seeming to suggest two distinguishable unities. There is only one, and it is at once local and universal; and the local is only real as far as it expresses the universal (and vice versa). Yet the organs and modes of the two aspects of unity differ, and the task of establishing unity differs in detail in the two cases. And the practical problem here is that of trying to keep the two searches—for local unity and for the wider unity—abreast of one another. In this, the existing unities provided by "confessional" families must continue to play a significant part. For at the moment it is only within those families that the same *depth* of unity, in both its local and wider manifestations, can be maintained.

I do not say such unity *is* necessarily maintained within these families of churches. Again I cannot speak for others; but I can say that the profound unity of full communion within the Anglican family is very far from fulfillment. We are often so separated by national boundaries (to say nothing of cultural, linguistic or even theological divisions) that our full communion may be no more than a phrase permitting an occasional, exotic, Eucharistic fellowship. Indeed a principal task before Anglican Christians at this time is precisely the exploration and fulfillment of our obedience to the unity God has given us, beyond our deserving.

But there is something to be explored and obeyed which now exists. It is not the limit of our obedience, but it is the deepest expression of unity now open to us. It is, in its implications, a deeper expression of unity than any federation of local unities could be, for it transcends "federation," at least potentially, with all the implications that federation has of being a voluntary action of men, and confronts us with the fact of our indivisible unity in the sacrament which, with Baptism, is the deepest of all unities given us in this world. Yet at the same time, in this unity across the world, there is room also for the proper expression of local unity, and the responsible autonomy and expression of local and national traditions.

What is true of the Anglican Communion is doubtless also true of other Christian families. They would say, I am sure, that the particular and limited expression of unity within confessional families is by no means anything more than the utmost that is now possible in a divided Church. As such it is necessarily incomplete and imperfect. But it has within it the seed of a universality which is different in kind than what I call a "federation of local unities"; and I am persuaded that this seed is an indispensable element in the whole ecumenical task, precisely because it persistently confronts us with the necessary corrective and balance to our emphasis on local unity. And if the Church is not again to become the captive of nation and culture, this corrective must be steadily and unremittingly supplied.

Is not the WCC a truer expression (because wider and more inclusive) of this corrective balancing sense? It would be, if it were the Church rather than a fellowship of churches. It would be, even as a fellowship of churches, if it were a unity of "the whole Christian fellowship in all places and all ages in such wise that ministry and members are accepted by all and that all can act and speak together as occasion requires for the tasks to which God calls his people." It is not that (although by God's mercy it may lead us to such a unity). It has its own nature as a fellowship of churches, and there can be no question of our absolute duty to take our places within it. But it would be romantic to suppose that the whole tangled ecumenical problem of communication and understanding and discerning of God's will and obedience to it can be miraculously by-passed by any meeting of churches, however wide.

It is important, I think, for the full articulation of our problem that it is churches and not confessional families which are members of the WCC. A federation of confessional families, so I think most Anglicans would feel, would compound the problems of Christian unity, and tend to perpetuate precisely the divisions we seek to destroy. It is churches (as far as that word has validity or meaning in the plural) which are to be brought into fellowship, that the Church may be visible. It is local unities, local churches, which need to find the other face of unity. It is for this reason, doubtless, that "confessional" representation in ecumenical bodies would seem to Anglicans both untrue to the nature of the Church, and also to add still another difficulty to those we now face in the search for unity. This would not preclude the usefulness of asking a member of a particular Anglican church, for example, to try to perform some practical service of interpretation or whatever, to the extent that one person could do so, on behalf of all Anglican churches. From time to time I am asked to do this, as are others. But it is characteristic of the Anglican Communion that my membership of the Assembly at New Delhi was as a bishop of the Protestant Episcopal Church in the United States of America, and not as an "Anglican representative."

To return to my final question, the point to be explored is that of the true balance of local and wider unities and the ways in which this balance is to be maintained and fulfilled. This is an extremely wide field of exploration. It involves the whole question of the basis of unity of these world families of churches and the degree of reality they have as expressions of the universal Church. It involves their own inner life, and the part separate churches play within it, and the degree of responsible freedom of dialogue and partnership they achieve. It involves most of all, the question of the meaning of full communion (presumably a distinguishing mark of most such families) and the way this should be developed and fulfilled within each family and even more, among Christians as a whole.

But this exploration—so imperative and significant—must be set within its largest and truest dimensions, those of the paradoxical nature of unity itself, at once local and universal. The confessional families are one way, and at the moment the deepest (but not the only) way in which this exploration of unity can go on. In my view, they are an indispensable stage in this exploration, not contradictory of the wider claims of ecumenical life nor to the absolutely essential local unities. The looked-for consultation on these problems cannot fail to bring help and guidance to Christians, if it is based on a recognition of the essential problem of unity itself and its two faces. So far, much of such discussion has seemed to be based on a feeling that unity is something which must be created by men in one place and then extended to other men and other places. From an Anglican point of view, this is not the way unity is given us.

31. WITH PRAYER AND BOLDNESS*

BY FAR THE MOST EXCITING ASPECT of the World Council of Churches Assembly at New Delhi (to this delegate, at any rate) was the leadership given by the Orthodox. There were many high points in the Assembly—some of them curiously undramatic and even flat, in the event, such as the extraordinarily "managed" marriage of International Missionary Council and the WCC; some of them, like Dr. Joseph Sittler's remarkable address, requiring more time for appreciation than those brief days afforded. But through all the days there seemed to run a new buoyancy of spirit, a new aggressive vigor of expression, a new and virile intent to be involved in the ecumenical debate and to affect it, change, stretch, broaden it, on the part of the Orthodox delegates.

It was not that there was anything new in their presence—there has been wide and generous Orthodox participation in ecumenical life from the beginning. It was not their numbers, although the addition of the delegates from the Soviet Patriarchate and others did make a visible difference. It was rather what seemed a new spirit, a new willingness to witness for their own insights in the shock and melee of the dialogue, where so often in other years, they had seemed inclined to withdraw at critical points.

Doubtless the most vivid instance of this new spirit was the notable presentation by Nikos Nissiotis of "The Witness and the Service of Eastern Orthodoxy to the One Undivided Church." Mr. Nissiotis, a young lay theologian of the Greek Orthodox Church, attacked at the outset "fashionable" ecumenism and its complacent slogans, and drove to the heart of the matter, which is the given and existent unity of the Church, the unity without which there would be no Church at all. "The Church does not move towards unity through the comparison of conceptions of unity, but lives out of the union between God and man realized in the communion of the Church as union of men in the Son of Man. We are not here to create unity, but to recapture it in its vast universal dimensions."

---

* From *The Living Church*, February 11, 1963.

It was thrilling to me, in great part, because it spoke so profoundly to our deepest Anglican thoughts about unity. It cannot be said often enough that amid all the confusion and blindness and often downright silliness of Anglican life, we never quite lost the essential secret of unity, that it does not consist in people thinking alike but in people acting together, especially in the great central actions of Holy Baptism and the Eucharist and the supernatural life growing out of those Sacraments. It is to God's glory and not our credit that we have managed to hold on to that noble truth through our visissitudes (and the Prayer Book has been His chief instrument in this). Nonetheless, we have never really forgotten it, nor what underlies it—that profoundest sense that the Church and its unity is entirely God's creation and gift.

When a voice comes from another tradition and says these things, there is an immense and jubilant recognition of brotherhood. So it was with me. I do not foolishly suppose that we shall resolve our historical problems of disunity easily, just because we recognize that there is a given unity in Christ infinitely more real than our divisions. What came out of that might be nothing more than the swifter destruction of our little churchlets by that terrible unity. All I say is that in the welter of conflicting theories about the Church and defensive confessionalisms and contrived solutions to the problem of getting people to accept unfamiliar and unpalatable ideas and institutions—in this tumult it is life-giving to be led once again to see God and His united and unifying action, and then to seek Him in company with others.

All of which leads me to wonder anew at why Anglican and Orthodox Churches do not press unremittingly and urgently toward full communion and a more profound unity among themselves. Friendship among us has been a happy fact for a good many years, notably in the past half-century. Theological conversations have increasingly been matched with the humbler experience of living side by side in mutual support, especially in the United States. Visits are exchanged with growing frequency and warmth, and it was characteristic that Archbishop Fisher's journey to the Vatican followed a similar pilgrimage to the Ecumenical Patriarchate in Istanbul.

Yet, for all this undoubted cordiality and indeed affectionate comradeship, the fact is that we still feel ourselves to be strangers from one another far more sharply (for more Western Anglicans at any rate) than we do from our neighbors of other traditions from which we are often much more remote, theologically. Why is this so? No doubt in part it is because of differences in language and national culture—certainly in America the Orthodox Christian (in the first generation at least) seems a very exotic person indeed compared with the familiar and safely-Anglo-Saxon Presbyterian or Methodist who shares Rotary with us. This begins to pass with the generations, no doubt, and as Orthodoxy becomes "indigenous" it loses much of its strangeness in our provincial eyes—indeed, Anglicanism in America had nearly as rough a time becoming "indigenous."

No doubt a deeper factor is that the Anglican tradition is so solidly Western—much influenced by the Reformation which Orthodoxy never knew, much molded and formed by the medieval political history of western Europe, much the child of the missionary condition and necessities of the early Church in the West. And to us, steeped in that cultural broth, Orthodoxy seems often far more remote than even the intricate legalities of Rome. But such things ought be a stimulus and not a barrier to discovery and companionship in our narrow world, all the more because of the rich and often-unsuspected depths of common faith and practice shared by us both.

At all events (and I am writing this on New Year's eve), I find myself praying with great sincerity that this year may bring a new seriousness to the Anglican-Orthodox friendship—a new and more intent drive toward that full communion which would mark so great a step forward in what Nissiotis called the "recapture" of unity. This is partly a task for theologians, drawn from all the Anglican and Orthodox families and prepared to do more than merely compare traditions. But it is also, and very seriously, a task for plain Christians in our parishes and dioceses—particularly where, as in America, we share together the single life of many of our communities. Anglicans and Orthodox hold in common infinitely more than they do separately. Our feeling for national tradition, our liberal and flexible organization, our sense of historic continuity, our respect for the part and ministry of the laity, perhaps most of all our abiding sense of the unity already given mankind in God—all these great elements run through the lives of both our churches. May it be that we shall be given the gifts of prayer and boldness we need, to work without impatience but without ceasing, until the day comes when we can break the Bread of Life together!

Index

315